SCORPIONS STING

THE STORY OF No.84 SQUADRON

ROYAL AIR FORCE

1917-1992

by Don Neate

An Air-Britain Publication

1994

Published in Great Britain by

Air-Britain (Historians) Ltd
1 East Street, Tonbridge, Kent

Sales Dept: 5 Bradley Road, Upper Norwood,
London SE19 3NT

Correspondence to the editor:

J. J. Halley, 5 Walnut Tree Road,
Shepperton, Middlesex, TW17 ORW
and not to the Tonbridge address

ISBN 0 85130 222 X

Printed by Hollen Street Press
Berwick-on-Tweed

Cover painting by Dugald Cameron

SCORPIONS STING

CONTENTS

FOREWORD

by Wg Cdr A M GILL OBE DFC AE MRAeS FIPM MBIM

I am honoured to have been invited to write the Foreword to this book about No.84 Squadron, Royal Air Force, when so many are better qualified than I.

All those who read this book will owe a debt of gratitude to Don Neate for giving up so much of his time to research the history of this famous yet, in some quarters, little-known squadron. It is perhaps surprising that a man who never served in the RAF or with No.84 Squadron should go to so much trouble to trace its history. Don Neate's research has entailed writing hundreds of letter, many of which were never answered, visiting the Ministry of Defence, the Public Records, and travelling hundreds of miles in the United Kingdom and to Cyprus at great expense to delve into the Squadron's records. No mean task.

No. 84 Squadron first achieved fame as a fighter squadron during the First World War when it played a prominent part in the defeat of the Germans. It became almost infamous between the wars when, based at Shaibah, it helped keep the peace in Iraq for 20 years from 1920 to 1940.

The Squadron was badly mauled during the early years of the Second World War in Greece and the Far East when it very nearly disappeared without trace. But it arose again from the ashes because no enemy (or Air Marshal) was able to crush the spirit of the 'Famous 84th', a spirit which had been created over a very long period by those great characters, from the humblest 'erk' to certain squadron commanders, who had served their Squadron and their country so magnificently.

In World War 1 and again in World War 2, the men of 84 were recruited from many nationalities from far and wide, including English, Irish, Scots and Welsh, Australians, Americans, Argentinians, Canadians (both British and French), New Zealanders, Rhodesians and South Africans. We were certainly a cosmopolitan bunch who, strangely, blended well together to form an unusually close-knit unit.

One aspect which has always stood out like a sore thumb was that, despite all the hard work and sacrifice put in by those gallant men of 84 Squadron over the years, very little credit was given to individuals. Admiral of the Fleet The Earl Mountbatten of Burma, the Supreme Allied Commander South East Asia, wrote that, although he had agreed with his Commanders-in-Chief that they would process recommendations for decorations and awards through their own Service Ministries and could quote his full support, the RAF authorities failed dismally to give adequate recognition to their own airmen. For example, of the many officers, NCOs and airmen of 84 Squadron who were recommended for awards after their successful victory over the Japanese in Burma, less than a handful received any recognition, and not one Mentioned in Despatches, for their courage and hard work under appalling conditions. Yet, as Lord Louis Mountbatten said, "Without the Air Forces, the Army could not have defeated the Japanese". Perhaps it was considered by the powers that be that to serve with 84 Squadron was sufficient honour in itself. If so, they were probably right.

No.84 Squadron has spent its entire lifetime operating overseas, first in France, Belgium and Germany, then the Middle East and Far East and now in Cyprus. "Out of sight, out of mind". Maybe that is why the Squadron is not as famous as some other better-known squadrons which achieved fame overnight but which did not survive for so long.

I am very pleased that Don Neate has now redressed the balance to some degree by writing this long-overdue account of one of the RAF's best-loved and longest-serving squadrons. There are many characters who contributed greatly to this success but whose names do not appear in this book. This is partly because the thousands of young men who served with 84 over the years - many still alive and others who are no longer with us - could fill a book many times the size of this one. But there is no doubt that the life of every man who served with 84, whether his name appears in the book or not, has been changed in more ways than one by the experience and comradeship he gained whilst serving with this remarkable Squadron - myself included.

The election of Don Neate as an Honorary Member of No.84 Squadron Association was well-deserved and greatly applauded by all those who have come to know him. I wish him good luck in his next venture.

S.E.5As of B Flight lined-up at Bertangles on 6 August 1918

CHAPTER 1 - THE FORMATIVE YEARS

When the formation of the aeronautical branch of the Armed Forces was first proposed, it was hailed more enthusiastically by the politicians than by the Service chiefs. The Generals and Admirals, with few exceptions, viewed flying and its adherents with scepticism if not with suspicion. The flimsy machines were regarded as contraptions likely to be of little military use except for observation purposes. In this respect it was argued that they might, in time, be an improvement on the static balloon used for 'spotting', but few foresaw the potential of aircraft as fighting machines. Thus, apathy was not the least of the obstacles in the way of development in the early days.

The Secretary of State for War, Lord Haldane was, fortunately, one of the more far-sighted minority and in 1911 he convinced the Committee of Imperial Defence that it was desirable to create an aeronautical service without more delay. So, on 13 May 1912, the Royal Flying Corps was born. Initially it consisted of a Naval Wing, a Military Wing and a Flying School. At this time there were barely twenty trained pilots in the Royal Navy and Army put together, with a handful of assorted aircraft for them to fly - and that was all.

The few enthusiasts who gathered at the Central Flying School at Upavon in Wiltshire had an uphill task ahead of them. Haldane had seen to it that the Secretary of State for War should be ultimately responsible for this new venture and the RFC should thus come under his authority rather than the heads of the two services. However, complications immediately arose because the Naval Wing came initially under the Admiralty and that meant under Winston Churchill as First Sea Lord. Meanwhile, the War Office, with its responsibility for the Military Wing, was now represented by Colonel J R Seeley, later Lord Mottistone.

The relationship between these two old Harrovians was cordial enough but the more forceful character of Churchill usually seemed to produce more evident results for his own branch and, in the early days, the Naval Wing had an advantage over Seeley's Military Wing. This probably did not amount to a great deal, for the appropriations that the Government made for the RFC during 1912-13 were pitifully small, but the Military Wing felt the disparity existed. Added to apathy, there was the parsimonious attitude of the Treasury. It was not surprising, therefore, that when war broke out in August 1914, the RFC had only four squadrons in a doubtful state of readiness for immediate action. The position

became critical, due to the lack of basic equipment for the training of recruits who were eagerly volunteering for service with the Flying Corps.

The strength of the Military Wing was by now 860 officers and men. Rapid expansion was vital and Major (temporary Lt Col) Trenchard, now in command of the Military Wing at Farnborough, was thinking in terms of raising a further 30 squadrons. Seeley left the War Office in 1914 and it might be regarded as fortunate that his place was taken by Lord Kitchener, for that soldier had a lively interest in the Flying Wing and he immediately authorised that Trenchard's projected squadrons should be increased to 60. By June 1916, the RFC had nominally doubled in size during the previous three months. But, by this time, casualties at the front were mounting and rose to one aircraft and its crew per day. With losses of this nature, the front-line strength came to a bare 26 squadrons. Six months later, in December 1916, the total strength in France, including reserves and some squadrons lent by the Admiralty, amounted to 36 squadrons. The powers in Whitehall were not especially helpful, but a different attitude was developing and during the autumn of 1916, Lord Curzon, who was nearing the end of his time as President of the Air Board, was furiously defending the rights of the RFC against the Admiralty, who still seemed to be getting preferential treatment.

So the battles on the Western Front and in Whitehall continued, casting a double burden on Trenchard and his staff, particularly the elegant but efficient Brancker who was responsible for supplies. This officer did a great deal for the RFC in the way of organising supplies, not an easy task in those days, but with the backing of Kitchener he fully justified the trust Trenchard had placed in him. At first sight he gave the impression of being affected, but Major Sefton Brancker and his glittering eyeglass was a man to be reckoned with. Trenchard supplied the aggressive attitude in France and Brancker an equally aggressive diplomacy at home, and between them they maintained a precarious balance of power between the RFC and the German Air Force. The programme of expanding the Flying Corps gained momentum and new squadrons were formed in ever-increasing numbers.

Early in 1917, Major Hazelton Nicholl of No.8 Squadron, who had been a flight commander at the Central Flying School in 1916, was detailed to form No. 84 Squadron at Beaulieu in Hampshire. At the advanced - by RFC standards - age of 34, he

Flight Commanders in November 1917: from left: Capt E.W. Pennell, Capt. J.M. Child, Capt K.M. Leask (S. Leslie collection)

B4876 "H" in October 1917, missing some essential components but showing the upward firing Lewis gun mounting (C. Ashworth)

was already known as 'Daddy' Nicholls. He was aided by Lt R A Denne as adjutant, Capt S Dalrymple as flight commander and Sgt Major McIntosh in charge of discipline. The Squadron came into being on 16 February 1917. It was equipped with a miscellaneous collection of training aircraft including three B.E.12As, a couple of B.E.2Cs, a Curtiss 'Jenny' and a Sopwith 1½-Strutter.

The policy was for squadrons to train their own pilots during formation and, when up to strength, 84 Squadron was to be sent to France equipped with S.E.5s, at that time the most advanced fighter in the RFC. Lt H B Hope and 2nd Lts O W Manning and C F Jex arrived as instructors, a case of the blind leading the blind. This is of interest as it shows some of the problems facing the RFC, in that quite junior officers with little flying experience were being appointed as flying instructors.

By 22 March 1917, with eleven officers and three NCOs, the five-week- old unit were posted to Lilbourne, near Rugby, where it joined the 25th Wing. Further changes took place in equipment with Avro 504s, Nieuport two-seaters and 1½-Strutters being used for training. Supplies were still short and each incident must have caused dismay at the time. One trainee pilot having made a poor landing was instructed to take-off and this time make a good job of it. He 'revved' up and promptly ran straight into a lorry, both resulting in 'write-offs'. While the Squadron was at Lilbourne, Capt Dalrymple was joined by Capts R H Mayo and C E Foster as flight commanders. Amongst the pupils posted to Lilbourne were 2nd Lieutenants P J Maloney, C L Stubbs and A W Proctor a diminutive South African, who was later to become the Squadron's sole Victoria Cross holder. Training of the Squadron was intensified now that a complete unit was taking shape, and the training by Major Nicholl was invaluable. During July 1917, Captain Kenneth St G Leask arrived to take over duties as Senior Flight Commander; over the following days he was joined by Capts J M Child and E R Pennell. The S.E.5s with which the squadron was to be equipped now began to appear but, soon after they were delivered, certain technical faults became apparent and they were returned to the factory for modifications to their engines. The V-8 Hispano-Suiza engines, made under licence by Wolseley, were to prove excellent in the coming eighteen months but, at this point, troubles were found which set them back for several weeks.

So it was that on 8 August, Major Hazelton Nicholl handed command of the squadron to Major Sholto Douglas. At 24 years of age, he had already served two years in the RFC. Just over six weeks later the Squadron was sent overseas. During that six-week period, the modified S.E.5 began to arrive, this time with the geared Wolseley-Hispano engine. For armament, it carried a .303" Vickers gun mounted on top of the fuselage firing through the propeller by means of the Constantinesco gear. In addition, there was a Lewis gun on a Foster mounting above the top wing. Major Douglas had, in the early part of 1916, already formed No.43 Squadron so he was well able to cope with the final birth pangs of No.84 and he completed the task in time to take the Squadron overseas on 21 September 1917. Apart from the Commanding Officer, the only officers with previous overseas experience were the three flight commanders, Leask with 'A' Flight, Pennell with 'B' Flight and Child with 'C' Flight. The majority of the remaining pilots had little flying experience and several had only just received their wings when the move took

place. Two days later, the Squadron was placed under the command of the 9th Wing and based at Estrée Blanche. The three weeks that followed were taken up with formation flying, mock dog fights and general local navigation flying. They share the airfield with 56 Squadron, also equipped with S.E.5s, so that No.84 had an immediate challenge from a rival and far more experienced squadron.

The first operational flight took place on 11 October and consisted of patrols along the line Dixmude-Armentières, which were uneventful. On 14 October, the squadron practised formation flying over the Ypres salient. This activity might not compare with modern notions of formation flying, since there was no radio contact and the Flight Commander had to rely solely on hand signals from his open cockpit. Lack of experience produced some distinctly loose formations in the early days. The following day the squadron was ordered to cross the front line for the first time, its mission being to act as escort to six D.H.4s of 25 Squadron which were bombing Harlebeke dump. It was also the first encounter with the enemy, 2nd Lt Krohn having the distinction of destroying the first enemy aircraft credited to the Squadron. Unfortunately, 2nd Lt Lord was lost, but was later to be reported as a prisoner of war.

Three days later, on 18 October, Capt Child led an escort patrol for D.H.4s with only three aircraft, the other three being forced to return with engine failure. 2nd Lt Park did not return from this patrol and was last seen flying south. Between 19 October and the end of the month, the Squadron lost seven more pilots. 2nd Lt Watts failed to return from the morning patrol on the 20th and a day later 2nd Lts Steele, Yeomans and Hempel went missing from the afternoon patrol. Although the Squadron had lost three of its members, both Leask and Maloney claimed victories. 2nd Lt Rush went missing on the 28th but was later reported a POW. On 31 October, Leask led a patrol consisting of Ralston, Payne, Powell, Gray and Maloney and they attacked four enemy scouts, only to be attacked by a further twelve of the enemy. Gray and Powell were quickly shot down. Leask and Ralston claimed victories over a mixed formation of Jagdstaffel 2 and 4. The early work of the Squadron was summed up by Major Sholto Douglas: "All through October we fought up and down the Menin Road to the east of Ypres. It was a hard school for the new and untried squadron and, at first, owing to the inexperience of the pilots, we suffered casualties, but bitter experience is a quick teacher".

Too often the weather ruled out flying for days on end to the annoyance of the pilots, for the Third Battle of Ypres was building up and the ghastly struggle for Passchendaele Ridge was raging. The first week of November was marked by low cloud, heavy rain, mist and fog and only once, towards the end of the battle, was No.84 able to play an active part in that appalling and disastrous episode. On that occasion, Capt Child and Lt Brown combined to drive down a two-seater out of control over Westroobeke. This was cancelled by the loss of 2nd Lts Deans and Kingsland.

On 10 November, the Third Battle of Ypres ended and two days later No.84 was transferred to the 13th Wing of the 3rd Brigade at Le Hameau. A British advance was planned and launched against the enemy at Flesquières on the morning of 20 November. An attack was to be launched at Cambrai at 06.00 hours; Camels, Pups and S.E.5s were all to take part. But once again the weather was to curtail operations. However, on the ground five villages were overrun by combined tanks and infantry. The morning patrol of 22 November resulted in a battle with elements of Jagdstaffel 5. Brown and Child aborted with engine troubles, leaving Leask and Maloney struggling to reach the safety of cloud after being under attack. Maloney had to force-land in the front line with a bullet wound in his thigh. He was later awarded the Military Cross.

Success came later in the day when a patrol under Capt Child attacked a DFW C-V and forced it to land near Flesquières. On interrogation, the crew said they were stationed at Busigny and belonged to Flt Abt 269, and had only been at the front a month.

On 23 November, three patrols were flown. On the second, 2nd Lt David Rollo was shot through his hand whilst, it is believed, he was thumbing his nose at the enemy. The 26th brought better fortune when the American Lt 'Swede' Larsen and Lt W H Brown succeeded in driving an Albatros down out of control. Out of 19 sorties flown, seven had to abort through engine problems. The Battle of Cambrai ended on 3 December and the withdrawal to a more compact line was completed by the 7th. Throughout the battle, the role of 84 Squadron was chiefly protection to low- flying machines, the fighting usually taking place between 300 and 2,000 feet.

The Commanding Officer of No.84 Squadron encouraged the closest co-operation between his pilots and, as the weeks went by, it became frequent practice for the entire squadron to fly offensive patrols as a complete unit. The tactics devised by Sholto Douglas and his flight commanders in order to maintain superiority in the air were for each of his three flights to be allotted a particular role in the team when attacking an enemy formation. The leader of the patrol, 'A' Flight would fly at 15,000 ft, to the rear and on one flank would fly 'B' Flight at 16,000 ft while 'C' Flight would be on the other flank at 18,000 ft. The duties of 'B' and 'C' Flights were to get involved only if the occasion demanded it, otherwise they were there primarily to stop enemy reinforcements from joining in. Pilots and flights were switched regularly so that everyone had a chance of leading. It has been officially recorded that these tactics were used with much success by No. 84 Squadron.

The first week of December brought to the Squadron 2nd Lt H W L Saunders MM (later to become known as 'Dingbat'), who became one of the Squadron's more distinguished sons. Hugh Saunders admitted, many years later, in correspondence with the Squadron Association's President, the late Owen Greenwood, that he flew his first patrol after only two days with the squadron but, owing to lack of experience, it was not until the middle of January 1918 that he felt he was able to pull his weight, that is to know what was happening in a fight and to be able to look after himself.

Little flying took place during December, snow, fog and frost being common, although it is known that the new 'Sidcot' flying suit was tried out by Major Douglas and Capt Child. On 29 December, the Squadron moved south to Flez where they joined the 22nd Wing of the 5th Brigade. Patrols were shared with 48 Squadron (Bristol Fighters) and 54 Squadron (Sopwith Camels). The orders were that the whole Army front, Lesdain-Beaurevoir-Sequehart, was to be kept clear.

Although patrols began on 2 January, it was not until the next day that any combats occurred. Patrols were flown in pairs and one consisting of Lts Larsen and Proctor found two enemy two-seaters over St Quentin. They engaged and had the satisfaction of seeing them both hit the ground. It was Proctor's first kill.

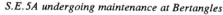
S.E.5A undergoing maintenance at Bertangles

Aircraft N in the snow during the winter of 1917/18

Replacement pilots arriving over the Christmas period included several who went on to become 'aces'. Capt Robin Grosvenor, a nephew of the second Duke of Westminster, was credited with at least ten victories either destroyed or forced down out of control. 2nd Lt Edwin Clear and 2nd Lt Jack Sorsoleil scored eight and twelve victories respectively before being posted to Home Establishment. 2nd Lt John McCudden was the younger brother of Major J B McCudden VC, DSO and MC. In the few short weeks of his life on the Squadron, he had six victories to his credit.

January brought few victories but the 13th was lucky for Sorsoleil (his first) and for Ralston who became the first on the Squadron with five victories. Two more fell to the guns of Saunders and Krohn on the 25th morning patrol and Travers and Johnson shared another after lunch. The 29th brought mention of an attack on a series of balloons, forcing the observers to jump. They also had the satisfaction of seeing the 'drachen' hauled to the ground.

The next twelve days proved relatively uneventful, owing to bad weather. Patrols were flown regularly but little enemy activity was seen. On 5 February, the Squadron was taken off patrol duty, with no flying permissible. The 6th to the 9th were similar with only kit inspection and football matches to enliven the day. This continued through the week and it was not until the 15th that patrols were resumed. A flight of four was despatched that afternoon, Proctor and McCudden sharing a two-seater. The 16th brought even more rewards on the morning patrol. McCudden attacked a two-seater which was seen to crash in flames and Sorsoleil shot down one of its escorts near St Quentin. On the next patrol, Capts F E Brown and Grosvenor encountered four Albatros near La Fère, Brown sending one down out of control, followed by a two-seater in flames. Saunders, Larsen and McCudden also claimed victories to bring the total enemy aircraft destroyed or forced down by the squadron to fifty.

Capt Grosvenor claimed a double on 19 February. His combat report makes interesting reading: "Whilst patrolling the line south of St Quentin, I worked my patrol, which was at 15,000 feet, around into the sun and dived on the enemy who were at 10,000 feet, a two-seater went away north-west. I followed and got directly behind him in the sun. As I was getting my sights on him he stalled directly in front of my machine. I fired a long burst from my Vickers and he went down in a vertical nose-dive. I watched him crash in the forest below. My Vickers was now jammed so I turned west to rectify it. As I turned a V-strutter came straight at me without firing, he apparently did not see me until we almost collided, then zoomed up over me. I fired about 50 rounds from the Lewis and he rolled over and started to fall out of control. I did not watch the machine fall far but I am certain he was out of action".

Over the next week, the weather turned against the squadron and it was not until the 28th that the next victory was recorded, with Proctor claiming an Albatros. Unfortunately, Krohn went missing on the same patrol, last seen being chased down by three enemy scouts. Jagdstaffel 12, consisting of 12 Albatros, claimed three S.E.5s that day, Leut Hermann Backer being credited with Krohn's death. This was the Squadron's first loss since 13 January, when 2nd Lt Davies was shot down and taken prisoner.

The March 1918 Squadron records state that replacement S.E.5As were now being fitted with the 180 hp Wolseley Viper

Personnel of No.84 Squadron at Flez in about February 1918. Back row: Capt K. Leask, F.E. Brown, G.O. Johnson, T.F. Northcote, J.V. Sorsoleil, C.T. Travers, H.O. McDonald, A.W.B. Proctor; kneeling: H.A. Payne, not known; front row: E.A. Clear, Lunnon, C.L. Stubbs

engines, which were ungeared versions and far more reliable.

On 9 March, Nos.48, 54 and 84 Squadrons attacked enemy airfields at Busigny and Escaufort, No.84 acting as cover while the other two squadrons dropped over fifty 25-lb bombs, causing damage amongst transport and setting hangers on fire. The accuracy of low-level attacks by fighters was to say the least haphazard but what must have been one of the first examples of dive-bombing occurred on the 13th when 2nd Lt W H Brown attacked ammunition barges in a near-vertical dive. On his second attempt on the 14th, his skill paid off, with the result that one of the barges was sunk.

The 13th brought further victories to the Squadron. Capt F E Brown and his patrol caught up with a formation of Albatros attacking three Camels. Within minutes, Brown had shot one down which crashed near Homblières. Stubb's shot another off a Camel's tail and Hobson, seeing one on the fringe of the melée, attacked and it blew up in front of him.

Two days later, Proctor added to the Squadron's tally when he forced down a two-seater DFW C-V near Villaret. Later patrols accounted for three more. On the 17th, three formations from No.84 acted as escorts to No.5 (Naval) Squadron bombing Busigny. Seeing a flight of V-strutters flying west, the top flight attacked and Capt F E Brown, with two out of control, brought his score to ten. Another was seen to crash near Maretz. Further attacks were made on Molain and Busigny.

The bombing raids of No.5 RNAS D.H.4s and a surprise attack by Nos.54, 62 and 84 Squadrons enticed the enemy into the air. Units of Jagdstaffels 3, 4, 5, 6, 10, 16b (Bavarian), 34b (Bavarian), 37, 47 and 56 combined to act as a single unit under the command of Rittmeister Manfred von Richtofen. The group put up a total of 150 aircraft. Controversy over the numbers lost and gained varied but it is known the five Camels, two S.E.5As and one D.H.4 were lost from the British squadrons. The Germans admitted losing four, however, No.84 Squadron alone claimed seven, Larsen, Clear and W H Brown claiming triplanes, and Leask, F E Brown, W H Brown and Johnson claiming Albatros. Unfortunately, 2nd Lts McCudden and Payne were lost, McCudden being shot down by Ltn Joachim Wolff near Escaufort. Payne's loss was a mystery. Many years later in the magazine *Cross and Cockade*, an article written by Leut Max Holtzem of Jagdstaffel 16 had this to say: "I followed a S.E.5 down and saw him land right side up, so I flew home and rushed to the site with a truck and mechanics. After a quick inspection I found the aircraft in a fit condition to fly away, except that in our excitement we forgot to paint out the cockades. I made it to the Staffel airfield at low altitude, being shot at from the ground by everybody with a loaded rifle, but instead of being credited with it I got an official reprimand". This battle is detailed in Sqn Ldr C P O Bartlett's memoirs *Bomber Pilot 1916-1918*.

The long-awaited German attack began on 21 March 1918. After several hours of destructive artillery barrage, divisions of the Second, Seventeenth and Eighteenth Armies began their attack. All No.84's forces were concentrated on low-flying strafing attacks against the advancing enemy; bombs of every kind were dropped and machine guns blazed off into the grey advancing infantry at very close range.

It was the start of four moves in twelve days. An interesting incident on the 22nd was the shooting down of an enemy aircraft by 2nd Air Mechanic Knight whilst on forward observation duty. His report reads: "Between 1400 and 1625 on the 22 March, 2nd Air Mechanic Alcock and myself were patrolling the Beauvais-Lanchy road on our motorcycle when we observed an enemy aircraft over the line. We took cover and opened fire from approximately 500 feet with our rifles. He circled us and we continued firing. Suddenly he appeared to be in difficulties and within a short time landed about 500 yards away. We immediately mounted the motorcycle and rode towards him. We saw the pilot get out and start to run away but he was caught and brought back by members of the infantry. We took charge of the machine but orders came to retreat and burn it".

On the 23rd the Squadron moved to Vert Galand and four days later to Conteville. The last days of March proved stormy, which made patrols difficult. Several indecisive combats followed with Capt F E Brown crashing on landing and being taken to hospital. The 31st saw the end of Capt K St G Leask's service with the Squadron and his posting to Home Establishment. He recalled later: "That this was my last day of active service in the Great War and I had three force-landings on that day, the first on 24 Squadron's airfield where repairs were done. I then took off to continue the patrol but the engine cut clean out and I managed to get down on our own field. I took another kite and after 20 minutes the engine seized and I once again force-landed, this time near Boves". During his time with 84 Squadron, he had flown 99 sorties, with two destroyed and six driven down out of control.

No.84 Squadron on 14 November 1918.
Back row: K Johnstone, J J Coots, C H Wilson-Laing, W E Evans, Lionel Stubbs, J M Bacon, R A Whyte
Front row: A E Ansell, A Sippe, L de S Duke, C W Pickthorne (CO), H O Macdonald, F H Taylor, J A Jackson
(Photo courtesy L de S Duke)

CHAPTER 2 - A NEW NAME BUT THE SAME WAR

On 1st April 1918, No.84 Squadron, Royal Flying Corps, became one of the founding members of the Royal Air Force.

It is of interest to go back and see how this event came about, for, although it did not have an immediate effect on 84 Squadron at the time, developments at home were to influence the whole policy regarding the air service as part of the armed services and eventually had a considerable effect on the future of No.84. As early as the spring of 1915, bombing was becoming an accepted role of the RFC and only the lack of funds and raw materials held back the production of more bombers, for which the Army leaders had been crying out.

Trenchard had never ceased demanding that the harassed Brancker should organise the building of more and more aircraft and, although these were to be mostly fighters, as 1916 passed fresh demands showed that the proportion of bombers was to increase. This, at least, was the theory, but in practice the supply of aircraft of all kind continued to fall far short of the urgent requirements of the Royal Flying Corps.

To put a stop to this bitter controversy between the service chiefs in Whitehall, General Haig wrote what Trenchard described as a real 'snorter' and made it absolutely clear that fighters were to be the first priority. That was in October 1916 and he was primarily concerned with refuting the ideas of Colonel Barès, the head of the French Air Service, who favoured a more determined bombing offensive and the Admiralty, who wanted 200 naval aircraft for bombing in France.

All of this goes some way towards explaining why No.84 was so much involved in low-altitude bombing when it was not engaged in its normal fighting role. Sholto Douglas and other leaders in the field were coping with the immediate problems which beset them on the spot and can have had neither the time nor the inclination to consider the bickering that went on at home. But the future was being decided nonetheless and in particular the future of No.84. Meanwhile the battle continued.

In London, developments of a different kind were taking shape. The Chief of the Imperial General Staff, General Sir William Robertson, who was known to thoroughly dislike the RFC, astonished everyone by suddenly declaring himself in favour of a massive and immediate expansion of the RFC and the formation of a full-strength Department of State for Air.

Thus it was that that remarkable man, General Jan Smuts, was asked to review and produce a report on this proposal. At the end of a mere two months this report was circulating in Whitehall. Three or four years previously, the authorities, particularly the Generals, were less than lukewarm in their appreciation of flying machines and the cranks who flew them. Now the report stressed the almost boundless potential of aircraft as weapons of war. Yet in spite of all this, there were further vacillation among the politicians, though it is fair to say that this was less concerned with the actual recommendations than in their timing.

The balance of power in the war zone was finely poised and as we have already seen, the Germans were to launch an offensive which was to need all of our strength to contain and, if possible, to repel it. It was felt, even by Trenchard himself, who must have

The remains of Richtofen's Fokker Dr.1 behind the hangars at Bertangles

been delighted with the report as a whole, that the timing was wrong. There was some furious fighting to be done and this might well be hampered by ministerial wrangling in London. While Lloyd George was resting at Criccieth, Bonar Law was rather ineffectually acting, or failing to act, in his stead. The Secretary of State for War, Lord Derby, while agreeing with the scheme was, like Trenchard, opposed to the timing. Against this background, and thanks very largely to Smuts, with the support of General Henderson, the scheme was eventually brought into operation and the Royal Air Force was born as a separate service on 1 April 1918.

The first week of April saw Travers off to hospital and W H Brown posted to Home Establishment. Of the originals, only Major Sholto Douglas and 2nd Lts Larsen, Proctor and Stubbs remained. The 10th brought a celebration when it was learned that Hobson, Johnson and Proctor had all been recommended for the Military Cross. The week also saw the Squadron move to Bertangles where they were to stay until September. It also saw the slowing of the German offensive.

The next day, in spite of the evening's celebration, the Squadron was in very good shape. A patrol led by Capt Tatton ran into an enemy patrol of eight triplanes, Tatton, Duke and Sorsoleil claiming victories. Next day brought further claims but it was tempered by the loss of 2nd Lt McCann who had only been with them a few days. Lt G O Johnson left on 17 April to become a Flight Commander with 24 Squadron but the following week four American pilots came as replacements, Lts Eckart, Mathews, Hammer and Newhall. Capt Tatton, who had been with the squadron less than a month, was shot down by ack-ack on the morning of the 20th, falling to his death near Glisy.

A short memo in the Squadron's War Diary records the death of Baron von Richtofen on 21 April, with photographs showing the famous red triplane in a sorry state behind the hangers at Bertangles.

Signs of another German attack were imminent on the 21st when the squadron dropped bombs on the airfields at Wiencourt and Marcelleine. Beauchamp Proctor, recently promoted to Captain, was leading 'C' Flight when they saw triplanes over Foucaucourt. Joined by 'A' Flight, they succeeded in firing at the leader, a triplane with a black tail and green wings, from 200 yards. It went into a dive and was seen to crash by Stubbs. Three others were also claimed and Proctor's comments on Duke's victory are worth recording:

" While on patrol over Framerville Lt Duke attacked one of a formation of ten triplanes. He was immediately attacked by another which cut two of his flying wires and wounded him in the arm. Despite this, Duke succeeded in manoevering the aircraft on to the enemy's tail and put in several bursts at very short range. It fell away, out of control, stalling and spinning but, due to Duke's injury, he did not see it crash. It was timed at 16.35".

Four days later, Lt Lister-Kaye was wounded in a battle involving 30 aircraft, Grosvenor saw a Pfalz break up after being attacked and Sorsoleil witnessed the pilot jumping to his death. Later that week, a patrol led by Lt Saunders forced a two-seater to land at St Gratien. This aircraft was also claimed by members of 70 Squadron.

Records show that on 4 May an attempt was made by two flights to rouse the enemy fighters from their field at Cappy. Fifty 25-lb bombs were dropped but they failed to get the enemy into the air. The following day the Squadron escorted D.H.4s from 205 Squadron on a bombing raid on Chaulnes railway station. Enemy triplanes tried to interfere but were driven off. On the 10th the enemy were more fortunate when a three-man patrol led by Leut Loewenhardt shot down three D.H.4s after others drew the escort off. For the next four days, weather curtailed operations. On the 15th, the day started early, the first patrol taking off at 0325, attempting to intercept bombers heading for Amiens. Proctor writing in his log states: "On climbing to 6,000 ft I headed for the point of convergence to fly east in the hope of intercepting them on their return journey. Observing three red flares, I glided down to 3,000 ft and hung around until 0355 when an AEG twin passed just above me. I got on his tail and started firing but I was now down to 2,000 ft and broke off the engagement. The enemy aircraft was still diving but, as far as I could see still under control".

A patrol which took off at 0935 saw three enemy two-seaters taking off from their field at Vauvillers. One of these was shot down out of control by Lt Roy Manzer while a second was compelled to land downwind by Lt H W Saunders. Other patrols encountered enemy aircraft but, all combats proved indecisive. After a patrol left to escort a formation of D.H.4s, it clashed with five triplanes. One crashed near Herleville (Manzer) and a second near Rosières (Capt H P Smith). On the way back, Smith felt a blow on the right ankle and found he had been wounded by a triplane which had attacked from behind. Almost at the same time his petrol tank was hit and his engine stopped. He at once dived for the lines, kicking his rudder as he went, and eventually crossed the lines at Villers-Brettoneux at a height of 100 feet and crashed in 'No-man's-land'. Whilst extricating himself, he was hit in the left ankle and his left arm was broken by a machine-gun bullet. He managed to roll over into a shallow depression and was finally pulled into the trenches by Australian infantry.

The month of May continued to demand everything that No.84 could give and it is clear that they responded with great determination. On the same day as Capt Smith's injury, a noon patrol met eleven V-strutters near Hangest. Proctor and Saunders accounted for two of them which crashed, while two more were shot down out of control by Lts Biccard and McDonald. On into the third week of May we read in the official records of continued victories for the pilots of 84 Squadron. Grosvenor shot down two on the 18th and the next day no fewer than 35 German aircraft were encountered, three being shot down over Vauvillers. It was in this engagement that Lt E M Hammer was killed.

The German Air Force was now busily engaged in supporting their own ground forces whilst the British squadrons were making this task as difficult as possible. Proctor avenged the death of Hammer by destroying an Albatros scout and another fell to the guns of Lt 'Bim' Oliver.

A fine performance was put up by Lt Roy Manzer on the 28th when, having already shot down a V-strutter, a second one attacked him. He got on its tail and managed a burst of fire from about 30 yards. He then overshot his target and caught the enemy's right top plane with his undercarriage. Manzer's aircraft was thrown upside-down but he was able to right it in time to see the enemy fall to earth. Saunders and Wilson downed two others. A second patrol of eleven of No.84's S.E.5As met ten of the enemy and, in the resulting fight, Lts Clear, McDonald and Lunnon, with the American S B Eckart, each accounted for one. Lt B Stefansson was less lucky and was badly wounded in the face, though he managed to get home. Bad luck also befell Proctor, who had his propeller shot away, but he landed safely at Allonville.

Some well-earned promotion came through for Saunders and Sorsoleil, who were both made Captain to replace Capt Smith, who had died from his injuries and Grosvenor, who left the Squadron to go into hospital. The same day brought to the Squadron Lt George Vaughn USAS, who was to claim seven victories before transferring to the 17th Aero Squadron USAS as a flight commander. He claimed a further six before the end of hostilities.

On 1 June, Proctor fired a balloon to the south-east of Fricourt. Wreaths of blue smoke appeared from the gasbag and the observer was seen to jump. A few seconds later the balloon was in flames, whereupon the observers in the neighbouring two balloons also jumped out. A little later Proctor forced a fourth observer to leap to safety.

Captain Jack Sorsoleil celebrated his promotion by shooting the top right plane off a triplane which then crashed. He followed this by driving one down out of control. Following his success on the 1st, Proctor set ablaze two more balloons on the 6th, one near Proyart and the second over Bruay. This was followed on the 13th by yet two more, one being set on fire, the second killing the observers.

Mechanics rescue A4553 after an undercarriage collapse at Izel-le Hameau in November 1917

On 15 June, Capt Proctor and Lt Clear left the Squadron for a well-earned rest in Home Establishment. Early in June, Lt Newhall left to join No.3 Squadron USAS and Lt Sam Eckart to 148 Squadron. There was also a toll on the newcomers, Wilson to hospital, Fyfe and Neilson missing, Henderson, Jones and Rivers all leaving after being with the Squadron for only days.

Capt J Ralston returned to the Squadron on the 15th. He had been posted during January of that year to become flight commander on 24 Squadron. His return was welcomed by those who remembered him. He celebrated his return by shooting down a D-V on the 18th, with Capt W Southey and Lt Manzer making it a treble.

A brief spell of bad weather curtailed patrols on the 23rd for four days, though the 25th brought a victory for Sorsoleil. A two-flight patrol which went out at 0630 on the 27th found no enemy aircraft, but a patrol which followed at 0815 had quite the biggest fight of its existence. Capt J S Ralston, who was leading the formation of fifteen machines, noticed white anti-aircraft fire, and in due course spotted a LVG at work near Morlancourt. As there were several formations of enemy scouts about he had to wait for his opportunity. When this presented itself, he dived on the two-seater with his bottom formation and fired about 75 rounds. Two other S.E.5s also fired at it. Small formations of the enemy began harassing tactics and it soon developed into a running fight in which all the aircraft were engaged. Many reinforcements arrived and the fight lasted nearly an hour. Ralston's report states: "Towards the end I charged one formation of Pfalz; one opened fire hitting me in the petrol tank. I was blinded, so I spun the aircraft and switched on the emergency tank. I just got the engine started again when I was attacked from the rear, so I swung around but my engine cut again, and I had no alternative but to get away the best I could. At 2,000 feet my machine caught fire and I landed at once near Cachy. Half a minute later it went up in flames". Lt D B Jones was lost in this battle.

Capt J V Sorsoleil, who had kept his flight as long as possible above the conflict, was forced by superior numbers to dive to the assistance of the lower flights. He estimated that there were between 30 and 40 V-strutters and Pfalz in the melee. At 3,000 feet he was able to single out a Pfalz which he shot down two miles east of Villers-Brettoneux. He was immediately attacked by six EA and was forced to dive within 50 feet of the ground to contour-chase home. 2nd Lt Nel attacked a V-strutter which he forced down. The final rally was made over Villers-Brettoneux, where what remained of the patrol made a stand of about twenty minutes duration, but eventually had to give up due to a shortage of ammunition and the fact that many of the machines had been badly shot about. Capt H W Saunders, with both guns out of action, was chased by three of the enemy to within three miles of Longeau.

The Squadron took a well-deserved rest for the remainder of the day. The next day's morning patrol found Saunders leading five S.E.5As east of Albert. Spotting two LVGs working within a mile or so of each other, they attacked. One crashed near Fricourt; the other, attempting to force land, hit a shell hole and turned over. Later the patrol encountered seven enemy scouts which were attacked with no results.

On 2 July, a limited attack by the Australian infantry gained its objectives. They were helped by the Squadron dropping over 150 bombs and firing over 15,000 rounds of ammunition. This small war was the preliminary to the operation for the disengagement at Amiens, their capture of positions east of Hamel and Vaire Wood, and the clearing of the Villers-Brettoneux plateau. It was successfully accomplished by the Australian Corps with the aid of the 33rd American Division and 60 tanks.

Bad weather and the absence of enemy aircraft resulted in the first half of July 1918 passing relatively quietly as far as No.84 Squadron were concerned. The only occurrence worth mentioning was on 9 July when some balloon observers were forced to abandon their balloons.

On 16 July, a Wing raid on Foucaucourt set hangars on fire and scored many direct hits on transport and living quarters. All aircraft returned. In the course of a squadron patrol next day, Lt N Mawle attacked three balloons; one he shot down in flames, the others he forced to the ground. An evening patrol on the 18th found no EA so they dropped 40 bombs on Mericourt and fired 1,500 rounds of ammunition into batteries and ground targets.

Following a day of bad weather on which flying was impossible, the Squadron record for the 24th says: "At last, a formation of EA!". This consisted of seven Fokker biplanes which Capt J Ralston observed approaching our lines at about 4,000 feet. One was crippled by Ralston and finished off by Mawle; another was shot down by Nel. An evening patrol encountered a further nine over Péronne and, climbing to attack, Lts Falkenburg and Vaughn each shot one down out of control. The same evening about 0830, Capt W Southey was lost in the rain clouds. Diving

Flt Lt P W Lingwood joined the Squadron in April 1919 and was later killed flying a D.H.9A in 1922

from 15,000 feet down to 500 feet, he became completely disorientated and his instruments had packed up. He flew for about ten minutes and crossed a river which he took to be the Hallue, so he glided down and landed. Just as his wheels touched the ground he was fired on from all sides. He took off immediately and with the aid of a small light he struck the Amiens-Foucaucourt road and flew along it till he reached his field. Later he stated that he thought the river he had crossed must have been the Somme and that he had landed near Péronne.

The next day, Ralston, who had led the morning patrol, was attacked by an enemy scout and was wounded, but he was able to crash land on our side of the lines and from there he was taken to hospital. The 26th and 27th proved uneventful but the 28th brought victories for Falkenburg, Vaughn and Saunders. The Squadron record comments for the last day of July: "Only a few EA seen far east, which went still further east on the approach of the patrol".

August 1918 opened well for the squadron. A morning patrol spotted six enemy scouts over Bruay which attempted to climb away but Southey managed to force an engagement at about 13,000 feet. He singled out a Pfalz, which tried to make a landing at Suzanne airfield, but at about 8,000 feet it burst into flames. Three others were shot down by Falkenburg, Biccard and Mathews. On 8 August 1918, the offensive commenced which was destined to end the war. Preliminary instructions to prepare to attack east of Amiens at an early date had been given to the Fourth Army Commander, General Rawlinson, whose front of attack extended from just south of Amiens to Morlancourt. For the offensive the squadrons of No.22 Army Wing, V Brigade, were allotted to Corps fronts as follows:

III Corps
No.80 Squadron (Camels)
No.48 Squadron (Bristol F.2b)
Australian Corps
No.201 Squadron (Camels)
No.84 Squadron (S.E.5As)
No.41 Squadron (S.E.5As)
Canadian Corps
No.209 Squadron (Camels)
No.23 Squadron (Dolphins)
No.24 Squadron (S.E.5As)
Cavalry Corps
No.65 Squadron (Camels)

All these squadrons, with the exception of No.65 Squadron, were to send out their machines in pairs at half-hour intervals commencing 20 minutes after zero. In addition, Nos.24 and 84 Squadrons were to detail one flight to stand by from zero hour for the sole purpose of attacking enemy balloons. These were to be either chased down to ground level or set on fire. Pilots were also to try to obtain as much information as possible about the ground situation and to ensure that this information reached the proper quarters as soon as possible.

In the event, the airmen saw little of the opening attack. From the moment of zero hour at 0420 until nearly 1000, fog shrouded the battleground from above. The assault, however, met with little resistance as the enemy were taken completely by surprise and,

under cover of the heavy mist, the first objectives were gained rapidly. The German batteries were completely over-run and their reserves were rounded up and captured in great masses.

One can see from the foregoing that No.84's area of operation was the front held by the Australian Corps. As soon as the fog lifted, the trail of S.E.5As began. Each aircraft was loaded up with the usual four 25-lb bombs and amply supplied with ammunition for low-level ground strafing. The Squadron kept up a continuous patrol from 0930 to 2045. Mawle, who left at 0945, sighted two enemy balloons being towed by a team of horses east of Harbonnières. Heedless of machine-gun fire, he dived to within 25 feet of the ground to set them on fire, the blazing mass falling on top of the horses. He next turned his attention on a party of retreating German infantry, causing heavy casualties, but in this attack he was wounded in the stomach and only just succeeded in reaching his own airfield before he collapsed.

Proctor, who had rejoined the Squadron on 6 August, also shot down a balloon, but later combats proved indecisive. In the evening, 2nd Lt S W Highwood claimed his first victory when he shot a Fokker biplane down out of control.

The work next day was a continuation of the day before. The first ground strafers left at 0545 and then at regular intervals throughout the day. The last machine took off at 2000 and returned 40 minutes later. On 10 August, except for the first patrol of two machines, the Squadron resumed individual flight patrols and completed five. Numerous formations of the enemy, mainly Fokker biplanes, were met but only one combat proved decisive, when Capt W Southey drove one down out of control.

Patrols on the 11th increased the Squadron's tally by six victories. Of twelve enemy machines engaged, three destroyed were credited to Capt D Carruthers, Lt C Falkenburg and 2nd Lt C Thompson. Three others were considered to be have been shot down out of control. 2nd Lt Lobley was forced to land at Boves with engine troubles. "Six EA for one forced landing, a scrap worthy of the Squadron's traditions" reads the squadron records.

August continued with the Squadron escorting No.205 Squadron's D.H.4s on a bombing raid on Péronne station. In the course of this attack, a formation of 15 enemy scouts was encountered but they were driven off and the bombers escorted back to their base at Estrées, where the Squadron joined forces with the S.E.5As of No.92 Squadron. The two squadrons then turned back to attack the enemy which by now had increased to 20-plus machines. In the resulting fight, Proctor shot one down in flames and sent a second down out of control. Another was believed to have been sent down by Carruthers.

Lt J L Payton, who had joined the Squadron on 8 August, was killed on the 16th, when the wings of his S.E.5A were shot off by a LVG and he died in the crash.

On the 21st, a patrol led by Capt A W Beauchamp Proctor was detailed to engage enemy balloons on the 111 Corps front. Taking advantage of the sun, he dived on the balloons from the south-east and, selecting one over Assévillers, he fired 150 rounds with his Vickers, followed by a further 50 Buckingham rounds from his Lewis. The balloon went down in a flaming mass. He next engaged a balloon over Hem and, although the observer jumped, it did not catch fire. Proctor continued up the line and forced all of the balloon observers to jump. He then returned to the line, put on another drum of Buckingham, and got his flight together. Observing that the balloon over Hem was still up, he decided to engage it and once more dived for the line, maintaining fire until he saw smoke curling from its side.

A raid by a solitary German aircraft on 24 August on the airfield caused the death of Lt Alexander Mathews and the wounding of 2nd Lt Bateman. Mathews, one of the original USAS members, was credited with having destroyed two EA. On the morning of the 25th, Capt Proctor's patrol shot down a Rumpler which was seen to crash near Vrely. 2nd Lts Reid and Nel sent a second down out of control. The following morning, with orders to engage balloons over the Australian front, Proctor with the aid of Boudwin and Corse (both of the USAS), succeeded in sending one down in flames. They were then chased back over our lines by a flight of Fokkers.

The following day, the Squadron shot up targets near the bend of the Somme above Péronne where the retreating Germans were making efforts to stem the advances of the Australian Corps. Pilots who returned from later patrols reported no enemy movements on the roads east of the Somme. The evening patrol dropped bombs on batteries at Cerisières. On the same patrol 'a foolish Fokker' flew into the middle of the formation. It was immediately engaged by several pilots who drove it earthward to crash in the neighbourhood of Brie.

Péronne was occupied by British troops on 1 September and two days later it was reported that dumps at Manancourt and Etricourt were going up in flames. It was now evident that the enemy were retreating towards the Hindenberg Line and their retirement was expedited by ground strafing by all available aircraft. No.84 Squadron contributed a great deal to this work during the day when targets were easy to see and easy to hit.

Patrols on the 4th and 5th each accounted for balloons and they later escorted No.9 Squadron on a low-level reconnaissance. Coming down to 1,000 feet over Roisel, they were struck by the total absence of road movement and the slight and very inaccurate ack-ack fire. Going lower, they engaged small parties of the enemy and succeeded in clearing the way for our infantry. Bombing and shooting up ground targets were now the order of the day. Southey's flight caused motor transport and horse transport east of Cartigny to ditch between Tincourt and Marquaix.

The 6th brought an organised balloon attack. Major Douglas's statement in the records says: "We were always liable to be interfered with by hostile enemy patrols and as it was usually necessary to go down to 1,500 feet or below, we had to devise a system of security. This was done by an adaptation of the formations we employed on offensive patrols. 'A' Flight was made up of the five most experienced pilots, who could be trusted to shoot straight and fend for themselves. This was the striking force. 'B' and 'C' flights were simply a covering force. It was found preferable for 'A' flight not to rendezvous after an attack but for each pilot to make his way back independently. The whole operation took about ten minutes from the time the lines were crossed until the pilots were safe again over friendly territory.

Carrying out this scheme on 7 September resulted in four balloons being destroyed in flames, one each for Proctor, Highwood, Christiani and Corse.

In view of the advances made on the ground, the squadron moved to Assévillers, about five miles south-west of Péronne. They also made use of the advanced landing field at Proyart. Three more balloons were destroyed on the 14th, Southey, Highwood and Rees being the victors. Thompson was twice wounded after attempting to shoot one down on the 15th, but succeeded in getting home.

At 0815 on 17 September, Sgts A Jex and F S Thomson failed to return from a morning patrol. They were later reported as prisoners. Later patrols dropped bombs on transport north of Fontaine and 2,500 rounds of ammunition were fired into pockets of the enemy at Fresnoy-le-Grand.

Between the 24th and the 29th September, 15 balloons were sent down in flames, newcomers to the squadron Christiani, Millar, and Coots all claiming. Unfortunately Christiani was killed after a ground strafing attack on the 29th. His fellow pilots, Highwood and Millar, in their reports state that they were flying up and down trenches at a height of ten to twenty feet until their ammunition was exhausted.

Offensive patrols were resumed on 1 October when a squadron formation met 30 colourful Fokkers and three two-seaters. Two fell to the fire of Proctor. During the following days, four EA and two balloons fell to No.84. On 8 October, Capt A W Beauchamp Proctor, after leading a patrol on which he sent down a two-seater in flames, attacked ground positions, and was wounded in the forearm by ground fire. Notwithstanding this, he proceeded to attack an enemy balloon but without success. He then returned and landed safely at the airfield.

The same day, the Squadron moved to Bovincourt, some five miles north-east of their old field at Flez. The next day in the course of ground strafing, Sgt Dowdell was attacked by enemy scouts. Turning, he shot one down to fall behind our lines at Troisvillers. The work of the Squadron at that time is well described by Wing Commander Sholto Douglas: "The only unusual task that fell to No.84 Squadron was a spell of low-level reconnaissance work during a foggy week in October 1918. The line had been advancing very rapidly; communications from the front were bad and General Rawlinson was often uncertain of his position of his advanced troops. At this time No.84 Squadron were carrying out a series of low-flying attacks on the retreating enemy. The movement employed was as follows. As it was impossible to fly across country without losing one's way, the only thing to be done was to follow the road just above the tree-tops. At this time, the front line of the Fourth Army were about five miles east of Le Cateau. From here the roads radiate eastwards; so making Le Cateau the base point, we flew along the roads until we saw enemy troops or were fired upon. Each road was prospected in turn and by this means half-a-dozen points were obtained which, if joined up, gave us the approximate position of the front line. The information obtained proved to be of the highest value to the Army commanders".

It might be added that Major Douglas himself did many of these reconnaissances. After the Hindenberg Line battles in early October, the Germans realised that the only way of averting complete disaster lay in a general retreat from France and Belgium. The only avenue was through the bottle-neck at Liège. To protect this movement, the enemy transferred the bulk of his Air Force to the Northern Front. This left the Somme area relatively sparse and consequently, as the end approached, air fighting became less and less intense on this front.

October 23rd turned out unusually active when a squadron formation found nine Fokker biplanes. After a dog fight, one was shot down in flames near Fontaine by Capt W A Southey. Two days later the squadron moved to Bertry, about five miles west of Le Cateau. "Not a bad place, we are all in good billets in the village" (Squadron records).

After a quiet day on the 26th, the enemy were in evidence again on the 27th when a morning patrol encountered 25 aircraft in several formations over Canal de l'Cise. They tried to avoid combat and, when forced, did so in a very half-hearted manner, one being shot down by Southey. A little later that morning, the CO went up alone on 'Aerial Sentry'. Whilst flying low, near Engelfontaine, he noticed heavy shelling and climbed to investigate but was suddenly attacked by three Fokkers.

Douglas at once turned west and contour-chased back to his own lines. After reaching them, he turned on one of the three who were chasing him and succeeded in getting in a telling burst. The Fokker's nose went down and it crashed on the edge of Forêt de Mormal.

The 30th brought the busiest day for a long time, Highwood and McDonald claiming victories on the morning patrol. Southey, Millar and Stubbs added to the day's tally. Unfortunately 2nd Lt H J Thorn died from his wounds after crashing in the French lines. Sgt J M Tarver was also twice wounded but succeeded in getting his aircraft home.

The first mention of an enemy pilot using a parachute occurred on 3 November 1918 when Lt Taylor attacked a Fokker which burst into flames, 2nd Lt C Wilson claiming a second on the same patrol.

Five days later, Major Sholto Douglas left the Squadron on promotion to Lieutenant Colonel. He was succeeded by Major C E Pickthorne who assumed command from 8 November 1918.

Two days later, he led a patrol which encountered four Fokkers and a LVG. Two of the Fokkers were shot down, one by Major Pickthorne, the other by Lt Taylor. These were to become the last added to the long list of victories of No.84 Squadron. It also brought the last war casualty. 2nd Lt Rosenbleet was shot down west of Mariembourg; he was probably the guest of the Germans for the least possible time.

In the course of fifteen months active service in France, the Squadron claimed 323 victories, 54 of them by Captain A W Beauchamp Proctor. 24 other pilots were credited with five or more victories. They also became the Royal Air Force's top balloon-bursting squadron with 50 being destroyed through fire.

The Squadron stayed at Bertry for a further month after the Armistice on 11 November 1918, moving to Thuillies, south-west of Charleroi, on 3 December. On 9 April 1919, Major Pickthorne left to be replaced by Major C M Crowe. The Squadron next moved to Bickendorf during May and on 6 July 1919 they crossed the Rhine to Eil. Soon afterwards, the Squadron was reduced to a cadre and embarked for England on 12 August, arriving at Tangmere. At the end of the year, the Squadron moved to Croydon on October 1919 and from there to Feltham, back to Croydon and then to Kenley, where it was disbanded on 30 January 1920.

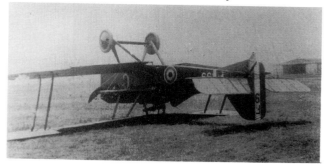

An S.E.5A overturned at Bickendorf in 1919

A F W B Proctor, VC, DSO, MC, DFC in a captured Fokker D.VII 817/18, 1918 (via Chaz Bowyer)

CHAPTER 3 - PROCCY TO HIS FRIENDS

Andrew Frederick Wetherby Proctor was born on the 4 September, 1894 at Mossel Bay, Cape Province, South Africa. He was the second and younger son of Mr and Mrs J J Proctor.

He was educated at George, Mafeking, and the old South African College (later to become the University of Cape Town). Matriculating in 1912, he commenced a course of study for his engineering diploma at this University. In 1914, he was granted a second year pass and on 1 October he became No 6348 Signaller Proctor of the Duke of Edinburgh's Own Rifles. He took part in the South West African campaign against the Germans, later becoming transferred as a signaller to the South African Field Telegraph and Postal Corps but, after three month's service, he was 'demobbed' in August 1915. For the next year, he continued his studies and completed his third year of the course.

It was in early 1917 that he met Maj A M Miller, DSO RFC, who was on his second recruiting tour of the Province. Proctor became one of the first volunteers for the RFC from this tour. On 12 March he attested as Third Class Air Mechanic and sailed for England. On arrival, a fortnight later, he was sent to No.6 Officer Cadet Battalion at South Farnborough. From there, he went to the School of Military Aeronautics at Oxford, where he underwent basic training. This was on 13 April and, six weeks later, he left for No. 5 Reserve Squadron at Castle Bromwich. It was here that he received his initial flying training. On two days, the 25th and 29th May, with Flt Sgt Perry as instructor, he flew a Maurice Farman Longhorn doing circuits and landings.

It was during this period that he dropped the name Frederick, on account of its German sound, and added the name Beauchamp, a link with some past relatives.

On 2 June, he was posted to No.24 Reserve Squadron at Netheravon, where the Commanding Officer was Maj B McEwan. From the 3rd to the 10th June, he flew on eleven occasions, totalling four hours and twenty-four minutes, all under instruction from 2nd Lt Pyecroft. He flew solo on 10th June. It was a notable

flight, for he crashed, writing off the undercarriage and the lower wing. From the 10th to the 16th, he went solo on every possible occasion and his flying time arose to nine hours fifty minutes.

During the month he was posted to Lilbourne where he joined the 'working-up' of No.84 Squadron under Maj H R Nicholl. His log book reads that he was flying an Avro 504 on 24 June with Lt Matthews as passenger. During the following month, when he was officially given his wings, he gained experience on Avros and 1½-Strutters. One of his instructors during that time was Capt Foster, one of the original flight commanders of the Squadron.

On 8 August, Maj W Sholto Douglas took command and 84 Squadron, which was originally intended to be a bomber squadron, became a fighter unit. Proctor continued his training but it is noticeable in his log that changes from the 1½-Strutter to fighter aircraft became more frequent: 4.50 hours on the Nieuport 12, 6.05 on Sopwith Pups and a 1.30 on a Sopwith Camel are all mentioned. He also flew S.E.5 A4867 for 40 minutes on the day before the Squadron moved to France on 21 September 1917.

One of his early jobs was to collect S.E.5A B56 from St Omer. A fortnight later he wrote off the machine when he attempted a forced landing due to a seized engine at Zupteens, west of Cassel. At the time he was flying a line patrol under Capt E R Pennell. On 18 October, a further patrol encountered eight enemy aircraft and broke up the formation, little occurred except another engine failure causing him to land at Bailleul but he returned to his own field later that day.

During the month, between 21st October and 22nd November, Proctor flew nineteen missions acting on four occasions as a cover to the D.H.4s of No.25 Squadron. On 11 November, the Squadron moved to Le Hameau which was in the 3rd Army area, and on the 22nd when 84 Squadron were assisting in the Cambrai advance, Proctor, who was paired with Capt Pennell, helped to bring a balloon down and forced another to be lowered. He later lost his bearings and landed at Belle Eglise where he wrote off the

Flt Lt Andrew Beacham Proctor

undercarriage. He later collected B539 from No. 2 AD at Candas, again being forced to land at Bellevue due to falling oil pressure.

Although records do not show it, Proctor was convinced that he opened his account on 5 December. He was testing his engine at 10,000 feet when he met an enemy two-seater. It was about 2,000 feet above him and he closed to within 200 yards and opened fire. The two-seater put its nose down and Proctor saw it enter a vertical dive. Unfortunately he could not follow, because the enemy rear gunner had managed to shoot through his tailplane and control wires. Proctor was convinced that this was a 'probable' and entered it as such in his log book.

On 15 December he wrote off B539 when he crashed due to fuel problems, wrecking the radiator, propeller and top planes. It was on 3 January that he claimed his first victory. On patrol with Lt Larsen they engaged two two-seaters and after a short battle both were shot down. A week later Proctor left for a fortnight's leave in England.

He returned on 28 January and resumed offensive patrols, commenting in his log that the Huns were very 'timid'. Weather conditions curtailed offensive patrols and it was not until 15 February that he and Lt J A McCudden engaged another two-seater which they promptly shot down after killing its gunner. On the 17th, his log states that he forced a V-strutter down out of control and then engaged a two-seater with no definite results. Two days later he had another Albatros when twelve aircraft of the Squadron mixed it with 15 enemy scouts. McCudden confirmed the kill for Proctor.

By now, Proctor was leading patrols consisting of Krohn, Duke and McCudden. Over La Fère, they engaged what seemed to be a patrol of six enemy scouts, but they turned out to be a decoy. A further twelve quickly entered the melée, forcing Proctor to retire, but not before one was driven down out of control. This may well have been Leut Lubbert of JG11, who was wounded after being in combat with a S.E.5. Further patrols on the 1st and 6th March proved indecisive, although a fight on the 6th brought considerable damage to Proctor's aircraft. Both of the left-hand struts and holes in the top plane and tailplane bore witness to the battle.

On the morning of 17 March, three formations acted as escorts to the D.H.4s of No.5 Squadron RNAS on a bombing

mission to Busigny. It was to be Proctor's best day, getting a Pfalz and an Albatros out of control and forcing another Pfalz to crash. During a fight with the fourth he was hit in the engine causing him to break away. At this time he was four miles over the lines and was forced to dive, being hotly pursued by the enemy. His engine finally cut over his own field.

The German offensive which was launched on 21 March gave 84 Squadron a new role - harassing the advancing infantry. That day Proctor's patrol of five aircraft, each carrying four 25-lb bombs, bombed an ammunition dump at St Quentin. On a second patrol they shot up and bombed troops near Houton Wood. Making two patrols on the 22nd, four on the 23rd and two or three daily up to the 2nd April, Proctor was kept very busy. Besides the patrols, the Squadron changed airfields three times. On 4 April they moved to Bertangles where they were to stay for five months.

Proctor's log book states that over this period of intense activity very few enemy aircraft were seen, and his primary task was ground strafing. On the 7th, Proctor left for ten days leave, but not before he had learnt that, together with Lts P K Hobson, W H Brown and E A Clear, he had been awarded the Military Cross. Capt F E Brown was awarded a bar to the Military Cross the same day. During his well-earned leave he was gazetted Captain.

He returned to the Squadron on the 16th and next day led his own flight on a ninety-minute patrol. On the 23rd, his patrol engaged nine enemy triplanes. Selecting the leader, Proctor got within 200 yards without being seen and opened fire. The 'tripe', which had a black tail and green wings, went into a dive and shed its wings. The rest of the month he led patrols on bombing and ground strafing missions.

9th May brought Proctor his 11th victory. While returning from a bombing mission, he saw a pair of S.E.5s being attacked by eight Albatros. On joining the scrap, both Proctor and Stefansson claimed victories, his twelfth followed a day later. On the 18th, the patrol he was leading engaged eleven enemy aircraft. Choosing the leading aircraft, he fired a burst. The Albatros fell over on its side and started a dive from which it never recovered and it crashed near Hangest.

A day later, when returning from an escort mission, they were attacked over Vauvillers. Three of the enemy were shot down, one by Proctor. The evening patrol brought him another Albatros which was seen to crash near Bachy. The next week proved uneventful due to poor weather conditions, but on the 27th over Mezières, Proctor shot down an Albatros and engaged two two-seaters without results. The following day a stray shot in a fight over Villers-Bretonneux forced Proctor to land at Allonville. The propeller and both guns were shattered and vibration caused a longeron to break.

Over Albert on 29 May, Lt Mathews confirmed his fifteenth victory. It is interesting to note that during May he put in 63 hours 25 minutes flying time. During a patrol on the 1 June a water pipe burst, necessitating a return to the airfield. A mixed formation of 20 enemy aircraft were encountered during the evening patrol on 3 June, one of the Pfalz being forced down on the airfield. He notes that he had a twenty-minute flight in the Pfalz the next day but he does not record his impressions.

On 7 June, a recommendation to the Officer Commanding 22nd Wing was sent by Maj Sholto Douglas regarding the immediate award of the DSO for Proctor. Its final paragraph states that: "Capt Proctor has served for nine consecutive months in France as a fighter pilot and has now accounted for 26 enemy aircraft. He is a remarkably fine patrol leader and has on many occasions when leading large formations shown the greatest skill in aerial tactics. His keenness and courage are beyond praise".

11th June added to Proctor's victories. Flying near Montdidier he attacked an Albatros which went down out of control. He followed this with a Pfalz, which caught fire as he closed with it and it dived into the ground near Cayeux. 2nd Lts Nel and Fyfe witnessed these victories. On the 13th, he attacked a balloon near Contoire which burst into flames. He then attacked a second, but was forced to break off due to heavy machine-gun fire from the ground. It is known, though, that the observer was either killed or wounded as he was seen to fall back into the basket as he attempted to jump to safety. His third patrol that day was the last of his tour, and he departed for a week's leave, followed by a short recruiting trip.

His Log Book continues: "Landed 6 August 1918. My second effort in France".

On the next day, 7 August, there opened the offensive which was destined to end the war. A new tour and Proctor was flying a new machine, D6856. Orders contained information that all EA were to be chased right down to the ground and, if possible, set on fire. This was exactly to Proctor's liking, and he carried them out the same day. Whilst flying with Maj Sholto Douglas and 2nd Lt Boudwin, he attacked two balloons near Rosières. After the first was set on fire, the second fell on horses which caused them to stampede. Bombing and ground strafing were the order of the day and on the 9th, Proctor claimed two probables; although one was witnessed by pilots of 92 Squadron, official records gave no indication of these victories.

On the 11th and the 14th he led flights escorting D.H.4s from 205 Squadron on bombing raids. Returning, they noticed enemy scouts trying to get on the bombers' tails. Closing on the D.H.4s, they succeeded in shepherding them back across the lines to Estrées. With help from 92 Squadron, they returned to their fighter role and Proctor claimed a red-fuselaged Fokker biplane in flames followed by a second out of control. (These could be the two victories logged for the 9 August; official reports tend to vary over these few days, perhaps because of the work load).

He notes in his log book that on the 20th he had a mock dog fight with the CO flying a captured Fokker D-VII. The next day he shot down a Albatros two-seater which crashed near Fay.

On the 22nd, Proctor's flight was detailed to attack balloons on the Third Corps Front. Taking advantage of the sun, he dived on the first over Assevillers and shot it down in flames. He chose the second over Hem and emptied the rest of the drum into it; it failed to catch fire. Proctor continued to attack the remaining four balloons and forced the observers to jump overboard. He later returned to the one at Hem and set it ablaze.

Two days later he tangled with a Fokker, which was one of a flight of five. After getting on its tail, he fired a short burst from about 20 yards; the enemy stalled and dived into the ground near Tempaux.

On 25 August, Proctor was again recommended for the DSO. Douglas stated that: "since 7 June when he was first recommended, he had increased his tally to forty, including seven balloons. He has a wonderful power of seeing through enemy ruses and crooked tactics, which has often stood his patrol in good stead". The award finally came through on the 29 October 1918.

Two more balloons fell to his attacks on the 27th, while on the 28th a D-VII which had strayed into the formation was set upon by the patrol and crashed near Brie. On 4 September, close cooperation with ground forces enabled his patrol to attack enemy trenches near Hancourt. Flying low enough to see ground signals, they were able to wipe out several machine-gun posts. Three days later, the flight, consisting of Proctor and 2nd Lts Highwood, Christiani and Corse, attacked balloons between Cambrai and St Quentin and fired the lot.

Five days later Proctor was nearly shot down when, after attacking one Fokker with no result, another latched on his tail and started shooting from close range. It was only the intervention of Capt C F Falkenberg, who broke off his own battle to engage the attacker and forced it to break away, that saved the day. Yet another balloon fell to Proctor's guns on the 24th, together with six more to the flight he was leading. The 27th brought him another balloon but, although Proctor was flying several patrols a day, very little was coming his way.

Work was resumed in the upper air on 1 October when a squadron formation met thirty Fokker D-VIIs and three two-seaters. The Fokkers were all brightly painted, with yellow, red and blue striped tailplanes. The two-seaters had orange noses. Two fell to the guns of Proctor; one with a blue tail crashed near Fontaine, the second with a red tailplane exploded into flames.

The 6th and 7th proved uneventful and on the 8th the Squadron moved to Bouvincourt. Later the same day Proctor found a Rumpler north-east of Maretz and, following it down, he saw it crash and burst into flames. He was wounded in the forearm by fire from the ground returned and landed safely at the airfield.

This was to be the end of the war for Capt A W Beauchamp Proctor, and he went into hospital to have his wounds treated.

A further honours recommendation dated 14 October refers especially to the exploits which took place on the 28 August. Proctor was given particular credit for the balloons shot down on the Australian Corps front. 29th August, 7th September and 1st and 2nd October were all mentioned in the award recommendation. Witness statements from Capt Carl Falkenberg, Lt F H Taylor and 2nd Lts Hill and Whyte were all added to the Commanding Officer's statement, and it is obvious that the combined effort led to the award of the Victoria Cross on 30 November 1918.

The *London Gazette* added: "In all he has proved himself conqueror over 54 foes, destroying 22 enemy machines, 16 enemy balloons and driving down out of control a further 16 aircraft. Capt A W Proctor's work in attacking enemy troops on the ground and

in reconnaissance during the withdrawal following the Battle of St Quentin from the 21st March 1918, and during the victorious advance of our armies commencing on the 8th August 1918 has been almost unsurpassed in its brilliancy and as such as made an impression of those serving in his squadron and those around him that will not easily be forgotten".

Proctor was discharged from hospital in early March 1919, and immediately left on a tour of the United States to aid the Liberty Loan Drive. On returning to England in July, he attended the RAF College at Cranwell, being granted a permanent commission as a Flight Lieutenant in November. On the 27th of that month he was invested at Buckingham Palace with his Victoria Cross, Distinguished Service Order and Distinguished Flying Cross.

The following February found Proctor on a boat to South Africa, arriving at Cape Town on the 20th where he was given a hero's welcome. Returning to England at Christmas 1920, he was posted to No.24 Squadron. Research does not give us a date for Proctor's posting to Upavon, but from a acquaintance of the author who lived at nearby Pewsey and met Proctor, it must have been early in 1921. From a chance encounter it seems that a friendship started between Proctor and the author's family, leading to their acquiring Proctor's log book and photograph albums when they were disposed of after his death.

Opinions vary as to the reason Proctor was stationed at Upavon. Reports in the local press state that he was on an engineering course, but both ACM Sir Theodore McEvoy and Gp Capt Cahill say that it was more likely to be on a temporary basis, training for his part in the forthcoming 1921 Air Pageant.

Here it was at Upavon, while flying a Sopwith Snipe, that Proctor was killed. It is known that Proctor was only 5 ft 1 in tall, and coupled with this is the fact his rudder pedals were always made up with blocks of wood. The Snipe was not equipped with them, and whilst attempting a roll off the top of a loop he lost control and dived into the ground at Enford, a mile or so away from the airfield. He was twenty-five years old.

He was buried at Upavon after a funeral service with full RAF honours. Later his body was taken to his home in South Africa.

The memorial bought by public subscription in memory of Beauchamp Proctor in Mafeking cemetery

D.H.9As of No.84 Squadron over the Tigris near Basra

CHAPTER 4 - A NEW ROLE FOR 84

For many years, going back well before the 1914-18 War, a wild and rebellious character known as the 'Mad Mullah' had been creating problems in British Somaliland. It was the responsibility of the British Government to curb, and finally put an end to, the Mullah and his disruptive activities. But in the aftermath of the Great War, there was no money and little enthusiasm for taking up arms and committing thousands of men in a campaign which had already lasted too long and cost far too much. Chief of Air Staff Lord Trenchard pointed out to Lord Milner, then the Secretary of State for the Colonies, that the situation was just the kind the Royal Air Force could handle cheaply and effectively. Against strong ministerial opposition, but with the valued support of Winston Churchill, Secretary of State for War and Air, Trenchard argued his case and was given the go-ahead.

In January 1920, Group Captain R Gordon and Wing Commander F Bowhill flew to Somaliland and, with one bomber squadron, subdued the Mad Mullah and his lawless tribesmen. Bombed out of one fort after another, the rebel leader finally escaped to Abyssinia only to be killed shortly afterwards. Peace had been restored to Somaliland and all within three weeks, at an overall cost of less than £80,000. The operation has been described as the cheapest war in history. Here was a role that the RAF could play better than anyone else and when trouble broke in Iraq, Whitehall soon realised that this called for similar action, but on a much larger scale. The stage was set for the RAF to take up arms in the desert.

The success at such a small cost of the operation in Somaliland had convinced Whitehall that Trenchard's ideas were not to be dismissed out of hand. Despite much opposition it was eventually agreed that the Middle East and India would make ideal proving grounds for his revolutionary proposals. India already had its own army and this would be supplemented by squadrons of the RAF. But both Iraq and Palestine were new mandates thrust upon Britain by the League of Nations, a fact which almost precipitated a violent rebellion in Iraq early in 1920. It cost over £38 million in a single year to suppress this uprising, with 92 units of British and Indian troops and four RAF squadrons.

Trenchard was quick to seize this opportunity to show how the Air Force could police Iraq at a fraction of the cost, reducing the army units by no less than four-fifths and cutting expenditure to a mere £7.5 million. All he asked was that the RAF should be increased to eight squadrons. In this way began more than two decades of control without occupation, and it must be regarded as one of the major achievements of the Royal Air Force. No.84 Squadron was to play no small part in carrying out Trenchard's scheme over the next twenty years.

The rebellion referred to proved an expensive introduction to the British mandate. Although the Army strongly disapproved of the notion that air power could replace strong forces of soldiers on the ground, the circumstances in Iraq made this a practical proposition and the financial savings was the overriding factor. The rebellion that had started in May had been more or less quelled by August 1920.

During the 1914-18 War, British and Indian troops had fought a violent battle against the occupying Turks in the Southern Desert of Iraq at a spot called Shaibah, some 18 miles inland from the port of Basrah. There still remained the ruins of a Turkish fort and a few huts which had been erected by the British. Beyond that nothing - nothing but flat shimmering desert of hard baked earth in all directions and a climate almost beyond description, from freezing nights in winter to roasting heat up to 125 degrees in summer, with appalling humidity if the wind was blowing from the Gulf and long-lasting dust storms thrown in for good measure. But as the Bedouin had shown, human life could survive there, so 84 Squadron was sent to do just that and it continued to do so for year after blazing year for 20 years.

To be strictly accurate Shaibah was not in Mesopotamia, as the name means 'between two rivers' (Tigris and Euphrates). It was nearly 20 miles from the Shatt-el-Arab, the name given after the two rivers had joined. Apart from the few huts, the decision was made because of the firmer texture of sand. A well was sunk but it was found that only brackish water was forthcoming so a pipe line was installed from Basra.

During the intervening months, an ex-Naval flyer, Sqn Ldr B L Huskisson DSC, had been sent to Egypt where he gathered about him the nucleus of a new squadron and then embarked for Basrah.

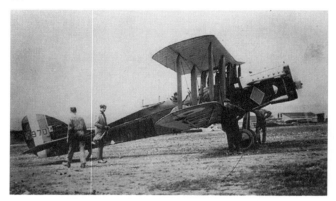

F970 with "Diamonds" marking running up at Shaibah
(S. Leslie Collection)

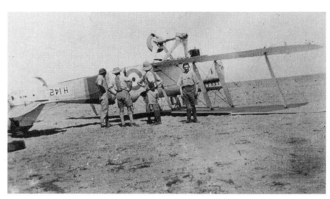

H142 overturned, presumably having lost a wheel on landing.
(via A. Thomas)

After an uncomfortably hot journey down the Red Sea to Aden and then around Arabia to the Persian Gulf, the party disembarked at Basrah and proceeded to Baghdad.

In the heat of a Mesopotamian August (promises of a trooping season in the cooler winter months had not yet come into operation), re-formation of the Squadron continued and on 15 August 1920, No.84 was once again an operational squadron after only a few months in cold storage.

The unit was now equipped with the D.H.9A bombers, or 'Ninaks' as they were called. They were appreciably larger than the S.E.5As of the wartime years, being two-seater biplanes with a twelve-cylinder 'Liberty' engine behind a big rectangular radiator. The original D.H.9 had incurred some caustic comments from Trenchard towards the end of the Great War and he compared it unfavourably with the D.H.4. However, the D.H.9A was a considerable improvement and appeared to have an adequate performance for the unusual duties it was to perform in Iraq. It was also suitable for ground strafing. The Squadron was now defined as a bomber squadron with its official designation being No. 84 (Bomber) Squadron, RAF.

Based on the aerodrome at Baghdad West, No.84 was involved in the final stages of subduing the anti-British tribesmen who were still active in various parts of the country, particularly in the Central Region and in the North around Mosul. In the latter area, the terrain was especially difficult, being extremely mountainous with deep gorges affording plenty of cover for the Arab forces on the ground and with little flat land suitable for emergency landings.

Within days of reforming, No. 84 (Bomber) Squadron wrote off one of its aircraft, E8601 being compelled to force-land at Hillah; due to its inaccessibility it was impossible to retrieve. Three weeks later, a more serious incident occurred when the crew flying H2838 was shot down while attempting to drop food to a stranded Bristol F.2b crew. They force-landed in the river at Dangatora, 20 miles south-west of Sawawa, Iraq, and, though seen to wade ashore, they were taken prisoner and killed. The same day H58 was shot down near Khidr; it is not known if the crew survived.

On 1 November, another crew was lost when an aircraft taking-off accidentally dropped one of its bombs. Not only was the aircraft and its crew lost but E779 immediately below was also destroyed. So, within three months of reforming in the Middle East, No.84 Squadron had written off six of its aircraft.

For some reason, the official records, not only of 84 Squadron but of Iraq Command as a whole, seem no longer to exist. Fortunately it has been possible to fill some of the gaps from other sources and from verbatim reports of former members of the Squadron who served with No.84 during the early and middle twenties. No sooner were the rebels in the north persuaded to give up their unfriendly habits, than trouble started in the south. On 20 September 1920, 'A' Flight moved to Nasiriyah. It was commanded by Flt Lt Henry Thorold DSC, DFC, AFC, another ex-Naval pilot who finished his RAF career as an Air Vice Marshal.

After dealing with the troublesome Sheikh Mahmud on the northern borders of the country, which included parts of the undefined area of Kurdistan, No.84 now had to deal with tribesmen who were creating a disturbance in the south of the country. Just over a month after they became operational at Baghdad West, Headquarters and 'B' Flight moved south and took up residence at Shaibah which was to become their home for the next twenty years. They were soon joined by 'C' Flight and on 14 December, 'A' Flight rejoined them from Nasiriyah. On 14 January 1921, none other than Flt Lt Hugh Saunders was appointed to take command of 'C' Flight. At the same time Flt Lt C V Porter took command of 'B' Flight.

A crew member was killed on 2 February 1921, when attempting to swing the propeller after the aircraft landed at a desert landing strip. A few days later, H117 crashed and overturned when landing at Nasiriyah.

Domestically, the life of No.84 after its arrival at Shaibah was less than happy. Apart from the unspeakable living conditions and the climate, there was the rather unattractive job of dealing with the Arabs in an unfamiliar country and with very little experience to guide them. Shaibah soon became a legend in the RAF and remained so until it was handed back to the Iraqis in 1956. Its isolated situation, its climate and its complete lack of amenities soon caused it to be regarded unofficially and quite inaccurately as a 'Punishment Station'. Even as late as 1940, sympathy was not lacking for those that had the misfortune to be posted to No. 84 Squadron at Shaibah.

It was not easy to draw the line between the political and racial troubles and the continual tribal bickering amounting at times to outright war between the Arabs themselves. In the initial stages during the rebellion, it was obvious that British forces were confronted by a population which found itself under the supervision

D.H.9A E803 displays its "Clubs" marking. Note spare wheel

J7027 over Shaibah. (S.Leslie Collection)

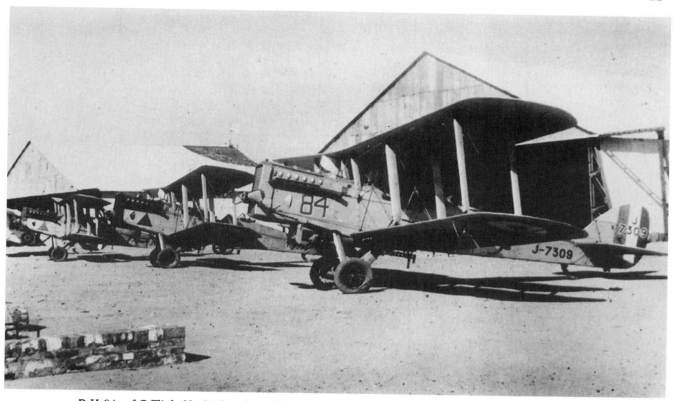

D.H.9As of C Flight No.84 Squadron. J7309 carries the squadron number in lieu of a Flight marking

a foreign power and it did not relish the idea at all. Having endured the domination of the Turks for so long, it was not unnatural that the average Iraqi should feel that he might now run his own country and he resented very strongly the intrusion of foreign troops and diplomats telling him what he could and could not do. Needless to say, it was not that simple, otherwise the League of Nations would not have set up the mandate in the first place. It remained for the British troops to see that peace was maintained and general order set up amongst the tribes who seemed to thrive on indiscipline and, frequently, ruthless crime.

Gradually the army was withdrawn, to the great satisfaction of the population. Few could have realised that military occupation was far from over, for it was replaced by a form of policing which would prove far more effective. It was to come from the air. It was now the job of the Air Force to subdue the warring tribes and convince them, by force if necessary, that they must obey the rule of law, which was not in their nature at all.

It was the custom of many Sheiks and their unruly followers to indulge in pillage and theft almost as if it was a national sport. But often their approach was so ferocious as to be completely horrific and this had to be curbed. The task facing 84 Squadron was not an easy one and it had to be learned from scratch. Patrolling the desert sounds simple enough but a method had to be devised of locating trouble and for dealing with it efficiently.

The desert in Iraq is featureless, especially from the air. A map reference is of little use to a pilot whose knowledge of the terrain is negligible. The first problems were to find the rebels and, when some tribesmen had been spotted, ascertain that they were in fact the rebels and not a friendly tribe. This was soon painfully clear to a young Army officer who was on special service in Iraq. His name was John Glubb. At the age of 25, he had been in Mesopotamia since July 1920 and had already established a close relationship with many of the Arab tribes. His experience was to become invaluable and he quickly formed a link with the RAF.

Operating chiefly in the south of the country, part of which is known as the Nejd, he soon realised that the two-year tour of the RAF was insufficient time in which to become familiar with the desert, which provided no landmarks to untrained eyes. He quickly appreciated the fact that ground forces might depend on air patrols for locating nomadic tribes, but the former could gather information from friendly tribes on the ground which pilots in the air would never be able to obtain. There was thus a strong case for the closest co-operation between the native troops and the police on the ground and the men in the air. Over the ensuing years, Captain Glubb and his meagre forces moving around the desert worked closely with the RAF and with No.84 in particular. It is known that

Glubb often flew with Flt Lt Jenkins of No.84 Squadron.

Policies decided upon in the capital, Baghdad, were of no use if they could not be carried to the recalcitrant sheikhs who must be compelled to observe them. In the vast area which was involved, this was no easy job but the aircraft of 84 Squadron were found to extremely useful in this role. Leaflets could be dropped on the camps of those that created trouble. Sometimes this would be sufficient to deter the tribes. If threats were ignored, a flight would be sent over to drop small 20-lb bombs to emphasise that the government meant business.

It was incidents such as this that showed up the political delicacy of the role of the RAF. Glubb, who knew exactly what he was doing, must have endured a great deal of frustration and this must have rubbed off on the shoulders of members of 84 Squadron with whom he worked so closely.

October 1921 brought a change of Commanding Officers. Sqn Ldr Huskisson was posted home and replaced by Sqn Ldr 'Bill' Sowrey. The existence of the troops in Shaibah was causing considerable discontent and the atmosphere was far from happy. The Arab raids in various parts of the desert still continued and the aircrew had a busy time patrolling hundreds of square miles of barren land and, when necessary, taking part in the punitive raids themselves.

The same month a bomb exploded just after an aircraft took off. Not only were the crew killed but the crew of E9919 parked nearby were severely injured and their aircraft damaged beyond repair.

In the early twenties, many of the young officers went on to make a name for themselves and rose to high command before and during the Second World War. Henry Thorold went on to AVM, Tony Paxton, who won the DFC, also reached AVM rank. Hugh Saunders became an Air Chief Marshal during the fifties; others to reach senior ranks were C E Porter, F J Mellersh, F Inglis and P Wrigglesworth. F J Fogarty, who joined the Squadron in November 1922, later became its Commanding Officer during the thirties and retired as Air Chief Marshal Sir Francis Fogarty.

Command of 84 Squadron changed again on 6 May 1922, when Sqn Ldr Sowrey was replaced by Sqn Ldr S V Brown who, at the age of 33, was regarded as positively elderly. He was not happy with what he found at Shaibah and soon set about making improvements at the camp to alleviate the lot of the long-suffering airmen and their officers. The Headquarters at Hinaidi were made aware of the shortcomings of the camp at Shaibah and local labour was engaged to carry out building. The result was that the camp gradually became more habitable and morale improved. In consequence the Squadron became far more efficient.

Shaibah in the 1920s. The landing area is to the top right hand corner of the photograph. It did, however, have its own railway.

Vernon Brown, or 'VB' as he was generally known, having decided that living accommodation was the top priority, soon had things under way. One of his first improvements was the construction of the fire pool which, apart from its duty as a water tank, doubled for swimming and water polo. Nothing could be done about the climate except to take all possible steps to keep cool. During the hot season, work began soon after dawn to take full advantage of the cool hour or two before breakfast. This meal, at 0800, usually started with hot porridge, although there were cereals as an alternative. Eggs and bacon followed and there were always gallons of scalding tea.

A working parade followed at 0900 after which everyone dispersed to their own particular section until after lunch-time. 'Tiffin' was always a hot meal, in spite of midday temperatures of well over 100 degrees. During a heat wave, temperatures of 132 degrees were recorded. Normally work then finished for the day and apart from the signals staff and a handful of men on special duties, everyone got their heads down till 1600, when mugs of steaming tea arrived. This was brought around by the 'chicko', the younger of two natives allocated to each hut. With the temperatures now falling (80 degrees), the evenings were spent in civvies where McEwans Export was readily available.

Life in the Officers' Mess was on similar, if more elegant, lines. In this elaborate building there was a spacious ante-room with a fireplace made from stone taken from the ancient city of Ur of the Chaldees. There were also two mounted skulls labelled 'Winner of the Dive Bombing Competition' and 'Winner of the Delayed Parachute Drop'.

Later years brought further amenities in the shape of a cinema/theatre where films were changed once if not twice a week. The alternative to the cinema was a rather dubious snack bar in a little hut within the camp's Indian quarter which a trusty Indian ran as a restaurant. The menu was limited and often consisted of egg and chips fried in ghee (the local substitute for fat). Otherwise there was nothing for it but 'a night on the beer', which at three hours an evening for seven nights a week worked out rather

expensive, beer being a costly beverage. Those higher up the social scale could indulge in whisky at a much lower price. The anomaly in prices brought rumours of discontent from the average erk.

It must be remembered that the pay of British other ranks, even in the middle thirties, was only about three shillings a day. A recruit in the UK received two shillings a day (10p) which was slightly increased after he had completed his initial training. From this princely amount there were always deductions for things like barrack damages.

One of the more peculiar items of the social calendar at Shaibah was a ball organised to greet the newcomers on their draft from England and to bid an alcoholic farewell to those who had completed their tour of two years. They were managed by an elected Mayor and Mayoress, their councillors and 'Dapper Dan'. Suitable clothes were often made by the Indian tailors on the camp. The men of the new draft on arrival by train from Basrah would be met by a huge sign reading 'Abandon hope all ye who enter here' and were confronted by a rampaging horde of lunatics and savages, all obviously under the influence of tropical fever and alcohol. Having been escorted into camp by the rabble, they were assembled on what served as a Barrack Square and addressed by camp dignatories wearing full civic regalia made from strings of bottle tops. At the camp dance, prizes were given by the Commanding Officer for the best-dressed couple.

In June 1922, E786 stalled and spun in after take-off, followed a few days later by E9909 being forced to land in a sandstorm en route to Samurah in Iraq; although it was repaired on the spot, it was destined to last only another two months. Returning from a raid, it crashed on landing at Shaibah and was written off.

It is noted that about this period the first indication of the playing card symbol began to appear on 'A' Flight aircraft. Whether the good luck symbol of the vertical swastika and the coloured triangles of 'B' and 'C' Flights appeared at the same time is not known. The first mention of these appear nearly two years later.

In April 1923, a rebel sheikh confined to the Nasiriyah area

No 84 (Bombing) Squadron, Shaibah, Iraq, 1927.

Officers of No.84 Squadron in 1927. These have been identified as:
Back row; Matheson, Glenn, Doc Smith, Nuttal, Tomkins, Sandiford, Von Nichol
Front row: Porter, De Burgh, Robertson, Vincent, Russell, Barrett, Goldie
(Photo: T. Mellor-Ellis)

absconded. Leaflets were dropped but bombs were necessary before he returned. A few months later, a dispute over grazing rights was also sorted out by a display of force from the air, with support from the Armoured Car Companies. Even this did not have the desired effect, for a number of tribes in the Samawa area began a revolt in the October of that year. After patrolling the area, the 'Ninaks' of 84 Squadron then engaged in offensive action. Within days, a revolt which could have spread rapidly was brought under control.

No doubt mistakes were made, but the cost of capture by Arab or Kurdish tribesmen must have helped to concentrate the minds of aircrews and fitters alike. If captured, the rumoured punishment was castration in non-clinical conditions, usually by women of the tribe. Hence the introduction of the famous 'Goolie Chit'. Written in Arabic, Persian and Kurdish, it guaranteed Turkish gold coins for the safe return of the downed airmen. As one old gentleman who flew the Vincent many years later said to me, "The problem was finding someone who could read".

Although Sqn Ldr V S Brown almost completed his two-year tour, he was followed by a series of officers, none of whom stayed longer than a few months.

Strangely, I can find no mention of any accidents during the whole of 1923 and it was not until 25 February 1924 that F2856 was compelled to force-land during a duststorm, overturning as it touched down. This occurred near Jalibah in Iraq and Jalibah was again the area where H147 landed south of the town; the crew was never found.

On 11 August 1924, D.H.9A J7253 flew into the ground and overturned near Shaibah; fortunately the crew were released before it burst into flames. What is quite noticeable is the number of minor mishaps which occurred; in most cases the aircraft were returned to the Aircraft Park at Hinaidi for rebuild or refurbishment before they were sent out as replacements for another aircraft, perhaps from Nos.30 or 55 Squadrons. Some aircraft have even returned to 84 Squadron after a lapse of several years and after several rebuilds.

During March 1926, F970 crashed, resulting in loss of life. In the same month, H138 swung on take-off, not only causing damage to two other aircraft but demolishing part of the perimeter fencing.

Later that year, H142 and H143 collided during taxying,

H143 being written off. H142 was returned to Hinaidi where it was adapted for dual-control. It was to reappear at Shaibah later in its long life.

During the early twenties, it was common practise for crews to wear a topee over the standard flying helmet. They had also to wear spine pads under their shirts as protection against sunstroke. The discomfort caused by these were often extreme. The slipstream playing on top of the topee caused the goggles to vibrate and any movement of the head outside the protection of the windscreen allowed the slipstream to get under the brim of the topee, often giving the neck a nasty jerk. First the spine pad and then the topee was discarded and their place was taken by tinted goggles and sun visors. Medical science had reached the conclusion that it was better to protect one's eyes than the head or the back.

It was not until Sqn Ldr F J Vincent DFC arrived in March 1927 that one can refer to the official records, soon after Flt Lts N M Russell, J F Barrett DFC and M W Ridgway took over as flight commanders. The same year brought an increase of 23 personnel to the Squadron.

On 2 August, Flt Lt N M Russell with two machines was detailed to remain at Nasiriyah to keep a look-out for Flt Lt C R Carr, who was engaged on an England-India flight. The following day he returned to Shaibah having learnt that Flt Lt Carr had failed in his bid by crashing in the River Danube.

The same month, it was rumoured that hostilities were to break out in the Nasiriyah area. All three flights were put on stand-by and were to be prepared to move at two hours notice. A reconnaissance carried out over the following days reported that tribesmen were fleeing towards the railway. Five aircraft were detailed to proceed, the pilots being Flt Lt J F Barrett DFC, Fg Offs M W Goldie and F E Nuttall and Sgts V G Wilson and M W Foy. Three were to carry out the reconnaissance, the others to remain at Abu Ghar in reserve, all carrying a load of 20-lb bombs and Lewis guns and ammunition. Later it was learnt that it was all a false alarm and that the rumour had been circulated by a local sheikh in order to induce members of his tribe at Busaiyah and Jamamah to join him. Further unrest followed in October.

On 13 October, a new draft of three officers and 50 other ranks arrived on the Dorsetshire. The 14th was given over to the 'handing over' and 'taking over' by the relieving personnel. Two days later Fg Off R W Glenn and 54 airmen left the station for other overseas commands.

Notification was received from Air Headquarters Baghdad on 16 October that the Squadron must stand by and be ready to proceed to Nasiriyah at short notice to relieve the crews and aircraft of 55 Squadron, who were there on reconnaissance duties. The unrest in this vicinity had been smouldering for some time and the climax arrived when natives refused to surrender to bail. Four aircraft, led by Sqn Ldr F J Vincent, left the following day. Ultimatum messages were dropped on all villages in the Al Hatim area. This had little effect and on the 20th bombs were dropped with satisfactory results.

It has been estimated that No.84 Squadron had an area of 25,000 square miles to patrol. An incident on 6 November resulted in the occupants of a police post at Busaiyah being massacred, the perpetrators fleeing to the Nejd area and to safety. To cover the re-occupation of the police post at the centre of a series of armoured car patrol routes, a small force was formed under Sqn Ldr F J Fogarty DFC, CO of No.84 Squadron. The force known as Vincol (Vincent's column). He was allotted a flight of D.H.9As which flew to the advanced landing ground at Abu Ghar, protected by two sections of armoured cars sent out from Basra. For supplies, he was given the use of two Victorias from No. 70 Squadron. With this small but effective force, the post at Busaiyah was reoccupied on 18 November.

It was noted that Ibn Saud was unable to prevent his tribes from continuing raids across the border and action was authorised on 3 January 1928. It was obvious that a much larger force than 'Vincol' was needed. To cover this, HQ Iraq devised 'Akforce', allotting 26 aircraft and 46 vehicles based at Basra, with its operational advanced HQ at Ur Junction under the command of Air Cdre T C Higgins CB CMG. To drive the Akhwans back, Higgins proposed two main RAF posts in the desert, No.55 Squadron flying in from Hinaidi to Busaiyah to form 'Buscol' under Sqdn Ldr H A Whistler DSO DFC, whilst No.84 Sqdn under Fogarty went to Shulman to form 'Nucol'. To form a supply column, forty Ford Model T vans were sent by rail from Basra and Baghdad for local use at Ur. The mobile column plus the Victoria transports were known as 'Supcol' under Wg Cdr H R Nicholls (No.84 Squadron's first CO). The Fords set out from Ur on 9 January, but were soon brought to a halt by a gale which threatened to blow them over. All flying was grounded.

Warning notices were dropped on the 11th, telling the tribesmen to retreat to a distance of four days march from the Iraqi border, failing which any persons found would be liable to air attack without warning. Seven days were allowed for the notices to be completely understood. Daily aircraft patrolled the areas looking for signs of movement and on the 18th the first nudging began. At first they seemed willing to comply but they soon had to be encouraged by a series of bombing raids around their encampments. Cattle would be stampeded and some stock killed.

On 27 January, a party some 300 strong raided Kuwaiti tribes 70 miles south-west of Basrah and next day RAF aircraft joined in their pursuit, finding and attacking one large party near Hafah. On his return, Sgt Hale crashed on landing, writing off J7847. On the 30th, six aircraft located 100 camels and approximately 40 men eight miles from Hafah. 24 bombs were dropped and 950 rounds of ammunition were fired, the estimated casualties being eight men and ten camels. During the attack Fg Off Kellett was forced to land only 400 yards from the Wadi where the party was hiding. Realising his difficulty, Flt Lt Barrett landed his aircraft and picked up Kellett under fire. Barrett was later to receive the DSO for his

bravery.

The expected attack from the Akhwan came on 19 February near the town of Jarishan. It fell to the aircraft of 84 Squadron based at Shaibah to bomb the raiders' main camp as a reprisal. During this attack, the leading D.H.9A was hit and the attack was broken off. It was resumed on the 20th, when a D.H.9A was shot down and the pilot killed. More armoured cars were despatched from Shaibah and on the 21st the crew of one car captured a wounded Arab who said that the main body of raiders was moving south to concentrate on Es Safa to distribute their loot.

On 24 February, on receipt of orders from Akforce, Sqn Ldr Vincent proceeded to Rukhaimiyah with six aircraft to prepare for a raid on Es Safa, the distribution centre for the raiders. At 0720, fifteen aircraft consisting of twelve D.H.9As and three Victorias left the airfield, the three Victorias in the lead, with the D.H.9As of 55 Squadron on their port side and the six from 84 Squadron on the starboard. Due to adverse winds, the outward journey took 3½ hours. A total of six 550-lb and 141 20-lb bombs were dropped, obtaining several direct hits on the fort and other hutments. All aircraft returned safely.

In May, No 84's Ninaks took part on a raid on the remote island of Gubbah, on the Hammar Lake, which had become part of a rebel sheikh's stronghold. Deliberately bombing the surrounding bank, it enabled the lake to flood the rebels out of their positions. In June of that year (1928), he finally gave a written undertaking to restrain his tribes from raiding and by 3 June, Akforce had ceased to exist. All units withdrew to their normal bases and duties. Over the five months of its commitment with the unit nearly 2,500 flying hours were amassed. These anti-Nejd operations were typical of the RAF's duties in Iraq during the twenties. It was remarkable that, with the stress of flying over areas which were not even mapped, the ever-conscious fear of an engine failure and primitive conditions, that the morale of the Squadron's crews never faltered.

Ten years after they were designed, the D.H.9A was still the work-horse of the Iraqi command. Over the years it was burdened with spare wheels, tropical radiators, bed rolls and other personal gear when on detachment, water bags and external bomb racks - all of which lessened its performance. Other loads included bulky hand-held cameras necessary for the unending task of reconnaissance and aerial mapping. The maximum bomb load could amount to 740 lb. Two machine guns were often carried and, in later years, some aircraft were fitted with experimental wireless sets.

Over the last few months that it was becoming obvious that the Ninaks were coming to the end of their service career, mishaps were becoming more frequent and often it was the case of having only six aircraft on strength. In February, H3515 had virtually collapsed on landing; in March, J7882 lost its undercarriage after hitting a ridge while making an emergency landing at Nugrat Salman. Later that year J7872 was struck by E963 on take-off, both being considered beyond repair. Two more were written off when one taxied into another while preparing for a night exercise.

By the late summer 1928, the obsolescence of the D.H.9A was finally recognised by higher authority and by September two of No.84's flights were equipped with the Westland Wapiti. As far as is known, the last incident involving a D.H.9A of 84 Squadron occurred on 29 September 1929, when J7054 crashed on landing. Although it is generally thought that all of the Ninaks had left No.84 by the end of 1928, there are references to J7872 still on the Squadron's strength on 14 October 1930 and an even later mention was H142, the aircraft which was adapted for dual control, being used during September 1931.

ان هذه الطائرة انكليزية والضباط الذين فيها م انكليز والذي يصادمهم فى اثناء طريقهم ويتشبث بحركة صدم والذي يلحق بهم ادنى ضرر يعاقب بالجزاء الصارم ويضرب بالقنابل الشديدة من فوق . اما الذين يعينوم عند اللزوم ويساعدهم فى امرهم عند طلبهم لذلك فان الحكومة ترتاح لهم جداً وتلطفهم على احسن صورة .

٣٠ آب ١٩٢٣ بغداد

القائد العام ومشير الطيران

و انكليز طياره سيدر واى عنده ده ادماره ده
الانكليز ضابطه بدر . و نظره دشمنلق ايدن
وكنديلرينه ضرر ورن كيمسه لر الك اغير
بصورتده جزا كورورلر وقارودن اوزرلرينه
ومبال آتيلور . اما ايستعلكرى وقتده
كنديلرينه يارده ايدنلره مساعداتده ولو نائلرى
حكومت كمال ممنونيتله تلطيف ايدر .

٣٠ اغستوس ١٩٢٣ بغداد

باش قوماندان
ومشير طيران

امه طياره انكليزه وام بياواتش ضابطان
انكليزان . هر جي كي اذيئيان بدا و دشمنايتيان
لكل بكات جزاى كردى ادرينى وه يوما
له مرهوه عوا كردتهوه . اما هر جي كي له
وقي حاجتدا مساعده ويار دهيان بدا حكومت
ممنوني انى ومكافاني جا كيان ادانى .

باش قوماندان ومشير طيران

٣٠ آغستوس ١٩٢٣
بغداد

Blood Chit

No. 84 Squadron Wapitis over Ashar, Basra, at the end of 1933. J9838 has been fitted with floats for operations along the Gulf coast but this scheme was not pursued.

CHAPTER 5 - STILL AT SHAIBAH, BLOODY SHAIBAH

The general purpose military aircraft grew out of the practice in the World War 1 of utilising the same type of aircraft to do a variety of different jobs. It was not uncommon for the same machine to be used for light bombing, artillery observation patrols and other reconnaissance flights involving the use of wireless and cameras, for carrying out individual personnel duties, including the occasional use as an ambulance.

Despite the reluctance of the authorities to sanction financial outlay for new types of aircraft on the one hand and the reluctance of the RAF to surrender their beloved old-timers on the other, replacement became inevitable. In the case of the D.H.9A this came in 1927 when a competition was held at Martlesham Heath to decide upon a replacement. One of the requirements issued by the Air Ministry was that the new aircraft should use many of the spare parts of the D.H.9A which were available at many of the RAF stations, particularly those which were overseas.

The prototype Wapiti had wings, tail surfaces, ailerons and interplane struts which were all D.H.9A components. The fuselage entailed considerable redesign to meet service requirements, being wider and more than a foot deeper. The engine used was the well-proven Bristol Jupiter which offered the pilots an all-round improvement in flying performances.

The Wapitis issued to No.84 Squadron were the first to enter RAF service. Four aircraft arriving at Shaibah during October 1928 (J9078, J9086, J9088 and J9091).

In the same month, Sqn Ldr J J Breen replaced Sqn Ldr F J Vincent as Commanding Officer, who moved to command No.45 Squadron. Other new arrivals included Flt Lts E Bussell and E Drummond and Fg Offs N M Pleasance and J Harris. Departures included Flt Lt J F Barrett DSO DFC and Fg Off R Kellett.

On 24 November, the Squadron football team won the Basrah Cup, a week later they were hosts to teams from HMS *Effingham* which was paying a courtesy visit to the port. The Squadron was also visited by the AOC Middle East Command, Air Vice-Marshal Sir Robert Brooke-Popham KCB CMG DSO AFC.

It is interesting to note that the total hours flown during 1928 numbered 5,286. It is also noticeable that more NCO pilots are being posted to the Squadron. On 20 February 1929, Flt Lt Lock led 'A' Flight to Busaiyah; eight days later they returned to Shaibah. During the time they were away the Squadron played host to the Chief of Staff Air Commodore C S Burnett CB CBE DSO, who was visiting the Iraqi airfields.

In connection with the operations against the Akhwan tribesmen in the Southern Desert, Iraq, from November 1927 to May 1928, the Distinguished Flying Medal was awarded to Sgt Edward Coleman and LAC Colin Reeve. Sqn Ldr Francis John Vincent DFC, Flt Lt Michael Ridgway and LAC W J Singleton were 'Mentioned in Despatches'.

On 16 May 1929, the Fairey Long Range Monoplane, flown by Sqn Ldr A G Jones-Williams and Flt Lt N H Jenkins, landed at Shaibah on its return flight from Karachi. This was the first non-stop flight from the UK to India. It resumed its flight on the following day.

On 24 March, two Wapitis were allotted to the Squadron for conversion to floats. It seems likely that only one (J9838) was converted. Trials took place during 1931 and 1932. Normally kept on the slipway at Basrah, it was maintained by 203 Squadron. In 1934 it was converted to a normal undercarriage and was based at Hinaidi.

During September, 'A' and 'B' Flights received the Wapiti IIa and this was celebrated by winning the Sassoon Cup for bombing at Hinaidi. The year ended with three Wapitis fitted with long range tanks leaving Baghdad on a trial flight to Cairo non-stop. The flying time was 9½ hours, the return flight, also non-stop, being completed in three-quarters of an hour less.

In April 1932, Sqn Ldr Hardstaff, who had recently been promoted to Wing Commander, left the Squadron, leaving Flt Lt E E Arnold in temporary charge.

On 1 June, assistance was given to a French Air Orient airliner which had force-landed in the salt marshes 25 miles south-east of Shaibah. A series of sorties were made, dropping bundles of chittai (matting) which, when spread on the soft sand, enabled the machine to take off and resume its flight.

Sqn Ldr P L Plant arrived to take command of the Squadron on 3 September 1932. Recently, in correspondence with John Wolstenholme, who served under him, John wrote: "Plant had the habit of changing into Arab dress and mysteriously wandering about in the middle of the night with the object of making contacts

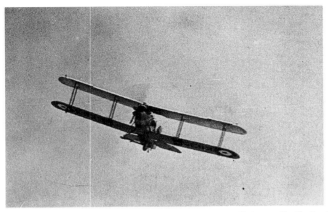 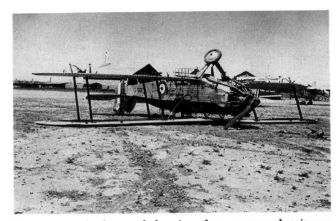

Wapiti K1135 left a wheel behind on take-off from Shaibah. Landing on one wheel caused the aircraft to overturn but it was repaired and returned to service

for intelligence purposes. Whether this was true is debatable, for he resigned from the service five months later, once again leaving Flt Lt E E Arnold in charge.

Three months later on 20 May 1933, Sqn Ldr S F Vincent arrived to take command. Vincent writes in an unpublished manuscript: "The position entailed the command of the Squadron and the station with its many commitments - military and civil - with the rank of Squadron Leader with an adjutant, which now would, I am sure, have meant a Group Captain and staff!"

"In spite of everything it was a happy station. We did a great deal of flying, and entertainment provided meant doing it yourself. I managed to scrounge a projector and films for a one night a week treat. Concerts and dances were held regularly (men dancing together to a gramophone on the sandy ground) but most of all every form of sport was played. Hockey and football played in temperatures which were well over 100 degrees and our 12-hole golf course was in regular use. Clubs were hired from the NAAFI at a few pence per round and small boys from the surrounding villages very soon learned the duties of a caddy. Bathing was allowed in the fire pool (at that time there was no swimming pool). Water polo was played a lot, officers v sergeants, corporals, airmen etc, and the main idea as far as I was concerned seemed to be to duck me - as CO - to the bottom of the pool as often as possible!

Wolstenholme continues with his memories: "One of Vincent's many virtues was his ability to play the piano in the mess". By all accounts he composed a new Squadron song during his time as CO. Wolstenholme still recalls the words after nearly 60 years:

Sing a song of 84
Shout till the rafters ring
Stand and drink a toast again
Let every 84 man sing
Sing to all the flying hours
Flown by night and day
Sing to who are absent from The Squadron of our hearts always.

By all accounts, there were many more verses but one must admit that it has not got the same punch as "Shaibah Blues" or "Hoot and Roar, 84"

In correspondence to the author, Wg Cdr C H Beeton RAF (Retd) relates the details leading up to his joining the Squadron in April 1933. He writes: "After completing my flying training at No. 4 FTS, Abu Sueir in January 1933, I had to pay my own fare home to the UK on leave. I returned to Abu Sueir in early April to learn that I had been posted to 'C' Flight, No.84 Squadron at Shaibah. I travelled by train to Amman and then got a lift in a Victoria to Hinaidi via Rutbah. Again by train from Baghdad to 'Shaibah Junction', a stop in the desert with not a building or person in sight. Fortunately, after a short wait a Trojan van appeared in a cloud of dust and conveyed me to the camp where I was to spend the next twenty months".

"At the time the Squadron was commanded by Sqn Ldr S F Vincent. The Flight Commander was Flt Lt E Arnold, shortly to be replaced by Flt Lt A C Evans-Evans. Other pilots in 'C' Flight were Fg Off Supple, Plt Off Allsopp and Sgt Johnson. Over the following months, we flew frequently on training missions, long distance flights to Muscat and routine inspections of desert forts. On one of these flights K1408 crashed at Al Barit and was

completely burnt out, probably because we were carrying long range petrol tanks on our bomb racks. Fortunately both pilot and air gunner were uninjured. At the time we were out of W/T range so the flight commander flew off towards Hinaidi to summon aid while I and my gunner stayed with the stranded crew of K1408. The following day aircraft of 'A' Flight arrived with spare seats to take them back to Shaibah. We had spent a very cold night in the desert".

"While at Shaibah, I was foolish enough to get myself court-martialled for low flying along one of the tributaries of the Shatt-el-Arab. I came down below the level of the palm trees and carried away a telephone wire crossing the water. As I was afraid it might foul my propeller or ailerons, I landed to clear the wire which we found had caught on the Holt flare brackets. The trouble was that, being hot, we could not restart the engine, with either bag and rope or handle. We just had to wait and let it cool. Meanwhile, back at Shaibah, a message had been sent to Air HQ that 'one of our aircraft was missing'. Needless to say that when we did get back the fat was in the fire! Fortunately the CO of the Armoured Car Company at Shaibah defended me and somehow, with the aid of my Flight Commander, I was acquitted. I had thought that was going to be the end of my flying career".

With the lessening of internal troubles, emphasis was given to improving and varying the training. Besides patrolling the Persian Gulf, long-distance flights were carried out in January 1934. Four Wapitis accompanied by two Valentias from 70 Squadron left Shaibah at daybreak on the 15th. Leaving Flt Lt Rodwell in charge at Shaibah, the formation reached Sharjah the first day. In stages they proceeded via Karachi, Jodhpur, Allahabad, Jinsi to Calcutta and into Malaya via Akyab and Rangoon. They arrived at Seletar airfield on Singapore Island on the 26th. The pilots were Sqn Ldr S F Vincent, Flt Lt C Walter, Fg Off C W Williams and Sgts Scrase and Christmas. Sqn Ldr H V Rowley of Air Staff HQ was taken as a passenger ordered to report on the route from an operational point of view. They left Seletar on the return flight five days later.

During the months, inter-flight competitions were organised to sharpen up the crews. Bombing trials from 3,000 to 14,000 ft and target firing from 200 ft using a 10 x 10 camera gun to compare results. This all added to the friendly rivalry between crews and their ground staff. By all accounts the prizes were crates of beer!

One rather curious note in the Squadron history occurred when a certain Sergeant McGee was posted 'due to over-officiousness'! The Orderly Officer at the time was a Fg Off Burton.

A personal experience which John Wolstenholme vividly remembers was on a flight to Air HQ at Baghdad. He writes, "As crew to Fg Off C W Williams, we left Shaibah, only to run into a sandstorm which necessitated landing at the emergency landing ground at Ur. These ELGs had a telegraph station and a fuel stock, and were manned by a couple of Arabs acting as caretakers. A wire was despatched to Baghdad for a weather report and we hung around awaiting a reply. A favourable report eventually arrived so we prepared for take-off. The Hucks starter was usually used for starting the engine, but no such thing was available. Fg Off Williams told me to stand on the wing and turn the magneto furiously, while he primed the engine from the cockpit. Several attempts were made with no luck. So Williams said, 'You'll have to swing the bloody prop", directing me how to form a chain with the help of the two Arabs. After two or three tries, the engine spluttered into life, sending us head over heels! No chocks were on

Wapiti J9848 of B Flight in 1931. The 84 Squadron scorpion is on the nose with the number "84" and the swastika (yet to acquire evil connotations) is on the fin and under the wing

the wheels so the aircraft moved slowly forward".

"Running to the rear to climb aboard, I stopped to put my tunic on, only to have it whipped out of my hands and sent flying across the desert by the slipstream of the aircraft. Meanwhile, Williams was looking around only to see me chasing after my tunic. In spite of all my efforts, I remember the 'rocket' I received from Williams when I eventually climbed aboard". Wolstenholme closed with the remark: "Such was flying in those days".

In the early part of 1934, some Persian sailors violated a British-held island in the Persian Gulf. The British Government, fearing that this might have some political repercussions among the neighbouring Arab tribes, decided to show the naval and air strengths of the British Empire. It was decided to carry out a combined operation at Sharjah with the Indian Ocean Squadron of the Royal Navy and a Royal Air Force Squadron from Iraq.

Wg Cdr C H Beeton takes up the story: "At that time I was still serving with No.84 Squadron at Shaibah. Our first learning of trouble was the fitting of long-range fuel tanks on the Wapiti. We were told that the Squadron was to carry out a flight to Sharjah and return and that 'C' Flight was to take a vertical and oblique camera".

"The flight to Sharjah was uneventful. Flying in open formation we crossed the coastline to avoid crossing any part of Saudi Arabia. As we neared our destination we could see that the Royal Navy squadron had already arrived and was anchored off a creek close to the town of Sharjah. Many of us had previously landed at Sharjah and we soon had our aircraft refuelled and picketed down. The following morning, Sqn Ldr Vincent called the pilots together and said that we were to give a demonstration that morning over the assembled warships on which the local chiefs were being entertained. On being asked what form the demonstration was to take we were told that it was to consist of formation drill. He would decide on the programme when we arrived over the ships. This was not very helpful, especially as we had not practised formation flying for many months and the Squadron now included many new pilots".

"In due course, the Squadron led by the CO arrived over the ships in a reasonably good 'vic' formation and we decided to fly up and down the lines of anchored ships at sea level. Being unrehearsed, the display probably compared unfavourably with those seen at Hendon. To those on the warships, the low altitude and the close proximity of the aircraft must have made the display

almost impressive. To the pilots and air gunners it was a most frightening experience. There was far too little room to manoeuvre and to attempt to maintain an element of formation whilst dodging ships' masts and aerials brought many a hairy moment. Fortunately it was all over in a few minutes and we returned to the airfield at Sharjah".

"From the airfield we were in visual communication with the naval squadron and, as soon as we had landed, a message was flashed to the ships asking what they thought of the demonstration. The reply came quickly. The lower deck had enjoyed it immensely but unfortunately the Arab chiefs were out at sea, aboard the flagship, witnessing a gunnery demonstration. We did not know whether to be amused or angry. We had flown 1,000 miles to give a demo only to be told we had given it at the wrong time. It was suggested that we remain overnight and repeat our performance when the flagship returned but the CO would not agree. He decided to leave straight away and spend the night at Bahrein. So with a final salute to the Navy we started our homeward journey".

"At Bahrein there are two main islands. On the larger one, or Bahrein proper, live most of the population and the rest houses, both RAF and Imperial Airways, are stationed there. Close to the town, there was a small landing ground which we had never had occasion to use, using instead the Imperial Airways airfield at Muharraq. However, the CO evidently decided that we would put down on the strip alongside the rest house. He signalled us to break formation and land individually. He was the first to touch down and shortly after came to an abrupt halt. His undercarriage disappeared and he was left with the fuselage of his aircraft flat with the ground. Fortunately there was a road running alongside the landing ground and, having ensured that it was free from obstacles, we all landed. With the help of a number of natives, we succeeded in lifting the CO's aircraft only to find that the undercarriage was intact and the aircraft could be wheeled away, the only apparent damage being a broken propeller. When we examined the ground we found that it was only a thin crust extending some distance into the sea".

"The following morning the CO decided that, except for 'C' Flight, the Squadron would return to Shaibah. 'C' Flight could remain at Bahrein and take mosaic photographs of the harbour area. It was decided that the best results would probably be obtained by one pilot doing the whole mosaic in one flight and as early in the day as possible. It was also decided to take them from

Personnel of No.84 Squadron in 1930. Sqn Ldr J Stewart (fifth from left) was killed on 5 January 1931. The two flight commanders, Flt Lts. Burke and Drummond are farthest left and seventh from left respectively

12,000 feet. Not having been previously warned of this operation, none of us had any warm clothing apart from some grey flannel trousers and pullovers which we always carried in an emergency. For the first hour all went well but by then the rear gunner and myself were so cold that we had to give it up and return to the ground. The operation was concluded the following day".

Beeton concludes by saying that both stories show examples of unplanned operations. The story of a flight that had taken a week to complete and had accomplished nothing beyond a series of photographs. Even those could have been taken in one day had they been warned of the possibility of their requirement before leaving Shaibah. At the end of May 1934, Fg Off J H Supple died from malignant malaria. Commenting, Beeton writes: "Supple's refusal to take quinine tablets undoubtedly did not help".

On 9 August, 'A' and 'B' Flights left on a eight-and-a-quarter hour flight to Mosul; a few weeks later, 'C' Flight flew a similar time flight to Muscat. During these months, the ground crews spent summer camps at Ser Amadia, north of Mosul, for a change of scenery and relief from the constant heat of Shaibah. And, of course, they were always looking forward to 'the boat' which

would take them home. Almost everyone had a 'DTG' (days to go) calendar. Even so, as Wolstenholme comments: "They were happy days and a splendid spirit existed between the officers and the men".

In October 1934, three D.H. Moths en route to the Bombay Flying Club strayed off route and lost themselves in the desert. Their leader managed to drain sufficient petrol from the tanks for him to take off and find the railway line which took him to Shaibah. Later the Squadron took off on the usual search procedures but without success. After two days they called in help from 30 Squadron at Mosul and 55 Squadron at Hinaidi. As their pilots did not know the Southern Desert, 84's pilots acted as flight commanders and led them to cover a square search operating from Ur. The Moths were eventually found by members of 'C' Flight 15 miles north-east of Ansab, refuelled and escorted to Shaibah, much to the relief of the crews who had started scribbling their last messages on the aircraft. November brought the rumour that No.84 Squadron were to be issued with the Vickers Vincent. The Wapitis had given good service but it was time for a change. On 12 December, the first Vincents arrived.

K1130 of A Flight appears a wreck but, as frequently happened to Wapitis, it was rebuilt and put back in service.

Heavily-laden K1405 carries its scorpion on the fin and the swastika on the upper nose

Two of No. 84 Squadron Vincents share the tarmac with Valentia bomber-transports of No. 70 Squadron

CHAPTER 6 - THE VINCENT YEARS

The official records state that the initial delivery of the Vickers Vincent to No. 84 Squadron was on 12 December 1934. As early as December 1932, a converted Vildebeest was sent on a tour of the RAF stations in the Middle East for trials as a general purpose aircraft. In due course, an initial order for 51 GP Vildebeests was given and the name Vincent was chosen as the role of the aircraft was to be completely different from the torpedo-carrying Vildebeest.

The all-metal aircraft, with its very reliable Bristol Pegasus IIM3 engine, fitted the role admirably, the main difference being the external fuel tank of 125 gallons in place of the torpedo. The normal tankage of 150 gallons carried in two tanks in the top mainplane, plus the extra fuel tank, gave a range of over 1,000 miles and a duration of between nine and ten hours. In practice, this was liable to be limited by the oil consumption because a Pegasus engine past its first flush of youth might well use more than a gallon of oil an hour and, as it only had fourteen gallons in the oil tank, the engine would rapidly overheat if the oil level got too low. Fuel from the belly tank was fed up to the engine from a propeller driven pump, so it could only be used at normal air speeds, and never at taking-off or landing when one had to use the main tanks which were gravity fed.

The first batch of Vincents was serialled K4106-K4126 and many of these were not struck off until the middle of 1939, which says a lot for the aircraft's suitability for the harsh conditions of the desert.

For the two weeks preceding Christmas, barrack rooms were not inspected and prizes of crates of beer were awarded by the CO to the best-decorated room. Vincent writes: "Out of the two Christmases I spent with No.84 Squadron, the best I saw was the Signal Section's conversion to the Court of King Arthur. Cement-washed four-gallon cans had been given the appearance of stone walls complete with portcullis entrance and a large hearth with 'open fire'. King Arthur and his knights were all in chain mail emblazoned with coats of arms, shields and swords and helmets were all fashioned. His Queen was dressed in a long flowing robe complete with crown whilst Merlin, court jester and serving maids were 'all present and correct'. The long table had bowls of steaming punch (hot Japanese beer) to be served to all and sundry".

On Christmas afternoon, there was the annual polo match between officers and other ranks, riding donkeys and using hockey sticks with a football. Later a ball was held when ladies from the Consulate, banks and the RAF hospital at Mangie, near Basra, were invited.

In February 1935, Sqn Ldr F J Fogarty arrived to take command of the Squadron. It was his third tour with No. 84, the first as a flying officer back in the mid-twenties. At that time he was renowned for his demonstrations of crazy flying at the Hendon Air Displays. Later on, he was remembered by having one of the camp roads named after him at Shaibah.

He was to find many changes since his previous tour with the Squadron. The working hours had been amended, starting at 0500 and finishing at 1100. Duties were few, but daily flights were flown. Junior ranks were still flying as observers and air gunners in their desire to get the coveted 'flying bullet' on their arm.

Sport was encouraged; tennis, cricket and athletics were pursued and Inter-Station games held at regular intervals. A new golf course was laid out with browns instead of greens, one of the hazards being that, with the drifting sand, it was never the same course two days in succession. Away matches were played at Mosul (30 Sqn), Hinaidi (70 and 55 Sqns) and Sharjah (Imperial Airways).

In April 1936, LAC Sid Sills joined the Squadron. At the time he had a steady job at Hinaidi, assembling radio components for the new RAF station being built at Habbaniyah. But in his heart, he wanted to become an air gunner. So here he was flying down to Shaibah in a lumbering 85 mph Valentia wondering if he was doing the right thing. He was awakened from his dreams by the words "Shaibah below". Looking out of the window all he could see was a motley collection of buildings and aerials surrounded by a whole lot of nothing.

Since Sill's foremost aim in life was to become an air gunner, the fact that he was a main station w/t operator was a problem. It meant that he was on a roster of varying watch hours as part of a team. Also, air gunners were only accepted and paid their extra one-and-six (about 8p) when established on a flight so vacancies

Vincent K4112 carries the swastika on an access panel in the nose. Times have changed and it now points the other way from the Nazi Swastika. For once, an 84 Squadron Vincent becomes acquainted with grass.

New arrivals at Shaibah are greeted by a welcoming committee that must confirm their worst fears as to the effects of service at Shaibah.

Raschid Ali, Regent of Iraq, disembarks from a Valentia of No.70 Squadron at Shaibah. In 1941, he led a revolt in collaboration with the Germans but failed

K4111 stalled on landing at Baiji landing ground on 21 July 1937. Although damage appears to be minor, it was struck off charge as "time-expired", RAF aircraft at that time having a set number of flying hours before being retired.

only occurred when those in the seat moved on. He also had a third handicap to overcome; the Flt Sgt in charge of Signals had no intention of allowing any of his watch-keepers time off for flying. It eventually took LAC Sills a year to commence training, after scrounging flights and ingratiating himself with the Flt Sgt who told him he could apply, providing he did the training in his spare time.

The Squadron's first fatality since it was re-equipped with the Vincent occurred on 22 June 1936 when, after making a bombing run on the range, a Vincent stalled from low level. Although its pilot survived, its air gunner, LAC Borthwick, was killed.

There was a major incident on 29 August when the Imperial Airways H.P. 42E G-AAUC, *Horsa*, after departing from Basrah on route to Bahrein with eight passengers and a crew of four, was compelled to force-land. Owing to a combination of factors, moonless night, Bahrein Airport unlit, strong tailwinds and an error by the D/F station, *Horsa* overflew Bahrein and landed some 40 miles south of Salwa Wells, damaging its starboard undercarriage struts in the process. Flights were sent out to cover the ground, but it was not until two days later that the aircraft was found by Flt Lt O C Bardon and his crew. After signalling the good news and calling for help, they landed nearby to find the crew and passengers unharmed but suffering from exhaustion. After abandoning the aircraft, they had sheltered under the broad wings of the H.P.42. Other Vincents had landed nearby with vital water supplies. The passengers were later flown back to Bahrein by a Valentia of 70 Squadron and they continued their flight to Karachi aboard A.W. Atalantas which had been sent from Karachi to join in the search.

The only female passenger on the flight had been the American novelist, Miss Jane Wallace Smith, who had doubtless kept up the morale of the eleven male passengers by disposing of her dress in favour of a makeshift bikini consisting of bra and panties. Such was the prudishness in those days that when photographs later appeared in the press, a shirt had been 'touched-in'. Some time later the frustrated members of No.84 Squadron learnt that Miss Jane Smith was to pass through Sharjah, flying westward. They 'arranged' to be at Sharjah to meet her, entertaining her to a party and persuading her to part with a pair of similar garments, suitably autographed, to be added to the Squadron's trophy cabinet. She was reported to have inscribed

them with the words "To 84 with love from Jane" in what was termed three strategic places. Suggestion has it that this could have been the inspiration for the *Daily Mirror* strip cartoon of the thirties and forties where the heroine 'Jane' had a regular habit of disposing with her clothes at the drop of a hat.

For the forthcoming Inter-Services flight to Singapore in the following January, No.84 undertook a series of comparatively long-distance flights. On 30 August, two Vincents left on a flight to Egypt and back, the total flying time being 28 hours 55 minutes. On 7 September, four Vincents left on a similar flight, arriving back on the 15th, the round trip taking 23½ hours. Ten days later the Squadron commenced a series of flights which logged nearly 3,500 miles in all and taking 34½ hours. This was followed by a further flight to Egypt, with the Air Officer Commanding as a passenger.

While the routine duties of the Squadron were continuing, LAC Sid Sills was still endeavouring to train for his 'bullet'. In his spare time, with the help of the armourers, he learnt the secrets of the Lewis gun and how to strip and assemble it with and without gloves, flying blind, and how to fire it with some degree of accuracy. He learnt about bombs, their sizes, their colour codes and how to drop them. He was introduced to the Williamson camera, both hand-held and mounted vertically; how to arrive at the focal length and the correct shutter speed; maps and charts, course and speed calculations; compass tracks, wind speed and direction - all were included in the course, first in the classroom and later in the air. It was followed by the Mk IX course and speed setting bombsight.

It has to be remembered that the air gunner was responsible not only for firing the Scarff-mounted Lewis gun, both as an attacker and defender, but was also responsible for aiming and dropping the bombs.

His experiences could vary every day. Anchored firmly by a metal pigtail to the floor in the rear cockpit, he would exercise by firing at ground targets or, occasionally, the odd target of opportunity like a turkey buzzard or even a stationary bush. As the pilot was often a flight lieutenant there was no arguing. One day a peacefully-grazing donkey was hit and the aircraft returned to base. Three days later, Sills was up before the adjutant. He confirmed it was he who had shot the donkey and was promptly asked for £3.00, which he gave to a rather irate Iraqi who had carried the

Passengers from Imperial Airways H.P.42E Horsa await rescue on 29 August 1936 after a forced landing 40 miles south of Salwa Wells

donkey 15 miles to demand recompense.

It took Sills just a year to get the prized 'bullet' over the years he was stationed at Shaibah. His letters recall vividly his experiences, ending in what he calls the highlight, the Inter-Command Flight to Singapore in 1938.

An exercise, which demanded skillful flying, was photography. Flying low over the area where the Rivers Tigris and Euphrates met, photographs would be taken of the Abadan refineries and tankers proceeding up the Persian Gulf. The exercise would sometimes be enlarged by making a mosaic map. An area would be selected and by flying similar courses over parallel lines for set distances, a complete picture could be obtained. During the planning stages for the new airport at Basrah, the Squadron took hundreds of pictures of the area for the Civil Aviation Authorities.

On 13 January 1937, the Squadron, consisting of twelve Vincents, left Shaibah for exercises in Singapore. They arrived on 25 February.

An air search for a party of five civilians was organised by No.84 Squadron on 2 June 1937, following a request made by the Provincial Governor of Basrah through the air liaison officer. The party, consisting of five members of an influential Arab family, had set out by car on 28 May to visit relatives at Batha, near Nasiriyah, and a search by police vehicles on 1 June had failed to locate them.

The search by two aircraft began at 14.25 and covered the obvious route the car was expected to have taken. The area to a depth of 30 miles was searched with no success and the aircraft returned after 3½ hours. On the following day the search was resumed to follow car tracks leading off the Shaibah-Busaiyah road. The car was eventually found abandoned in the sand belt. A message was immediately sent to the Governor and a party with guides was organised. Five bodies were eventually found near Rih Balak, about 20 miles south-east of the car. The action did much to raise the prestige of the Squadron in the neighbourhood.

Two months previously, Sgt Plt Charles Whitelock had joined the Squadron straight from No. 4 FTS at Abu Sueir. His letters gave lively descriptions of life with No.84 during the late thirties and the problems of the Vincent are exceptionally well-portrayed. He states that it was an easy aircraft to fly, but had very little inherent stability, having to be flown all of the time. In the severe turbulence at the height they used to fly, it could be physically very exhausting and definitely a 'brown paper job' at times for those in the back with nothing to take one's mind off it. Even the pilot, who sat in front of the mainplanes, had problems. After several hours a day on a long trip, those parts of his face not covered by the helmet or goggles were baked dark brown. Whitelock himself always carried a pot of vaseline to rub on his face at intervals. The Pegasus engine was a great oil slinger and, on occasions, when he was without the vaseline he was reduced to rubbing his finger along the windscreen and collecting oil to put on his face: anything better than roasting.

Whitelock also comments that a thoughtful pilot would do much of his flying as possible using the belly tank. It was much easier filling it from the four gallon cans stored at the relief landing grounds than having to lift them up to the top tanks which were fourteen feet off the ground. This was a three-man job and, with temperatures quite often in the 120s, there was no shade. Petrol burns were frequent when the fuel spilled and were aggravated by

the sun.

Another disadvantage of the Vincent involved the WOP/AG, or any other unfortunate person detailed to start the engine. He had to stand on a fold-down panel just behind the engine, about eight feet off the ground and only two feet from a very large propeller. Using a starter handle unfolded from inside the panel, he had to wind up the inertia starter (a sort of flywheel) until a whining pitch was reached. The pilot would then shout "Contact", whereon the operator would stop winding and pull out a wire toggle. With luck the engine would start. If not, the operator, still balanced on his little shelf, would have to go through the whole procedure again till the engine fired. When it did, the operator would then have to stow the handle, close the panel and step down via a smooth and very slippery wheel on to the ground, not forgetting that the 'prop' was still ticking over a couple of feet away from him.

On 26 October 1937, three Vincents of 'A' Flight led by Plt Off McGlashey, with Sgt Plts Frame and Whitelock in support, left Shaibah on a landing ground inspection trip down the Gulf and along the coast as far as Salalah, the limit of No.84's parish. McGlashey carried a passenger, Wg Cdr Rickards, the political liaison officer from AHQ. They spent nights at the rest-houses belonging to Imperial Airways at Sharjah, Muscat and Masirah before continuing their flight to Salalah, calling at Khor Gharim and Merbat on the way. Khor Gharim, being a minimal size airstrip with corners marked by concrete 'L' strips, had no buildings and no windsock.

On approaching KG, they followed the usual drill of a widely-spaced, echelon to starboard, left hand circuit at about 1,000 feet. McGlashey went into land on to what he judged to be into wind, with the other two ready to follow him in. But as his wheels touched down he must have realised he was landing cross-wind and he opened up to go around again. He climbed away but, on turning to port at about 500 feet, he stalled and entered a spin from which he could not recover. There was no fire, although it was possible he was carrying in excess of 200 gallons.

Frame and Whitelock circled the accident but saw no sign of life. After they had landed it took them nearly an hour to reach the wreck, having to circle the marshy lagoon area. The three occupants had been killed instantly. As neither of the other aircraft had been equipped with W/T, it was agreed that Whitelock would fly back to Muscat leaving Frame and his crew to do what they could. The following morning, Whitelock flew back to the wreck with orders to await the arrival of a Valentia from 70 Squadron. In the meantime, Frame and his crew had extricated the bodies, wrapped them in fabric from the aircraft and buried them under a ledge of rock bordering the lagoon. Little is known of Wg Cdr Rickard's duties, but surprisingly-large amounts of silver rupees were found in the wreckage. Rupees and Maria Theresa dollars were the commonly-used currency during those years.

A day later, the Valentia arrived carrying the Station Commander, Sqn Ldr C H Stevens, and they returned to Shaibah together. Sgt Frame and Cpl Bougourd, who had been a tower of strength, were later awarded the MSM.

Later reflections by the now Sqn Ldr Charles Whitelock gives a possible reason for McGlashey's crash. He puts forward the theory that if McGlashey had failed to switch over to his top tanks before going in to land on his first attempt, when he had to open up to go around again, his airspeed would have been too low to drive the belly tank pump. He would have immediately lost engine power, tried to turn to attempt a landing but lost speed, stalled and spun in. Though this was never put forward at the enquiry, Sqn Ldr Whitelock thinks that this was the likely cause of the accident.

The highlight of No.84's year was undoubtedly the Annual Inter-Services Flight to Singapore. Although the 1937 trip has been documented, the 1938 trip is given in detail due to the fact that three of the author's correspondents took part in it. Apart from the two already mentioned, Sgt Plt Charles Whitelock and LAC Sid Sills, Sgt Plt Peter Ault has added details.

The flight was led by Sqn Ldr C H Stevens, the Station Commander, with Flt Lt H Simmonds leading 'A' Flight. Not all of the names are remembered but Fg Off Towgood (later to be killed in Greece) Sgts Winward, Worsdell, Nobbs, Ault, Whitelock and Honeyman were some of those taking part. On the morning of 11 January 1938, the nine Vincents left, each festooned with spares hung from the bomb racks: charguls (skin bags) of water strapped to the main wing bracing struts and, internally, filled with the personal belongings of a crew of three. The first stop was Bahrein, not yet a full airport but a cleared strip on the island of Muharraq and joined to the mainland by a causeway. A quick stop for a meal and refuelling and then off to Sharjah where they stayed the night, courtesy of Imperial Airways.

To show off the Squadron, the aircraft took off the next morning in line abreast. Over the Straits of Hormuz and after skirting the mountainous coast of Oman, they landed at Gwadar to top up the tanks. Then on to the RAF station at Drigh Road, Karachi. Although long-range tanks were fitted, flight distances were restricted to conserve both pilot fatigue and engines.

The next day's flight was only a short one to the city of Jodhpur. Thanks to the generosity of the local Maharajah, they were received in a large and colourful marquee and fed on an enormous buffet of cold meats, curries and fruits. They were then left to sleep it off in a highly decorated and very warm tent. Breakfast was an unlimited supply of hard-boiled eggs, freshly-baked bread and gallons of rich sweet tea. The day continued with the flight to Cawnpore, which took them over the Taj Mahal.

From Cawnpore, they flew to Calcutta via Gaza, where they landed to refuel. It proved to be a complete contrast to Jodhpur, their being allotted a cold and unfriendly army post in which to sleep. They were not sorry to move on to Akyab, before flying down the Burmese isthmus to the airfield at Mingaladon, Rangoon. Unfortunately, time did not permit a visit to the city of golden pagodas, for the next morning they set course for the island of Mergui and then on to Victoria Point for the night stop. The main memory that lingers of Victoria Point was the ability to lean out of the billet windows and pick fresh oranges.

The next day took the Squadron to Alor Star, where they stopped for refuelling. Here they were issued with special white linen flying suits with the Squadron crest on the pocket, ready for the inspection at the end of their 5,000- mile journey. It was a pity that half-an- hour out, one of the aircraft signalled that it was losing oil pressure and another was detailed to escort it back to land at Taiping. Two days later they rejoined the Squadron at Singapore in very dirty flying suits, much to the annoyance of the Squadron Commander.

The next three weeks might almost have been considered a holiday, for only about twenty flying hours were logged, carrying out pseudo-attacks on shipping and generally doing the same training but under far more pleasant conditions.

The return flight on 8 February proved a bit of an anti-climax. The flight up through Burma, across India and finishing at that same featureless desert, all seemed so ordinary. The nine Vincents all arrived back on time, full of memories and souvenirs. It was never to happen again!

In April 1938, Sqn Ldr C H Stevens left the Squadron and was replaced by Sqn Ldr D H Barnett (later to become ACM Sir Denis Barnett). Sqn Ldr Barnett was only with the Squadron for seven months but, in a recent interview, he relates the story that he was at his desk one day when a telephone call from AOC Middle East told him that he had rather an odd request to make. Evidently the daughter of an old 84 Squadron member had written stating that a request in her late father's will was for his heart to be buried at Shaibah. After a discussion, it was agreed that, if it turned up, they would do their best to see that the request was carried out. Sure enough, three months later, the heart pickled in formalin, turned up on his desk. Sir Denis went on to say that later, when there was no one else about, he took out his No. 9 iron and buried the heart. As far as he knows, it is still there!

Two other stories are told about No.84 in the late thirties. The first was handed down by Sqn Ldr Keith Passmore to Sqn Ldr Bill Russell. It concerns the welcome given to newly-arrived officers. After a long and trying journey from the port of Basrah, they were ushered into the Officer's Mess and in the ante-room, to their astonishment, they saw the Squadron's officers in greatcoats, huddled in front of a roaring fire, who roared at them to shut the door and keep out the draught as it was so ruddy cold! The poor new boys were so bewildered, as the temperatures were well over 100 degrees in the shade. This particular practical joke ceased after one of the jokers went down with heat stroke!

The second story concerns the officer in charge of pay who, when he had to pay the crews of the Armoured Car companies detachment out on patrol, would hitch a lift in the back of a Vincent. By all accounts, they used to land alongside the cars where the officer concerned would take a table and chair from the Vincent and set it up so that the crews could line up and sign for their pay, all according to the book.

On 27 September 1938, the whole camp was mobilised and put on a twenty-four hour alert. Vincents were hurriedly camouflaged and stores readied for immediate despatch. However, after a few weeks, a degree of normality was resumed.

One unpublished incident was the landing at Shaibah by Clouston and Ricketts in their D.H. 88 Comet on their UK - New Zealand record trip. Looking for Basrah, they put down at Shaibah. When told they could see the control tower at Basrah from Shaibah, they did not believe it.

On 15 November, Sqn Ldr D L Thompson took over command of the Squadron from Sqn Ldr D H Barnett.

Just prior to Christmas 1938, Sgt Plt Charles Whitelock was detailed to take his crew, ACs Holding and Prior, to fly to Hinaidi and collect twenty turkeys for the Christmas dinner. He insists that for some peculiar reason, smells in the Vincent always travelled from the rear to the front of the aircraft, finishing in the pilot's cockpit. He goes on to say that after ten minutes flying, the stench was appalling. After that, chemical warfare held no fears. It evidently took weeks for the smell to finally disperse from the aircraft.

In the New Year, a search was laid on for a 30 Squadron Blenheim which went missing on a flight from Habbaniya to Ismailia. The search was unsuccessful but the aircraft was later found 60 miles WSW of Habbaniya in very small pieces.

A few final thoughts on the Vincent by Sqn Ldr C Whitelock. When a flight of Vincents went away on a trip, only one would carry a W/T set. The only communication between aircraft was by 'Zogging', a primitive method of Morse code by hand signals between the pilots in formation. It is unbelievable that the Squadron was all packed up ready to fight the Italians with such systems at a time when they had modern fighters! This was the period of the Munich crisis.

Toilet facilities were minimal - pee tubes to atmosphere. It was all right for the boys in the back but for the pilot, relief was difficult due to the parachute harness, the safety harness and the flying suit. One could be quite desperate after a six-hour flight in the cold. So the first priority on landing was to make a bee-line for the tail region. This habit resulted in a memo from the engineering staff for crews to take care and avoid the tail wheel, as serious corrosion to the bearing could result.

A narrow-brimmed pith helmet was tried once but, when sticking his head out into the slipstream, it nearly took the pilot out of the cockpit. He never tried it again!

Sgt Plt Whitelock's tour was over in March 1939, one month after the Squadron received its first Blenheim. To finalise, he says: "My memories of two years at Shaibah rank among the best of my 31 years service. Life was rarely very comfortable and luxuries were few, but frequent renderings of the 'Shaibah Blues' were enough to get the grouses out of the system. Fortunately there were never visits from MPs and no social workers came to stir things up and tell the troops how deprived they were. It was a different world in those days".

As for the Vincents, they were allotted to No.8 Squadron; six were struck off during March 1939 and the rest were given to the Royal New Zealand Air Force, where they were used for coastal patrols, flying in some cases until 1944.

The wreckage of K6336 which crashed on 26 October 1937 at Khor Gharim landing ground, killing the crew of three.

Believed taken at Heliopolis, No.84 Squadron's Blenheim I line-up shows the dust filters fitted under the engine cowlings

CHAPTER 7 - THE ERA OF THE BLENHEIM

February 17th, 1939, heralded the start of a totally new type of flying for No.84 Squadron - no more open cockpits, fixed undercarriages or the oil-spurting Bristol Pegasus engines. Instead it brought the arrival of the first Bristol Blenheim I, powered by two 840 hp Bristol Mercury engines. It had a range of just over a thousand miles, a top speed approaching 280 mph, double that of the Vincent. It had a wing span of 56 feet, only seven feet bigger than that of the Vincent, but what a difference. It was equipped with a retractable undercarriage, variable-pitch propellers and a fully-enclosed, partially- retractable, rear gun turret with a single Lewis gun. Later this was changed to twin Brownings.

Before the Squadron was issued with the aircraft, it was decided to incorporate controllable gills on the engine cowling and improve the carburettor air intakes. The locking of the tailwheel in the down position was also introduced because being retracted added to the maintenance without improving speed. It also brought the role of the navigator/wireless operator into the Squadron.

There was no mention of which was the first aircraft received. Stan Humphrey in his book *Press on Regardless* mentions that the first one received was the subject of an accident when the transporter carrying the crated fuselage twisted going over a ridge, causing the shell to fracture. It was sufficient to cause its write-off. It is probably easier to say which one it was not rather than the other way round.

It was not until 3 June that No.84 Squadron was up to Establishment with twelve Blenheim I bombers and six Mk.IF fighters. The Commanding Officer was Sqn Ldr D L Thompson, with his Flt Commanders being Acting Flt Lts O Godfrey, R A Towgood and L P Cattell. Other officers were Plt Off K Passmore, G J Stonhill, A F Mudie, D H Walsh and J Evans. Soon to join them were Plt Off G R Colenso, R V Whitehead, N W Pinnington and Sgt Plts W E Smart, W S Sidaway and G Horsham.

On 3 September, war was declared but, apart from initial rumours that the Squadron was to move, training continued. The need to maintain maximum serviceability meant that only necessary trips were undertaken. Cases for packing stores were checked and re-checked and every preparation was made for a quick move. Life became very sober but gradually returned to normal.

Between training, four crews led by Flt Lt R A Towgood flew to Mosul and other Northern Iraqi airfields on an inspection and photo-reconnaissance flight, returning on 3 November. There are mentions in the Squadron records that there were now 16 aircraft on strength, although 18 had been received, which suggests that two were written-off. One of these could possibly have been the

one mentioned in the earlier paragraph, the other being involved in a crash on 3 August. It seems likely that they were L1394 and L1384 respectively. There was another incident on 22 November when L1380's undercarriage was retracted after landing. It was later repaired.

During November and December, there were constant changes of personnel, D H Walsh being posted to No.4 FTS at Habbaniya, N W Pinnington moving to HQ, being replaced by Fg Off J M Mahler and Plt Off J M Christie. The New Year brought more changes, Sgt Plt J Balch arrived on the 11th, replacing WO J Smith. Two days later Sqn Ldr D G Lewis arrived to replace Sqn Ldr D H Thompson. The same train brought Sgt Plts Bradley, Gordon and Bratton. Later that week, Sgt Plts Horsham and Smart left to join No. 4 FTS, followed a day later by Plt Off G Stonhill. Sqn Ldr D G Lewis assuming Command on 28 January 1940.

On 30 January, there was a tragic accident when AC1 Hampson died from heat exhaustion after passing out while working inside a Blenheim. A ruling was introduced that on no account should only one man work alone inside an aircraft.

The Squadron strength was now up to 216 personnel, made up of 20 officers, two WOs, nine Flt Sgts and 185 airmen. Six more Sgt Plts joined the Squadron on 9 February, Williams, Thomas, Shaw, Nuttall, McVea and Cazalet.

On 1 March 1940, Handley Page H.P. 42 *Hannibal*, with four passengers and a crew of four on route from Jask to Sharjah, was lost without trace over the Gulf of Oman. Search flights made on the 2nd and 3rd were to no avail. As a result of this loss, the three H.P.42s based at Cairo were withdrawn to Whitchurch in England.

Early May saw recently-promoted Flt Lts O Godfrey and M G Stevenson leave on a posting to HQ Middle East. Over the next three months, the Squadron's strength was gradually increased and by the end of May had risen to 251, even though the number of officers on strength had dropped to sixteen. June 1940 brought more shuffling within the Squadron, Sgts Sidaway, McVea and Williams being posted to the UK. Flt Sgt R B Bryan was commissioned and became the Officer in charge of the Technical Branch. Plt Off Streatfeild (Wop/AG), the Intelligence Officer, was posted to HQ Middle East.

Orders were received on 21 June that four aircraft were to proceed to Sharjah via Bahrein. There were rumours that an Italian submarine was operating in the area. The aircraft were flown by Sqn Ldr D G Lewis, Flt Lts R A Towgood and L P Cattell and Sgt A Bailey. At Sharjah, Towgood and Cattell took off on a patrol at 0600 returning at 0945 with nothing to report. Later Sqn Ldr Lewis

The Squadron's first mishap with a Blenheim, the result of pulling the undercarriage release instead of the flap lever

and Bailey took off and found HMS *Yarmouth* doing a surface patrol. On the 22nd, they received a signal that they were to return to base after finding small oil slicks, arriving at Shaibah at 0730 on the 23rd. On the 24th, it was learnt that the submarine *Galvani* had been sunk by HMS *Dartmouth* when it took no avoiding action after being caught on the surface; 31 survivors were picked up. During this action, No.84's crews were accommodated at the British Overseas Airways quarters. The aircraft flown were L1378, L1382, L1379 and L8362. A further sighting by an overflying BOAC aircraft resulted in Sqn Ldr Lewis leading Towgood and Cattell (L1385, L8362, L1383) on a patrol. No submarine was sighted.

July brought the arrival of Plt Offs D R Bird, Keble-White and Linton, also the return of Sgts Sidaway and Williams.

On 25 July, a Blenheim flown by Sqn Ldr D G Lewis with Flt Lt R A Towgood, Fg Off Trevor-Roper, WO Blackburn and Sgts Keen and Stevens flew to Habbaniya en route to visit operational squadrons in Egypt at their war stations, visiting Maaten Bagush (113 Sqn), Fuka (55 Sqn), El Daba (211 Sqn) and Ikingi Maryut (30 Sqn), returning to Shaibah on 2 August.

An order was received on 10 August calling for a flight commander and his crew to fly to Habbaniya and then on to Heliopolis. A further five crews were to follow in a 216 Squadron Valentia, the reason being to ferry aircraft to Shaibah. The following morning, Flt Lt Cattell with his crew, Sgt Taylor and LAC Sergeant, took off at 0800. On their return, flying the southern route via Port Sudan, when nearing Kamaran Island they encountered a Savoia-Marchetti SM-81, which they attacked from astern. After all six Blenheims had attacked, it was seen to catch fire and dive into the sea. It cannot be ascertained which person or crew was responsible for the victory but it is probable that Flt Lt Cattell who made the first attack, killed the rear gunner and set one engine on fire.

The other crews were made up as follows: Plt Off J Evans, Sgt Somerville, LAC Round, Plt Off K Passmore, Sgt Hibband-Lord, LAC Chick, Sgt Gordon, LAC Edwards, LAC Foster, Sgt Cazalet, Cpl Chadburn, LAC Holding, Sgt Balch, LAC Wincott, LAC Crowe.

On 10 September, Flt Lt Mudie, who with Towgood and Cattell had just lost their acting rank, led 'A' Flight on a photo-reconnaissance flight to Muscat. On their return, it was announced that 84 Squadron was at last to move, leaving Shaibah on the 23rd and arriving at Heliopolis in Egypt on 25 September 1940.

Each flight was allocated a 70 Squadron Valentia in which to carry the ground staff and tool kits. The flight would take them first to Hinaidi and from there following the oil pipe line past the various pumping stations known by 'H' numbers to Haifa. The next morning they left Haifa, following the coast to Port Said, from where they flew down the canal and over Cairo into Heliopolis. The remainder of the squadron left Shaibah in a convoy of military transport, escorted by the Armoured Car Companies, their route taking in Baghdad, Rutbah, Amman, Beersheba, Ismailia to Heliopolis.

On arrival at Heliopolis, it was learned that 'A' Flight was to remain in reserve, while 'B' Flight was to fly to Fuka on detachment to 55 Squadron for war experience flying. The same applied to 'C' Flight, which left for El Daba where 211 Squadron were based.

While it is not my intention to include in this chapter the political reasons leading up to the Italian invasion of Greece on 28 October, I feel that a short precis would not come amiss.

As early as 1924, the Italian dictator, Benito Mussolini, in his

egoistic desires to rebuild the Italian Empire, had cast envious eyes on the Greek mainland. One of his first acts was to demand an official apology and retribution for the actions, supposedly by Greek forces, resulting in the assassination of the Italian President of the International Commission and four of his staff who were motoring through Greek territory.

Understandably, Greece denied all knowledge of this, blaming factions of the Albanian regime. However, they agreed to the rendering of military honours to the Italian flag by the Greek fleet and to the holding of an inquiry into the incident by an Italian officer. Coupled with this they refuted all suggestion of any indemnity. Consequently, on 31 August 1924, the Italian fleet bombarded Corfu, causing the death of several of its people before its troops occupied the island. Later the International Commission of Enquiry demanded an immediate withdrawal and reluctantly the Italians agreed.

On 7 April 1939, the Italians annexed Albania, bombarding Durazzo from the sea. At the same time aircraft dropped leaflets invited the surrender of other towns and villages. On 16 April, King Victor Emmanuel accepted the crown of Albania. Just over a year later, the Italian Dictator led his country into World War 2, crossing the border into the south-east corner of France before the cessation of hostilities.

By the summer of 1940, Mussolini, the junior member of the Axis Alliance, was anxious to prove himself. His East African Empire was under threat. Malta had not been subdued, which meant that supplies to his army in North Africa had ground to a halt and, worst of all, his famed Mediterranean Fleet was unable to leave harbour due to the might of the British Navy.

Over the following months the Italians had initiated a series of incidents against Greek shipping. During July they had bombed and machine-gunned a lighthouse tender, followed by attacking a destroyer which had gone to its assistance. Early August two destroyers were bombed in the Gulf of Corinth and days later the cruiser *Helle* was torpedoed at anchor by an unidentified submarine. All these actions were denied by the Italian authorities but, after the war, records disclosed Italian guilt.

It was agreed that the intended assault on Greece would take place on 26 October. By 20 September, the Italian garrison in Albania had risen to 40,000 troops but, due to the Italian economic situation, little had been done in Albania to facilitate the proposed attack. Only six airfields of note were available; other landing strips had little in the way of buildings and other facilities.

At 0300 on the morning of 28 October, the Italian Minister in Athens handed to Prime Minister Metaxas a note from his government complaining in the strongest possible terms of alleged Greek assistance to the Allies and demanding for the Italians the right to occupy certain strategic bases in Greece. General Metaxas regarded this note as an ultimatum which he promptly refused. A few hours later Greece was at war with Italy.

Unlike the Italians, the Greeks were badly prepared for war. They had little in the way of modern equipment. In fact only 150 aircraft of ten different types were available. These were backed by a hundred or so trainers and other elderly reconnaissance Their regular forces were at their peacetime stations and mobilisation had not been ordered. However, the initial advance by the Italians was slow for, although they had massed large forces on the Greek frontier, the attitude of the Greek Government came as a

Using an RAF armoured car, the 'Mayor, Mayoress and Aldermen of Shaibah' address No.84 on leaving Shaibah

L1391 VA-J, Doughnut Doris *at Menidi in December 1940. (Wg Cdr B.R. Wade DFC)*

complete surprise, as it had been presumed that it would be a diplomatic victory and a peaceful advance into Greek territory.

On 30 October, the British Minister in Athens sent a telegraph to General Wavell indicating that, while Greek morale was comparatively high, aid was essential if resistance was to be sustained. The Greek Government, however, thought that as long as it was only the Italians they were fighting, they had little wish for the help of the British Army, reasoning that their own troops were quite capable of withstanding an Italian attack through Albania and that the landing of British troops on the mainland of Greece would only bring upon them the hostility of the Germans. Air Chief Marshal Sir Arthur Longmore, the Air Officer Commanding, Mediterranean, was at that time strongly opposed to spreading his squadron strength any more widely. Nevertheless, there were political and military arguments for sending at least a token force to support the Greeks. When the request came for help, Longmore despatched a mixed squadron of bombers and fighters (No.30 Squadron) to defend Greece. Four days later, he received a memo from the Chief of Staff saying that it had been decided to give Greece the greatest possible material and moral support at the earliest possible moment.

Consequently, the result was to draw upon the resources in Egypt and to replace them with units from the UK. Detailed orders followed and before the end of the month two more Blenheim squadrons (Nos.84 and 211) and one Gladiator squadron (No.80) were sent to join No.30 Squadron. Air Vice-Marshal J H D'Albiac DSO, the Air Officer Commanding Palestine and Transjordan, was sent to Greece to command the forces.

One of the main difficulties was the scarcity of airfields suitable for use by modern aircraft, especially all-weather strips. For political reasons, he was not allowed access to fields in the Salonika area. In the Larissa area, there were suitable sites but, unfortunately, in November the rains had started with the result that they soon became flooded. Finally it was decided to use Eleusis and Tatoi for the bomber squadrons. Eleusis was still under construction and rubbish and filth of every description was strewn all over the place. Tatoi, or Menidi as it became known, was on a plain about twelve miles from Athens. It was flanked by mountains rising to about 4,000 feet covered with pines. At each end were orchards of olive trees and eucalyptus. There were three hangars on the field, two for the use of the RAF squadrons, the other housing three Ju 52/3ms belonging to the Greek Air Force.

It proved to be a bizarre situation because the Greeks were not at war with Germany as they were with Italy. However German Embassy propaganda and intelligence machines were working overtime and were able to report accurately on the Order of Battle

of the British Forces, as well as to fabricate slander and rumour about them for Greek ears. It also encouraged subversive elements to monitor our activities and to spread false rumours. They also tried to persuade the Greek population not to fraternise with the British. Accordingly our troops were depicted as degenerate, weak in battle and liable to desert their Greek comrades. All Greeks at the front and behind the lines were warned about the licentious British who were a danger to their families.

In reality, the absurdity of the propaganda, as far as the RAF was concerned, was recognised. Our reputation at war was very much appreciated and many friendships were formed between Greek families and RAF personnel. When in uniform they were welcomed in restaurants and night clubs like The Argentina or Maxim's where every effort was made to make their stay enjoyable.

On 8 November 'A' Flight, led by Sqn Ldr D G Lewis and consisting of Flt Lt W F Mudie, Plt Off D R Bird and Sgts Balch, Nuttall and Sidaway, left Heliopolis to fly to Greece. Each aircraft was not only carrying the crew of three but also three ground staff. Leaving at 0800, they touched down at Maleme on the island of Crete before flying on to Eleusis, where they were billeted at the Britannia Hotel on University Street before moving on to Menidi.

Two days later, the Squadron moved to Menidi where the officers were billeted in a summer residence a few miles from the airfield and the ground crews under canvas amongst the pinewoods to the north of the airfield. On the same day, the flight attacked targets in the Valona area but because of poor visibility no results were seen. Following this, on 12 November, Durazzo was attacked. Bombing from 8,000 feet, they hit warehouses where fires were started.

Meanwhile, back in Egypt, the rest of the Squadron were preparing to leave Heliopolis, staying overnight at Sidi Bisr near Alexandria before boarding HMS *York,* SS *Clan MacArthur* and the Dutch ship *Jan de Witt* to sail to Piraeus, which they reached on the 15th. They arrived to find that there had already been losses in the Squadron. After bombing Valona and Argyrokastron on the 13th with very little opposition, three crews were detailed to bomb bridges and troop concentrations near Koritza. The bridge was destroyed, effectively denying the movement of troops but Flt Lt Mudie and his crew, Flt Sgt Hibband-Lord and LAC Chick were killed when they flew into a mountain in L1389. Sgt Sidaway, flying L1378, was also killed together with his crew, Sgts Friend and Hoare. Sgt Nuttall returned but his aircraft was extensively damaged. Witnesses agreed that had the action taken place in Northern Europe, Flt Lt Mudie's bravery in pressing home the attack would have warranted a posthumous award.

Flt Lt W.T. Russell's L4819, The Musso Menace *with C Flight's Cleo motif on the nose panel*

A strike on Durazzo on 23 November was aborted due to the worsening weather. It also brought the arrival of part of No. 211 Squadron, followed on the 24th by the remainder of the Squadron, together with 'B' and 'C' Flights of 84 Squadron. With the arrival of the Gladiators of No.80 Squadron, the RAF force was now at full strength.

Six aircraft from the Squadron made a raid on Valona on the 26th. They were intercepted by three G-50s but low flying enabled Fg Off J F Evans to escape. It also enabled him to spot a line-up of enemy bombers on the airfield which he bombed. Flt Lt Towgood also escaped the three fighters, his gunner claiming hits on one aircraft. On the 28th, the Squadron put up nine aircraft to bomb Durazzo, refuelling at Araxos. Several of the aircraft, unable to find the target under cloud, attacked Elbasan. Sgt Jim Hutcheson flying L1892 recalls: "After letting my two 500-lb bombs go, I was set on by a couple of CR-42s but fortunately I got clear". Plt Off Dickie Bird in L1385 was forced down, landing in a dried-up river bed. He was taken prisoner along with Sgts Stan Davis and Eric Scott. Unfortunately Scott later died from a throat infection whilst in the camp, but both Bird and Davis were allowed out to attend his funeral.

The following day, the Squadron again put up nine aircraft on a strike against Tepelene but this time they were escorted by six Gladiators of 80 Squadron. On 4 December, 84 Squadron, carrying 250-lb bombs, attacked roads and buildings near Kelcyre. Light ack-ack was experienced during their 3½-hour round trip.

On 7 December, six aircraft took off at 1220 to raid Valona, followed at 1300 by nine aircraft from 211 Squadron. Due to extremely bad weather, No.84's first formation of three aircraft was forced to return through heavy icing. The second three were intercepted over the target by CR-42s. Flt Lt L P Cattell and his crew, Sgts Taylor and Carter, in L8455 and Sgt M P Cazalet with Sgts Ridgewell and Foster in L8457 were shot down immediately. Fg Off K Linton in L1381, with his crew Plt Off Dunn and Sgt Crowe, force-landed near Sarande after a long burst from a fighter had set fire to his port engine. From the first two aircraft, only Sgt Foster was to survive, joining Stan Davis in a POW camp. Two of 211 Squadron's Blenheims were also to perish in this action.

Three days later on the 10th, Flt Lt W (Bill) Russell arrived with his crew, Sgts Ken Dicks and Alan Blackburn, to join 84 Squadron. In his letters, Bill Russell recalls: "We had been serving in 107 Squadron in the UK when we stupidly volunteered to fly a brand-new Blenheim IV out to the Middle East. We thought we would be posted to a squadron with this beautiful aircraft which had all the latest gear, two guns in the turret and a blister gun under the nose. Barely had we got our kit out of the aircraft at Abu

Sueir than it was whisked away never to be seen again. After a week we were posted to 84 Squadron, flying to Menidi in a rather clapped-out old Blenheim I. The impression changed and eventually I thought a lot of the Mk I in spite of its limitations".

The mission on the 11th was abortive due to heavy icing, Jim Hutcheson jettisoning his bombs before landing. The conditions were to continue over the next week and it was the 19th before No.84 could resume operations again when they attacked Valona and Krionero. Despite heavy gunfire and being intercepted by four fighters, bombs were dropped and fires started amongst motor transport. Three of the aircraft were damaged in the raid.

During the week, Flt Lt Tony Plinston and his crew, Sgts Jack Tozer, navigator, and McLoughlin, Wop/AG arrived on the Squadron. Writing from his home in New Zealand he comments: "One pleasant feature was that the rate of exchange was about 120 drachma to the pound, and beer and cigarettes were cheap. The cigarettes (Papa stratos) took some getting used to. My first operation was a squadron raid on Valona on 19 December. It was a beautiful day, no cloud over the Gulf of Corinth, cloud over the mountains, and then clear skies again over Valona. A ship was moored alongside the quay but regrettably there were no direct hits. On the way back, three Italian fighters came up to have a look but did not press home their attack. It served to remind me how an enemy fighter helps to improve your formation flying".

Nine aircraft from 84 Squadron left Menidi on 22 December to bomb the Kucera oil fields from 9,000 feet. Two Blenheims were lost, L8471 going down with Fg Off P F Miles and his crew while Fg Off J Evans in L8374 managed to bale out near Koritza. Five other Blenheims were damaged, amongst them Flt Sgt A Gordon flying L4818, his observer Sgt G Furney suffering a bad head wound. Despite the damage, Gordon flew back to base. Fg Off J Evans also returned to base to tell his story. Both he and his observer, Harry Offord managed to bale out, Evans landing in a stable yard where a mule was tied. To add insult to injury, the mule lashed out and kicked Evans on the leg, breaking his thigh. He was found there by his observer and, with the aid of some Greek soldiers, carried to a nearby village. After treatment, four soldiers were detailed to carry him down the mountain to the nearest town, a journey which took three days. From there he travelled to Athens by train. Offord, his observer, was later to rejoin the Squadron. On the same raid, Flt Lt Russell flew L1382 and Sgt Plt Ingham-Brown L8501.

Recently, Wg Cdr Russell wrote these comments on the 'raid': "Navigation was very primitive, dead reckoning plus map reading, as we had no other aids. Even the D/F radio bearings were difficult to obtain and not reliable due to the mountainous terrain. Target maps were either non-existent or laughable e.g. for the raid on the Kucera oil wells on the 22nd we were shown a hand-drawn sheet of foolscap with everything written in Greek. This masterpiece failed to show us that there was an airfield within ten miles of the target".

A couple of days before Christmas there was a collection of all spare kit and boots, as it was heard that the Greek troops on the island of Corfu were suffering from frostbite. This was the RAF's answer to their request for help. On the 25th, a flight of three Blenheims led by Flt Lt Bill Russell dropped the clothing over the Greek lines. There were many moans from the ground crew because the leather jackets had only just been issued.

Supply flights into Menidi were undertaken by Greek Air Force Ju 52/3ms

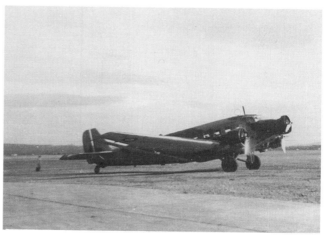

On 5 February 1941, Flt Lt Towgood suffered fatal injuries in this crash on the edge of Menidi airfield on return from Elbasan

Continuing Wg Cdr Russell's comments on the situation: "As a result of the hammering we had received from the G-50s on 22 December, Flt Lt Towgood and myself decided to start experimenting with extra guns. He fixed up a Lewis gun firing backwards from an engine nacelle while I got one attached rear of the bomb-bay, the idea being to load a full drum of tracer to hose rearward at any fighters repeating their tactics of the 22nd, which were to cruise along astern and below and pick us off at their leisure. Before we could try the system out, Sqn Ldr D G Lewis got to hear of it and we were both bawled out for making 'unauthorised modifications to aircraft' and that was the end of that. I often wondered if he had ever heard that around the same time, 14 Squadron operating out of Aden over Eritrea in the Wellesley, which were even more impotent than the Blenheim, fitted Lord knows how many unauthorised mods on, in and around their aircraft, and consequently had quite good results against the Italian fighters".

The year ended with local formation flying, the weather was worsening and the forward airfields like Larissa were either underwater or frozen over. On 1 January, an intended raid on Tepelene was abandoned due to low cloud and bad visibility. At 0830 on 2 January, six aircraft took off on a raid on Durazzo, followed at 1215 by a further six to bomb Elbasan. Hutcheson's log book states: "Extremely bad weather with snow and sleet creeping up the valley. Surprise attack but plenty of accurate ack-ack, 250-lb bombs dropped".

At 0810 on the 5th, Sgt Plt Nuttall with his crew, Sgt Maplesden and Air Gunner Thistle, was detailed to make a photo-reconnaissance of Valona. On reaching Corfu, he was obliged to return through continuous heavy rain which forced him down to sea-level. Two days later a surprise attack on Elbasan was made. AA was experienced up to 30 miles away from the target. The weather was so bad that many aircraft did not see the results. On the 10th, there is mention of a raid on Kelcyre, in Flt Lt Russell's log book: "Beat up retreating Italians from ground level, rain and snow heavy".

Early in January, the Greek General Staff realised that it seemed probable that the Germans intended to make a move through the Balkan states. They were already infiltrating into Rumania and it seemed a possibility that in the spring they would be facing the enemy on two fronts. With this in mind, they considered it essential that the Italian campaign should be brought to an end before such a possibility arose. With Italian morale at such a low level, it was decided to shorten their front line enabling them to have available troops ready to strengthen their forces in Macedonia.

Berat was bombed on the 13th by six aircraft from 84 Squadron. Notes say that results were seen from 5,000 ft. A further attack on the 19th brought these comments: "No fighters but ack-ack was waiting for us, sticky, but no one was hurt, flight led in line astern through the valley".

It was soon after he joined the Squadron that Flt Lt W T Russell introduced to 'C' Flight a Walt Disney character painted on the nose of the Blenheims. Photographs show a dolphin named Cleo, his own aircraft showing a rather fancy print compared with the standard drawing on the rest of the flight, Russell's was the *Musso Menace*, Passmore had the *Queen of Shaibah*, and another was the *Caliph of Shaibah*. All characters were painted by AC2 Bauman, a Palestinian sign-writer who was serving in the Squadron. Later when Russell took over 'B' Flight, he introduced the Bulldog on to their aircraft.

At 1035 on the 21st, six aircraft took off to bomb Elbasan, Sgt Ingham-Brown having to return with engine trouble. Next day, six aircraft undertook an operational reconnaissance of the Kelcyre-Berat road. Bombing from 6,000ft, they were intercepted by two G-50s but succeeded in getting clear. On the 24th and 25th, Bulcar

The cockpit of Flt Lt Towgood's Blenheim shows where the propeller blade penetrated

Menidi airfield in the winter of 1940/41

The surface and surroundings of Menidi, December 1940

and Boultsov were bombed with negative results. On the 31st, Russell led a formation of six aircraft on a raid on Tepelene and Dukeaj, attacking the camp under cover of a snowstorm. All aircraft bombed and strafed the target, a later raid bombing buildings on the Tepelene-Valona road. A raid two days later on the same targets was abandoned through extreme weather conditions.

Early in February, the Greek armies in Albania started a fierce onslaught in the direction of Valona. Unfortunately, bad weather intervened and the Italians were able to bring up reinforcements and the advance was held up north of Tepelene. Before this the policy of bombing had been against lines of communications, ports and aerodromes to the rear, reducing the flow of reinforcements and supplies to the army in the field. Pressure from above forced D'Albiac to change his attack to close support of the Greek forces. Due to continuous bombing attacks, the severe winter and the recent death of the Premier Metaxas, morale of the Greeks had been severely shaken. It was therefore thought that by bombing the Italian forces in the same way would be a stimulus to the Greek army.

On 5 February, three Blenheims led by Flt Lt R A Towgood took off to bomb supply depots in the Valona area. They became separated and bombed individually. On their return, Flt Lt Towgood had engine failure and crashed near the boundary fence. Towgood was killed immediately, Sgt Somerville was unhurt but suffered from shock while the gunner was unhurt.

Two days later Fg Off Angus Nicholson, flying L1393, left on a lone midday operation. The weather rapidly deteriorated and he was obliged to ditch off an island in the Gulf of Corinth. In the crash his gunner, Sgt Hollist, was killed; his other crew member, Plt Off Day, was not a strong swimmer and was drowned before he could open the dinghy. Nicholson alone managed to inflate his dinghy, was rescued by islanders and was taken to hospital. On the 7th and 8th, flights were flown on search missions before news came through that Nicholson had been rescued.

Twelve aircraft from 84 Squadron were sent on detachment to Paramythia on 12 February to bomb troop concentrations on the Kelcyre-Berat road from 9,000 feet. Tony Plinston writes: "Refuelling and rearming were a little primitive at Paramythia. Four-gallon cans were manhandled on to the wing and tipped into a large funnel, with a chamois leather filter. Fortunately tank capacity on the Blenheim was limited to about 50 gallons a side. Bombing-up required somebody with a strong back and legs, being loaded by two others and then getting up to get the bomb high enough to hook on to the release hook".

A second raid bombed road transport at Tepelene. The following day raids by the twelve aircraft continued bombing and strafing missions against troops. All crews and aircraft returned to Menidi on the 15th.

It was obvious that if successful close support was to be provided, reorganisation would be necessary and it was decided that the aircraft needed for such a role should be based nearer the front. So it was that, on the 18th, Wg Cdr P B (Paddy) Coote arrived to set up an Advanced Operations Wing at the base. This was to be known as 'W' Western Wing, comprising a Blenheim detachment from 30 Squadron, the whole of 84 and 211 Squadrons and a further detachment from 11 Squadron which was to arrive later. A further detachment of 37 Squadron's Wellingtons and six Hurricanes from 80 Squadron would be joined by six Gladiators from 33 Squadron, the Wing Headquarters to be based at Yanina.

At 1015 on the 20th, six aircraft led by Flt Lt Russell left for a raid on Tepelene. Russell aborting after take-off through hydraulic problems on L4819. At 1515, 17 Blenheims (eight from 84 Squadron) escorted by two Hurricanes, bombed Berat from 5,000 ft, demolishing a bridge over the Rover Osem. G-50s from Berat airfield were scrambled but the Hurricanes led by Flt Lt Pattle disposed of four of them. One of No.84's Blenheims had engine failure on the return flight and belly-landed on the airfield. On the 26th, Blenheims from 11, 84 and 211 Squadrons escorted by six Hurricanes bombed Buzat near Tepelene.

Paramythia was honoured by a visit from ACM Sir Arthur Longmore, General Sir John Dill, Sir Anthony Eden and General Sir Archibald Wavell.

On 28 February Sqn Ldr D G Lewis left the Squadron, being posted to AHQ. His replacement was Sqn Ldr H D Jones, who had been seconded to the Royal Egyptian Air Force. He had no operational experience and, more important, no experience of the mountainous terrain over which he was to fly. Before he was eventually killed, he nearly 'bought it' when attempting to take a short cut through cloud, thinking he could fly across a saddle between two hills only to find that there was no saddle there. He climbed desperately, just scraping the ridge before managing to regain control. Fortunately he and his crew escaped with cuts and bruises.

The night of 28 February/1 March was noted for the most severe earthquake Greece had suffered this century. At Larissa, rifts had opened the length of the airfield; buildings and hangars had collapsed and personnel had been buried under the debris. After salvaging as much as they could, the RAF personnel worked throughout the night rescuing people from the shattered villages. Next morning, Blenheims flew in with much needed relief supplies and RAMC doctors. Members of the Squadron remember the problems of landing where there were giant cracks, also sleeping in tents on the following nights, feeling the ground shake and rumble due to after shocks.

There was little let up in the war, for on 2 March aircraft from 84 and 211 Squadrons took off to bomb parked aircraft on the airfields at Berat and Devoli. On the 4th, five Blenheims from No.84 joined nine from No.211 in a raid on five Italian naval vessels (identified as two cruisers and three destroyers) which were shelling the coastal road near Himara, under cover of a strong force of G-50s and CR-42s. The bombers were escorted by Hurricanes and Gladiators from Nos.80 and 112 Squadrons. The Blenheims attacked in line astern and, although near misses were seen, no hits were recorded.

March 9th heralded the start of a new Italian offensive, immediately putting the stretched Greek forces under pressure. The Greek C-in-C at once requested that the RAF bombers operate in direct support of the ground forces and although D'Albiac considered this a misuse of air power, he reluctantly agreed. The next four days were given over to tactical targets.

By now the Germans had completed their domination of Rumania and were repeating their penetration tactics into Bulgaria. It was realised that it was only a matter of time before they were on the Greek northern borders. Later, both Rumania and Bulgaria joined the Axis Powers. The Greeks, fully realising the seriousness of the situation, were in no doubts that if they allowed British troops to enter the country, war with Germany was inevitable. To their credit, they preferred to accept such a situation rather than have to submit to a tame capitulation in face of overwhelming

L1391 VA-J suffered a near miss while flown by FO Barry Wade (Wg Cdr B.R. Wade)

How near can you get? Bullet holes in the mid-upper turret of a Blenheim, February 1941

force. In consequence, a British force was rapidly assembled in Egypt and British and Commonwealth troops arrived in Greece on 7 March.

On the night of 12 March, five aircraft from 84 Squadron bombed Calato airfield on the Island of Rhodes. Hutcheson's log book reads: "First attack on Rhodes, four 250-lb bombs dropped". On the 15th, taking off at 1325, seven Blenheims from 84 and 211 Squadrons set out from Paramythia to bomb Devoli airfield. Reports say that three Ro-37s were destroyed and three G-50s damaged. Later eight aircraft left at 1730 to bomb Valona. The mission was repeated on the 16th. The Squadron Commander, Sqn Ldr H D Jones, led a low-level attack on Tepelene on the 19th. Russell's log book states: "Good results but five out of the six hit by ack-ack, possibly due to admiration of the scenery". On the 23rd, six Blenheims from No.84, escorted by Hurricanes from 33 Squadron based at Larissa, attacked the airfield at Berat, approaching at low-level due to cloud at 1,500 ft. Later that day, military camps at Buzi was attacked, Hutcheson's elevators being hit by ack-ack fire.

Members of 'B' Flight left Menidi in a Bombay to fly to Heliopolis to collect replacement aircraft, the first mention of Blenheim IVs (Z5860 and Z5861) issued to 84 Squadron. They returned on the 26th.

The airfield at Calato was attacked again on the 27th, when six aircraft took off at 1335, Ingham-Brown flying T2340 having to return through engine problems.

A report by a patrolling Sunderland came through on the morning of the 27th that elements of the Italian Fleet were steering south-east towards the Greek shipping lanes. The British battlefleet put to sea that night from Alexandria. On the morning of the 28th, they were 150 miles off the southern coast of Crete. The first sighting of the Italian Fleet was by a patrolling Albacore. So began the Battle of Cape Matapan. A further report by a Sunderland which had sighted two battleships and three cruisers resulted in three Blenheims from No.84 being despatched to attack the ships. Although the bombs fell close, no hits were recorded. Later six aircraft from 113 Squadron took off but with the same result. The log book of Ingham-Brown's navigator states: "Operations against Italian battleships south of Greece. Bombed with four 250-lb from 3,500 ft. Intense and heavy ack-ack but not very accurate, no one hit". Although No.84 had little to shout about from the operation, the morale of the Squadron rose. In all, 29 missions had been flown by Blenheims and 13 tons of bombs had been dropped.

On 30 March, ten Blenheims from No.84 left to bomb Elbasan. Sgt Ingham-Brown, flying in one of the Blenheim IVs (Z5861) reports that he attacked from 10,000ft with 500-lb bombs. Two fighters attacked but did not press it. However Jim Hutcheson, flying L1388, was hit by ack-ack which necessitated him force-landing at Neapolis. His navigator, Ken Irwin, writes: "After both engines failed there was little alternative but to hit the deck. Sgt Jim Hutcheson did a great job and put it down just short of a ravine. I had braced my feet up against the bomb aimer's seat which was just as well as the bottom of the aircraft parted like a piece of cake. Both engines came adrift and there was petrol everywhere. So we got out pronto. I had always had misgivings about the size of the hatches on the starboard side of the Blenheim but I am sure that I never touched the sides on the way out. We had difficulty getting Sgt Jacky Webb, the air gunner, out because his hatch was jammed but we eventually succeeded and legged it away

before the kite blew up. About a hundred yards away a Greek soldier appeared and started firing at us, so deciding that discretion was the better part of valour, we stopped and put our hands up. We tried to get through to him that we were 'Inglese' and showed him the roundels of the aircraft. Meanwhile two cars appeared with a couple of Greek army officers and a Greek Orthodox priest. The latter spoke English and agreed to take over proceedings and away we went to the village of Neapolis. We spent an uncomfortable night in a bare room at the local taverna and next day were taken to Kozani. Meanwhile we had contacted Menidi and they said that if we could get to Koritza they would send an aircraft to pick us up. The next day, a driver, whose main ambition was to put the fear of God into us, took us over the Florian Pass with its hair-pin bends and sheer drops. After a debriefing with the Greek Air Force, we were told that they always avoided the area around Pogradec due to its heavy ack-ack. We were flown back to Menidi in a Greek Ju 52".

Others who were damaged in the attack were Fg Off I P Goudge flying T2427 and Sgt G Bailey in L1391. Sgt Blackburn in Flt Lt Russell's aircraft reported that he thought that he had shot down one of the attackers, which he had seen diving away streaming smoke.

On 1 April, the Squadron lost its Senior Flight Commander, Flt Lt D G Boehm, when he and his crew were killed in an accident near Kiphissia, north of Athens.

On the morning of 6 April, the German forces started their attack, moving west from the Struma valley and filtering by every available road into valleys and gorges. The first air reports indicated that an attack was being made in the area of Mt Beles and the Rupel Pass. At this point it was only 50 miles from the second biggest city in Greece, Salonika. During the night, Petrich and Simitli were bombed by Wellingtons and Blenheims flying from Larissa. In spite of severe weather some of our aircraft were able to bomb troop concentrations with good results.

Sgts Balch, Dicks and Fermor, Menidi, February 1941

An abandoned armed Greek Air Force Avro Tutor

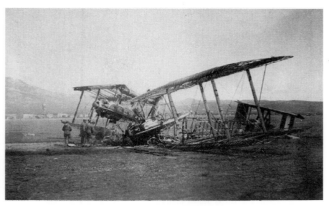

The wreckage of Valentia J9764 SH-T at Menidi

The speed of the German advance was such that on the next day it was admitted that troops had already crossed the border and were surrounding the city whilst others were turning west and threatening the Monastir Gap, the main road and rail link between Yugoslavia and Greece. At the same time, German divisions from Austria and Hungary invaded Yugoslavia, driving quickly through Zagreb and Sarajevo in their efforts to meet up with those crossing from Bulgaria and turning west and north.

That same evening, Ju 88s and He 111s bombed the port of Piraeus. At the height of the attack the *Clan Fraser*, which was unloading ammunition, was hit, with the result that the explosion lifted the ship out of the water. Moments later the *City of Roubaix*, which was lying alongside, also exploded. In all, eleven merchant vessels were destroyed and the port devastated. The series of explosions were so severe that windows in Athens were blown out and the blasts heard 150 miles away.

On the 9th, Salonika fell to the German Army, despite resistance from the Greek forces. The same day a Blenheim was despatched to Sarajevo carrying a Greek General to ascertain the position and see if any concerted action might be possible. The following day, nine Blenheims took off to attack columns of enemy troops on the Prilep-Bitolj cross-roads, one observer being hit by ground fire. Later six aircraft bombed tanks and other transport in the Monastir Pass. Hits were obtained but all six were severely damaged by ground fire, Flt Sgt Nuttall being killed after crashing. The log book of Sgt Gerry Maplesden reads: "Bombed railroad crossing 3 miles N of Mogila, hits on road and rail, little opposition". His second raid, five hours later makes for different reading: "Bombed railway crossing South-West of Lake Petrov, no results seen due to them waiting for us, sticky".

Blenheims from all squadrons on the 12th continued their attacks on the Bitolj-Veles road. On the 13th, six Blenheims from 211 Squadron were sent unescorted to bomb Prilep; caught by German fighters all six were shot down. Amongst those lost were Wg Cdr Paddy Coote, who had gone along as an observer. Only two of the crew were to survive. Later nine aircraft from 113 Squadron escorted by Hurricanes were sent to bomb the target. On the 14th, six aircraft from No.84, escorted by Hurricanes, attacked road transport at Ptolemais. They suffered intense flak and were attacked by Bf 109s. Four Blenheims were damaged. This was the last raid by Sgt Ingham-Brown and his crew before they were evacuated on the 21st.

On the 15th, Wg Cdr D G Lewis arrived at Paramythia from AHQ with instructions to dissolve the Western Wing and arrange evacuation from Yanina and Paramythia. The same day, Blenheims started to fly out ground personnel (nine to an aircraft). This operation would take three days to complete. The main effort by the German Air Force was now directed against the RAF, which had been delaying their military activities and taking toll of their aircraft. Large numbers of Bf 109s roamed the Larissa Plain and ground-strafed Niamata, where 113 Squadron was based, on two separate attacks. All of its Blenheims were destroyed.

The strength of the Blenheim squadrons at that time was: 84 Sqn, nine aircraft, 11 Sqn eight, 113 Sqn none, 211 Sqn five and 30 Sqn fourteen.

Meanwhile the German forces were advancing with such speed through the mountain passes in Northern Greece that the morale and organisation of the Greek army collapsed. Within a week Yanina had capitulated.

On the 16th, an attempted raid on Kozina was chased off by a standing patrol of four Bf 110s over Larissa. At this point, it was decided to bring all the remaining Blenheims under the control of 11 Squadron at Menidi. On the 18th, fourteen Blenheims, six each from 11 and 84 Squadrons and two from 211 were sent to make individual attacks on transport in the Katarine and Grevena areas. During one such sortie Sqn Ldr H D Jones, flying L1391, was attacked by two Bf 110s in the Larissa area. He was chased out to sea, where he was forced to ditch. Local villagers saw the crew climb into their dinghy but, before a local boat could put out to pick them up, one of the Bf 110s strafed and killed them. Later the bodies of the crew (Sqn Ldr H D Jones, Flt Sgt Jacky Webb and Sgt Harry Keen) were recovered and buried in the cemetery at Keramidi.

Further raids took place on 19 April and on the 20th the remaining aircraft concentrated as far as possible on evacuating key personnel. As far as is known, the last raid by any of the Blenheims occurred on the 21st when Sedes was attacked and four enemy aircraft destroyed.

Two strafing attacks by Bf 109s on Menidi on the 21st resulted in four Blenheims being destroyed, two from each of 11 and 211 Squadrons and one from No.84 was seriously damaged. Later attacks caused further damage.

Eight of 84 Squadron's Blenheims left for Crete on 22 April. They were led by Flt Lt Plinston, the others being Fg Offs Passmore, Linton, Goudge, Nicholson, Plt Offs Wade, Shand and Keble-White. Flt Lt Russell, who as senior flight commander had taken over command, writes: "Plt Off Shand was detailed to fly out in L1872 which had been undergoing repairs. I think it was the replacement of the outer panel of the wing, which was not quite finished. He made one of the quickest circuits ever, saying that the aircraft was uncontrollable in its present state, lacking fairings and other parts. So I let him fly T2340 which was my aircraft".

With the evacuation of the majority of No.84 Squadron's aircraft to Heraklion on the 22nd, Sqn Ldr Russell stayed on at Menidi with three of the ground crew working on L1872. Watching the rest depart, they were left with a feeling of loneliness and their main thought was to get the job completed before the Germans arrived. After surviving a strafing attack at dawn on the 23rd, Sqn Ldr Russell, with the three fitters, took off to catch the Squadron at Fuka. Their only aid to navigation on this four-and-three-quarter hour flight was an Admiralty chart of the Eastern Mediterranean.

At the same time as Sqn Ldr Russell was flying his lonely way across the Mediterranean, the formation of eight Blenheims were leaving Heraklion. Touching down at Fuka, they flew on to Heliopolis where they rejoined their Commanding Officer. Three days later they left for Aqir in Palestine, where they waited for their ground crews to arrive after their evacuation and to regroup. This was a painful process as they had little left in the way of kit.

CHAPTER 8 - THE EVACUATION

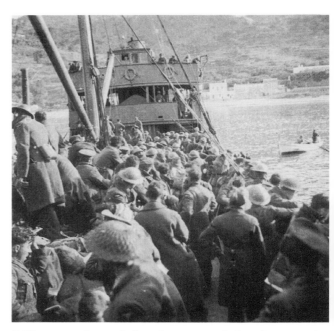

RAF personnel crowd aboard a coaster during the evacuation from Greece

It is fitting that I begin this chapter with the name Barry Paterson, for he was not only one of the last to join 84 Squadron at Menidi but he was also one of the first to be evacuated. He arrived at Menidi only three days before orders came to leave. The first news he received on landing was that German troops had broken through passes to the north from Bulgaria and Yugoslavia. He recalls that it was complete chaos and that his sole contribution was the handling of a Chance light, enabling the Blenheims to take off and land at night. Unfortunately, the Bf 110s used to shoot up the aircraft as they were doing so. Paterson was only there for three more days before he embarked on a destroyer for Piraeus, later landing at Suda Bay on the island of Crete.

On 18 April, Owen Greenwood recalls that just three days before the final evacuation, a small party of armourers under a NCO was sent to Sta Andrea (Marathon) to prepare a re-arming base for fighter aircraft on a small isolated airstrip. It was a case of 'Too little, too late', for four days later Menidi and Eleusis were empty; all the aircraft which were serviceable had flown off.

It was a totally different story for the ground crews. Reports from those who were there show the many problems that were to be experienced. It started as early as 1100 on the 20th for Corporal in Charge Orderly Room, George Thwaites, when the CO came in and said, "Corporal, destroy everything. The Germans are advancing quicker than anticipated. The Army are unable to hold them, we are moving out after lunch". Before they could start, the Bf 109s and Ju 87s were back, shooting and strafing anything that moved. He went on to recall: "It showed how vulnerable the RAF was to air attack, especially to its installations on the ground. The raids happened so quickly there were no prior warnings and the only time one was able to fire was if they made a second pass. There were no defences at all except for a couple of Lewis guns".

After the attack, it was remarkable how quickly the office staff cleared everything. Even the Squadron history went up in smoke! By 1300 the destruction was complete and an hour later they were ready to move off. Thwaites was lucky to find room on the canteen truck which was loaded with chocolates, cigarettes and beer. It was guarded by his friend, Charlie Burrell, the NCO in charge of accounts, with a loaded Lewis gun on his lap. Setting off at the tail of the convoy, they made their way through Athens and along the coast road to Corinth. They could see wrecks of ships still burning in Piraeus harbour and it was obvious that there was no way that it could be used for the evacuation.

The coast road to Corinth had been cut into the cliff side for virtually its entire length. This made it impossible for the convoy to be attacked, but every inlet showed burning ships. Credit must be given to the Military Police who seemed to be at every point where assistance was needed. As Rolly Duncan recalls: "It was a great pity that it could not have been so well.organised in advancing as it was in retreating. As we approached Corinth, the hills to the north were covered in columns of our troops making their way to the canal.

After crossing the canal, part of the convoy turned into the town of Navplion. Others moved to high ground overlooking the town, where they stayed the night. The following afternoon brought a renewal of the attacks by Ju 87s, their noise being frightening if you were on the receiving end. Luckily for the convoy, it was the ships in the harbour which were the target. The sky was lit up by the continuous explosions, the biggest of which was when a ship carrying ammunition blew up, scattering red-hot debris over a wide area. We heard later that it was one of those earmarked for the evacuation.

Back at Menidi, the few ground staff which remained were systematically destroying everything that would have been useful to the enemy. All the bombs were rendered useless by driving tractors over the tailfins two or three times until they were smashed beyond recognition. A trench was dug and all detonators, flares, signal cartridges and fuses were piled in. Petrol was poured over and the lot ignited. Later the earth was pushed back over the remains. At 0130 on the 23rd, they left Menidi and by 1000 hours they joined the others in convoy, reaching Argos at 1600.

At Argos, the few Hurricanes which remained were ordered to take off for Maleme the following dawn. At the same airfield, Sgt Jock Cruickshank had found space for himself and others aboard three Lodestars belonging to 267 Squadron which had flown into Argos under cover of darkness to remove key personnel.

Dawn on the 24th, the column which had spent two days at Navplion were told to prepare to move and make for Kalamata, a small port on the south coast of the Peloponnese. The journey involved driving around Argolis Bay, hugging the coastline. Passing Argos, where the fighters had been based, they could see extensive damage, but they passed the area without further problems. The journey took all day as the roads were very narrow and quite unsuitable for military transport. On reaching Kalamata they were billeted in the local brewery. As George Thwaites went on to say: "The one blessing was that for once a decent meal was available. RAF cooks had set up a kitchen in one corner and a choice of meat and vegetable stew or tinned sausages with bacon and eggs were there for the asking, together with gallons of tea. It was obvious that the British troops would put up with most things provided they had their tea!"

Word had filtered through that Sunderlands of 228 and 230 Squadrons had flown in and taken forty of the top personnel, including AVM D'Albiac and General Sir Thomas Blamey, Commanding Officer of the Australian Forces, from Scaramanga to Suda Bay on the island of Crete. They also learned that the Greek forces in the Epirus had capitulated and as a result of these setbacks, the Greek Government had handed to the British Minister a note stating their inability to resist further and asking that the Imperial forces should leave the country. Rumours abounded, but it was obvious that this was what they were trying to do. German armoured divisions were crossing at each end of the Gulf of Corinth and the only way for the British to leave was by sea, and to be quick about it.

The second group, after spending two days at Argos, left in a convoy on the morning of the 25th, as WO Blackburn writes: "It was not a very pleasant experience owing to the very persistent attacks by 'Jerry'. However we got away arriving at the small town of Esprokona just before dusk. The vehicles were dispersed around the lanes under such cover as could be used to advantage". The following afternoon, the RAF personnel were taken in to Kalamata to rejoin their mates.

Operation 'Demon', the code name for the evacuation, was already well under way. Six beaches had been nominated for the embarkation points, Beach 'Z' being Kalamata where the majority of the No.84 Squadron personnel were waiting. But as witnesses tell: "it was more a case of getting on when and where one could". Sunderlands and the 'C'-class flying boats Coorong and Cambria were running a ferry service from Crete, arriving with only sufficient fuel for the short return trip, and on occasion carrying 84 passengers.

On the evening of 26 April, WO Blackburn was detailed, together with WO Stevens and a party of 600 men, to be prepared to depart by ship. He continues the story: "We had lined the men up at dusk and proceeded to put them in the transport provided. We had not gone far when we met transport coming from the quay with the news that the ship had pulled away. On arrival at the quay we were told that the ship was overloaded". Meanwhile Rolly Duncan and others had boarded a small coastal vessel. He recalls that: "The holds seemed full of straw, but none of those in the hold worried, for even before they sailed the majority were asleep". They were awakened by the rattle of an anchor chain, only to see that they were in a small steep.sided bay, where a number of cottages were tucked into the cliff face. They were told it was the island of Kythera and that the captain had no intention of sailing to Crete during daylight hours. The bay, having no jetty, meant that we had to be rowed ashore. It was to be their home for the next few days, the vessel having been set on fire from a solitary air attack.

Back at Kalamata, Blackburn states: "Things were now becoming serious. One of the senior officers, Gp Capt Lee, told us to pack rations for seven days and make up a small party. It consisted of four officers and fourteen airmen. Leaving Kalamata, we moved up into the olive groves behind the town. All that day we sat in the hills and watched the bombing of Kalamata. There being no opposition, the carnage was frightful. Once or twice, aircraft came towards us spraying with their machine guns, and once a stick of bombs was dropped on houses about 300 yards from our parking place. That night we put a guard out to waken us if any naval vessels came in. Nothing in the way of rescue came and, at 0800, we reluctantly decided to make our way down to the coast".

"The party set off and soon came to the village of Pergus Dyrrou and also to the end of the track. Here we awaited the return of Gp Capt Lee who had gone into Kalamata to report. When he returned, he brought with him a survivor from a crashed Sunderland who had refused to stay in hospital. He could walk but was obviously in pain. Despite this he remained cheerful and uncomplaining".

"From there, Gp Capt Lee and Plt Off Lewis went into the village and came back with the good news that they had obtained a boat. So after a quick meal, we packed the truck with kit and set off to the nearest point we could get to the boat, which turned out to be a 40.ft kerosene.driven yawl, which was very well hidden in a small cove a mile the other side of Pergus Dyrrou. This we packed with our kit and rations. We also kept our rifles, as the Gp Captain wished us to walk to the next bay as he thought that the Germans would not proceed further than the end of the track. The yawl was to be put out that afternoon and, provided it did not get bombed or machine.gunned on the way, would pick us up in the next bay. However, news reached us that the Germans were closing in on the landward side, so we boarded the boat at 1500 on the 29th. The party now numbered 32, including the crew and a small number of army personnel who had come along as we were loading up. Luck was still with us as we set off at a steady eight knots, and it was a relief when darkness fell".

The next morning they drew into the island of Kythera where they were surprised to find three of No.84's main party, Fretwell, Wilson and Merrick. They told us that a destroyer had called at the island at 0200 and had taken off many of the RAF personnel. They had been left behind because they were on the mountainside exploring. At 1900 that evening we loaded the party from the yawl on to a Greek auxiliary vessel and sailed, reaching Crete on the

morning of 1 May. Others were rescued by a destroyer whose job it was to collect anyone from the islands off the Greek coastline".

George Thwaites, with his mate Charlie Burrell, was one of the thousands who were still waiting at Kalamata. Information that those leaving would be on a selective basis with Group I tradesmen (fitters, riggers and armourers) going first. As he recalls: "Being a Grade 4 clerk GD meant that we were at the back of the queue. Every evening we were marched down to the quay in the hope that a boat would be there. On the third night, the 26th, we set off as usual, but this time we were marched to a small jetty which was jutting out into the sea. We waited in the darkness among thousands of other troops squashed into a small area when suddenly the orders came for us to board the destroyer, HMS Defender, which was moored alongside. When it became impossible to cram any more on board, we shoved off and sailed into the darkness. Soon we could see the outline of two large ships. As we drew alongside, I could see the nets over the side. It was now obvious why we could not bring our kit with us. It would have been all right if I had been the only one climbing, but thousands had the same idea. In their eagerness to get aboard, no one cared whose fingers were trod on and I was not sorry to reach the railings".

Dawn came to find that they were aboard the City of London and, apart from the Costa Rica which was some way behind, the sea was empty. Around the railings were troops with Lewis and other machine guns at the ready. Suddenly out of a clear blue sky, Ju 87s attacked. After what seemed an eternity, they disappeared as quick as they came. The Costa Rica had been hit and it was learnt later that she had sunk. Fortunately all of the troops she had been carrying were taken off before she eventually went down 20 miles off the north coast of Crete. As the days passed they got farther from the Greek mainland and felt more at ease, even though they were not escorted. After three days, on 29 April, the ship docked at Alexandria. Later it was revealed by General Wavell that the evacuation had been carried out successfully and out of a total force of 60,000 Imperial troops, over 43,000 had been rescued. So much for success.

I have already mentioned that the aircrew in their Blenheims had left Crete on the morning of the 23rd. But many of the ground crew, like Rolly Duncan, Barry Paterson and Cpl Tommy Spencer, the Squadron wit (more about him later), were still there. Barry Paterson recalls: "I was evacuated in an old Greek coaster manned by volunteers because the original crew had deserted. Just outside Suda Bay we were bombed and many were killed. After drifting behind in a solitary lifeboat we eventually landed at Kolfanini. Use of a steel mirror eventually attracted a Greek destroyer which came and picked us up".

On 9 May, those who were on the island of Crete were taken on board the SS Nieuw Zeeland, a small freighter laden with aviation fuel. This entailed the 'passengers' living on deck for four days until they reached Port Said. Here they disembarked by tender as the authorities would not allow the ship to tie up at the quayside owing to the dangerous nature of its cargo. The men were then taken to the Middle East Pool at Geneifa and on 17 May to El Qantara. They crossed the Suez Canal and proceeded to Aqir where, on 18 May, they rejoined No.84 Squadron.

I have made no attempt to give an overall picture of the evacuation from Greece and Crete. Far better to leave it to other historians. What I would say is that I have tried in this chapter to give the experiences of half.a.dozen members of No.84 Squadron. Perhaps the reader should know that other survivors were turning up along the Egyptian and Palestinian coasts for weeks afterwards.

I cannot finish without giving an insight into the lighter side. The following was written for a Squadron reunion during the 1950s by the Squadron wit, Cpl Tommy Spencer, for which I give him credit.

The Zeeland *embarking ground crews from a destroyer*

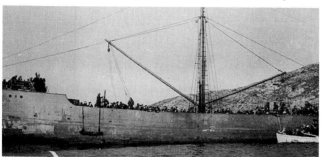

The evacuation beach at Kalamata, now a popular holiday resort

"There have been two baffling mysteries of the sea, the *Mary Celeste* and the SS *Zeeland*. The first I have only read about, the second I personally experienced. The SS *Zeeland* was an extraordinary little freighter, seldom visible to the naked eye, as it was permanently shrouded in a haze of petrol fumes. This phenomena was due to an error in design as it had originally been constructed in some dubious Latvian shipyard to convey mundane materials such as slabs of cow cake, vats of pickled walnuts or piles of polished mahogany pit props.

Unfortunately, while it was wallowing vacantly up that well-known creek, a sadly deranged Palestinian storekeeper loaded it with large cardboard cartons containing frail two gallon tins of petrol that leaked. The SS *Zeeland* was so tightly packed with this lethal cargo that there was little room below. So everybody lived, slept and ate on the open deck, with the exception of the engine room staff, entombed for all eternity in a reeking vault of sodden cardboard cartons. Fumes from those many millions of leaking containers seeped up through the cracks of those ill-fitting deck planks and kept everyone in a grinning, semi-carbon monoxide stupor. In fact, it soon became apparent to us all that the SS *Zeeland* was a sea-going 'Molotov Cocktail' shunned by the beaten British, the triumphant Third Reich and the swaggering Italian Navy, backed by five million bayonets, as Musso said at the time.

The Captain of the *Zeeland* was a frightened and bewildered little man who, thanks to his global maritime unpopularity, had become an inarticulate cross between Uriah Heap and Godfrey Wynn. He occasionally appeared on the bridge to polish his dark glasses with a shell.torn piece of signal bunting, hang his white stick on the boatswain's leeward epaulette, then, stumbling over his guide dog, would grope his way into the wheelhouse.

But the *Zeeland*, rejected by every harbour master from Ramsgate to Rangoon, performed one great, all-redeeming act of humanity; it saved the struggling remains of the 'other ranks' of the immortal No.84 Bomber Squadron from being butchered by the crack German Airborne Divisions on the hillsides of Suda Bay, Crete.

I had been sitting on the hillside for several days, accompanied by the famous 84 Squadron's wandering ground staff. Existing on a plentiful diet of boiled bully beef, rice and apricots, dispensed by a field kitchen situated in an orange grove and run by a chronically-eccentric RAF Warrant Officer called Long. This odd character swaggered up and down the hillside and seemed to enjoy every moment of this chaotic situation. His trousers were tucked into the top of some costly Australian's parachutist's boots; he carried a service .38 revolver in a khaki webbing holster attached to a light blue lanyard. He loudly bragged that he had been taken prisoner by the Turks in the First World War, forced to march barefoot from Basra to Belgrade and had written a book called *The Other Ranks of Kut*. His cultured cry: "I got left behind once before but I ain't sodding well getting left behind this time" often echoed around Suda Bay.

One day in the late afternoon, we 84 Squadron remnants were herded together and rushed down to the harbour jetty to be bundled upon a small motor-driven lighter bound for yet another unknown destination. I looked upward at my tall distinguished-looking comrade, Owen Greenwood, whose academic clowning never failed to elevate the Squadron's morale in moments pregnant with doubt and doom, such as this. Cleverly disguised as a RAF corporal, Owen Greenwood's faultless Oxford Don's accent and regal bearing instantly crushed any rank below Air Marshal to an agonising pulp. Mere Field and Air Marshals petulantly addressed him as 'Sir' and saluted.

After several moments perplexedly loafing on the lighter, we were sped out to the middle of the bay where we almost collided with the SS *Zeeland*. The ship had turned around to return to Egypt, as she had been refused sanctuary in yet another harbour by ashen-faced authorities, this time none other than General Freyburg VC, head of Crete, sharing the opinion of the rest of the world that the dreaded SS *Zeeland* was a menace to all mankind.

Once we were aboard, several days were passed sprawling on the open deck languidly inhaling the petrol fumes and munching corned beef. Owen Greenwood relieved the tedium by drawing my attention to a heavily-bolted and barred door leading to God only knows where. Owen suggested that it led to an armoured padded chamber that housed the 'Monster of the *Zeeland*', a hideous mutation that was the ghoulish result of the captain's illicit relationship with some far-flung oriental whore who made Fanny Hill look like the Virgin Mary. And though this 'Frankensteinian' atrocity had once escaped and strangled the ship's cook, the captain could not shoot it because it reminded him of his mother. So it was doomed to sail the seven seas with him for ever.

When we eventually sailed into Alexandria harbour, the *Zeeland* was once again refused berth and we had to be taken ashore in another lighter. Even today, hardened merchant seamen speak with awe of a phantom little freighter that they swear appears in a sort of mist in the Mediterranean.

FO Turner, PO Streatfeild and Sqn Ldr Passmore with their Blenheim Queen of Shaibah

CHAPTER 9 - BACK TO IRAQ AND THE WESTERN DESERT

Whilst a few of the early arrivals from the Greek evacuation were given a few days leave, others literally stepped off the boat at Alexandria and were immediately drafted to new duties. Cpl George Thwaites was one of those who, having disembarked, was taken by coach to Aboukir where they found that tents had been erected on the sports field. Equipped with spring beds and complete with sheets and pillows, each bed had soap and towels! So showers and a good scrub down was the order of the day!

Being the admin clerk, his first job was to try and compile a nominal roll. He soon found that many of the Squadron had yet to arrive. Over the following days, airmen started arriving in ones and twos and all had vivid stories of their escape. Many had found their way to Crete in small boats and from there were evacuated in naval vessels. Others had island-hopped and landed as far afield as Mersa Matruh and Fuka. It was surprising that after a few days, everyone had been accounted for. It was annoying to many that the Accounts Section would not accept other than Greek paper money. The Corporal in charge of the cinema receipts had collected all the takings (mostly coinage), carried it across Corinth, through Kalamata and scrambled up the side of the boat, only to find that no one wanted it when he arrived at Aboukir. Evidently his language was something to be wondered at!

On Friday 2nd May, the airmen arrived at Rehoveth station in Palestine and boarded buses for the RAF camp at Aqir. This was a permanent base with brick-built billets. Thwaites remarks that the standard of cooking had improved since his last visit to the station. It was also pleasant to be back with the aircrews who had been there since 26 April, primarily re-equipping. They were now up to full strength with several new aircraft and a few new faces. The same day, Plt Off Shand flew a reconnaissance over the Mafraq - Rutbah section of pipe line. These recces were mainly to check on whether the Iraqis were sending a force out to Rutbah Wells.

It is beneficial to the story to backtrack a few years. As long ago as 1936, Raschid Ali, an Iraqi politician, had fostered ideas of removing the hated British from the territory. In key positions he had invited German scientists, teachers and administrators, each spreading their own form of German thinking. Germany was only

too willing to go along with these arrangements. Not having any oil of their own, they were quite prepared to give Iraq every encouragement. This continued over the following years, although Raschid Ali's career was somewhat chequered.

On 3 April 1941, Raschid Ali, backed by four of his army generals, seized Baghdad. The Regent, Abdullah Allah, scenting danger, had fled first to the American Embassy and then to the RAF station at Habbaniya from where he was evacuated. To this change of regime Britain could hardly be indifferent, already knowing Raschid Ali's sympathetic feelings towards the German cause. Action of the promptest kind was now necessary if Britain was not to be excluded from the oil fields in Iraq and faced with an Axis advance from an entirely new direction.

On 16 April, Raschid Ali was informed that we intended to avail ourselves of the treaty right to pass military forces along the Iraqi lines of communication. By the 29th, Ali's attitude was so menacing that steps were taken to evacuate 230 women and children from Baghdad. On the morning of the 30th, Habbaniya and its airfield were dominated by guns of the Iraqi artillery. The same day an Iraqi Commander, under a white flag, approached the airfield and presented a note to the effect that the camp was surrounded and that flying should cease immediately. The AOC immediately replying that on no account would he cease flying and that firing on an aircraft would constitute an act of war and would result in immediate reprisals.

RAF Habbaniya had been built before the war and was the showpiece of the Middle East Command. Situated in the bend of the River Euphrates, it had the river to the north and Lake Habbaniya, where the Imperial Airways flying-boats used to touch down, to the south. Permanently stationed there was Air Headquarters Iraq, an aircraft depot with two large repair hangars. No.4 Flying Training School consisting of a miscell-aneous collection of training aircraft, accommodation for about 1,000 Levies who were assumed to be loyal to the British and a first class hospital manned by members of Princess Mary's Royal Air Force Nursing Service.

It also had accommodation for airmen and civilians, both

Sgts Francis, Holbrook and Morris in the desert
(D.O. Morris)

A Blenheim is written-off at Habbaniya, May 1941

British and Iraqi, plus families. Compared with other stations, it was 'Shangri-La'. There were wide avenues of trees, lawns, flower beds, swimming pools, cinemas and churches. It had a large shopping centre, appropriately named after an area in London called 'Cheapside'. Buildings were of brick and their lofty proportions housed ceiling fans and large windows, allowing the air to circulate.

Adjacent to the main camp were tennis courts, riding stables, a polo field and a golf course. A pack of hounds was based there for the benefit of those that hunted and there was a yacht club on the lake.

The base was situated on the main road, being about 200 miles from Rutbah and 50 miles from the capital, Baghdad.

It was assumed that Raschid Ali had the backing of about 9,000 fully-equipped troops and about 80 operational aircraft. No.4 FTS consisted of Oxfords, a wooden twin-engined trainer, Audaxes, Gordons (normally used for target towing), 24 dual-control Harts and three time-expired Gladiators.

During April, the majority of these aircraft were adapted to carry small bombs and crash courses had begun in bomb-aiming and air gunnery. To fly this motley collection of aircraft, there were 35 qualified pilots and flying instructors and a few of the more promising pupils. The other pupils, it was decided, would be used as air gunners, bomb-aimers and observers.

It was realised that the Vichy French, who held Syria, could act as a foothold to German forces coming from Greece. It could also create a bridgehead to the Middle East oil fields.

This was the scenario on 2 May 1941. Unknown to those at Habbaniya, a relief force was being formed at Amman to be known as 'PaiForce' (Palestine and Iraq). Barry Paterson takes up the story: "Seven days leave, but only one had been used before we were being recalled to our unit. MPs were going around Tel Aviv collecting all the airmen and returning them to camp, I was detailed to act as a guard on a convoy through Jerusalem to Jericho, across the valley of the River Jordan, crossing the Allenby Bridge and up the long climb into Transjordan. Pith helmets were issued to protect the head from temperatures reaching 115 degrees when crossing the Boulder Desert. As the convoy crossed the border into Iraq, our escort from the Arab Legion turned back and we were met by the armoured cars of No. 1 Armoured Car Squadron with their 1928 Rolls-Royces".

At Habbaniya, No.4 FTS had already gone into action; bombing had begun at 0500 and continuing around the clock. At the end of the first day, 193 sorties had been flown and 22 of their aircraft had either been shot down or so seriously damaged they needed more than the occasional patch. Far more serious was the fact that ten of the 35 pilots available had been either killed or were in hospital. Over the next four days, this continued with a lessening number of crews flying a rapidly diminishing number of aircraft. Of the 27 Oxfords at the start, only four were serviceable. The same ratio applied to the Audax and Harts. On the fifth morning a reconnaissance Audax reported that reinforcements were approaching from the direction of Baghdad.

FO Scoones landed across the runway to avoid Iraqi fire but both he and Sgt Blackburn survived

A Blenheim IV of No.84 Squadron over the Western Desert in December 1941

Curiously, and certainly very fortuitously, the Iraqis appeared to have had enough. At any rate, those retreating met their reinforcements about five miles east of Habbaniya, whereupon every aircraft set about them. In the next two hours, 139 sorties were flown and it was reported that when the last pilot left, the road was a strip of flame more than 250 yards long. There were ammunition limbers exploding and cars were burning by the dozen. One Audax was lost.

During that five days, the FTS had flown 647 sorties, dropped over 3,000 20-lb bombs, 200 250-lb bombs and fired 116,000 rounds of ammunition. A total of 13 aircrew were killed and 21 too badly wounded to work, with four other pilots grounded through strain.

To those who wish to read the full story of the Habbaniya siege and subsequent details, I would recommend AVM Tony Dudgeon's book *The War that Never Was.*

Meanwhile, on the 7th a detachment of No.84 Squadron had left Aqir for H4, an airstrip alongside the pipeline. From there, four aircraft led by Flt Lt Tony Plinston raided Rutbah. He writes: "The Group Captain who was conducting the operation did the whole thing stylishly. First we had to take off at dawn and drop the fort commander a message, telling him to surrender or else. So off we went. We got to the east of the fort and went in low with the sun behind us. Even then one of the natives fired a bullet which came in the front and disappeared between Jack Tozer and myself. After that we went off on another reconnaissance and saw nothing but desert. On our return, the fort was still occupied, so we dropped our bombs one at a time. The idea was to get at least one bomb to burst inside the fort. I think there were four aircraft, each making two trips. Of the 32 bombs dropped, not one succeeded in bursting inside the fort".

Fg Off Goudge was shot up and had to land at H3. Raids continued on the following two days. On 12 May, six aircraft led by Plinston flew to Habbaniya. The following day, they bombed the railway line between Mosul and Tel Awainat. Plinston writes: "We were to drop 11-second delay bombs into a sandhill alongside the rails. The idea was to send the sand sliding down to cover the tracks. An unfortunate railway official was sent with me to identify the right spot. We took off in the evening, timed to bomb at dusk. All went well until we went in at low-level. All the bombs hit the sandhill, but went off as soon as they hit. The first one spattered us with shrapnel and we sat in trepidation waiting for the other three. Of course, as the sandhill rose, the bursts got nearer. Despite being severely shaken, and spattered with bits of bomb, the aircraft was still flying and nothing vital had been hit. The observer's window in the nose had shattered so it was very windy. With three in the front cockpit, it was quite crowded, but Jack Tozer crouched at the civilian's feet. Everything worked when I landed but the aircraft looked a real mess the next morning. While I was looking at the aircraft, an irate Sqn Ldr Armaments Officer came up to me and demanded a full report. So I wrote one, saying "The 11-second delay bombs went off instantaneously, thereby damaging the aircraft". After all, it was his men who had armed the bombs. All I had done was drop them".

Of those that remained at Aqir, Fg Off K Linton and Plt Off Taylor set out to bomb Palmyra, escorted by two Tomahawks, on the 14th. A day later eight Blenheims led by Sqn Ldr Russell dropped leaflets on Damascus, Rayak and Palmyra, their escorts losing them on the way. Two Dewoitines were seen but did not attack. On a further raid on Rayak airfield, Fg Off Linton reported that the runways were bombed, but that they were attacked by French fighters. Raids were also made on the 21st and 23rd. The same day the detachment left at Aqir rejoined their fellows at Habbaniya.

Those who had flown to Habbaniya on the 12th continued daily raids. On the 16th, three aircraft bombed Qugaghan rail-way station. On their return, the AOC Palestine gave a talk prior to their first raid on Syria from Habbaniya. On the 17th, six Blenheims escorted by six Gladiators bombed Raschid (Baghdad) aerodrome. Night raids were also made on Mosul airfield. On the 20th, a solitary shoot-up of the field resulted in the loss of a Blenheim with a further two damaged. Later that day five aircraft arrived as replacements.

The presence of German aircraft in Iraq was first known on the 13th when a Blenheim was attacked by a Bf 110 while reconnoitring Mosul. The German danger was, as yet, in the early stages. By way of nipping things in the bud, our aircraft intensified their raids on Northern Iraq, bombing the hangars at Raschid and the supply lines on the Aleppo - Mosul railway.

Despite this, three He 111s attacked Habbaniya on the 16th

and other German aircraft were seen at Rayak and Palmyra. Fortunately, through lack of supplies and insufficient replacements, the German danger lessened and early next month 84 Squadron moved to Mosul.

On the 23rd, orders came for the ground party under Plt Off Ashmole and Bongard to proceed to Habbaniya, the column to be known as 'HabForce'.

Operations continued with leaflets dropped on Diwaniya, Kut-al-Imara and Ba'quba. Goudge shot up a Heinkel on an airfield 50 miles North of Habbaniya while Passmore and Tulley bombed and machine-gunned Kirkuk airfield.

There were no operations on the 28th, the day being devoted to servicing the aircraft. Next day, Iraqi troop concentrations at Fallujah were bombed by nine Blenheims. An afternoon operation resulted in a strafing job on the Iraqi airfield at Raschid. Single aircraft reconnaissance flights were made over Haditha and leaflets dropped on Manmudiya and Ramadi.

Sgt Gordon and his crew failed to return from a reconnaissance flight on the 31st. Over the following three days, aircraft carried out searches but to no avail. It is noticeable that even after being under fire for several days, remarks were made by some of 84 Squadron that some of the staff at RAF Habbaniya seemed quite out of touch with reality and tried to assert their authority.

Barry Paterson comments: "It was a marvellous station but he was not sorry to move on owing to the 'Bull'. However the Squadron's stay there was short-lived. It was late May and they were told they were moving on to Mosul in Northern Iraq. Apparently they had been waiting for the British army units to deal with the Iraqis and an official armistice to be declared. After packing, they started out for Baghdad. Just outside of Ramadi a group of Iraqi troops opened fire on them. The road on which they were travelling was on top of a bund, which was a barrier built to hold back the flood water from the Euphrates. They bailed out as fast as they could and crouched beside the bank while troops from the King's Own Royal Regiment flushed the Iraqis out.

After some time, they set off again and eventually covered the 50-odd miles to Baghdad, where they waited for the train. Thwaites recalls: "For the journey, they were provided with rations including tea, sugar and tinned milk. Whenever they wished to have a 'brew up' they stopped the train and got water from the boiler. It was not the best he ever had but at least it was hot and sweet. They travelled through the night, sleeping where they could on the seats, luggage racks or on the floor. They were not sure whether Mosul had been cleared or not, but the Gurkhas had gone ahead two days earlier, so they felt reasonably confident".

It was 3 June when they arrived at Mosul railway station and marched to the camp, many of them wearing their blue serge which did not suit the conditions. However, soon after, their kit and other equipment arrived. Mosul had quite a history, having been occupied by the RAF soon after the first World War and then used intermittently over the years. Prior to our arrival, it had been used by the Iraqi Army, who had left it in a bit of a hurry and, in consequence, the camp was in a sorry state.

RAF Mosul covered a large area and in one part a double-storey building, surrounded on all four sides with a courtyard with plants growing and a lovely pool, was said to be a harem, but more likely to have been a brothel. It eventually became the Sergeant's Mess. All of the other buildings were single-storey. Fortunately it did not take long to settle in.

The second ground party led by Plt Off B Ashmole left for Mosul on 6 June, arriving on the 8th. That day three aircraft led by Flt Lt Passmore bombed Aleppo. Comments in Gerry Maplesden's log book reveal that as Plt Off Keble-White's observer, his bombing was not all that accurate. His log states: "Four 250-lb bombs dropped, all missed the target". Over the following days, raids continued against targets in Vichy French-held Syria.

Aleppo became the main target but reconnaissance flights covered Tel Kotchek, Balad Sinjar and Ainzala areas. On the 13th, a dusk attack on Aleppo was interrupted by three Dewoitines and one of the Blenheims was damaged in the getaway. Deir-ez-Zor airfield came under attack and at the same time leaflets were dropped over a wide area.

As Sqn Ldr W T Russell writes: "Operations over Syrian targets were unescorted and not very pleasant. We had had several accidents, but eventually we got some of the aircrew who had been captured back. We had been detailed to send two or three aircraft to rendezvous with, and escort back to Mosul, a Vichy Air Force aircraft which it was hoped would desert in accordance with some secret deal made by the powers that be. Unfortunately it did not turn up. However the day before, we received a fighter Blenheim

which had been cast off by some squadron or other and I thought it would be a good idea to take this (L9335) in case we were ambushed. On the way to the R/V, I seemed to recall that the fighter boys used to test their guns with a short burst, so I did likewise. Unfortunately, I did not realise that the guns were improperly aligned and all four in the box underneath were pointing up into the nose! The first I knew, my navigator Sgt Somerville was bouncing up and down in his seat in the nose amidst a cloud of dust, his feet were being bounced by bullets entering the nose and ricocheting off his shoes".

In the same letter, Sqn Ldr Bill Russell comments that it was the practise to carry your topee when you were flying. As a result of the accident in the previous paragraph, his was holed in a couple of places. Some days later, he was in the local store with his bearer acting as interpreter, when they were met by the store manager. He goes on to say that his bearer was very proud of being with the 'CO Sahib' and tended to throw his weight around. When the manager asked about these holes in his topee, Russell hoped that he would be regaled with some stirring tale. But to his mortification the bearer said "Oh that! CO Sahib fell out of his aeroplane on to his head".

Further raids were made on Aleppo on the 29th and 30th, Flt Lt Passmore leading the first on a dawn attack. Records show that it was well timed and one aircraft was set on fire. Later attacks by Sqn Ldr Russell state that all bombs fell in the area, Ingham-Brown shooting up motor transport on the return flight.

Sgts Shaw and Ingham-Brown carried out recce flights over Moslimyva and El Bag. Strafing attacks on Nasrullah were carried out and later strikes on airfields in the region. It was a bad day for the Squadron on 2 July when Flt Lt Williams and his crew (Plt Off Eidsforth and Sgt Crowe) failed to return from a visit to Aleppo. The same day, Sgt 'Banger' Balch and Sgt Bill Wright was lost over Nasrullah. Two days later there was another loss to the Squadron when Plt Off Ryan and his crew were shot down on a photo-reconnaissance flight to Aleppo. Searches were carried out over a wide area but it was not until several days later that the wrecks of two Blenheims were found.

Both Williams and Ryan, with their respective crews, were eventually returned to the Squadron after an armistice in Syria had been signed.

July 6th brought one of those accidents which happen occasionally, either through lack of communications or insufficient information. Sqn Ldr Russell was summoned to the Station Commander who said that AHQ Iraq had their suspicions that a force of Vichy French were moving towards Raqqa from the Turkish border. One aircraft was to recce 50 miles down the road and attack any forces seen. "Whereupon I was told to take Sgt Bud Shaw as my No.2 and recce as far as Raqqa. Unfortunately, we saw nothing until we reached Raqqa itself, which had a load of vehicles scattered around its airfield. So we got stuck in with gay abandon until Shaw got a bullet through his windscreen that nicked his shoulder harness. So we packed it in. Unfortunately, there were no markings on the vehicles to indicate that they belonged to the Gurkhas.

On 3 July 'HabForce' captured Palmyra and the ceasefire occurred on 12 July. The crisis which had begun in April 1941 was over. Cyrenaica, Greece and Crete had been lost but Egypt and Iraq had been saved and Syria had passed into our hands. With the Middle East firmly under British control, the struggle for control in the Mediterranean could begin in earnest and all forces available could be directed on a single front.

Meanwhile, back at Mosul the RAF were making themselves at home with their customary thoroughness. Conditions seem to vary considerably because some were billeted in old Iraqi barracks, with walls about 2ft thick which kept them very cool, while others had to make do with tents smeared with oil and sand and camel thorn leaves thrown over them. Fortunately, the new Corporal's Mess was well under way. Named 'The Belly Tank', it was equipped with ex-German long-range fuel tanks cut down to form chairs and tables. As always, beer was plentiful and at the opening ceremony more than half of the members proved to be incapable and were charged with throwing the Station Warrant Officer into a slit trench. Barry Paterson recalls that approximately half of the Squadron were put on a charge. It was found that, on analysis, the locally-brewed beer was about five times the normal alcoholic strength.

Later, when the charges were dropped, the NCOs were lucky in the fact that they had served only two days of their punishment whilst the erks who had gone through the same process a few days before had completed theirs.

There were also based at Mosul a small group of about 30

Blenheim IVs of No.84 Squadron lined up in preparation for their flight to the Far East

men calling themselves a 'P and C unit', found later to mean 'parachute and cable', supposedly a form of defence against dive-bombing. Within a few weeks, they had packed up and gone elsewhere.

At the end of July, Sgt Ken Lister and his crew, Alan Sharrott and Ron Pile, joined No.84 Squadron. Their first job was to deliver a replacement Blenheim IV from Abu Sueir. At the briefing, Lister remembers being handed the maps for the first part of the flight across Palestine and along the pipeline as far as Rutbah, but no printed maps were available for the final leg from Rutbah to Habbaniya, where they intended to night stop. They were given a rough sketch and told that they were bound to see Lake Habbaniya and could not miss the airfield. As luck would have it, they missed the Lake and found themselves over the River Euphrates not knowing whether to turn North or South. Deciding to turn south they flew for several minutes without seeing the airfield. After a short time they turned through 180 degrees and found Habbaniya, only to be met with the words "What kept you so long".

The next day they continued their flight to Mosul. On taxying into the field it was interesting to see a He 111 left behind from the German occupation. Having tested the excellent facilities at Habbaniya, Lister found Mosul a bit of a shock. Sleeping accommodation was a large tent which they shared with three other sergeants. Bed consisted of three planks with two supports to keep them six inches off the ground. They were issued with two rough army blankets, a mosquito net, a mat to either sleep on or to put on the floor and a straw-filled pillow. The following day, they were advised to go to the local store and purchase camp beds which had obviously once been in army stores.

Local flying continued in their efforts to familiarise themselves with the neighbourhood. They also learned how to use the siren with which the aircraft was fitted as a means of scaring villagers who had done something which had upset those in authority. Sqn Ldr Russell had decided, soon after settling in at Mosul, that aircrews would help out the armourers by doing a stint in the armoury. On visiting them one day to make sure that they had turned up, they were surprised when Passmore had turned on this 'screamer' device and beat up the airfield from zero feet. Rumour has it that Passmore was nearly lynched on landing.

Later the Squadron had a lot of trouble from thieving by the local Kurds. On occasions, the hurricane lamps used for a flarepath went missing. They even took to stealing ammunition from parked aircraft. After experiencing this on several occasions, the Squadron enlisted help from the Gurkhas who acted as guards. They were so efficient they were always notified if anyone went out after dark, as

it was probable that you would have a kukri at your throat at the same time as hearing "Who goes there?"

During July, the Squadron establishment was changed from a Sqn Ldr CO plus three Flt Lt flight commanders to the UK establishment of Wg Cdr CO plus two Sqn Ldr flight commanders. In connection with Iraq Command Operations of 8 August 1941, 12 Blenheims complete with crews and one extra passenger proceeded to Shaibah to operate under Basrah Wing in forthcoming operations against Iran. The 12 Blenheims left Mosul at 0800, flying in box formations of four, and all but one aircraft reached Shaibah safely. The missing aircraft, flown by Plt Off Shand, force-landed at 1250 hours 20 miles from Shaibah with engine trouble. The ground maintenance party of 55 NCOs and airmen were moved on the same day by aircraft of 31 Squadron.

This differs considerably from Sgt Ken Lister's account of the flight. In his letter he writes: "We flew down in formation with no problems until our arrival, when we found a duststorm blowing across the field which prevented several of the aircraft from landing. Some diverted to Habbaniya and others landed on the open desert. It was noticeable when we landed at Shaibah that all the copper-embossed Scorpions which had decorated the walls of the control tower, etc. had been removed. The home Squadron was not amused when painted scorpions appeared on every hangar wall and crossroads. Needless to say, it was not No.84 who had done this dastardly deed!

Plt Off B Ashmole assumed command of 84 Squadron personnel at Mosul. On the 21st, Plt Off G Milson was appointed to act for Committee of Adjustment in respect of Sgt S E Wilson and Sgt S Clough, killed in a flying accident at Shaibah. A few days later, the committee held a sale in the Officers' Mess of the personal effects of Plt Off Webster.

Also based at Shaibah were the Hurricanes of No.261 Squadron and the Vincents of No.244 Squadron. All had been brought together for Operation 'Y'. During that four-day skirmish, the Hurricanes and Blenheims attacked Ahwaz airfield, destroying motor transport and setting hangars and barracks on fire. They also flew tactical reconnaissance flights over the oil refinery at Abadan and dropped leaflets at Isfahan and Shiraz. One Vincent was mistakenly shot down by a Hurricane, wounding its pilot. After the Shah of Persia had ordered an end to the hostilities, 261 Squadron left for Mosul while No.84 returned to Habbaniya with a detachment at Amriya.

The following decorations were awarded for devotion to duty while serving with 84 Squadron to Fg Off Trevor-Roper DFC, Sgt F D Round and Sgt G Bailey DFM.

On 28 August, Sqn Ldr W T Russell flew his last mission

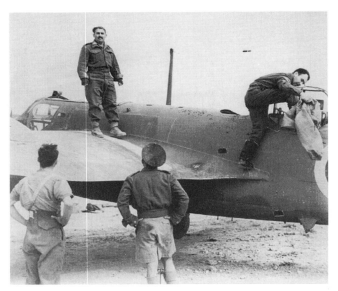

Wg Cdr Clayton Boyce on wing and Sgt Alan Chenery climbing out of turret, Western Desert, December 1941
(AVM Boyce)

with No.84 Squadron and left to join AHQ. In his letters he was severely critical of the system employed by Middle East HQ. He writes: "My final comments, for what they are worth, cover two points. First, in the UK operational tours were clear cut. 30 operations or three months on ops and you were then rested. In No.84 some of the aircrew were with the Squadron for eight months continuously with no leave at all. It was a disgrace how some of them were treated. I remember one chap who was in such a state he used to vomit due to nervous tension before every sortie. Another I knew never flew on ops again. And as for decorations, one of my first acts on taking over the Squadron was to prepare citations for several of the aircrew and other ranks on leaving Greece. Many got them but many were ignored completely".

Wg Cdr C D C Boyce took over command of the Squadron at the end of August 1941.

Ken Lister refers to the period spent at Shaibah whilst flying with the Hurricanes. He writes that an exercise was mounted to give No.84 practice in defensive manoeuvres against fighter attacks at medium and at low-level. After the medium-flying exercise, they split into individual aircraft and, whilst trying to evade attacks from a single Hurricane, his crew saw that one of the Blenheims had crashed on the salt flats. His observer, Alan Sharrott, took a fix and they returned to Shaibah to get help. As a consequence, a sergeant from sick quarters and himself were flown out in a Vincent. Because the ground where the crash occurred was dried salt, the pilot made a couple of dummy runs to see if it was hard enough to land on. He decided it was safe enough and landed quite close but, just as it was about to stop, the Vincent went up on its nose. They scrambled clear and went over to the wrecked Blenheim only to find that one of the crew was dead. The pilot had a badly smashed leg while the other crew member was not too bad. By this time, another Vincent had dropped tents, blocks of ice, food and other supplies to keep them going until help could arrive.

"Having got the injured as comfortable as possible, we wrapped the body in a hessian bag that had held the tent and buried it by sinking it in a hole in the surface of the brine lake. The Flight Lieutenant pilot of the Vincent conducted a funeral service. It was nearly dark when the rescue party arrived, because they had to walk several miles, leaving their transport on hard ground". Later, Lister was to run into the pilot again when he returned from Sumatra, finding him in hospital where he was recovering from his amputated leg.

It is worth recording that this period at Shaibah was the hottest time of the year, with temperatures well over 100 degrees Fahrenheit and 100% humidity. So hot that an egg could be cooked on a piece of metal left in the sun. Flying took place in the early morning and the aircraft were normally back on the ground by 1030. It was also normal to wear gloves when climbing in or out of the aircraft to avoid burning oneself.

He also recalls that on a flight to Kuwait, there was in those days a large fishing village with no Custom duties where cameras and other desirables could be bought in the local souk (covered

market) at very low prices. There was a landing strip just outside the town and permission had been given to the Squadron to fly down and do some bargain hunting. A very pleasant day was spent by most of us but, unfortunately, one aircraft crashed on landing. Plt Off Keble-White had forgotten to lower his undercarriage. The aircraft had to be left behind, which must have left someone with some awkward questions to answer.

On 26 September, the personnel who had remained at Mosul rejoined the Squadron, their few aircraft preceding them. From Shaibah the Squadron moved up to Habbaniya on 28 September, preparing for their move to the Western Desert. On reaching Habbaniya their days were taken up by extensive training under their new flight commanders, Sqn Ldr James and Flt Lt Passmore. Amongst those who joined the Squadron during October were Fg Off Arthur M Gill, who was later to command the Squadron in India, Ceylon and Burma.

On 25 October, two Bombays arrived to transport essential equipment and personnel to Aqir. The following day, the 20 Blenheims on strength left for Amriya, three returning to Aqir with engine problems. A Valentia carrying some of the squadron equipment crashed at Burg-el-Arab. Later James landed nearby to help salvage the equipment.

Ken Lister writes: "When the move took place, the aircraft were flown to Amriya just outside Alexandria with an overnight stop at Lydda which enabled the crews to see Tel Aviv and enjoy an evening out on the town". After their arrival at Amriya, the air party had to await the arrival of the ground crews who were travelling in a large convoy of trucks across the desert through Jordan and Palestine. Amriya was a horrible place with the most primitive of conditions, infested with flies and subject to frequent dust storms. As we were living in tents there was little protection from either; so every opportunity was taken to get into Alexandria which catered for all kinds of entertainment, legal and otherwise.

A reconnaissance flight was made by the two flight commanders on 31 October to inspect the proposed landing strip allocated to No.84 Squadron. They were to move there on 19 November. Notes in the PRO state that the main party arrived at Haifa on the 9th and then travelled by train. On the same day, motor transport arrived from Helwan preparatory to moving to LG.116. An advance party led by Fg Off Bongard, the Equipment Officer, left on the 19th, followed on the 23rd by the main party led by Flt Lt B Ashmole and Flt Lt Ryan. They arrived at 1730, minus four vehicles. Two had broken down, two others had lost their way reaching Mersa Matruh and had to return via Sidi Haneish.

The aircraft arrived the next day and, operating from nearby LG.75, flew their first operation on the 25th, bombing motor transport in the Bir Schefferzen - Gazr-el-Abid triangle. The following day, eight Blenheims escorted by 20 Hurricanes bombed troops at Magen Bel Hared. Sqn Ldr James led nine aircraft on a bombing raid on the El Cuscia area. Log Books report it was very successful. The Squadron suffered its first loss on the 27th when Flt Sgt Ingham-Brown was shot down by AA fire.

In his letters, Sgt Ken Lister records that No.270 Wing, in which 84 flew, consisted of Nos.45 and 211 Squadrons plus a Free French Squadron. As far as he remembers, all raids were in formations of 6, 12, 18 or 24 aircraft, with all bombs being released when the formation leader's bombs were seen to leave the aircraft, thus creating a heavy concentration in a relatively small area. The normal bomb load was four 250-lb with instantaneous fuses at the nose and tail. The nose fuse was generally fitted with a ten-inch extension rod, which meant that the explosion took place just above ground level, giving the maximum horizontal blast effect.

Six aircraft, in conjunction with No. 14 Squadron and the Free French Squadron, targeted the Sollum-Tobruk area on the 30th. Chaos was created, prior to a proposed raid on 4 December, when, due to bad briefing, three Blenheims from No.45 Squadron started to take off from the end of the dirt strip nearest their dispersal area. At the same time, the first three aircraft from the Free French 'Lorraine' Squadron started their take-off from the opposite end. Fg Offs A M Gill and G Milson, who witnessed the accident, realised that nothing could be done to stop them. They had no telephone or Very pistol with which they might have been able to fire a red warning flare.

Suddenly the two leaders saw each other. They just missed by swerving, the next two pulled up so rapidly that one stalled and crashed, the last two collided, one of which caught fire and exploded. A total of four aircrew were killed and others were severely injured. Only two were saved. As Ken Lister, who was flying overhead recalls: "In view of what followed, it should be

No. 84 Squadron personnel in the Western Desert

Standing L to R: Flt Lt John Wyllie; Flt Lt A M Gill; Sgt Stan Owen; Sgt J Ellis; unknown; FO George Milson; unknown; Sgt H Hough; three unknown; Wg Cdr C D Boyce; Sgt Wakefield; Sgt B Bennett; Sgt Cosgrove RAAF; unknown; PO R Millar RNZAF; two unknown; Sgt Ken Lister; unknown; PO Streatfeild; Sqn Ldr Keith Passmore; Sqn Ldr Tayler; FO Eidsforth. Kneeling L to R: Sgt Craddock; PO J Hawke RAAF; Sgt Bill Proctor; Sgt B Winchester RAAF; two unknown; Sgt Jenkins; unknown; Sgt A Blackburn; Sgt Ron Pile; PO J Goldfinch RAAF

noted that radio silence had to be maintained and that all communications between aircraft was by hand signals. In any case the radio equipment was virtually useless and successful speech transmission to the aircraft next to you in the formation was very rare".

A raid by 24 aircraft of Nos.14, 45 and 84 Squadrons attacked troop concentrations at Sidi Rezegh on 6 December. Over the target, they were set on by Bf 109s, losing one aircraft on the return flight. It was followed by a full squadron raid on motor transport at El Adem. From photographs, it was estimated that 53 vehicles had been destroyed. Unfortunately, four of the escorting Hurricanes were lost. On the 12th, Sgt Bayford and his crew were killed when they flew into an escarpment. The 12th also brought a change in the Wing structure, Wg Cdr H R Kellett DFC AFC being promoted to Group Captain and given command of 270 Wing.

Raids continued on the 13th, attacking motor transport and armoured vehicles. They were attacked by enemy fighters, losing a Tomahawk from the escort. Sgt Brackpool was forced to ditch in the sea during an attack on the 14th; luckily both he and his crew were rescued. Five Blenheims from 84 Squadron joined three from 14 Squadron on a raid over Derna, attacking the road which runs from north to south, with the intention of starting a landslide. Although hits were obtained, no landslide resulted. Four Hurricanes were shot down when attacked by twelve Bf 109s. At the same time, four of the enemy were claimed by the escort.

No.84 Squadron moved to Gambut on the 18th; Sgt Ken Lister's comments about Gambut are well worth recording: "At Gambut most of us found ready-made accommodation in large packing cases sunk to just below ground level which had recently been occupied by the enemy and which were still occupied, as they found later, by another adversary - FLEAS. An intensive campaign with Flit and flea powder was waged and won in a very short time. I shared quite a large and superior packing case with my observer, Alan Sharrott, my gunner Ron Pile, Ken Dicks, Alan Blackburn and two others. The case measured about twenty feet long, nine feet wide and seven feet high. On entering through the end door,

one had a small ante-room about eight feet long with a table and benches along the walls and through the door at the end was sleeping accommodation with tiered bunks".

"One of the great trials of life was the shortage of water as most, if not all, of the wells were contaminated or put out of action. What water we did get was brackish and heavily chlorinated and limited to two pints per man per day. Every wash was nothing more than 'a lick and a promise' with emphasis on the promise. Tea tasted foul with salt and chlorine. Despite this water shortage, No.84 lived up to its reputation in providing a regular supply of thirst-quenching liquids at all times. This was achieved by having two three-ton trucks regularly running between the main forward supply depot and wherever we were based. Also, whilst at Gambut, we found we were close to an abandoned enemy stores depot which I believe provided a source of wines by the carboy for those with a taste for the better things of life".

"Christmas Day was spent at Gambut and, as it was supposed to be a war between civilised nations, all fighting stopped for the day and we enjoyed something approaching a traditional Christmas dinner with lots to drink and a celebratory photograph behind a swastika flag".

From the 27th to the 31st, there were daily attacks on the town of Bardia, prior to its being taken late on 31st December. On 2 January 1942, orders came through that 84 Squadron were to be withdrawn from the desert and be prepared for departure to the Far East. The command of the Squadron was handed to Wg Cdr J R Jeudwine. From researches, I can find that 27 operations were flown between 25 November and the Squadron's recall from the desert on 2 January 1942.

A note in the Public Record Office contains the following memo: "From the time the Squadron left Iraq on 26 October 1941 to the time we left the Western Desert, I would like to say that the morale and fitness of the personnel were excellent. Most personnel enjoyed the hard life, even with the abundance of dust and the lack of water, because they were doing a job of work - HITTING THE ENEMY - and it was with regret that most of us left the desert: Signed, Boyce".

Palembang P.1 airfield, Sumatra (Royal Netherlands Air Force)

CHAPTER 10 - THE FLIGHT INTO CHAOS

On 5 November 1941, Emperor Hirohito of Japan presented a statement to the Japanese civilian cabinet and the military authorities with the aim of starting warlike proceedings against the United States, Great Britain and the Dutch East Indies. On the same day, Admiral Yamamoto, Commander of the Combined Fleet, made known his plans for the attack on Pearl Harbor. Two days later, Yamamoto told his staff officers that the attack was to be made on 8 December.

Belatedly realising the worsening situation, Britain decided to send two capital ships and an aircraft carrier to the Far East in November 1941. HMS *Indomitable*, the carrier chosen, was delayed due to a mishap in the West Indies. As a result, HMS *Prince of Wales* left Cape Town with her attendant destroyers on 18 November, dropping anchor next to HMS *Repulse* at Colombo on the 28th. This small squadron, which sailed with no air cover, became known as Force 'Z', with Admiral Sir Tom Phillips in command.

From records, it is clear that both Britain and the United States were very well informed of Japanese intentions, yet little was done to reinforce the area. A classic example of this way of thinking concerned Japanese fighter strength. As early as the summer of 1940, reports were coming in from China of the seeming invincibility of the Mitsubishi Navy Type 0 carrier fighter (later known as the Zero). It was faith in the ability of this aircraft to wrest control from the enemy in air fighting that gave the Navy its confidence of victory in the initial campaigns. This information was available to both the United States and Great Britain but was largely ignored because it seemed unbelievable. A statement by William M Leary in an article "Assessing the Japanese threat" reads: "Allied pre-war intelligence in Japanese aviation was abysmal. Blinded by complacency, chauvinism and arrogance, it reached dubious conclusions about the state of Japanese Air Power".

Two RAF fighter squadrons were hurriedly formed, together with two from the RAAF and another from the RNZAF, all of which had to wait for pilots to arrive from training establishments. It meant that Britain and the Commonwealth went to war in the Far East with just 158 aircraft; these included 24 obsolete Vildebeest.

On the morning of 4 December 1941, two Japanese convoys left the shelter of Samah harbour on the island of Hainan. On the 6th they were sighted by a Hudson of No.1 Squadron RAAF. Already at sea were the 32 ships forming the force allocated to the

attack on Pearl Harbor with orders that, if they were detected before 6 December, they were to return to port. No one saw them!

The initial act of war was the shooting down of a RAF Catalina on 7 December, 14 hours before the attack on Pearl Harbor. 12 hours and 40 minutes later, Japanese troops landed on beaches on the North-East coast of Malaya.

This heralded the start of what proved to be one of the bloodiest and most horrific wars ever known. It was also the beginning of one of the most glorious episodes in the history of the RAF, RAAF and RNZAF.

At the end of the last chapter, it was stated that No.84 Squadron was withdrawn from the Western Desert on 3 January 1942 in order to re-equip prior to its transfer to the Far East. The aircraft were flown to Heliopolis, near Cairo, and the personnel were moved to Almaza Training Camp. As the camp was found to be unsatisfactory, the airmen were accommodated under canvas on the perimeter of Heliopolis airfield.

The Squadron was re-equipped with 24 Blenheim IV bombers in three flights, with an establishment of 484 ground staff and 33 complete crews. As no person approaching the end of his overseas tour was to proceed to the Far East, a considerable number of its original personnel were posted away.

Wg Cdr C D C Boyce handed over command of the Squadron to Wg Cdr J R Jeudwine on 5 January 1942.

Airmen of No.206 Group inspected the aircraft on the 5th and passed ten fit for further service. The 14 aircraft required to bring the Squadron up to strength were collected from Nos.103 and 108 MUs on the 12th, 13th and 14th January. All aircraft were fitted with a 55-gallon overload petrol tank carried in the bomb-bay, its contents to be pumped into the main tanks by a Zwicky pump fitted on the starboard side of the pilot's cockpit. The tanks were fitted for Operation 'Crusader', which was to locate the aircraft carrier HMS *Indomitable* off the coast of Java and escort the Hurricanes of Nos.232 and 258 Squadrons to a shore base.

The first flight was inspected by Air Marshal Sir Arthur Tedder, Air Officer Commanding Middle East, on the afternoon of 13 January and wished "Good Luck". They were to need all the luck that was going!

Briefed at HQ Cairo, the air parties left in four flights on the 14th, 15th, 16th and 18th. Each aircraft carried two groundcrew beside the aircrew, together with personal kit, spares and tool kits, the all-up weight of each aircraft being 14,000 lbs.

The route planned was as follows; Heliopolis, Habbaniya, Bahrein, Sharjah, Karachi, Calcutta (Dum Dum) via Bombay, Hyderabad or Allahabad, Toungoo, Rangoon (Mingaladon or its satellite field Zayatkwin), Llo'nga (Sumatra), Medan or Pakan Baroe to Palembang (KNILM airfield). The stage Rangoon to Llo'nga was over the Andaman and Nicobar Islands.

The first flight of five aircraft left Heliopolis on 14 January 1942. Unfortunately, Plt Off John Goldfinch was delayed due to a burst main tyre. He rejoined the flight, leaving the following day. Trouble began at Habbaniya when Plt Off Macdonald's Blenheim suffered a collapsed right oleo, causing the aircraft to ground-loop. Fortunately no casualties occurred. He was to continue the flight in a Blenheim left by 113 Squadron. Flt Lt Gill also had problems. Struggling to lift his heavily-laden Blenheim off the runway at Sharjah, he hit an oil drum, damaging his tailwheel which collapsed on landing at Karachi. Collecting the necessary spares from the RAF depot at Drigh Road, he and his crew worked all day to repair the aircraft. He caught up with his flight at Toungoo and reached Palembang (P.1) with the first aircraft on 23 January. Plt Off Mort Macdonald missed Palembang completely and was forced to ditch in a swamp at the mouth of a river, miles to the south of the airfield.

On arrival over Sumatra, the flights found that the position of Llo'nga had been incorrectly plotted and although a correction was sent by signal, no notice was taken off it and this faulty briefing caused the loss of one aircraft from No.84 Squadron and another from No.211.

The second flight was also having difficulties; Sgt Bill Cosgrove force-landed at Ramadi with his starboard engine seized. It was to be a further four weeks before he and his crew reached Palembang. Sgt Howard Hough was the unfortunate pilot mentioned in the previous paragraph who, through incorrect briefing, ran out of fuel and force-landed in padi fields. He and his crew eventually reached Palembang on 9 February. Sqn Ldr Keith Passmore, leading his formation, reached Medan successfully but taxied into a loosely filled-in bomb crater, damaging both undercarriage and airscrews. Shortage of spares necessitated a seventeen-day delay before the aircraft was considered serviceable. Sgt Ken Lister became the fourth member of the second flight to have problems. At Allahabad, flap failure caused difficulties which were never solved. Reaching Mingaladon, the aircraft was taken by another crew which subsequently crashed on its approach to Llo'nga. Lister and his crew reached Palembang on 7 February.

The third flight, led by Flt Lt "Dutch" Holland, experienced few difficulties, all crews arriving at Palembang by 26 January. The Command-ing Officer, Wg Cdr Jeudwine, left on the 16th and, by making the first two stages Heliopolis-Shaibah (via Habbaniya) and Shaibah-Karachi (via Sharjah) in good time, caught up with the second flight at Karachi and the first flight at Calcutta on 20 January.

Of the fourth flight, Sqn Ldr T James reached Pakan Baroe, where his aircraft was strafed by enemy fighters. Sgt Headlam crashed at Rangoon, killing himself, Sgts Odgers and Lloyd. Sgt Farrer the Wop/AG was badly burned but was later able to rejoin the Squadron on its return to India. Sgt Aubrey Pedlar, after experiencing fuel problems, was finally compelled to force-land in a field alongside the River Ganges. Neither Pedlar or Sgt Jack Prentice, who had similar problems, were able to join their Squadron before the route was closed. Both rejoined the Squadron on its return to India.

The result was that of the 24 Blenheim IVs and crews which had left Heliopolis, only 16 reached Palembang. Three reached Sumatra but never reached P.1. Two crashed on the flight, one with fatal results. Three were held up by engine defects and never flew beyond Burma. Two crashed on arrival, another was crashed by a Hudson pilot and a further three were destroyed by enemy bombing. Thus the greatest number ever available for operations was ten.

The sea party left Heliopolis at 2100 on 16 January under the command of Flt Lt Bongard, the Equipment Officer. Reaching Port Tewfik at 0400 the next day, they embarked on the *Yoma* and sailed at 1400. Little is known about the voyage except that No.84 Squadron occupied the forward hold and No.211 Squadron the aft. A comment made by 17- year-old AC2 Hugh McKinley was that his sole memory is the amount of time he spent in the crow's nest keeping a bleary eye open for enemy aircraft and submarines. They were to arrive at Oosthaven, a port in southern Sumatra, the day Japanese troops parachuted into Palembang.

The first five aircraft of the Squadron (Wg Cdr J R Jeudwine, Flt Lts J Wyllie, A M Gill and G W Milson and Plt Off B Fihelly, arrived at Palembang on the afternoon of 23 January, only to find

that the aerodrome had been bombed and strafed at 0900 that morning. The most noticeable thing was the general nervousness, approaching panic. Steel helmets were worn continuously and the arrival of aircraft was viewed with apprehension in case an air raid should follow. When the second formation landed at Medan, the refuelling party could not work fast enough to get the aircraft ready for departure. The officer in charge was beside himself with anxiety when, later, Passmore's aircraft was stuck in the middle of the airfield.

The first Squadron casualty occurred when AC2 Partington, the Intelligence clerk, was hit by bomb splinters during a Japanese raid. Partington was part of a small advance party which had been flown out by a Liberator of No.108 Squadron, arriving on 22 January. He died later in hospital and was buried at Palembang. Wg Cdr J R Jeudwine and Flt Lt G W Milson attended his funeral.

The news that Plt Off M Macdonald and his crew had been picked up by natives and were being returned to civilisation was greeted with relief. Owing to the build of the members of the party and to the fact that they had some Indian two-anna pieces with them, the first report was that some 'tall men with big feet and square money' had been picked up.

The reorganisation of the RAF in Sumatra was in its infancy. Gp Capt A G Bishop was in command, later superseded by Air Commodore H J Hunter. Except for one squadron leader in the operations room, the rest of the staff were officers who had lived in Malaya for some considerable time and who had little or no experience of the RAF. This lack of trained officers and the inability of the various heads of departments to make decisions were largely responsible for the muddles and delays which occurred. There were no aircraft or engine spares, insufficient refuelling facilities, shortage of bombs and fuses and an almost complete lack of transport. During the whole of the Squadron's stay in Sumatra the only transport which could be obtained was one decrepit 16-seater bus on loan from the Dutch, which was not obtained till early February.

The plan was that No.84 Squadron should be based at Palembang P.1, with a small maintenance party. The aircrews and the remainder of the maintenance personnel were to be quartered in the town some eight miles away. Accommodation was to be in the Maria Girls School which had been evacuated. In this were crammed the aircrews of three squadrons and the ground staff of one squadron. Conditions were appalling. Cooking arrangements were inadequate and the only means of obtaining a meal was to go to hotels where the prices were exorbitant. Crews slept on mattresses on the floor and it was not always possible to rig mosquito nets. The area was malarial and often the mosquitoes were very troublesome. If anyone was away for the night on operations, he would find on his return that his mattress had been taken by someone else and quarrels over sleeping space were frequent. The sanitary arrangements, which were also inadequate, soon broke down and it was only by good fortune that there was no epidemic. There was, however, considerable sickness from gastric complaints.

The small maintenance party was to be stationed at P.2, a satellite and secret airfield some 42 miles by road from the town and across a river where there was a ferry but no bridge. P.2 had only become serviceable during January and at the time its position was unknown to the Japanese. In making the airfield, nothing was done to interfere with the natural configuration. It was only drained and some essential clearing was done to the landing areas. Dispersal bays were cut into the timber on the perimeter with as little damage to the timber as possible. Laterite strips were run into the bays to eliminate the chance of bogging. During the three weeks of its use, eight bomber squadrons were based there. Conditions here were extremely bad, there being very little in the way of accommodation and at times no food. The airmens' billets were two miles away from the dispersal area and, as no transport was available until early February, much time was wasted walking between the billets and the aircraft.

The maintenance party's duties were to service the aircraft as necessary. All unserviceable aircraft were to be kept at P.2. In addition, the men were to handle the serviceable aircraft which were to be flown from P.1 to P.2 at dawn each day for dispersal, and back to P.1 at dusk. This left very little work for the ground party at P.1. But when this was pointed out to the authorities, it was stated that, owing to limited accommodation at P.2, the arrangements would have to stand.

As the only ground personnel available during the Squadron's stay in Sumatra were the passengers in the aircraft, there was none to spare for P.1, and only on two occasions were aircraft sent there for the night. On the second occasion, the Japanese made a dawn

The "secret" airfield at P.II, now known as Karangendah (Royal Netherlands Air Force)

raid on P.1 and three of the aircraft were destroyed, after which the arrangement was not observed. In spite of all the drawbacks, the ground personnel under Flt Sgts Slee and Barker did an excellent job of work and no praise can be high enough for them.

On the afternoon of the 25th, five crews were sent in reputedly serviceable Blenheim Is from No.27 Squadron to attack ships which were reported to be landing troops at Endau, 80 miles north of Singapore. Owing to delays in bombing-up, the aircraft could only get as far as Singapore when darkness fell and all landed safely at Sembawang. This turned out to be very fortunate as the oil consumption on two of the aircraft was so heavy that they would have force-landed on the way back from the target. The three others carried out a night raid on Kuantan, a further 80 miles north of Endau. The weather conditions were such that thick cloud stretched from ground level to 7,000 ft, making the target difficult to locate. Diving through cloud, they bombed from low level. The Blenheims returned to find that Sembawang had been attacked, causing multiple craters. The flare-path had been laid out downwind and Flt Lt A M Gill, with unserviceable brakes, overshot on landing, missed two craters but succeeded in straddling a ditch. Both props were bent and the starboard undercarriage collapsed. He later commented that this was his first crash.

It was found on arrival that the Blenheim Is of No.34 Squadron had also been fitted with long-range tanks and detailed for Operation 'Crusader'. Their state of serviceability, however, was such that two of No.84 Squadron's aircraft were flown to Batavia by Flt Lts Wyllie and Holland on 27 January. Although each aircraft urgently needed 40-hour inspections after their flight from Egypt, No.84's aircraft were the first to locate HMS *Indomitable*, the preceding pairs having failed to find the carrier in spite of perfect weather. Flt Lt John Wyllie in recent correspondence writes: "The other pilots had all tried to fly directly to a moving spot in the Indian Ocean. There was one obvious feature they had all overlooked. Christmas Island was no more than 50 or 60 miles from the point where we were expected to make our rendezvous. I decided, after discussing the point with Doug Argent, my navigator, to fly direct to the island to get a good fix and proceed from there. We found the carrier right on station and 16 Hurricanes were flown off and escorted to Batavia's Kemajoram airfield. A further two flights of 16 aircraft followed the next day.

The crews that had made the attack on Kuantan returned to P.2 on the 28th, Gill and his crew flying in on Wg Cdr J R

Jeudwine's aircraft. On arrival, they found that two of No.84's aircraft had been loaned to two Hudson pilots from 62 Squadron to carry out a reconnaissance and Gill's aircraft, the one he had flown from the Middle East, had crash-landed at Tengah (Singapore) and been written off.

While at Sembawang, some very illuminating glimpses were obtained of the conditions on Singapore Island. The aerodrome had been attacked but no very serious damage appeared to have been done. There were a number of craters, but one runway had not been damaged. There had been little attempt to fill in the craters or to clear away any of the debris. In fact the most remarkable thing about the station was the absence of personnel during the daylight hours. At this time, the Japanese were making three raids a day on the island, the first about 1000. At about 0930, the yellow warning would be broadcast, whereupon the great majority of the personnel, including officers, left the camp and hid in the rubber plantations, most of them remaining there all day. There was no system of spotters and there was insufficient slit trenches around the camp. Native labour was unobtainable, but no efforts were made to use the airmen to repair damage or to dig trenches.

On 30 January, six aircraft left P.2 for Medan and, after refuelling, bombed shipping and the submarine base at Penang.

All operational records were lost in the series of evacuations which took place from Sumatra and Java but operations were carried out against targets at Ipoh, Songkhla, Penang, the Anamba Islands and against Japanese troop transports off Sumatra. On the 31st and 1st February, aircraft stood by to continue raids but on both occasions were stood down. Five aircraft led by Wg Cdr Jeudwine took off on the 2nd to fly to Medan to refuel and to rest. At 2200 they took off and flew to Songkhla in Siam, where they bombed buildings and stores on a spit of land north of the airfield. Slight opposition from warships was encountered. Arriving back at Medan after a flight of four-and-a-half hours, the aircraft refuelled, returning to P.2 on 3 February, having flown 1,800 miles in 13 hours to drop four 250-lb bombs each.

The raids against land targets were all carried out at night and all except those against the Anambas were made via Medan. Medan had three airstrips, the longest being 1,100 yards. It also had considerable dispersal areas, being used by the Dutch who were equipped with Curtiss Hawk 75As. The raids from Medan proved to be very tiring; aircrews had to travel the 42 miles to P.2, where they were usually unable to get any lunch, and then be off the ground by 1300 so as to arrive at Medan before dusk. After a few hours on the ground, the aircraft would take off on a raid which could be from two to four hours, returning to Medan for a scratch meal and to be off the ground at first light to arrive at P.2 where once again there would be no meal and little chance of getting one in town. The day after their return from Medan the operation would be repeated. So every other day, crews would fly ten to twelve hours to drop four 250-lb bombs on targets of which they had little or no information. One good meal every 48 hours (for which they had to pay) and very little sleep. Yet very few complained.

The authorities were asked to allow one flight to be detached to Medan, where there were excellent dispersal facilities and concealment available. It was not approved because there were no bombs at Medan and no transport available to send any there and neither the RAF or the Dutch wanted aircraft based there in case it should encourage air raids.

February 4th brought a signal from Group HQ indicating that Japanese parachutists were likely to attempt a landing at Palembang. Accordingly, pickets were posted, machine-gun posts manned and all available officers and airmen issued with rifles or Sten guns. No crews were allowed to return to Palembang. In the early hours of the morning on the 5th, sirens were sounded and an attack appeared imminent. Action stations were taken and several Blenheims had their port engines started in order that their turrets could be used, but nothing further happened. A false alarm!

Later that day, eight aircraft took off at 1300 to fly to Medan in order to make a night attack on Songkhla. Very bad weather set in at 2200 as the aircraft were leaving, with the result that the raid was cancelled. At daylight on the 6th, they left for P.2. Nearing the airfield, they were attacked by 'Zeros', Sgt Gardner, turret gunner on Sgt 'Scotty' Thomson's Blenheim, mistook them for Hurricanes and was hit in the thigh during the attack. Thomson made a good landing with damaged elevators. On the 7th, Flt Lt Ken Linton of No.211 Squadron was shot down and killed as he was returning from a reconnaissance. His crew of Sgt Roy Crowe, who baled out at 300 feet, luckily survived with severe bruising, whilst Sgt Harry Offord was found badly injured and released from the crashed aircraft before being sent aboard a hospital ship. All three crew members had seen service in the Greek campaign with No.84 Squadron.

This heralded the start of daily Japanese fighter sweeps over Sumatra and Java to establish complete air superiority. Palembang was an important target for the Japanese, being the third largest oil producing centre in the Netherlands East Indies. Having found only the charred remains of the two based in Borneo, they decided to use paratroops in a surprise attack on Palembang to prevent the destruction of the refineries at Pladjoe. The attack was anticipated and constant patrols were flown by Blenheims from squadrons based at P.2. However, poor communications and co-ordination often hindered accurate reporting.

On the 10th, six crews stood by to make a night raid on targets in Malaya but it was cancelled two hours later. There were rumours on the base that a move to Lahat was planned. Lahat was about 120 miles to the south-east where there was supposedly more and better accommodation and where the Squadron could be all together. On 11 February, the Air Officer Commanding, AVM Maltby, visited P.2 and later P.1 where he told the assembled crews that "they were there to fight and that there was no intention of evacuating Sumatra". Members of No.84 Squadron Association 50 years later say that the visit was particularly ill-timed. "Where there were so few facilities available, there was little need to remind them that they were a scruffy bunch or that well-polished shoes were essential to maintain morale". As Wg Cdr Ken Lister comments in letters: "The AOC's knife-edge trousers and spotless uniform would have looked a sorry mess if he had to go through what the aircrews and the ground staff of the squadrons had had to do. He certainly did nothing to raise the morale of what was a gathering of very experienced aircrews with operational experience in Greece, Iraq and North Africa".

The second raid on the Anambas took place on 11 February. Led by Flt Lts John Wyllie and George Milson, the raid was to involve six hours flying and was timed so that the aircraft returned at first light. It also brought the first Squadron aircrew casualties. The Station Commander, Gp Capt McCauley RAAF, insisted on the flare-path being controlled from the watch office, which had the only telephone on the airfield, so that any notification of an impending air raid could be sent by runner to the officer in charge of the flare-path. In addition, his scheme was for each aircraft to taxi to the take-off point and then switch off. The officer in charge would then listen for any Jap recce aircraft and, if none was heard,

give the green light. The pilot would then start his engines, which was a sign for the flare-path (hurricane lamps) to be lit and the aircraft would then take off.

Apart from the impracticability of stopping and restarting engines, pilots were ordered to take-off at two-minute intervals. With the flare-path starting from the watch office, the last two flares were hidden by a hump in the airfield and the airmen in charge could not see when to light them. Consequently, the aircraft were liable to come over the brow of the hill and have no guidance for the rest of their run. Any slight deviation would point the aircraft at a belt of trees. On the night in question, one aircraft from 211 Squadron ran into the trees before becoming airborne. The aircraft exploded, killing Flt Lt Clutterbuck and his crew. A second aircraft of 211 Squadron also crashed, fortunately not bursting into flames, its crew managing to escape from the wreckage before its bombs exploded. The third flown by Sgt Hyatt of No.84 Squadron is thought to have hit a tree with his wing tip just after take-off and, in trying to regain the airfield, stalled and crashed. Sgt Joe Hyatt and Sgt George Mutton his observer were killed in the crash. The air gunner, Sgt Irvine was found the following morning nearly half a mile away where the fuselage had broken in half. He was found to be still alive, but badly injured. Sgt Allan Ross, turret gunner with Sgt George Sayer's crew remembers that he was told to move forward in the aircraft on take-off, even when the crew heard the brush of boughs against the aircraft.

Correspondence from Flt Lt John Wyllie mentions the fact that the mission to the Anambas was mentioned by Mr Winston Churchill in his biography, *The Hinge Of Fate*. He writes:" The fact that the Anambas lie 450 miles north-east of Palembang meant a round trip of nearly 1,000 miles. Instead of despatching a flight the previous night when a convoy had been spotted anchored, a 24-hour delay meant that it had up-anchored and disappeared. With no second pilot, well over six hours flying, of which at least five were flown on instruments, was a testing flight, especially when it was to no purpose".

Meanwhile, on the 12th, Flt Lt Gill led five Blenheims to Medan for the night. They took off at dusk but had to cancel the raid due to extreme weather conditions. In a brief history of the period compiled by Flt Lt Bernard Ashmole, the Adjutant, Flt Lt A M Gill and others on the return voyage to Colombo aboard the *Yoma*, it is stated that after Flt Lt G W Milson had taken off at night on this operation, he discovered his blind flying instruments were unserviceable, probably due to heavy rain or humidity. Letters from Milson state the problem was condensation in the pitot head and this would have affected both the airspeed indicator and the altimeter. He goes on to say: "The circuit around the sky, lit only by flashes of lightning, was not so shaky as it sounded, but it was good to get down in one piece. When I reported back to the ops room, the Station Commander, Gp Capt McCauley, thought that I should have carried on with the operation. I immediately suggested to him that it would have been rather difficult to do so and that if the Gp Capt had allowed air tests to be flown in daylight before night operations, perhaps my problems might never have happened. The Gp Capt went off the deep end and finished up by telling me to report to him in the morning". Later Milson reported the matter to his CO when he returned and was told to forget the order.

Flt Lt Milson also comments about the loss of the aircraft the previous night. "It has been suggested that the flare-path had been laid out badly. As we were on ops that night, I went out to look at it being laid and found that the flares were in exactly the same position as the previous night. One could see where the paraffin had marked the grass and, to me, it looked OK. I think that the aircraft met exactly the same problems as we had with unserviceable instruments and that they had tried to return but finished up in the trees".

On Friday the 13th, the Squadron was scheduled to move to Lahat. There was little advantage operationally in the move as there was no fuel or bomb stocks and the aircraft would have to fly to P.2 daily for orders. The move never took place, as it was rumoured that Japanese transports were approaching Sumatra and orders were received to prepare for immediate evacuation. Later the authorities decided to send a small strike force and the proposed evacuation was cancelled.

A little after 0900 on the morning of the 14th, the Japanese made their surprise attack on the oil installations at Pladjoe, Sungei Gerong and P.1 airfield. The paratroops were carried in Kawasaki Ki-56 transport aircraft, Lockheed 14s built under licence. These were actually seen by patrolling Hurricanes and taken for friendly Hudsons.

Sgt A Wakefield, Flt Lt J Wyllie's air gunner, recalls vividly the scene. "The one date I do remember is 14 February. Six aircraft, led by Sqn Ldr Passmore, left P.2 and flew to P.1 where a fighter escort was to be waiting. The target for the raid was a Jap carrier reported as being just off the coast. P.1 looked deserted and a red Very light was fired from the ground. The flight therefore set course for the coast. Soon after leaving P.1, a large number of aircraft were seen flying in the opposite direction and I looked back to see paratroops falling on P.1. The Japs must have taken us for some of their own aircraft returning from the dropping zone. We proceeded out to sea and eventually located ships of the Jap fleet headed by a cruiser. There was no sign of a carrier so we dropped the bombs from about 6,000 feet but unfortunately with no hits. On leaving the area, we came across the carrier on its own".

Flt Lt Wyllie backs up this account, adding that he thought as many as 150 - 200 troops were dropped. The actual figures were 330 in the morning with a further 96 later in the day.

Sgt Ken Lister, on a later mission, writes: "The Jap invasion fleet was reported to have been approaching the mouth of the River Moesi leading to Palembang. A sortie of six aircraft was detailed to attack the fleet, dropping instantaneous-fused bombs from 11,000 feet. The method of attack was pattern bombing in which the leading bomb-aimer takes aim, with all of the other aircraft releasing their bombs as they see the leader's bombs leaving the bomb-bay. I was flying as leader of the second vic with my nose tucked under the leader's tail. We made one bombing run across the target without releasing our bombs. So we turned and came back over the fleet at a lower altitude, once again without releasing. We were then led away from the fleet. As the leading aircraft turned we went into a shallow dive and over the target the leader dropped his bombs. I checked my height and noticed that the release height was just on 700 feet. We were still diving at the fleet with the three leading aircraft firing their single front guns. I was in a position from which there was no escape. The twenty-four 250-lb bombs released simultaneously had instantaneous fuses in both nose and tail pistols and could cause severe damage to any aircraft above them at heights up to 1,000 feet. We were about to pass over this pattern of bombs at between 100 to 200 feet! I can only remember being hit by a huge wall of spray and the aircraft being thrown about. When we emerged from the water splash and regained control, the first thing I heard was the broad Devon accent of Ron Pile from the turret asking "What the bloody hell is going on? I'm soaked through back here".

Returning to base individually, the aircraft flew at low level up the river with the gunners shooting up landing craft which were moving towards Palembang. As they passed over the town on the way back to P.2, they could see a huge pall of smoke rising from the burning oil installations which had been set alight by the Dutch.

Sgt Dave Russell also comments about the bombing on the 14th. Being turret gunner in Wg Cdr Jeudwine's aircraft he recalls: "As the Jap transports got nearer, I began to wonder if there were some form of professional rivalry between the CO and Wg Cdr Bateson of 211 Squadron. Had they mutually decided to hit the transports from as low as possible in order to inflict the most damage. It seemed an age before I heard "Bombs away". There was a pause, then the blast of the explosions caused the aircraft to buck and I rose from my saddle, hitting my head on the roof of the turret. I caught a brief glimpse of crowded decks at close range and weapons spitting upwards. Before I could depress the twin Brownings to fire, Jeudwine had pulled the aircraft back in a steep climbing turn towards P.2, probably as troubled as I was in case we ran into a crowd of Jap paratroops on their way to capture the airfield. Skirting P.1, we could see the smoke rising from the burning buildings and the collapsed parachutes on the jungle ceiling.

They returned to find that Flt Lts John Wyllie and Fg Off Dutchy Holland had grabbed their gunners and commandeered a couple of Blenheim I fighters and had set off to find targets to attack. After searching the river for Japs, they reached the coast to find the invasion fleet anchored. Sgt Archie Wakefield recalls how the conversation went: 'Slug' Wyllie's voice came over the intercom "Let's have a go", I replied, "Don't be a bloody fool". "What did you say?". "I said don't be a bloody fool". "Can't hear you" - and with that he immediately attacked troops who could be seen climbing down netting into invasion barges. Damage was caused to the aircraft by small arms fire, two bullets passing through where Doug Argent would have been sitting. Later, flying at zero feet above the river, they sighted a boatload of troops which Wyllie wiped out with a prolonged burst.

While this was happening in the air, the remainder of the aircrew were on standby at P.2. Sqn Ldr Taylor, Flt Lts Ashmole and Gill and Plt Off Macdonald were at the Maria school in Palembang. Plt Off G Maurice had gone to Group HQ to finalise the move to Lahat. Maurice later collected a lorry load of armed airmen and set off towards P.1, but was turned back by the Dutch Army. At the same time, Taylor, Gill and Macdonald, together with four officers and eighty airmen from other units, were sent to form a bridgehead at the ferry. On arrival they were informed by Air Commodore Hunter that Palembang was to be evacuated. Unarmed personnel were to move to P.2 and Lahat. Those with arms were to remain and guard the ferry. Only one ferry boat was operating. This could only take five vehicles at a time across the fast-flowing river. Owing to the number of private vehicles and people trying to cross the river, there was much confusion. Gill stayed at the ferry for the next two hours, organising the flow of traffic. He later commandeered a three-ton truck and drove back to Maria School, where he found Flt Lt B Ashmole, the adjutant, on his own.

After discussing the situation, they decided to drive to P.1 airfield to try to find any of the Squadron ground crew who might still be there. With nine airmen, they loaded the truck with food and water and drove eight kilometres to the last Dutch picket on the Palembang - P.1 road, which consisted of two Vickers machine-guns mounted on an open truck and manned by Dutch soldiers. As they were not allowed to drive any farther, they left the lorry and advanced in single file alongside the ditch for half-a-mile, armed with one Thompson sub-machine gun and the remainder with rifles. Suddenly machine gun fire opened up from about fifty yards and bombs landed from a trench mortar located in a nearby native hut. When the firing subsided, they were able to advance another 200 yards to an overturned petrol bowser, which had been trying to rush through to Palembang from the airfield with other vehicles loaded with No.232 (Hurricane) Squadron personnel. There they found several dead Japanese parachutists (including one hanging from a tree with his rigging lines wrapped around his neck) and dead and wounded RAF men, including Fg Off Wright, the Squadron engineer officer, and a dying airmen pinned under the back wheel of the bowser. Eventually the road block was cleared by Dutch native troops and three or four lorries loaded with wounded were driven to Palembang.

Whilst this was going on, two Royal Navy officers arrived in Palembang with instructions to the Group HQ. On arrival, they found it deserted. One of them had arrived from Singapore in a small ship towing five RAF launches. The ship had broken down, so they had come up the river in one of the launches, rescuing on the way the pilot and navigator of a Blenheim which had force-landed in the river, the gunner having being killed.

It was generally agreed that if a strong lead had been given by Group Headquarters staff, the road to P.1 could have been kept open another twelve hours, enabling armourers to have exploded the nineteen tons of explosives buried under the runway and designed to cause craters thirty feet wide and nine feet deep. The plans for these demolitions were not passed to the RAF by the Dutch authorities until the 16th, when it was too late for any action to be taken. The value of this cannot be overestimated because the bombing of shipping which was later sunk in Batavia harbour was by Japanese aircraft operating from P.1.

Early next morning, 15 February, the airfield was taken. The few remaining officers and men in Palembang loaded their kit, arms and ammunition into the Ford truck and a small van that Macdonald had scrounged and left for Lahat, in accordance with the last orders given by Group Headquarters on the 11th, but they decided to go via P.2 in case the orders had been changed. On reaching the ferry, they found considerable congestion. The Dutch were rightly claiming priority for a number of vehicles loaded with troops destined to deal with the Japanese, who were then known to be coming up the river in boats. The journey across the river and back took fifteen minutes and the Squadron's two vehicles were between 30th and 40th in the queue. With one Dutch officer, Gill took charge of regulating the flow of traffic and there was no panic. When it seemed possible that our vehicles might not be able to cross the river before the Japanese started bombing the ferry or arriving in force by river or road, it was decided to send all of the Squadron personnel with their small kit and arms across by foot. All of our men helped with the loading and unloading of wounded on both sides of the river.

During this period, large explosions could be heard as wharves, etc were demolished. Black smoke drifted across the sky from fires and the oil storage tanks, which had blazed all night.

Meanwhile, Japanese aircraft flew overhead in large numbers. It also appeared that Japanese aircraft were landing at P.1 but fortunately the ferry was not bombed. The Dutch native crew

The Pladjoe oil refinery on the Moesi River at Pelambang (T Kelly)

worked the ferry nobly and without panic until, just before mid-day, the captain announced the last trip. By this time, Jap fighters were flying low over the river but, surprisingly, did not open fire, maybe thinking that by then their own troops had reached the ferry. On the last but one ferry crossing came Plt Off Macdonald driving the Ford truck and, on the last ferry, Flt Lt Gill and Flt Lt Jackson of 34 Squadron who was driving the civilian van. On reaching the other side, a third vehicle was commandeered, which was used for the wounded and was driven by Sgt Hough. The party reloaded the vehicles and proceeded to P.2, arriving about 1500 hours.

Flt Lt Gill immediately reported to the CO, Wg Cdr J R Jeudwine, who telephoned Group HQ, being instructed that the party should proceed to the transit camp at Oosthaven and not to Lahat, as previously ordered. This was the first intimation that the complete evacuation of Sumatra was intended. Wg Cdr Jeudwine told Gill that he was taking the last eight serviceable Blenheims and the ground crew to Java. As Gill had no aircraft, he was instructed to destroy all bombs and ammunition and burn any secret documents before proceeding to Oosthaven. This he did and, at dusk, he and the RAF driver left P.2 in the Ford 3-tonner, overloaded with surplus aircrew and ground crew, including Flt Lt Ashmole, Plt Off Maurice, Sgts Lister, Craddock, Ellis, Pile, Longmore, Nourse, Thomson, Thomas, Sharrott, Duignam, Morris and Gardner. They drove the open truck for 300 miles throughout the night, in pouring rain, over the mountains and along precipitous roads to Oosthaven on the southern tip of Sumatra. There, about to cast off from the wharf, was the *Yoma* with the ground crew who had left Egypt on 17 January.

The aircrews who still had their aircraft were flying round-the-clock missions on the 15th. Sgt Dave Russell recalls: "With the dawn, the CO ordered every available aircraft to take off from P.2 on strafing operations. The airfield was in chaos and communications had broken down. We had no difficulty in finding the enemy, for up the river chugged a continuous flow of barges. Frank Cameron was on his belly in the front using the blister gun while I stood up in my turret directing my fire into an indistinguishable mass of khaki that flashed by. I knew that the aircraft had been hit several times, but comforted myself with the thought that the enemy were in a worse state than I was. Japanese sources state that the number of troops in the Tanaka force which were off-loaded into barges and entered Palembang via the Moesi and other rivers was 1,500. Returning to P.2, we found the place deserted except for a few from the Squadron. Wg Cdr Jeudwine was both touched and delighted that his few ground staff had not joined the general exodus and that his flying personnel had no intention of relieving him of their company".

He went on to comment that as both Nos.84 and 211 Squadrons had aircraft out on raids, it was impossible to reach Java before dark and so that night they bedded down beneath the wings of their aircraft.

Flt Lt John Wyllie continues the story: "We flew out at break of day, each aircraft being loaded with ground crews. Unfortunately, Sgt Geappen crashed just after take-off with only one survivor, Cpl Shaw. Ron Shaw was later taken prisoner when Java fell and became the only British airman to lose his life when the atomic bomb was dropped on Nagasaki on 9 August 1945. We flew straight to Kalidjati and to the billet of a hospitable manager of a tea plantation". Wyllie was extremely critical, commenting on the abject loss of morale which affected the military in the area.

"Whether the war fought by the British out there played a worthwhile part in delaying things long enough to build up their strength is a question for historians to answer. It certainly gave the natives throughout the area a different view of the white man who had played Lord and Master in the region for so long".

The *Yoma*, which had arrived in Oosthaven on the evening of the 13th, had brought all the Squadron's equipment and the air parties' kit. The three month's pack-up of Blenheim spares, which AHQ Iraq had sent for the Squadron, never arrived in Sumatra. In the sea party were Flt Lt Bongard, Equipment, Fg Off Jebb, Intelligence, Flt Lt Tierney, Medical, and Plt Offs McNally and Bishop, Cypher Officers. The following morning, only armed men were allowed ashore and some 250 men, mostly tradesmen, and all the above officers were sent about 30 miles north to act as a rearguard. LAC Tony Record writes: "After landing at Oosthaven, a group of us were ordered to make our way 60 miles up-country towards Palembang where our aircraft were supposed to be based. On the way we stopped at a rope factory near an important bridge. Those who were injured or were of poor sight were ordered to fall out and make their way back to the *Yoma*. The rest of us were given a pep talk by a senior RAF officer. From my memory, he told us that "today, 84 Squadron would go down in the annals of history, as the Squadron had been chosen to cover the withdrawal of Allied forces on their retreat from the island". You can imagine how I felt, I was just 21! We were told to sharpen our bayonets on one of the many grindstones dotted around the factory. Our job was to blow up the bridge when the last of the Allied forces had passed. Over the next few hours, several trains passed loaded with troops. What we could not understand was why we, who had little knowledge of explosives or demolition, were staying there when troops were making their way to Oosthaven. After nearly three days with no kit, no rations and no transport we were told to return to Oosthaven. We commandeered every vehicle we could find and eventually reached the port at 04.00 on the 17th".

On arrival at the docks they found that the *Yoma* had sailed. They were therefore embarked on the SS *Silver Larch*, which reached Batavia before the slow old *Yoma*. Due to the number of ships tied up at Batavia, the *Yoma* had to lay off from 1030 on the 17th until 1400 on the 18th. When the ship finally docked, the remainder of the ground crew and the surplus aircrew who had travelled from Palembang by road expected to disembark and that the Squadron would be reformed and re-equipped in Java. But no one was allowed off the ship as orders had been issued that all surplus personnel were to be evacuated. Preparations had been made for another 700 RAF to embark and these were expected to be the remainder of the Squadron. Instead, 170 civilians, mostly wives and children from Singapore, came aboard. The ship eventually sailed at mid-day on the 20th and joined a convoy during the afternoon, which finally left Java at dusk for Ceylon and India. The small convoy was escorted by the cruiser HMS *Exeter* and two destroyers through the Sunda Straits for a day and a half. They later returned and were sunk. Of the 605 Officers and airmen of No.84 Squadron who had left Egypt, only 132 returned to India.

From the many conflicting reports, the reader will appreciate how difficult it was to fight a war during those brief few weeks amidst the utter confusion and lack of leadership from above. To throw away crack squadrons in their prime, with the awful loss of life, when the war in the Far East had already been lost, was, in retrospect, an act of lunacy or worse.

A surviving Blenheim IV, probably at Kalidjati, repaired by the Japanese with Nakajima Sakai engines

CHAPTER 11 - JAVA AND CAPTIVITY

The evacuation of Oosthaven, the harbour of Teloekbetoeng at the southern tip of Sumatra, highlighted the panic which prevailed in some of the higher echelons of the forces in the Netherlands East Indies. Further administrative blunders added to the difficulties of an already disjointed Air Force and considerably reduced its capacity for fighting. The Dutch authorities at the port had already set fire to the bazaar and its adjacent wharves and destroyed much of the military equipment which had been gathered there. A black pall of smoke lay over the town and beneath it the airmen and troops strived to carry out their orders. They found themselves facing not only a situation created by the enemy, but by military embarkation officers who had been issued with orders which were treated as sacrosanct. Orders came that the evacuation should be completed by the 16th, with the result that they were to leave, as laid down by orders, without their motor transport or their equipment. In other words, they were to reach Java in a condition in which they would be quite unable to take any further part in operations. Left behind were the stores of No.41 Air Stores Park of 266 Fighter Wing and a complete Repair and Salvage Unit which had only just been unloaded. Anti-aircraft guns, together with ammunition, which had been brought from the airfields were all abandoned.

This departure, remembering that the Japs were still 250 miles away, can only be considered as panic. It was also quite unnecessary for, two days later on the 17th, Gp Capt G E Nicholetts at the head of 50 volunteers returned to Oosthaven by sea from Batavia in HMAS *Ballarat* of the Royal Australian Navy and spent twelve hours loading the ship to its gunwales with such air force equipment as could by then still be salvaged.

By 18 February, the evacuation from Sumatra had been completed and more than 10,000 men, belonging to a variety of units, had arrived on the island of Java. Reports vary considerably but recent researches indicate that the true numbers were as follows: 2,500 RAF personnel, 1,090 British and Australian troops, 700 KNIL troops and about 1,000 civilians left by ship for Java. In a narrative written by Sqn Ldr J E B Tayler, he states: "Arriving in Merak in Java, they entrained for Batavia and, shortly after dusk on the 18th, the men were billeted in Meester Cornelis barracks on the outskirts of the city". Batavia also became the RAF Far East Pool, where all unattached personnel were sent until they could rejoin their units. There followed a period of impatience, disillusionment and finally disgust.

Meanwhile at Kalidjati, an airfield about 100 miles southeast of Batavia and the main base of the NEI Flying Training School, 29 Blenheims had arrived, all that were left from Nos.84, 211 and 34 Squadrons, having flown in from P.2. There were 22 Blenheim IVs; the remainder were Mk Is, including two Mk Ifs from 27 Squadron. Nos. 27 and 34 Squadrons had effectively ceased to exist and a number of their crews were ordered to evacuate. On the 18th, RAF Headquarters at Bandoeng decided that all Blenheim squadrons in Java should be consolidated under the mantle of No.84 Squadron, commanded by Wg Cdr J R Jeudwine.

It was also decided that a total of 200 ground personnel,

including cooks and butchers and a few aircraftmen (GD), would be sufficient to maintain the aircraft and the running of the station, with 20 complete crews to operate them. It was rumoured that No.84's sea party had arrived in Batavia, so demands were made on WesGroup for the necessary number of tradesmen to be sent to Kalidjati. These demands were made daily without result until the 24th, when Wg Cdr Jeudwine travelled to Batavia to try to obtain the men. WesGroup denied all knowledge of the demands or the whereabouts of the men, but a search of the town resulted in finding the majority of the officers. They reported that they had been reporting to WesGroup daily asking for instructions, but they had been told that the whereabouts of the Squadron was unknown and they were not to come and worry people. WesGroup had left Singapore for southern Sumatra on 7 February; from there they moved to Soekaboemi on the 16th and to Bandoeng on the 23rd.

By the 26th, a selection had been made from the personnel to fill the revised establishment and they proceeded to Kalidjati. Accommodation for the ground staff had been arranged in houses made from the local material, atap and bamboo, on the edge of the airfield. Squadron and flight offices were also situated there. As there were no telephone facilities, a despatch rider service was maintained with Group HQ. Fg Off R Jebb was appointed adjutant, replacing Flt Lt B Ashmole, who had been forcibly evacuated with others by sea.

From 19 February, operations from Kalidjati were mainly cloud cover raids on shipping in the Banka Straits and attacks on the airfield at P.1. Four Blenheims led by Flt Lt M K Holland, three crewed by No.84 and a fourth by a crew from 34 Squadron, left to attack the airfield and fuel dumps at Palembang. The latter was compelled to abort with engine problems but the other three continued and, although P.1 was covered in cloud, two released their bombs over the airfield. Several aircraft were seen to be destroyed whilst others were severely damaged. Fuel installations were hit and set ablaze. Sgt Bob Bennett, turret gunner on Holland's Blenheim, writes vividly of the attack: "Broken white cloud increased as we neared the target. Formation flying was abandoned so we split up to make individual attacks. Eventually Doug Argent, our navigator, announced that we were approaching P.1 and 'Dutchy' Holland started to look for a hole in the clouds. Doug was spot on course and the airfield appeared ahead, rows of aircraft lined up on each side of the runway, wing-tip to wing-tip. We levelled out and dropped a stick of bombs amongst them. The lack of flak meant only one thing; there were fighters about. We turned on a course for home, hoping that cloud cover would hold for a while longer. At that moment there was a sound like a sharp fall of hailstones and the aircraft shuddered. There it was, in the blind spot under the tail. 'Dutch' banked to port and there, perched on top of a cloud, was our attacker, about 200 yards astern. Quick, perfect target-aim and both Brownings chattered. I saw pieces fly off the fighter and he fell into the cloud and disappeared, leaving a trail of black smoke behind him".

"Luckily no one was hit, but oil was beginning to spread over the starboard wing and, although the engines sounded rough, they were still going. We still had about 45 minutes flying time to do and it was vital for us to get back to Java before the motors packed up. The idea of three men in an inflatable dinghy did not appeal to us. Fortunately our luck held and we made Kalidjati before our engines failed".

Sgt George Sayer, flying one of the other Blenheims, dropped his bombs on a ship tied up in the river. He was also attacked by fighters, Allan Ross, his turret gunner, claiming hits on the aircraft when it was seen to sheer off.

This attack was repeated on the 20th on shipping in the Banka Straits. Four direct hits on transports were claimed. They returned to find the airfield had suffered its first raid by Japanese aircraft. It was to be the first of many over the next few days. On the 21st, the most southern airfield in Sumatra fell into Japanese hands. The same day, six Blenheims led by Sqn Ldr Keith Passmore took off to attack shipping and oil tanks on the banks of the Moesi river. Flt Lt John Wyllie, commenting on this raid, writes: "This was a 'must get through job' to blow up some storage tanks which had been overlooked in efforts to evacuate. It was memorable for the fact that I took three aircraft into a line squall. These weather fronts could stretch for miles and there is no flying under then, around them or over them. Only two aircraft came out the other side. The one I lost was a very young Australian, too inexperienced to fly on instruments alone through the massive turbulence these storms have in their immense rumbling bellies. I was lucky when the other equally-inexperienced Australian joined me on the other side. We left great clouds of oily smoke over the tank farm on returning. All the aircraft were attacked by Army Type 97 fighters, but returned safely to find that Kalidjati had again been bombed". Sgt J A Burrage of No.211 Squadron was the pilot of the aircraft lost.

On the 23rd, three aircraft led by Wg Cdr Jeudwine were sent to attack the airfield at P.1 and several enemy aircraft were believed to have been destroyed. On the return flight, three Jap submarines were seen on the surface and attacked, Fg Off Brian Fiheely claiming hits on one of them, causing possible damage. Flt Lt John Wyllie, another member of the flight, writes: "The Japs had two fighters flying cover and we played a game of hide-and-seek amongst the clouds. After dropping a stick of bombs on the lined-up aircraft, we returned via P.2 to see if the enemy had taken it over; once again fighters were lined up wing-tip to wing-tip. Dropping to zero height, Argent with the front gun and Wakefield in the turret proceeded to create chaos amidst the lined-up fighters".

Although there were more bombs at Kalidjati than in the whole of Sumatra, the supply of fuses were very limited and shipping was attacked using 11-second delay fuses which were not very effective unless attacking from zero height.

The following day, three Blenheims took off for a raid on P.1. Whilst they were gone, 17 Jap bombers escorted by 13 fighters bombed and strafed the airfield.

On the 25th, six aircraft were being prepared for a raid when the Japanese struck the airfield at Kalidjati. Two of the Blenheims were destroyed, reducing the number serviceable still further. Sqn Ldr Keith Passmore led three of the remaining aircraft on an attack on P.1, Fiheely and Cosgrove making up the flight. Sgt Eric Oliver, the turret gunner on Fiheely's aircraft, takes up the story: "The plan was for an attack on Palembang P.1 in an effort to cause maximum disruption to the Japanese Air Force, who were using it as a main base for operations against the allied airfields in Western Java. Aircrews were detailed for a cloud cover raid to get under way immediately. As we climbed aboard the truck to reach the dispersal area, we heard the roar of aircraft engines and six Jap medium bombers came into view at tree-top height. Inevitable panic set in and conflicting advice was shouted at the driver. With a sudden slam on his brakes, he stopped and we leapt off the truck and hurled ourselves into the nearest bomb crater. In less than four minutes the attack was over. Finding the truck still in working order, we continued to the dispersal area, only to find that our aircraft had a row of bullets the entire length of the fuselage. Within two minutes we found that Plt Off Macdonald's navigator (Plt Off G Maurice) had been wounded in the arm and, as it was policy to keep aircrews together, we were allotted the aircraft. Finally, three aircraft took off, to be reduced still farther when Cosgrove was forced to return over the Sunda Straits. We droned over the thick jungle of southern Sumatra for nearly two hours. As we approached Palembang we could see smoke rising from the refineries which had been set ablaze ten days before. The crackle of machine-gun fire forced me to look at Passmore's aircraft which was about 400 yards away on our port side. Three Jap fighters were snapping at his tail like terriers. 'Fighters' I yelled into the

mike of the oxygen mask and as we swung away to starboard, three more came into view sniffing at our heels. Tommy Gomme, with his customary coolness, dropped his bombs on the refinery, adding more smoke and flames to the already badly damaged silos".

"Aided by the nine pounds boost that Brian Fiheely had thrown in for the engines' absolute maximum power, we ran for home desperately looking for cloud cover. Tommy had got down in the nose firing his backward-pointing gun, while I was trying to manoeuvre the arc of incendiaries from my twin Brownings into what I hoped was a vulnerable part of their aircraft. Realising one of my guns had jammed, I groped for the cocking handle to free the stoppage, nudging it out of its position on to the floor. While I was reaching on the floor for the handle, I was well below the level of the turret. Brian had at last found cloud cover on our starboard side and banked towards it. The change of direction gave our attacker far more of the aircraft to fire at and he closed for the kill. At that moment I re-emerged from the floor to find that he was less than 100 yards away. I fired a continuous burst of about ten seconds and, at the same time, yelling for Brian to turn to port. Suddenly the fighter sat up like a begging dog, seemed to hover for a moment then slid away out of sight. The next moment we were in cloud, fortunately sufficient for us to lose our attackers".

"There were numerous bullet holes in the tailplane but the ones that made me sweat were four through the perspex of the turret. I puzzled as to why they had not taken my head off, then realised it must have occurred when I was on the floor groping for the cocking handle".

"The starboard engine was now running very roughly and a stream of smoke suddenly billowed from it. The feeling of relief turned to dismay as I felt sure that the smoke would turn to fire. Then I noticed that the tailplane was shiny and realised that an oil pipe had been severed and we were losing oil. With a lurch of the aircraft and a sudden bang, the prop dropped off and fell to the jungle below. Bailing out was out of the question; we were far too low. Fortunately, at that moment, Tony said he could see the sea ahead and within seconds we had hit the water about 100 yards from the shoreline".

On the 26th, three Blenheims were detailed to bomb shipping off Muntok on the island of Banka. It is believed that Sgt Bill Cosgrove obtained a direct hit on one of the transports but no explosion was seen. On the return flight, units of the Japanese invasion fleet was seen heading for Java. The same day a convoy was discovered (numbering more than 50 transports with a strong naval escort) to be moving through the Macassar Straits southward towards the Java Sea. The same day, the majority of ABDA Command staff and WesGroup left Java by air and sea for Australia.

Next day, Admiral Doorman sailed to intercept the convoy. Hopelessly outgunned and outnumbered, he fought a most gallant action, losing his entire fleet in the battle, a sacrifice that secured a respite for 24 hours. Amongst the ships which were lost were the cruisers *De Ruyter*, his flagship, and *Java*. The remaining cruisers, HMS *Exeter*, HMAS *Perth* and the USS *Houston*, were later sunk attempting to pass through the straits to escape to the south of Java. The Battle of the Java Sea, fought on 28 February/1 March 1942, went down in the annals of Naval history.

Three aircraft took off to bomb and strafe 30 bombers seen on the ground at P.2. Whilst two aircraft attacked the airfield, the third attacked shipping in the Moesi river leading to Palembang. No results were seen.

The Japs were closing in. The USS *Langley*, a seaplane carrier carrying much-needed replacement P-40 fighters, was sunk on the 27th. The freighter *Seawitch* with 27 fighters just managed to reach Tjilatjap. These aircraft were still lying where they were unloaded on the 5 March. The *Abbekerk* sailed from Tjilatjap with flying school personnel and any surplus RAF; some members from Nos.34 and 62 Squadrons returned to Colombo aboard the *Abbekerk*. The following day she was bombed and strafed but was fortunate in being able to reach first Fremantle, then on to Colombo.

It was realised that two separate fleets were converging on Java. The original, sighted off the Sumatran coast on 13 February, part of which had landed troops at Palembang, was now sailing through the Banka Straits to converge on either side of Batavia. The second had left Jolo Island in the Philippines and rendezvoused with fleet units from Balikpapan, on the island of Borneo, and Macassar. It was now due north of Rembang, 300 miles east of Batavia.

On the evening of the 28th, instructions were received to attack a large Japanese convoy approaching the coast to the north-west of Kalidjati. The attack was to continue all night with all available aircraft, but the aircraft were to land at dawn. By this time only six Blenheims were serviceable, plus two Hudsons. During the night, 26 sorties were flown, many of the crews flying at least two operations if not three. When they returned, they were replaced by fresh crews.

Due to blood poisoning in his left arm, Flt Lt G W Milson had not flown since his arrival in Java. He and Plt Off Ron Millar RNZAF, his observer, were in charge of night operations. In correspondence he writes of his duties: "To start with, we were in charge of laying out the flare-path, followed by the briefing of the crews. We were also responsible for the taxying of aircraft, making sure that the flare-path was clear before allowing an aircraft to take off. We also had control over the aircraft joining the circuit on their return and ensuring that two aircraft did not try to land at the same time. Finally, when all the flying had finished, we had to pack up all of the kit. All communication with aircraft was done by Aldis lamp".

Flt Lt John Wyllie distinguished himself during these attacks, destroying one ship and damaging two others. He was subsequently recommended for the DFC, which was later awarded. In recent correspondence with Flt Lt Wyllie and his turret gunner, Sgt Archie Wakefield, they gave a vivid account of the action. "On the first sortie we found the fleet. The Japs in return found and held us in a multiple cone of searchlights, enabling other aircraft to find them. It was a perfect bomber's moon, full, enormous and making sharp black silhouettes of every ship against the brilliance of its reflection on the water. We were in a hurry to get rid of our load of armour-piercing bombs and, as Argent had a warship in his sights, he let them go. Returning, we found the airfield heavily cratered from the previous day's bombing. The only strip in use was marked between two rows of hurricane lamps. Refuelled and bombed up with 11-second delayed action bombs we took off, flying a little north of east and intercepted a 7,000 to 8,000 ton ship with two light escort vessels heading for Tjirabon. We attacked from mast height, from bow to stern, Argent dropping all four 250-lb bombs and in a sharply banked turn to port, we looked back to see the outcome of our efforts. The 11-second delay meant that we were well clear of the explosion. As well as troops it must have been carrying explosives because the whole foredeck from foc'sle to bridge lifted into the air with an enormous burst of flame".

"We did not wait around to see if the ship sank, because we were under fire from other vessels. Back at Kalidjati we refuelled and loaded some more of the same type of bombs. As, by that time, there were already rumours of landings in the vicinity of Tjirabon, we headed along the coast and in a few minutes we found our second victim. There were a dozen vessels lying at anchor alongside each other. We took the first and made the same approach. There were lifeboats alongside and I realised they were ferrying troops ashore. This time I did not hang around but flew low and parallel to the beach to give Wakefield a chance to use his Brownings on the small boats crowding the shore".

Archie Wakefield added that they then handed their aircraft over to a fresh crew. Wyllie later found that, on return to Kalidjati, a message, delivered to Wg Cdr Jeudwine by despatch rider, stated: "Maintain maximum dispersal and await further orders". He realised then that Jeudwine had initiated all operations on his own without instructions from HQ.

It was learned later that the crew which had taken Wyllie's aircraft had been attacked by fighters and forced to land in a padi field. The crew, consisting of Sgts Sayers, Ross and Proctor, were all reported safe.

Statements made after the evacuation from Java add to the confusion. One credited to Wg Cdr Jeudwine states that considerable time was lost in the early stages of the attack in trying to locate the target. There was a lot of low cloud and the moon did not rise till after midnight. Also the reconnaissance report was inaccurate as regards the initial position of the convoy and the Japanese had employed warships as decoys. The main force of 15 transports was eventually discovered at Indramajoe at approximately 0200 on 1 March, after they had already made their landing at Eretan Wetan. This information was passed on to AHQ at Bandoeng at 0300 hours.

Three hours later the Station Commander at Kalidjati, Gp Capt Whistondale, informed Wg Cdr Jeudwine that the Dutch were evacuating all of their serviceable aircraft to Bandoeng and were destroying their petrol dumps. But RAF Headquarters at Bandoeng had ordered maximum dispersal as usual. This meant the removal of bombs from the three remaining Blenheims and putting these and the five other serviceable aircraft in such a position that at least five minutes taxying was required to get them to the only airstrip still usable. After confirming these orders with AHQ, Jeudwine

drove to Soebang to warn the spare aircrews to prepare to evacuate and proceed to Bandoeng.

Jeudwine then returned to Kalidjati and reported the situation at Soebang to the Station Commander, who decided to go to Soebang himself. Gp Capt Whistondale was never seen again. Arrangements were then made for the Squadron to be ready to move at short notice. Crews stood by serviceable aircraft and demolition parties were posted on the airfield. Ground staff were split into parties, each party allocated a lorry and told to disperse along the west side of the airfield. In the meantime, Plt Off McNally had driven to Soebang to find the village deserted. Later a party of Plt Offs Kewish and Bott, Flt Sgt McBride and four airmen were detailed to drive to Soebang and collect the kits of the aircrews who had spent the night at the field. This party never returned.

It should be noted that Kalidjati was 15 miles in front of the first line of defence. The few guns which were used as coastal defences between Batavia and Tjirabon were of little use against a determined attacker. At 0500 all Dutch and British commanders were notified that an attack on Kalidjati was imminent. At the same time attacks on the Jap fleet were suspended, awaiting better conditions later in the day. The small Dutch aerodrome defence party had withdrawn at dawn without notifying the RAF. Already considerable confusion reigned on the station due to the fact that Gp Capt Whistondale had not returned. Added to that, sporadic gunfire could be heard in the distance and by 0900 news came that Soebang was in Jap hands. Whether this news was known at Kalidjati is debatable but it is known that the Dutch Commander, Lt Col Zomer, had heard the news at Bandoeng. A signal from AHQ at Bandoeng confirmed that things were becoming serious and that the aircraft could be evacuated at the Station Commander's discretion.

At approximately 10.30, the first Jap tanks entered the airfield. Before any move could be made, the Admin buildings came under fire from mortars and small arms fire. By deploying along the north and east sides of the airfield, the Japanese tanks soon had the area covered. During this period, one Hudson had taken off. Wyllie and Macdonald had tried to start a Blenheim but a burst of bullets through the right hand side of the windshield caused a hurried, and not entirely dignified, withdrawal.

A narrative written by Sqn Ldr Tayler continues: "Whilst endeavouring to taxy an aircraft out of the dispersal area, the port wheel got bogged down in a partially-filled bomb crater. The enemy were already on the airfield but not in our line of vision. I realised then that we were isolated and that the remainder of the Squadron had probably withdrawn according to the scheme laid down that morning. We emptied a pan of tommy-gun ammunition into the Blenheim and told Cpl Doug Jeans to act as driver of the lorry placed at our disposal. Flt Lt George Milson, Flt Sgt Bill Slee, Sgt Bill Cosgrove and myself began to run the gauntlet across the southern boundary of the airfield. Midway, we stopped to help an ack-ack crew attach their gun to the lorry. This activity drew the attention of the enemy and they opened fire from about 300 yards. Bill Slee was hit in the shoulder. As he was being helped into the lorry, we were joined by another truck which careered off at a tangent". Tayler continues by saying that they continued their escape with an army driver, but a light tank firing its main gun shattered the windscreen killing him. A further burst went through the engine of the lorry. Tayler and Jeans continued their dash for cover to find they were on their own.

Flt Lt George Milson, who had been left in the middle of the airfield, was fortunate enough to make his way to Bandoeng. Flt Sgt Bill Slee was never seen again. In a letter from George Milson, he writes: "During the thirteen days the Squadron was operating at Kalidjati, I did no flying due to blood poisoning in my left arm and during this period I got to know Bill very well. I was with him in the hangar when the Nips dropped a stick of bombs outside the hangar door; the next second we found ourselves blown into one of the offices at the side. The night of 28 February was the last time the Squadron operated in the Far East before the world blew apart. Along with Ron Millar, we were in charge of the flarepath. I cannot stress how hard the ground crews worked turning aircraft around for the next sortie. When operations was stood down, one Blenheim was missing and Bill and I waited until we heard it had force-landed and the crew was reported safe. Wg Cdr Jeudwine, commenting afterwards, wrote: "With only a handful of men to do the work, with insufficient tools and spares, without any outside assistance and handicapped by lack of transport, Flt Sgt Slee was responsible for the maintenance of the Squadron's aircraft from 23 January to 1 March, and the results deserve the highest praise".

Wg Cdr Jeudwine, together with Flt Lts Wyllie, Owen and

Holland, seeing that the situation was chaotic, drove a battered car with the three passengers armed with tommy-guns firing from the windows, in the hope of drawing enemy fire. It had the effect of taking fire from two enemy vehicles loaded with troops. Fortunately the combined fire from the car prevented the Japs from getting too close. They were thus able to escape from the airfield where they joined other crews who had taken cars and other transport from the pool and were able to make the hazardous journey towards Bandoeng. Sqn Ldr Tayler and Cpl Jeans had made their way deeper into the bush. Over the next 20 hours they witnessed the arrival of transport aircraft escorted by fighters. Shortly after dawn the following morning, they started south in the hope of reaching Bandoeng. It took them four days before they were overtaken by a Dutch staff car which was out looking for refugees from Kalidjati. This vehicle may well have been part of 'Group Toerop' who on 3 March tried to re-occupy Kalidjati from the south and west. This group was supported by armoured vehicles and artillery. Unfortunately, due to Jap air support, the attack failed. This was not the only time the Dutch tried to retake the field as on the 2nd a group with light tanks had entered Soebang on three separate occasions but were repelled by Jap pressure. Sgt Sayer and his crew, after their crash, had found an abandoned truck and they too made their way to Bandoeng. Others like Cpl Porter and LAC Shaw, who were left behind at Kalidjati, managed to evade the Japs and walk to Bandoeng.

LAC Tony Record, writing from his home near Tiverton gives further details: "I was with Jock Middleton on the back of a truck heading to where our aircraft were parked. We could see the Japs pouring out of the jungle onto the airfield, sending mortars in our direction. The driver grasped the situation and made a bee-line diagonally across the airfield pursued by rifle fire. We could hear the bullets whistling around us as we reached the road"

It is believed that 19 people were lost, including Plt Off D W Kewish and his party and two sergeants who had not left with the spare aircrew from Soebang.

It was subsequently established that the force that attacked Kalidjati consisted of tanks and armoured cars together with 100-150 troops, most of whom were armed with automatic weapons. Rein-forcements soon arrived and consolidated the position, which was never recaptured. The day after, on the 2nd, Japanese fighter and attack aircraft were using the field for raids on Andir.

Referring back to Brian Fiheely and his crew's force landing, Eric Oliver recalls: "We learnt later that Brian was one of the few Australians who could not swim a stroke and thought it more prudent to land on terra-firma. His aversion to water had caused him to plan the landing as close to the shore as possible. Not being sure whether the aircraft would sink further into the mud, we abandoned it and took to the dinghy. What 'Charlies' we must have looked marooned six feet from our aircraft. Looking out to sea, we were reminded that the coast of Java was some 70 miles away, while behind us was an impenetrable wall of jungle which seemed to go on forever. The only gleam of hope appeared to be a fishing stake - a hut built on poles driven into the sea-bed. It indicated habitation and the possibility of assistance. Finally Tommy Gomme and I decided that we had the option of waiting twelve hours for the tide to turn or make a determined effort to crawl across the mud, swim along the coast and hopefully find help".

"The two of us flopped onto the foul-smelling mud and began our crawl. It proved to be a very slow, exhausting and extremely unpleasant method of propulsion. The situation seemed unreal as we lay there, side by side, spread-eagled whilst hundreds of mud-flippers (air-breathing fish with heads like frogs) skidded across the mud around us. As we reached a point about half-way to the waterline, I reached a point of utter exhaustion. Tommy insisted on going on alone, confident that he could reach the water where, after a rest, he would swim for help. After Tommy had dis-appeared from sight, I struggled back to the dinghy where Brian was waiting for news. We rigged one of the parachutes over the dinghy to keep out the incessant mosquitoes and also to act as a marker for our hoped-for rescuers. We seemed to spend hours peering out of our parachute tent and as time went by we felt more and more that Tommy had not made it and had drowned through exhaustion. In the midst of despair, I made out the silhouette of a small boat, a flashlight signalled 'Boat is coming' and from the depths of misery we raised a cheer."

"I don't know from where Brian produced paper and matches, but suffice it to say that he waved a piece of burning paper above our heads to guide our rescuers. Two figures appeared out of the gloom standing in a flat-bottomed boat. Progress was slow so Brian and I abandoned the dinghy and struggled to meet them. We found Tommy in a small boat, along with two other natives. With all four

fishermen at the paddles we made it to the fishing hut in good time. Climbing the ladder into the hut, we collapsed on to the floor, absolutely shattered. Efforts were made to express our gratitude but since neither could speak each others language we made do with the Moslem greeting As-Salaam Alaykum" which evinced some response. The following morning we were taken by a larger boat to the natives village where a young Indonesian who had worked for an English planter explained to us that we could not stop there owing to the fact that the Japs had threatened to execute anyone found harbouring Allied forces. They eventually found us an old decrepit skiff about 12 feet long with an 8-foot pole for a mast and sackcloth for a sail. For this, we had to turn out our pockets, offering a handful of Dutch guilders. Their parting gift was a biscuit tin holding water, another container holding boiled rice and three Chinese coolie hats".

"Our trip to the mouth of the river was hairy, to say the least. Several times we were near to capsizing but, by good fortune, we eventually paddled our way back to the fishing hut. Tommy, being the navigator, hazarded a guess that travelling down the coast would bring us to the narrowest point between Sumatra and Java. There, a short sea crossing of some 20 miles would return us to our own lines. We decided to stay the night at the hut and next morning we edged our way down the coast; at times we were moving freely, at others we were becalmed. It must have been on the 28th when we heard what appeared to be thunder but what later proved to be gunfire. Periods of scorching sun were frequently followed by periods of tropical rain, so heavy that we had to bail out with our drinking vessel - a half coconut shell".

"When dawn broke the next morning, we spotted a couple of islands lying to the west. Although they appeared to be very small we decided to make for them. The sun was beginning to set when we reached them; this leg of the journey had taken us the entire day. It turned out to be barely an acre in size and scarcely rose above the level of the sea, being completely over-grown with mangrove roots. What we did not know, as we guided our craft into the creepers, was that the shoreline was covered by razor-sharp coral which tore holes in the hull as we struggled ashore. We stayed there the night and despite our exhaustion we found it impossible to do more than doze due to the millions of mosquitoes which attacked continuously".

"The following morning we awoke with pangs of hunger; it had been four days since our rice and fish meal at the village. Little did we realise that the following three and a half years would teach us much about hunger and exhaustion. Returning to where the boat lay half submerged, it was obvious that it would have to be hauled out of the water for repairs to be made. Our view to the sea was blocked by overhanging branches so Tommy and I waded in to get a clearer view. The sight that met our eyes was nothing less than a miracle. Anchored about 300 yards offshore was a large white yacht which would have graced a marina in the south of France. Ignoring our intention to repair the skiff, we pushed off and paddled towards the yacht. As we neared the vessel we could see two figures on the deck, the taller was obviously European and dressed in white shirt and shorts, whilst the other was coloured. As we drew alongside, the man shouted "What nationality are you?" to which we cried "British - we're RAF". We were assisted aboard where we collapsed with exhaustion".

"In time, the skipper told us how the *White Swan* came to be anchored where she was. It seemed that a senior RAF officer had received permission for one of the minesweepers to tow out his private yacht from Batavia in order that he could sail it through the Sunda Straits and into the Indian Ocean. The sweepers had been sunk but for some obscure reason the *White Swan* was not attacked and she was able to pick up some 40 survivors from the action. Came the dawn, she was stopped by an enemy patrol and ordered to anchor off the island to await escort into captivity".

"After mutual explanations had been exchanged, the skipper ushered us below decks where we met our fellow survivors. There followed the usual comments after every military defeat, Dunkirk, Greece and now, Singapore. "The RAF eh! Where the bloody hell were you?" Questions came thick and fast until they realised we had not eaten for several days. The skipper offered us the use of the ship's dinghy to continue our voyage but we all agreed that we'd had more than enough open-boat experience to last us a lifetime. As dusk fell, we discussed with the skipper the feasibility of making a break for it and sneaking quietly through the Strait into the Indian Ocean. The skipper was undecided, as he bore responsibility for all on board. We decided to put our suggestion to the others to see what their reaction might be. Not unexpectedly, none relished the idea of becoming POWs".

"As I recall, the *White Swan* was about 60 feet long with a 15-

Kalidjati airfield, No.84 Squadron's base in Java

foot beam. She had two masts and two large square-rigged sails and was quite capable of ocean sailing. As darkness fell, the anchor was raised and with a gentle breeze we set course for freedom. As dawn broke we cleared the narrowest part of the Strait and were now covering the last few miles to the freedom of the Indian Ocean. With the coasts of Java and Sumatra receding in the distance, we were congratulating ourselves when the lookout shouted, "Destroyer on port bow" followed seconds later by, "Destroyer on starboard bow". Our spirits sank - so close to freedom. A shell exploded a few yards ahead of us. It was clearly a signal to heave to; a pinnace was lowered from the destroyer with a boarding party which climbed aboard. It was our introduction to the Japanese military machine".

"We all sat around feeling dejected while the Japs searched the yacht. As we speculated on our future, one of the Jap ratings strolled casually towards us. In pure American he said "Hi fellas". He told us his name was Hiroyama; though born in Japan, his family had moved to America where they owned a restaurant. A few months before Pearl Harbor, with a number of other Japanese/Americans, he had accepted an invitation to study the culture of their ancestors. They had not been allowed to return and were conscripted into the forces as interpreters. He told us that whilst the Japanese Navy would treat us in a civilised manner, we would not be so fortunate with the Army. Future events proved him right".

We were ordered to return to Bantam Bay on the western tip of Java, adding that if we made for Tjilatjap, this ship is dead!. It was a very dejected ship's company that turned about. There we sailed into the anchorage holding 30 or 40 Jap troopships, all frantically unloading tanks and other transport, much of it from ships emblazoned with the Red Cross in complete contradiction to the Geneva Convention. A Japanese naval surgeon came aboard to attend to our wounded. Immediately he left, a military escort took over and our party of would-be escapers were taken into custody. From that moment the treatment was rough and abusive."

It was to be nearly three years before Eric Oliver was to meet his fellow sergeants from No.84 Squadron at Changi again. Tommy Gomme died on Boxing Day 1991.

Many of the Squadron had arrived in Bandoeng during the afternoon of 1 March and were accommodated in barracks about ten miles from the town. It was assumed that the Squadron would be required to take to the jungle and arms were provided to wage guerrilla warfare. Instead, an order was issued by AHQ to the effect that the men were to be trained in arms drill! Volunteers were called for to travel to the satellite airfield at Pondoctjabi to fetch six Wirraways which were based there. Amongst the volunteers were Sgts Howard Hough and Geoff Dewey from 34 Squadron. A letter from Geoff Dewey gives the details: "The six

pilots, plus an engineer officer and two fitters, set off in a commandeered Chevrolet on the morning of the 3rd, travelling by minor roads. Eventually we arrived at this jungle strip and found the six Wirraways pushed under the trees. Whilst the EO and the fitters gradually got the engines running, Hough and I gave the other four pilots a quick rundown on the controls, cockpit layout and characteristics of the aircraft. The first four, escorted by Hough in the fifth, took off and set course for Bandoeng, flying at about 200 feet. I followed after about 30 minutes, having had problems getting the engine to start. Once airborne, I found that not only would the undercarriage not retract but the canopy would not close. I followed the railway line at about 100 feet, losing it a couple of times when the line went through tunnels. I reached Bandoeng about 15 minutes after it had been bombed. Two of the Wirraways had finished up in craters but Hough had guided the other two in safely. As far as is known they were never used".

On the afternoon of 3 March, AVM Maltby, the Air Officer Commanding, told Wg Cdr Jeudwine that there was a chance that more ships would be available for the evacuation of surplus personnel and as No. 84 was a complete unit, it would be evacuated if the opportunity arose. Next day an order was issued that all flying personnel were to proceed to Tjilatjap, the only port on the south coast of Java. Nothing was said about the ground staff who were to stay in Bandoeng together with the adjutant, equipment, engineer, medical and cypher officers.

By then, conditions in Java were too confused and desperate to make further defence anything but local and spasmodic. The surrender of Java was a foregone conclusion as soon as the Japanese had set foot on the island.

Research shows that between 20 and 30 ships left Tjilatjap between 26 February and 4 March. Amongst them were the *Kota Gedeh* which carried some personnel from Nos.34 and 62 Squadrons. Several of these were sunk.

On the 5th, an enquiry was held regarding the capture of Kalidjati. Allegations had been made that British troops had fled from the airfield and it was deemed essential that this should be looked into. Impartiality was important and British Army and Air Force officers, together with their Dutch counterparts, should make a joint report. It was agreed that responsibility should rest mainly on the shoulders of Higher Command as there were no protective troops between Kalidjati and the coast. The airfield was only about 22 miles from the coast where landings had been made and the speed with which the enemy had been able to land troops and tanks and reach a point so far inland in so short a time was never appreciated.

The matter was subsequently discussed between AVM Maltby and Lt Gen van Oyen. It was agreed that, whilst the whole incident was far from satisfactory, there was no evidence of the allegations

The Kota Gedah *was one of the few ships to escape for Tjilatjap after 26 March 1942 carrying RAF personnel*

Other RAF personnel from 84 Squadron had arrived on 5 March at Poerwokerto, a town about 30 miles inland from Tjilatjap. They were amongst a large contingent of nearly 2,500, mostly unarmed RAF and RAAF men. On the evening of the 6th, two trains, made up of a few carriages and tanks carrying high octane fuel, arrived. The first under the command of Wg Cdr Rae moved off about 1900. The second, with Wg Cdr N Cave in charge, followed two hours later. Both were packed with airmen making their way to Tasikmalaja airfield, 40 miles south-west of Bandoeng. At approximately 2200, the first was ambushed by a detachment of Japanese troops, attacking with mortars, machine guns and grenades. Several of the freight wagons were derailed, a number of airmen being killed or wounded.

Meanwhile, the second train, which had been forced to stop because of the derailed trucks, also came under fire and there were further casualties. Strangely the Japs did not press home their attack, retreating into the jungle. Survivors were now making their way along the track, the wounded being left in the hope of being collected later. After a few miles they came to a five-span steel railway bridge. As the earliest arrivals crossed, the Dutch colonial troops blew it, up causing more casualties. Apparently the defenders were under the impression that Japanese troops had arrived and were crossing. Later, attempts were made, which was ultimately successful, to rig a cable across the river. A great many more traversed the river by pulling themselves across the water. The last man had only just crossed when machine gun fire was heard and the remainder of the bridge was blown-up.

Of the wounded who were left by the derailed train, Cpl 'Butch' Finning had this to say: "We lay there for quite a time, then as it got dark I heard screams from the adjoining hut. The Nips had burst in and were bayoneting the men on the floor. I knew it was curtains for me. I wriggled close to the man nearest to me and turned on my side to take the thrusts on my ass and thighs. The screams from the men were terrible, but the Japs were just as bad every time they lunged with their rifles. When they reached me I feigned dead. The light was fading and I managed to wriggle clear from the rest of the corpses".

In all, Finning had received 14 bayonet wounds but amazingly was still alive.

When the Japs finally departed, he dragged himself to a window and managed to stagger off into the bushes. There he passed out and came to the following morning. Although in great

pain, he forced himself away from the scene and eventually lay exhausted on the side of the river. It was not the end for Finning, for natives found him and decided to finish off what the Japs had started. Trussing him up like a chicken, they put a noose around his neck. He went on to say: "This time I was convinced that I had had my chips. They had slung a rope around a branch and were trying to string me up. They got me off the ground and I found myself spinning. At that moment I heard a car and they dropped me back on the ground. I vaguely remember a strange man wielding a large sword and I made up my mind that I was to be beheaded instead of hung".

However the Japanese officer was his saviour. He had already picked up two wounded airmen who were sat in his car. He then cut Finning loose and helped him into the car, then he drove to the local POW camp which was full of Dutch internees. They, however, could do nothing to help him and it was due only to the fact that the Japanese officer returned, saw Finning's wounds and drove him to a nearby civilian hospital, that Finning eventually recovered. As far as is known, there was only one other survivor from this massacre. Cpl Hornblow of the RAF managed to escape prior to the actual killing taking place.

Of those who reached the comparative safety of the other side of the Tjitaroem river, transport was requested to take them to Tasikmalaja. Apparently two trains eventually arrived and one of these reached its destination. The second, however, was another victim of a bridge being blown up by native troops and it plunged into the River Tjimanoek. Once more there were casualties, many fatal.

On the night of the 6th/7th, four Lodestars and one DC-3 took off from a small airfield at Boeahbatoeweg to fly to Australia. Among its passengers were Lt Governor General van Mook and Lt Gen van Oyen, Commander Java Air Command. These seem to be the last aircraft to leave Java before the surrender.

On 8 May at 0900 came the news from the Dutch authorities that all organised resistance had ceased. In these circumstances the two Commanders, Maltby and Sitwell, had little alternative than to comply with the Dutch surrender. Four days later, they negotiated terms with the Japanese Commander, Lt Gen Maruyama, at Bandoeng. He undertook to treat all prisoners in accordance with the Geneva Convention of 1929.

In Chapter 13 you will read that their word was not always to be relied upon!

The port of Tjilatjap on the south coast of Java, starting point for the voyage to Australia

CHAPTER 12 - THE VOYAGE OF HMRAFS *SCORPION*

At dusk, on Saturday, 7 March 1942, Wg Cdr John Jeudwine and a crew of four officers and seven Australian sergeants set sail from Noesa Kembangan, an island just off the coast from the town of Tjilatjap. In addition to the officers already mentioned, Jeudwine had chosen Sgts P M Corney, W N Cosgrove, P A Haynes, A C Longmore, J A Lovegrove, G W Sayer and A C Snook. He had chosen them, not only for their fitness, stamina and morale but, also he thought that, as Australians, they should be given first refusal to make the voyage to their own country, especially as they had all volunteered to join the Royal Australian Air Force and serve overseas with the Royal Air Force.

Before leaving Tjilatjap, a considerable amount of rations and other foodstuffs had been collected; also a quantity of American tinned beer had been obtained from a Dutch canteen. The latter undoubtedly helped in the well-being of the crew, as water had to be strictly rationed and the beer was a food in itself.

It was estimated that the nearest spot on the North Australian coast would be Roebourne, approximately 950 miles away, and it was hoped that it could be covered in 16 days. For navigation, they had a ship's sextant, two compasses, one of which came from an aircraft, and a large-scale map; unfortunately no charts of the area could be found.

During the first day, the only signs of air activity was an appearance of a Zero fighter which made a couple of circuits before shearing off in the direction of the mainland. All next day, the group were becalmed off the coast, the lack of wind continued until early afternoon of the 9th when a gentle breeze sprang up. The lifeboat had just begun to make headway when to the horror of those on board a Japanese submarine surfaced about a mile astern. The conning tower opened and the escapees saw an officer scrutinising them through binoculars. Beside him stood another man, a rating at the breech of a 5.5-inch gun and a fourth man standing by a machine-gun which was fortunately pointing skyward.

Approaching to within 50 yards, the submarine made a half circle of the airmen while, all the time the officer continuing to examine them through his glasses. The number I-56 stood out plainly on the conning tower. Finally, to the relief of the airmen in the lifeboat, the submarine set course to the east and later submerged.

The rations were fixed at 10 ounces of 'meat and vegetables or camp pie', half-pint of water and four biscuits per man per day. Cigarettes were limited to three a day. It was found after the first few days that the crew were suffering from acute sunburn and that considerable mental effort was needed to move about, which was usually done on all fours. The breeze continued to hold and finally freshened but, because it was a headwind, the men were forced to beat against it. When the lifeboat was originally salvaged, the rudder had been damaged; on the third day it broke away.

Sgts Corney and Lovegrove volunteered to become the shipwrights but the limited tools available made lasting repairs difficult. Wire and floating salvage was used to good effect. During the time of the repairs, the course was held with difficulty by using an oar. About this time, the lifeboat was officially christened HM Royal Air Force Ship *Scorpion*.

After seven days at sea, they enjoyed an extra ration of water from one of the casks which had a tablet of Lifebuoy soap left in it. It was hoped that the soapy water would act as a laxative as most of the crew were suffering from constipation. Unfortunately the results were not as they would have liked. To help maintain morale, Wg Cdr Jeudwine instituted the Naval custom of 'Saturday night at sea'. All hands were given extra rations and a tot of whisky was issued. The King's health was drunk, followed by the toast 'Sweethearts and Wives, May they never meet'.

Their position became serious when it was realised that their water supply was critical; the tap on one of the casks had become loose and most of its contents were lost. A second cask was lost when it was accidentally tipped over and a further three had

The only known photograph of the survivors of HMRAFS Scorpion after arriving in Australia

loose and most of its contents were lost. A second cask was lost when it was accidentally tipped over and a further three had become contaminated with sea water. Miraculously, they ran into a tropical storm which enabled them to collect enough water to refill their barrels. During the storm the rudder again broke free; after 36 hours struggling and a lot of the time in the water, Corney and Lovegrove repaired it sufficiently well enough to last the voyage out.

Over the days that followed, they were becalmed for long periods but the noon positional check showed them to be gradually drifting north. The third week at sea brought a forced reduction in rations. It was found that some of the tins were corroding due to the heat, being continually under water and being shaken about. Competitions were devised to occupy the crew and reduce boredom but the mental exercise made them feel hungry and thirsty. The last of the cigarettes were smoked on 8 April when it was estimated they were 140 miles from Barrow Island and 180 from the town of Onslow.

Up to now the men had taken little notice of the whales which were often seen blowing in the distance. On the 34th day, a whale surfaced about 200 yards astern and then rapidly began to overtake the boat. About 60 feet long, it came alongside with its tail beneath the boat. Its head appeared about three feet off the stern and stared at the crew. After what seemed an eternity, the whale moved off and joined a larger one about a hundred yards away. Neither were seen again!

The first indication of land was the sight of a swallow-tail butterfly on 18 April. More were seen the following day and, at 2.30 am Perth time, they touched land on Fraser Island. A plate on a nearby beacon identified the site. When dawn broke through, they went ashore for breakfast.

Re-launching the lifeboat, they continued their course and in mid-afternoon an aircraft was sighted. All on board waved and flashed mirrors but little notice was taken. It transpired that the pilot had seen them, but thought they were a pearling lugger and took no further notice. Later they sighted a flying boat coming towards them. Waving shirts and other items of clothing they were delighted when the American Navy Catalina alighted nearby. The American was very wary and asked his questions from behind a loaded Colt .45, whilst Jeudwine was clinging to a rope in shark-infested waters. Finally, convinced by Jeudwine's story, he was allowed aboard the 'Cat' and, after discussion, the Catalina crew offered to take six of the crew back to their base.

Sgts Cosgrove, Haynes and Longmore agreed to go, but the rest were determined to sail the *Scorpion* into port. The following day, the Catalina reappeared and landed alongside with orders that the crew had to be picked up and flown to Shark's Bay. Gathering up their few belongings, they boarded the Catalina and the faithful old lifeboat was set adrift. It was a disappointment to the crew that after travelling so far, they could not complete the journey. The health of all was remarkably good. There were no signs of fever but ulcers and abrasions were common. There had also been considerable eye problems through exposure to the sun and the sea.

The crew of the *Scorpion* spent the night of the 22/23 April on board the USS *Childs*. On the 23rd, the whole party was flown to Perth where Jeudwine contacted the US Naval Authorities. Arrangements were made for the US submarine *Sturgeon* to call at 'Scorpion's Cove' on the island of Noesa Kembangan, Java, in an attempt to pick up the 84 Squadron aircrews who had been left there with orders to wait for two months if possible. Although the *Sturgeon* closed to within 50 yards of the beach on the night of 30 April, nothing was found except a deserted lean-to. There were no signs of a voluntary departure, so the fate of the stranded members of the Squadron was not known until three-and-a-half years later.

Wg Cdr J R Jeudwine was later to report: "Looking back on six-and-a-half weeks of trial, I can say that I would not, if the opportunity again occurred, alter one of the crew. They were magnificent.....we became staunch friends in adversity".

This story was printed in the March issue 1984 of *RAAF News* and caused a sensation in Japan. It referred to the incident where a Japanese submarine commander allowed four RAF and eight RAAF men to escape from Java. During recent visits to Japan, efforts were made through the media to find the captain of *I-56*. These eventually led to contact being made with the captain's younger brother. It was revealed that the decision to let the airmen escape had been made by Captain Katsuo Ohashi, who had made courtesy visits to Australia and New Zealand during the early thirties. Despite his compassion, Ohashi was to lose his life in the last fortnight of the war when the submarine *I-13* was sunk by allied bombers.

THE CREW

Wg Cdr J R Jeudwine: Killed flying a Typhoon, 1944
Sqn Ldr A K Passmore: Killed flying a Boeing Washington, 1952
Fg Off C P Streatfeild: Died natural causes, 196-
Fg Off S C Turner
Plt Off M S Macdonald: Died natural causes, 1958
Sgt P A Corney: Died 1962
Sgt W N Cosgrove: Killed, 30 Sqn RAAF Beaufighters, 1943
Sgt P A Haynes: Living W Australia
Sgt A C Longmore: Died natural causes, 1989
Sgt J Lovegrove: Living Bull Creek, W Australia
Sgt G W Sayer: Killed, 30 Sqn RAAF Beaufighters, 1942
Sgt A Snook: Died natural causes, 4 Dec 1991

The sextant used by FO Turner on the epic voyage of Scorpion (A W Cooper)

The Japanese prisoner-of-war camp at Kamiiso, 18 July 1944. Identities from top to bottom:
Neal, Ellory, Sanderson, Mathe, Noble, Munro, Hammond, Dixon, Cooper, Weaver, Barry, Passey, Stanford, Naylor, Horrocks,
Yearkess, Palmer, Glover, Blake.
Jackson, Hough, Higson, Robson, Shaw, Vacca, Day, Maskel, Brannon, Potter, Ross, Ford, Brown, Richdale, Smith, Clayton,
Pugh, Searle, Garrett.
Forbes, Holden, Watts, Hill, Dilworth, Ditchburn, Abbotts, Edwards, Greenan, Hughes, Jones, Hilton, Garrott, Roberts, Kedge,
Newton, Passey, Andrews, Peter, Alloway, Butler, Cooper.
Ashworth, Morris, Dixon, Biggs, Eames, Everell, Boyer, Roylands, Gough, Smith, Hart, Bentley, Lay, Diggins, Ward,
Farnsworth, Temple, Swainson, Robbins, Atkinson, Day.
Walsh, La'closh, James, Hirst, Redman, Glass, Chicweddon, Southall, Cropper, Bumgarner, Bancroft, Colenut, Aldous,
Crowther, Street, Lawrence, Bull, Grant.
Burton, Weakley, Thoroughgood, Boast, Gold, Cook, Anderson, Reader, Fyford, Farnes, Goodwin, Oakley, Cooley, Hobbins,
Harrisson, Sayerpoll, Evans, Walker, Dunne.
Inman, Record, Kennet, Winter, Lammin, Peace, Owen, Perrera, Sandy, Kennedy, Chalkley, Millsom. Evans, Morrison, Moore,
Bradshaw.
(Tony Record)

CHAPTER 13 - UNDER THE SWORD

Ambon, Horoekoe, Boel Glodok, Tanjong Priok, Macassar, Pakan Baroe, Hakodate, Moearo, Changi, Mukaishaina. These names, plus many others, are etched on No.84 Squadron memories, just as are Shaibah, Menidi, Kumbhirgram, Khormaksar and Akrotiri, the only difference being that the first ten mentioned were all prisoner-of-war camps where members of 84 Squadron and other units were imprisoned in unusually diabolical conditions.

The majority of these camps were in the Dutch East Indies. Ambon, of which we shall hear more later, was probably the worst, situated 1,500 miles ENE of Java between the islands of the Celebes and New Guinea. Hakodate is on the northern- most island of Japan whilst Mukaishaina is an island just off the coast of Japan, a mere 20 miles from Hiroshima.

It is difficult to ascertain the exact number of No.84 Squadron members who were to become POWs. It is possible that the number could be as high as 450 although the exact number of casualties in the latter stages of the Java fiasco is not known. It is known, however, that of those who left Heliopolis in mid-January 1942, only 132 returned to Karachi aboard the *Yoma*. A further eleven accompanied Wg Cdr J R Jeudwine on his voyage from Java to Australia, while several crews rejoined their Squadron in India from airfields strung across Burma and Malaya.

Fg Off Keble-White, writing in 1945 after his release: "To write a brief summary of the last three-and-a-half years as a POW is not an easy undertaking. Probably no man who has never experienced a long internment can imagine the long periods of complete boredom, the monotony of life, of food, the surroundings

and the people existing around you".

I am not making any attempt to give an overall picture of life under the Japanese but merely to give individual experiences of the few who have been kind enough to give me details of their own years of imprisonment.

Plt Off D F McNally RAAF in a statement dated 5 September 1945 writes that he, with Flt Lt Bongard, Fg Offs Jebb and Brentnall and Plt Off Bishop together with other RAF personnel were taken prisoner on 24 March. They were taken to the native prison at Boel Glodok. In cells, marked for occupation by 60 natives, were packed 140 POWs. For 42 days they were left without medical attention or toilet facilities. The floor rapidly became a cesspit and the men were forced to form a endless queue awaiting their turn for a breath of comparatively fresh air from the single window.

Eventually 2,400 British and Commonwealth prisoners were confined in this prison built for 600 native prisoners. Later, many of the personnel from No.84 Squadron were gathered together in two separate blocks and the officers did everything in their power to make life as pleasant as possible for the airmen. Others, from the very start of their imprisonment, were forced to join large working parties, either filling in bomb craters on the heavily-bombed Batavia airport or extending its runways for Japanese bombers. All work was done by hand, shovels and wheelbarrows being the only aids for the weakened prisoners. Food was minimal, a handful of rice supplemented by a type of green weed and the occasional piece of meat. On the odd occasion, eggs and bananas were bought from the Chinese market traders who were located on the edge of the airfield. But this often led to beatings if the person was caught bringing food back on to the camp.

Some, like LAC Julian Rogers, who had flown to Sumatra as groundcrew in Sgt Ken Lister's Blenheim, was one of those who never even left Kalidjati. After struggling through storm drains he surfaced from the culvert to find about 30 airmen lying flat on the ground being guarded by two Japanese soldiers armed with machine-guns. Putting their fingers to their mouths they gestured him to join the gang and indicated just where he was to lie. So started his life as a POW.

Roger's initiation into POW life was the Pamegaten tea plantations. Here the large drying sheds were used to house the prisoners. The sheds were like miniature skyscrapers with perforated zinc windows to allow the cooling wind through the structure. Eventually several hundred POWs were to start their period of imprisonment there. The hilly region, with its cool breezes, kept everyone in reasonable spirits. Their diet consisted of two meals a day of rice and green vegetables, with hot water to drink. The availability of native tobacco meant that soon there were cigarette factories set up amongst the prisoners, the Airmens' Testament being ideal for cigarette papers. This enabled them to buy rough brown sugar, fruit like bananas and papaya and medicine like quinine.

Pamegaten is remembered partly for the beauty of the area and the lack of illness. It was an easy-going camp where those imprisoned got used to their captor's habits and customs. As the picking season neared, the sheds were needed for the drying of the leaf. The 600 or so prisoners were moved out, taken by train to Buitenzorg, then marched to Semplak.

Flt Sgt Rice also comments on the comparative good health of those at Pamegaten. He was one of a draft which was sent to Boel Glodok in the conditions already described. In September 1942, they were joined by Sgts Hough and McKillop and Cpl Shaw who had been at Bandoeng. They stayed there until January 1943. During this time drafts were being constantly moved in or out.

The month of January 1943 brought the closure of Boel Glodok and the majority were moved to Tanjong Priok which, after a period of brutality and close confinement, was a pleasant change for all. Sam Crocker comments: "Working at the docks were reasonably OK but the 'good times' were not to last". Barry Paterson was another of No.84's ground crew who, after wandering about the southern part of Java, had eventually been picked up at Garoet. Here he was bound with wire and left outside with a large notice inviting the locals to throw their rubbish over him. Taken inside after dark, it was to be a further 32 hours before he was given a small loaf and a pot of jam. On transfer to Tanjong Priok, he met two others from No.84 Squadron, Sgt Eric Oliver and LAC Clement.

In September 1942, they left in a large party for Singapore where they were marched to Changi army base and accommodated in large concrete barracks. Most of the guards were Straits Settlements Sikhs who had gone over to the Japanese and were very prone to carry out their duties to excess, often beating up the prisoners. Soon after their arrival, they were awoken in the middle of the night and told to go to the latrines. It appeared that one of the Sikhs had beaten up a Gurkha. The Gurkha had turned upon him and thrown him into one of the sewage boreholes. It was the duty of the prisoners to fill the hole with fresh sewage.

On 9 October, Paterson left Singapore aboard the prison-ship Sombong Maru. The space allocated was one cubic metre per man. For four days they suffered in disgusting conditions before landing at Kuching in Sarawak, which was to be his home for the next three years. Further drafts were assembled and the first of these was sent to Thailand and put to work on the infamous railway from which few survived. Cpl Owen Greenwood, after serving nearly a year clearing sewage from a canal, was amongst a draft sent to an equally horrific railway, the Pakan Baroe line to be built across the jungles and mountains of Sumatra.

In an interview with the author he recalls vividly of his experience: "The sea journey from Batavia to Padang took four days, travelling in a small collier. The ship was filthy, especially in the holds where the POWs were housed, which were covered in a thick layer of coal dust".

He well remembers the journey inland across the equator in a convoy of Japanese Army vehicles. The roads were good but difficult as it crossed the mountain range and he was impressed by the driver's skill in negotiating the tricky road and its numerous hair-pin bends.

As far as he could recall, they stayed at Camp I for only a couple of days before the whole party, with the exception of some of the technicians, moved on to Camp Two, which had been hacked out of a rubber plantation. The trunks of the trees had been left standing as a supporting framework for the atap huts. Work from this camp became progressively more arduous and uncomfortable. Some miles further on through the jungle, a third camp had been set up, as a bridge had to be built over a river. It was here that Greenwood's activity on the line came to a halt when he contracted malaria, dysentry and general weakness. He was allowed to stay on camp but at the price of becoming a 'sanitary wallah'. Fortunately, it enabled him to stay on 'full' rations.

It is estimated that at least 6,600 POWs worked on the building of this railway. The death rate from malaria, beri-beri, ulcers, dysentry and malnutrition was high, and by the end of hostilities there was a large cemetery overlooking the valley where Camp Two was situated. The numbers were probably equally divided between the British and the Dutch, with a few Australians. The British Commandant at Camp Two was Wg Cdr P S Davis and the C of E padre by the name of Phillips was later to become Chaplain to the Bishop of Llandaff. Among the RAF prisoners on these camps were about a dozen from 84 Squadron and a similar number from 211 Squadron. In all, thirteen camps were built, the last and most infamous being Moearo. Work continued right up to the last day of hostilities when the Japanese vanished overnight. In the case of Camp Two, the date was 17 August 1945.

Another to leave Batavia in October 1942 was LAC Tony Record. He writes: "We were taken to the docks and boarded the Tufuka Maru. We were kept below decks all of the time except when using the latrines - slung outboard on both sides of the boat - or to bury our dead. Flt Sgt Barker, who was not particularly fit, would climb a stairway to read the burial service. We sailed, first to Saigon to refuel and then on to Formosa where we were caught on the fringe of a typhoon. At Formosa, we left a great many sick, whom the Japs said would be taken to hospital. From there to Honshu, by rail and ferry to Hakodate on the island of Hokkaido, where we had to march through a cemetery to a collection of timber bungalows which were originally part of an isolation hospital. For Christmas Day 1942, we had three bowls of rice and cabbage water. Whilst there, it was so cold that 'Tiny'Turner burnt his pith helmet. This was where 'Chiefy' Barker came into his own. Each day he read a lesson and prayers followed. The sermon he gave really sank into the hearts of the POWs. From there he was known as 'Get a grip' Barker, the continuous theme of his sermon. He was later sent to Sapporo military prison for 'taking a swipe' at one of the guards."

Record's first job was to unload ships in the nearby docks. He recalls: "Salt, bales of seaweed and boxes of frozen salmon were all unloaded into barges and, from there into refrigeration plants. Occasionally the boxes of salmon were dropped enabling the prisoners to carry large salmon back into the camp slung down their trouser legs. At camp they would be stood in a bucket of boiling water before being passed around as many men as possible and devoured with speed. In the spring of 1943, half the camp was moved across the bay to new wooden buildings adjoining a cement works at Kamiso. The Japs eventually took us off loading bags of cement on to the barges because of the number which finished in the sea. From there I was moved to a coal mine, one of four POWs allocated to each Jap, to load and unload the trolleys. Not being a success at this, I was moved to the electrician's shop where, in company with an army electrician, I was put on re-winding electric motors. I had never done this work before and as far as I recall none of the motors I wound ever worked! I was here until August 1945.

Referring back to January 1943, a draft of nearly 1,000 men was sent to what became known as the worst of all camps, the island of Ambon. Approximately 200 miles south of the equator, the prisoners task was to build an airfield. The original draft was made up of Hussars, Gunners and RAF personnel, most of the latter coming from 84 and 211 Squadrons. Due to an enforced two-day march, and subsequent primitive living conditions and a totally inadequate ration, a large number quickly became ill and many died. Out of the original draft, I am told that only 430 were to set foot again on the island of Java.

Warrant Officer L W Havard was one of those that survived. His narrative written at the conclusion of hostilities makes one wonder why there were no large-scale War Crimes Commission in Japan, as there was in Germany.

The Ambon draft left Soerabaya on 16 April 1943 and 84 Squadron was represented by about 50 men. The island of Ambon measured about thirty miles by forty and, even in peacetime, it could never have grown sufficient food for its own needs. To establish a camp for over a 1,000 men, it was not an ideal setting.

Conditions were as bad, if not worse, than any of the other bad camps. It had atap huts, which even when new could not withstand the tropical storms and the fused coral on which they stood was crippling to the feet. Think of everything a camp needs and none of it was available, even water. A bamboo pipeline which was eventually constructed, stretching over a mile-and-a-half, never supplied more than 400 gallons a day, the majority of which was drunk by the guards.

After six months, the number of sick and slowly-dying was such that arrange-ments were made to return the survivors to Java. Accordingly, in November 1943, over 300 men were drafted away. Unfort-unately the ship was sunk, believed by an Allied submarine; amongst those lost were Fg Off Brentnall and WO Wright. At about the same time, a party of fifty men were detached and sent to a camp on the south coast of the island. WO Havard being placed in charge. There, the construction of an underground Headquarters on the side of a hill was started. Two parallel tunnels, six metres high and seven metres wide and sixty metres apart were to be dug and a further tunnel was to join the two. The nature of the ground was such that, even after one metre had been excavated, it was obvious that roof falls were probable. The farther they dug, the more often it caved in. No actual injuries were sustained but cuts and bruises were the norm.

Food on this camp was even worse than it was at Ambon but thankfully the guards were more sympathetic. Eventually the project was abandoned after an outbreak of fever, believed to be blackwater, which caused the death of one airman and the return of 27 others, including Havard, to the main camp.

During the first year of captivity, a draft of about forty led by Flt Lt Bongard left Batavia for Japan, picking up a further 60 at Singapore. Amongst them were John Leavers and Fred Walsh. They arrived at the port of Moji on 24 November 1942. John Leavers remember well the conditions endured. The holds of old ships were so full of prisoners that once the covers were on, there was little chance of seeing the light of day until the destination had been reached. Several died on the voyage, their bodies not being found until the ship docked. On disembarking, they left for the small island of Mukaishaina where their job was the cleaning and painting of merchant ships. Another party saw the transference of Julian Rogers and Harry Ward to Japan. They were in a party of 600 which eventually landed at Nagasaki. They were to witness the damage caused by the atom bomb during their evacuation from Japan in August 1945.

In April 1943, Cpl Ramsden, together with 63 others, was sent on a draft to Horoekoe, arriving on the 4 May. Immediately a serious dysentry epidemic occurred. During the following two months, Cpl Smith and Warren, LACs Fisher and Robinson and ACs Holden and Tame died. Later Cpl Hough, LAC Johnstone and Webster and AC Warner also succumbed.

At Ambon, Havard recalls that by the beginning of 1944 food problems were acute and, despite the sick draft which had left, the hospital area was full to overflowing. During this time, LAC Hembridge had done wonders as medical orderly. A further draft left Ambon in May of that year; all were in a pitiful condition. From May onwards, conditions became indescribable and the camp was moved to the south of the island near Ambon town. Beri-beri, malaria and malnutrition was rampant.

In September 1944, the majority of the British prisoners who were still alive arrived back in Java, 30 being left behind. This small party eventually arrived on an island in the Celebes and from there dribbled back to Java by means of small craft. During the voyage of ten days to the town of Macassar, land was never out of sight. Here the Japanese Sergeant-Major in charge of prisoners commandeered all the welfare money and bought supplies of dried fish, tobacco, fruit and eggs to supplement the meagre rations. One wonders whence came this kindly thought!

On the first night out from Macassar, a RAF corporal was killed after being found in an unauthorised part of the ship. The following day, Havard himself was the victim of an unprovoked attack, being beaten up by the Jap Sojo. Reports say that he was repeatedly hit by saplings taken aboard as stretcher poles and consistently hit over the head by bottles and tea dixies. Dodging these wildly driven blows and threats, Havard apparently thought enough was enough. Giving prior warning to the Jap interpreter standing near, he broke away leaving a bemused Jap trying to follow. At this stage a ship's officer appeared and took the NCO away.

For days after this incident, the tension aboard the ship was high. This atmosphere lasted until the ship reached Java. Somehow, setting foot back on the island seemed to be so tremendous an achievement that it overshadowed all that the men

had endured. Havard, like so many others, saw the final part of his imprisonment at camps on the island of Java.

Meanwhile, Plt Off McNally, after leaving the confines of Tanjong Priok, had gone first to the Cycle Camp at Batavia and from there to Kampong Macassar. Later he returned to Batavia where he was joined by Sqn Ldr J E Tayler, Flt Lt J Wyllie and Fg Off R Jebb. Later Fg Offs Holland and Keble-White joined them and at the same time WO Jones arrived from captivity near Bandoeng.

During 1944, drafts left Java which took many of the prisoners to camps on Singapore Island, Wyllie becoming SBO at the Pulo Damar Laut, a small island just off the mainland. Here they were given on Christmas Eve 1944 a small black pig, a gift from the Emperor to share between 1,000 prisoners, It was at Changi that Eric Oliver was reunited with his fellow 84 Squadron aircrews, Davy Russell, Archie Wakefield, Bill Miller, Bill Proctor, Johnny King and Geoff Palmer. All were eager to hear how he had escaped from his forced landing and his subsequent adventures.

Flt Lt George Milson, in letters to the author, writes that his luck held even during his three and a half years of captivity. He moved from Java in September 1943 with a working party which included nearly all of the aircrew left by the CO on the beach at 'Scorpion's Cove'. From there he spent a few weeks in a transit camp before leaving for Singapore. Many of the party continued to Japan where they worked in mines, but Milson with about 20 others were absorbed into the Singapore administration. The last six months he spent at a working camp just short of the causeway, in charge of a party of about 250 airmen.

I have already mentioned that Barry Paterson spent nearly three years of his confinement at Kuching. In October 1942, the draft was greeted by a Colonel Suga. The character in the TV series 'Tenko' was said to be based on him. His first words were: "I am Colonel Suga, Commanding Officer of all POW and internee camps in Borneo. All men will work, you will obey orders or be severely punished. I am a kindly man, so I will give you three days holiday, yesterday (when they were at sea), today (it was now 0930 in the evening) and to-morrow (Sunday, normally a non-working day). It was a speech which will stay with me till my grave".

Their job was to extend the runway at Kuching. No heavy equipment was available so all the work had to be done by hand. Another job was the manual lifting by about 50 POWs of a complete bungalow. Dysentry affected about 99% of the POWs at one time or another. It was also the cause of most deaths. Here the heat was so intense that putrifaction set in after twelve hours and it was essential that burial took place within twenty-four.

Later, many in the original draft were shipped to Kuching in North Borneo. Of about 2,600 who were drafted, less than 50 survived. In early 1945 those that had survived the normal rigours of POW life were taken on a forced march and those that dropped out through illness or exhaustion were bayonetted where they fell.

On 25 May, leaflets were dropped by American aircraft saying that the war in Europe was over and that resources would now be devoted to bringing the Pacific War to an early conclusion. Spirits rose rapidly when Australian aircraft bombed the radio station and shipping in the harbour but during that time rations were cut still further and more deaths resulted, 68 in May, 80 in June, 136 in July and by 15 August when the Pacific War ended, a further 200 had died. On 5 September, LAC Clement died, only a day before aircraft had dropped Red Cross food parcels and medical supplies. A further 50 died before the camp was actually relieved on 11 September. The same day, Colonel Suga attempted to commit suicide (not very well, for his batman finished it off for him). Later, documents were found stating that all POWs were to be executed on 15 September, POWs by machine-gun fire and internees by the injection of air into the blood.

Later Paterson and others were evacuated on the Australian hospital ship *Wonganella*. At the end of a short convalescence, he was flown to Singapore where he was given VIP treatment by No. 84 Squadron, now based at Seletar.

A short tribute was printed in the closing paragraphs of Plt Off McNally's statement. He writes: "During our imprisonment, the personnel of the Squadron acted in a manner which was of the highest merit. Throughout the whole of the period of brutality, shortage of food, etc, their conduct made me proud to be a member of 84 Squadron".

"The Squadron can always be proud of the men who were left behind in Java and can be assured that they acted in a manner expected of members of the British forces".

The relations of the many that died have my deepest sympathy and they can remember their loved ones as true soldiers of Britain.

Vengeance AP137, with Sqn Ldr Gill at the controls, over Ceylon, 29 May 1943

CHAPTER 14 - THE SCORPION RISES FROM THE ASHES

The *Yoma* arrived at Karachi on Monday, 16 April 1942, having left Batavia, Java on 20 February. It had been a slow voyage as the *Yoma* could only achieve 12 knots on one serviceable engine which was vibrating badly. Initially, the ship had been in convoy with nine others, escorted by HMS *Exeter* and two destroyers. After escorting the convoy through the Sunda Straits, the cruiser and destroyers had turned back and were later sunk by the Japanese fleet after the Battle of the Java Sea. Being so slow, the *Yoma* had to proceed independently after the other, faster ships had left her far behind.

After unloading some 20 tons of aircraft spares, ground equipment and several tons of anti-gas equipment, the Squadron personnel were moved by road to the RAF Depot at Drigh Road, Karachi. Arthur Gill who, as an acting flight lieutenant, had assumed command of the remnants of the Squadron, was attached to No.301 Maintenance Unit as a test pilot, flying various types, whilst all the other airmen were usefully employed in their various trades at the Depot. So as not to lose their identity, all officers, NCOs and airmen paraded as a unit each morning before marching off to work. Gill's next job was to ferry 12 Hurricanes to Burma and, in April, volunteers were called for to return to Egypt for the purpose of ferrying Blenheim IVs out to India. Travelling to Karachi by train, the crews boarded the Empire flying boat *Cameronian* on 24 April to fly to Cairo, where they landed on the 25th after a night stop at Sharjah. Whilst there, they were billeted on a houseboat on the River Nile. Returning to India on 29 May, the flight was interrupted for three days while searching for a Boston which was reported missing, arriving at Karachi on 6 June. Whilst in Cairo, Air Marshal Sir Arthur Tedder, the AOC-in-C Middle East, sent for Gill and talked to him for a long time about No.84's annihilation in the Far East and questioned him about his old friend AVM Pulford.

When Gill arrived back at Karachi, there was still doubts about the reforming of No.84 Squadron and talk about posting the remaining personnel to fill vacancies in other units. So he flew to Delhi to visit Air Command where he met the Commander-in-Chief, Air Chief Marshal Sir Richard Pierse and his staff. He argued that No.84 Squadron had never been disbanded since the First World War and that, as the spirit and morale of the officers and airmen was so high, the Squadron should be reformed and given new aircraft. Surprisingly, this was agreed and Gill returned jubilantly to Karachi with the good news. There was still the problem with the supply of aircraft. So it was decided that the Squadron should move from the heat of the Sind up to Quetta in the cool of the mountains for training.

ACM Sir Edgar Ludlow-Hewitt, the Inspector-General of the Royal Air Force, visited the Squadron on 30 May and stayed chatting for a long time about 84 Squadron's past, present and future. Next day, Flt Sgt Watkins, Sgt Dicks, Blackburn and Owen rejoined the Squadron from Australia, having escaped with Sqn Ldr T James and others by sea from Java.

The move to Quetta was delayed due to the derailing of trains and damage to the railway track by insurgents. In the meantime, four pilots and their navigators were attached to No.31 Squadron at Lahore to start a communications flight. A number of airmen were posted home to the UK, having served overseas for four years.

On 2 June, Plt Off Hayward, who had joined the RFC in 1916 and served with 84 Squadron in 1922, visited the Squadron and spent the evening talking about the good old days he had spent with the Squadron at Shaibah. Next day the main party under Plt Off G Maurice, navigator and adjutant, left by train for Quetta. As the decision had been made to equip the Squadron with American-built Vultee Vengeance dive-bombers, Gill stayed behind at Drigh road to meet the Vultee technical representatives who had arrived from America and to discuss the new aircraft and gather as much information and servicing manuals as possible.

Lt Gen HRH the Duke of Gloucester arrived at Karachi from the Middle East on 10 June on his tour of inspection. He was met by ACM Sir Richard Pierse and the Governor of the Sind and others. As far as RAF Drigh Road was concerned, the war stopped for two days whilst HRH inspected the Depot.

Arthur Gill, Plt Off 'Pop' Walker the assistant adjutant, and the airman who had stayed behind, left Karachi on the *Quetta Mail* on 20 June to rejoin the Squadron. On arrival at Quetta, the Squadron immediately embarked on an extensive training programme to prepare for the arrival of the new type of aircraft.

SNCO's Cricket Team, Quetta, October 1942
Back row: Woodward-Knight, unknown, Alan Sherrott, Ken
Owen, Tommy Farr, Len Hart, Chuck Fou'weather.
Front row: Norman Smith, Timber Woodhouse, Ken Lister,
Stan Owen.

Whereas the Blenheim had carried a crew of three, pilot, navigator/bomb aimer and wireless operator/air gunner, the new Vengeance was a two-seater with a pilot who flew the aircraft and aimed the bombs whilst in a vertical dive and a navigator/air gunner who, in addition to firing the twin 0.5" machine guns, also operated the radio in the rear cockpit. All the observers had to be trained as Wop/AGs in addition to their navigation training and all air gunners were trained to navigate.

After an early morning parade, all personnel spent the mornings in the six large lecture rooms at East Camp, the Squadron's base at Quetta. The afternoons were spent playing sports, with concerts, dances and other entertainments in the evenings. Airmen attending training lectures were encouraged to take their trade tests for promotion.

Activities included all forms of sport, football, hockey, tennis, cricket, swimming, polo and mountain climbing, with Fg Off 'Feef' French as the Squadron's sports officer. In addition, horse riding was available using Army remounts and a course was organised by Sgts Nourse and Winchester who, in civilian life in Australia were horse trainer and jockey respectively. Meetings were held regularly in Quetta and because of his previous experience, Nourse soon became involved, with Winchester riding against native jockeys who did not take kindly to his success. Sgt Artie Nourse had bought his own horse which by all accounts was called "Double Scotch" and rumour had it that the princely sum of 100 rupees (£7.50) had changed hands for it. All of the sergeants in the Mess were kept well informed of the horse's progress and advised not to bet on it until it was ready. Just before the Squadron left Quetta, they were advised that the time was ripe and by all accounts a satisfactory amount changed hands when the horse duly won. In the evenings, personnel took part in dramatics, a Squadron concert party and male voice choir under the guidance of Sgt Doug Morris (Wop/AG). In addition, target practise was held regularly when it was discovered that many of the NCOs and airmen had never fired a weapon of any description.

Initiation Ceremonies were re-introduced and all new arrivals were initiated by His Worship the Mayor of Shaibah, ably supported by the Lady Mayoress, the aldermen and 'Dapper Dan the Lavatory Man' who knew all the squadron gossip! Over the weeks, aircrew and the odd airman who had been held up in India and Burma by unserviceable aircraft or crashes when they were on the way to Sumatra, rejoined the Squadron. Amongst them were Plt Off John Goldfinch and Jimmy Hawke, Sgts Aubrey Pedler, Mike Roberts, Mike Morris, Sgt Jack Prentice and his crew, Sgts Engall and Thomas. By now the squadron strength had reached nearly 300.

After completing their training and taking their trade tests, the airmen started courses in first aid, fire-fighting and passive defence. Soon after holding a fire-fighting exercise at East Camp, the treasury at Quetta was burnt down by members of the Indian Congress Party. Two days later, a large wooden hut on the camp caught fire, which the duty picket extinguished within seven minutes. So much for practice!

Quetta had been very much an Army preserve and No.84 Squadron were the first 'boys in blue' to be stationed there since the big earthquake in 1935 when so much of the city had been destroyed.

In athletics and sports, the Squadron beat most of its competitors. In the Inter-Unit Athletic Championships held in September, the Squadron was beaten at the last moment by the 8th Gurkha Rifles, having led the field by the highest number of points.

With the increasing number of delays over the delivery of the new aircraft, a problem arose over occupying the airmen and preventing boredom. As regular route marches were unpopular, the Squadron Commander changed them to 'mountain expeditions'. With Fg Off Dan Mayger in charge, all personnel became very enthusiastic. When one party became lost in the foothills and did not return on time, the CO borrowed a Lysander and scoured the mountains and valleys until they were found, safe and unharmed but very hungry. On 16 August, a party under Colin Papps made an attempt to climb the 14,000-foot mountain Murdar Ghar. Unfortunately four of them, including Papps, had to retire, but the three remaining led by Jim Farrer reached the peak by 17.00 hours, signing their names and the squadron number on the topmost rocks.

When the weather turned cold, all ranks were issued with khaki battledress 'borrowed' unofficially from the Army garrison, as they had no blue uniforms. In August, Quetta was cut off from the outside world, except by air, as the railway line had been washed away in 32 places and with floods 14 miles wide on the plains, the worst since 1929. It was not until November that the trains were able to run again. In the meantime, Quetta became very short of food and other necessities. Fortunately, mail from home, always a morale booster, was flown in from Karachi.

On 10th and 11th October, the AOC-in-C, Sir Richard Pierse, visited the Squadron with Air Commodore Gray, AOC No.223 Group, together with Major General Christison, GOC Baluchistan. Later that month, Doug Morris presented the Squadron's Concert Parties Show 'Bombs Away' in the Recreation Hall at Quetta. To advertise, the CO showered the city with leaflets from a Lysander. On 21 October, the Viceroy of India, His Excellency the Marquess of Linlithgow, arrived at Samungli airfield in a Douglas DC-3 and was met by the CO. During the week the Viceroy and his party were in Quetta, they were told about 84 Squadron's excellent variety concert and, as a result, the concert party were asked to put on a Command Performance of 'Bombs Away' for the Viceroy and his party. The hall was again filled to capacity and the Viceroy expressed his grateful thanks to the Squadron for a most enjoyable and entertaining evening.

In view of the Viceroy's interest in 84 Squadron, he asked to visit the Squadron in its new home, White Barracks, a larger and more modern camp. Whilst there, he listened to a navigation lecture being given to navigators and air gunners. He must have been a good omen because, on 30 October, Gill was officially given the command of No.84 Squadron and promoted to Acting Squadron Leader. Ten days later 59 NCOs and airmen left Quetta for RAF Drigh Road on attachment to No.301 Maintenance Unit to help with the assembly of the new Vultee Vengeance aircraft which had arrived by sea from America.

Letters were received by the Squadron Commander from Air Commodore F J Vincent (CO No.84 Sqn 1927-28) and Air Commodore S F Vincent (CO No.84 Sqn 1933-35) then AOC No. 227 Group, later to become AOC No.221 Group in Burma, wishing the Squadron every success and good luck in the future.

On 14 November, the advance party of 17 airmen under Flt Lt John Goldfinch (Flight Commander) and Flt Lt D J Hawke (Navigation Leader) left Quetta by train for Vizagapatam, which was to become the Squadron's main base on the east coast of India. The main party, under Flt Lt Bryan Lilly, the Adjutant, left on 17 November. Fg Off E F French and a small servicing party under Sgt Amy stayed behind in Quetta to complete the repairs which the Squadron had undertaken to a Hudson which had crashed whilst trying to land on Quetta's small airfield.

Sqn Ldr A M Gill also stayed behind to visit Air Cdre F J Vincent, AOC No.225 Group, who was on a visit to HQ Baluchistan District. He then travelled by air and rail to Karachi on 19 November and flew the first of the Squadron's Vengeance I dive-bombers (AP917) on 22 November 1942. So started a new chapter in the history of No.84 Squadron.

From Karachi, Gill flew to Bombay with his new AOC, Air Cdre Phillip Mackworth. From there to the Base Personnel Office to try and obtain more airmen to bring the Squadron up to strength. From Bombay, he travelled to the Squadron's new base at Vizagapatam. Several of the pilots were attached to Cholavaram, Madras, to do the conversion course on the Vengeance. At Cholavaram, the Squadron were allocated a Harvard trainer so that it could give dual instruction and check out the Squadron's pilots who had not flown a single-engined or any other type for so long,

Three brand-new Vengeances lined up at Quetta in December 1942

prior to flying solo in the Vengeance.

At Vizagapatam, the Squadron moved into its new "basha" accommodation and motor transport and other equipment began to arrive. The only other memory of Vizagapatam was the need to cover one's plate when carrying one's food from the cookhouse to the messroom. Failure to do so resulted in the food being pinched by one of the dozens of kitehawks which hovered overhead and were ready to swoop whenever opportunity presented itself.

The CO and some of the aircrew travelled via Delhi to Karachi by train to collect the first six aircraft. From Karachi, Gill decided to return to Delhi to try to obtain more technical personnel as the Squadron had no technical officers and few SNCOs. He took off from Karachi on 24 December at 11.00 in a new Vengeance (AN900) with Sgt Ken Dicks as navigator and arrived at Jodhpur at 13.20. After refuelling, they took off for Delhi but, 75 miles away, the 1,600 hp Wright Cyclone engine cut out, due, they discovered later, to problems with the electrical fuel pumps in each tank. They managed to keep the engine firing by madly pumping petrol manually from the tanks to the engine by using the wobble-pump situated in the cockpit. They arrived back at Jodhpur 50 minutes later with aching arms and made a perfect landing.

After spending Christmas Day evening dining with His Highness the Maharajah of Jodhpur at his new palace (which had taken 14 years to build) followed by breakfast at 04.00, Gill returned to Karachi to collect the necessary spares. He later returned to Jodhpur flying a Blenheim I fighter. After further delays, the Vengeance was passed fit to fly on 30 December. Proceeding to Delhi, Gill called on Air Marshal Sir John Baker, Senior Air Staff Officer, South-East Asia Air Command and visited the personnel staff. Here he met Group Captain 'Sparrow' Lewis SPSO and explained his problem. "No engineer officer, armament officer, signals officer, insufficient senior technical NCOs and a shortage of skilled tradesmen". The Group Captain picked up a glass ball on his desk and gazed in it for several minutes. Suddenly he said "Ah! I see an engineer officer, two Flight Sgts and four Sergeants; here, you have it" and passed the ball to Gill. Although the Group Captain had obviously been out in the sun for too long, he was true to his word, for arriving back at Vizagapatam with the first of 84's Vengeances, a signal awaited him from HQ, posting to the Squadron one Fg Off John Ramsden, the new Engineer Officer, Flt Lt Geoff Cooper the new medical Officer and numerous other officers, NCOs and airmen who arrived at Vizag on 5 January 1943.

On 7 January, a large pack of Vengeance spares and other essential equipment arrived from No. 301 MU, followed by Fg Off George Pattinson, the new Equipment Officer, a Geordie from Tyneside who later proved to be of immense value to the Squadron during its training period and eventually when it went into action.

On 26 January, the Squadron's main party moved by train to Cholavaram airfield, Madras. Next day, the CO with Flt Lt Jimmy Hawke navigating, flew Vengeance AN900 from Vizag to Madras. They found the troop train between Ellore and Bezwada and 'beat it up' for ten minutes to relieve the airmen of their boredom.

It was at Cholavaram that Sgt Plt Ken Lister and his crew left No.84 Squadron after being with it since Mosul, July 1941. In letters to the author, Lister writes that he and his crew wished to keep together after all their experiences together. Coupled with this he stated that the Vengeance dive-bomber looked like an aircraft the Americans would be pleased to see the back off.

On 1 February, the CO was informed that the Squadron was to receive 16 new Vengeances, including the improved Mk II, from No.301 MU, Drigh Road, Karachi and were to hand over their existing Mk Is to Nos.45 and 82 Squadrons. However, due to numerous technical problems with Vengeances in the early days, such as faulty electrical fuel pumps and high oil consumption because, it was discovered, the engines had not been inhibited before they left America and were not fitted with air filters, it was not until 29 March that the new Mk IIs reached the Squadron. The petrol pump problem was eventually overcome by Acting Corporal Childs. 'Curly' Childs as he was known because he had only a few strands of hair on his head, was always in trouble. One day as he stood to attention on yet another charge the CO said to him "Childs,,I am fed up with you always appearing before me for first one charge then another misdemeanour, I have decided to promote you to Corporal. Case dismissed". Childs was marched out with a dazed expression on his face muttering to himself "The old man must be mad, or am I dreaming?". Childs later became one of the best Corporals in the Squadron. He set up his own test rig in the corner of the workshop, took every electric pump to pieces and found that the seals around the impeller shaft had failed, allowing the pump to flood with fuel and fail to operate. Childs substituted neoprene washers that he had acquired from somewhere and the Squadron had no further problems with pumps failing. The Squadron was blessed with unique and unusual characters like 'Curly' Childs who were the salt of the earth and kept the aircraft flying in appalling conditions of heat, dust, torrents of rain and

'A' Flight at Cholavarum

Back row: PO Farrer RAAF; PO Tonkin RAAF; three unknown; PO Nowland RAAF; Sgt Craighill.

Middle row: PO Owen, PO J Prentice, PO C Darling; PO F V Bird; FO R Davies; PO C Papps RNZAF; PO A Blackburn; WO Keech, two unknown.

Front row: PO D Morris; PO B Engall; PO N Bruce RAAF; Flt Lt J Hawke RAAF; Flt Lt J Goldfinch; Sqn Ldr A.M. Gill; FO G Plumb; PO A Padlar RAAF; PO B Winchester RAAF; unknown.

mud, with never a grumble.

Flying and ground training continued and new aircrew arrived. Wop/AGs completed their navigation training and all groundcrew tradesmen continued to take their trade tests. By the end of March, the Squadron were up to strength in personnel, some 450 officers and airmen, and had received 12 of its establishment of 16 new aircraft.

Intelligence reports indicated that the Japanese were about to launch a seaborne attack on Ceylon. So on 19 April 1943, the Squadron moved to Ratmalana airfield, south of Colombo, Ceylon, to await the arrival of the Japanese fleet. The Squadron was now fully operational and raring to go. Training continued with vertical (85-90 degrees) bombing attacks from 12,000 feet on Gonagala Rock, half a mile from the shore, using 20-lb live practice bombs and live 250-lb bombs. New tactics were tried out from both high and low level, which the Squadron had to devise for themselves. No manuals existed and dive-bombing was unknown to the Royal Air Force at that time as it had been ruled out by the Air Ministry before the war. Formation flying in close flights of three aircraft stepped down were practised, which was the best form of defence against Japanese fighters. Practice attacks were carried out against shipping and Royal Navy warships, including the cruisers *Sussex*, *Newcastle* and *Kenya*, and 'attacks' made on harbour installations, oil refineries and other 'targets' and airfields on the islands. Attacks using live ammunition were also undertaken using the pilot's front wing guns and the gunner's rear twin Brownings.

After one such flight, the navigation leader, Flt Lt Jimmy Hawke, who flew as the squadron commander's navigator, said: "I could smell smoke during that low-level attack on that oil refinery. I thought my radio was on fire until I looked back and saw the smoke from the chimney we had just passed".

The Squadron lost two aircraft in Ceylon, the first when the propeller fell off Colin Papp's aircraft, resulting in a skillful landing on a tiny strip of land on the edge of the water. The second was when "Kiwi" Tonkin flew straight through the top of a large palm tree with Ray Hedley, medical orderly, as passenger. The Vengeance, being an extremely tough aircraft, made it back to base and landed safely.

In his spare time, Sqn Ldr Gill wrote a training syllabus with new dive-bombing tactics which the squadron had devised by trial and error. It was later published by Group Headquarters for circulation to other dive-bomber squadrons.

Air Marshal Sir Guy Garrod, Deputy AOC-in-C SE Asia Air Command, and AVM Lees, AOC Ceylon visited the Squadron on 10 July to discuss the work and problems. The Squadron Commander appealed to the Air Marshal that if the Japanese had changed their plans, could 84 be sent north into battle, instead of sitting around in Ceylon, training and swimming? The Air Marshal pointed out that flights of ten aircraft from the Squadron had flown to Yelahanka (Bangalore) the previous month on exercises but he would talk to the C-in-C to see what could be done.

The Air Marshal kept his word and the Squadron left Ceylon, by air and sea, for Ranchi in Bihar State, Northern India, on or about 18 August. The main party sailed from Colombo aboard the *Varela* to Calcutta and then by rail to Ranchi whilst the aircraft flew via Madras and Vizag. Sqn Ldr Gill flew to Dum Dum in order to visit the staffs of HQ No.221 Group and to meet the AOC AVM Williams and Air Cdre Rowley. On arrival at Ranchi, which was a large Army base and training area for XV Corps, a stream of senior Army officers asked to visit the RAF station to see and talk about the RAF's new dive-bomber. Many had experienced the Stuka in Europe, but no one had heard of the Vultee Vengeance before! Several flew with the Station Commander, including General Sir William Slim (later to become Field Marshal Viscount Slim) and HE Sir Thomas Rutherford, Governor of Bihar.

The officers of XV Corps were very keen to see the results of our bombing and whether or not 84 Squadron were as good as they claimed to be. In the past, they had not been well supported by the RAF and had little faith in their abilities. This was due to shortage of suitable aircraft at the time and the wrong use of the types available. Here at last was an aircraft which the RAF claimed was ideal for the close support of the army. The CO therefore suggested that the Squadron would be pleased to give the officers of XV Corps a demonstration of the Vengeance fire-power and accuracy. It was agreed that the Army would construct Japanese style bunker positions, at which they were very good, and trenches

Vengeances awaiting delivery at Drigh Road; AN796 in the foreground saw service with No. 84 Squadron

and pill boxes and fill them with dummies. Sites were selected on the Piska and Kunti ranges. Despite very wet weather, Vengeances were able to bomb the targets with 500-lb bombs and the Army were suitably impressed. Sadly, during one of these tactical exercises, the Army killed two of their own soldiers and injured another five with their own gunfire. Thankfully, all of 84's bombs landed in the target area except for one pilot who dropped his bombs 80 yards from the bunkers and forgot to 'arm' them, so they did not explode! But that is all part of the training.

At this time, the Squadron had a surprise visit by Mr Fenwick, the President of Vultee Aircraft Corporation of America, who was anxious to learn what the Squadron thought of his aircraft. The pilots and groundcrews were able to tell him a few home truths but also assured him that they liked the aircraft as a good, stable and very strong dive-bomber.

The Squadron had to find a suitable area and mark out its own bombing range nearer the airfield, where it could practice vertical dive-bombing daily from 10,000 to 12,000 feet. The gunnery leader and the CO spent some time searching the locality for a safe area and then marked out the target and quadrants. After the Squadron Commander had successfully bombed the new target on 20 September from 12,000 feet, WO Wacher RNZAF and Flt Sgt Goodfellow RNZAF also dived from 12,000 feet but failed to pull out the dive. The aircraft disintegrated and both crew members died instantly. This was the Squadron's first fatal accident with the Vengeance. They were buried next morning in Ranchi Military Cemetery and the impressive military funeral was attended by all officers and aircrew.

The actual cause of the accident was never discovered but experiments and practice in the techniques of dive-bombing continued until each pilot was able to achieve direct hits on the target. The early Vengeance was equipped with a telescopic sight mounted on the nacelle above the instrument panel. It was soon discovered that, with the pilot's eye firmly 'glued' to the rubber eyepiece on the sight, he had absolutely no idea what height he had descended to in the dive. Bearing in mind that the aircraft was diving at several thousand feet per minute, it did not take very long before he reached a height too low to pull out! It was discovered that the safe height at which to start to pull out a vertical dive after releasing the bombs was 3,000 to 3,500 feet, with 2,500 the absolute minimum. Even then, the pilot would be pulling 7g during

the pull-out. For the uninitiated, this was equivalent to seven times the acceleration of gravity or, in other words, the weight of the pilot, whose normal weight was 200 lbs would be 1,400 lb in his seat. As 'G-suits' had not been invented, the crew had to be exceptionally fit to withstand the strain on the body and not 'black-out' at that point. Both the pilot and, more so, the poor gunner in the rear cockpit almost invariably 'greyed-out' momentarily until the aircraft had levelled out at 450 mph. The speed was very useful later on in Burma when live bullets and ack-ack shells were filling the sky over the target area. It was extremely difficult for the enemy to hit a Vengeance either in a dive or as it pulled out and quickly disappeared from sight. The telescopic sight was therefore discarded and instead a 2-inch yellow line was painted along the engine nacelle from the centre of the armour-plated glass windscreen to the nose of the aircraft. This was a far better sight, simple as it was, and as the pilot picked out the target immediately he entered the dive, he was able to judge any lateral or longitudinal drift of the aircraft and correct it. As soon as the target appeared to be sitting steadily on the top of his nacelle, the pilot would be able to judge his height from the ground and release his 1,500 lbs of bombs in a salvo or individually in a 'stick' at about 4,000 feet.

No. 84 Squadron was now part of No. 221 Group, the Headquarters of which was now in Calcutta. The Air Officer Commanding at that time was Air Cdre H V Rowley, who frequently visited the Squadron at Ranchi. He would arrive in the circuit unexpectedly in his Hurricane using the callsign "Bullshit Zero". The duty pilot in the control tower would immediately ring the CO, if available, who would have to race down to the dispersal and greet the AOC before he had time to climb out of his aircraft. The AOC was a great cat-lover. Whenever Sqn Ldr Gill visited Group Headquarters, he would call on the AOC if he wanted approval, for example, to take the Squadron on a training exercise or change any standing orders. The AOC would never give an immediate reply but would turn to his cat dozing contentedly on a rug and say "What do you think, Cat?" This was a very serious moment and one would never smile but patiently wait until the AOC said "Cat says yes!" If the cat said "No", it was pointless arguing with it, because it had made up its mind and that was final. Many amusing stories could be told about this likable but, sometimes, very odd Air Officer but certainly not in print.

On 25 November, Air Cdre Rowley flew into Ranchi with the

74

news that 84 Squadron had been specially selected to support General Orde Wingate's Long Distance Penetration Group (known as 3 Indian Division). The Squadron Commander was informed in the strictest secrecy that General Wingate's columns were to be dropped far behind the Japanese lines in north Burma and, as they would be unable to take in heavy artillery, they would need the support of accurate dive-bombers with sufficient range to reach the targets that they would be given. Wingate's LRPG was then training at Gwalior in Central India and 84 Squadron were to move to a large unused airfield called Maharajpur.

At that time it was planned that the Squadron would move to the Arakan and operate from Chittagong against the Japanese. An advance party was in fact sent to Chittagong to prepare for the Squadron's arrival and had brought a large number of hens for the airmens' Christmas dinner! But the rains came and the airfield was under water so the advance party was recalled.

Next day, 26 November, the CO with Flt Lt Jimmy Hawke, flew to Maharajpur to inspect the airfield and its accomodation. It was a very good airfield with a 2,000-yard concrete runway and with good brick-built accommodation. On 30 November, Lord Louis Mountbatten landed at Ranchi in his Skymaster transport, accompanied by Madame Chiang, wife of the Chinese Leader Generalissimo Chiang Kai-Shek, where they were met by the Station Commander.

The move of the Squadron started on 6 December and training with 3 Indian Division began immediately. Major Purcell was appointed ALO (Air Liaison Officer) and moved into the Officers' Mess to work with the Squadron. He proved to be of the greatest assistance to the Squadron, arranging exercises and demonstrations and ironing out problems as they arose.

Sqn Ldr Gill met General Wingate at his Force headquarters and had frequent discussions on the tactics they were to adopt. The General had watched the Squadron's accurate bombing, which was not what the Army had previously experienced. The General asked "If the Commander of each column sent the map reference of the target he wanted bombed, could 84 guarantee to destroy it?" Gill tried to explain that from 12,000 feet the ground looked flat. If the target could be identified by a feature, such as a village or a river bend, he would have no problems finding it from a map reference. But if the target was hidden in dense jungle in which the LRPG was operating, it would be impossible to find it. Gill suggested that if the soldiers could identify the targets by firing smoke mortar bombs on to it, the dive-bombers could accurately bomb the smoke. Wingate argued it would entail each column would have to carry smoke grenades or mortar bombs instead of live ammunition. Gill replied that he would only require two smoke bombs, one at each end of the target area, at the appointed TOT (time over target), to be able to identify the target and to bomb it.

Wingate replied: "But what if the Japs use smoke too and lob it on to my troops?" To which Gill suggested "Then use coloured smoke or, if that will not be available, use a pre-determined pattern such as a triangle or square using three or four bombs. If your troops can identify the target accurately at the right time we are due over the target, we will be able to bomb it accurately". The General agreed. It was tried out successfully at Gwalior and adopted later in Burma.

On 13 December, the CO flew to Delhi to visit Air Marshal Sir John Baker at HQ SEAAC. Here he learned that 84 Squadron were to be re-equipped with the Mosquito FB.VI - just as the squadron were all ready to go into action against the Japanese forces in Burma! Gill was both pleased that the squadron would be able to fly the world-famous Mosquito and sad that, after all the sweat and long hours spent in mastering a 5-ton brute of an aircraft, they were not to be permitted to fly the Vengeance on actual offensive operations. Whilst in Delhi, Gill called on Air Cdre F R Mellersh (an No.84 old boy from the Shaibah years) to give him the latest news of the Squadron.

On 20 December, Arthur Gill and Ken Dicks flew from Maharajpur to Ranchi to collect Christmas fare for the Squadron. They returned on the 22nd in Vengeance EZ875 which could barely stagger off the ground, it was so full of 'Booze'! The bomb-bay and every spare foot of space was taken up by drink and other 'goodies'!

The following day, the Squadron Commander addressed a conference of 400 officers of 3 Indian Division, including General Wingate and General Symes and the GOC Central India Command, at Force Headquarters on the Vultee Vengeance dive-bomber - its capabilities and its limitations, its range and its choice of bomb load. The audience were well aware of its accuracy, which had become legendary, and were full of praise and great expectations. After the conference, Gill broke the news to General Wingate that

the Squadron was to be re-equipped with the Mosquito fighter-bomber. General Wingate was stunned, but said very little.

Christmas was celebrated in true 84 Squadron style. After 08.30 Holy Communion, followed by breakfast, the officers in fancy dress played football against the 'rest'. No-one can remember who won, not even what the score was! The senior NCOs visited the Officers' Mess for drinks before lunch. The officers then served the airmen's Christmas dinner with all the trimmings at 15.00 hours, after which photographs of all the Squadron personnel were taken. An Indian acrobat entertained the airmen, after which a camp-fire 'sing-song' was held during the evening. A good day was had by all! During the Christmas period the Squadron's male voice choir was invited to sing in Gwalior cathedral. The late Hugh Lowe recalls in letters that this was one of the highlights of his time in the Far East.

In the Squadron's Christmas magazine published in December 1943, there appeared the following forward by the Commanding Officer.

"There have been many changes in the personnel during the past year and I take this opportunity to welcome all those members who have joined the Squadron and to wish all those that have left us good luck in their new work. The Squadron has been highly honoured by the award of 'The Standard' by His Majesty King George VI, the Squadron having served nearly 27 years in the RFC and RAF. The enthusiasm and spirit of all ranks during the past year have been most gratifying and I rely on you all to continue to work hard with me for the success of the Squadron.

Signed A M Gill, Sqn Commander.

In the first week of January 1944, more dive-bombing demonstrations were laid on for the Army on their range at Jhansi, each aircraft dropping 1,000 lb of bombs. This was followed by Exercise 'Enterprise' when every crew did two sorties. The aircraft also shot-up the local Indian bazaar during a full scale ARP demonstration laid on by the local authority. On 8 January, Sqn Ldr Gill flew to Lalitpur to visit General Symes and Brigadier Brodie and also to visit the Americans, the 5307 Provisional Unit, known as the Air Commandos, under the command of Colonel Philip Cochran, who had achieved fame in the USA by the strip cartoon which traced the adventures of 'Flip Corkin'! Initially Cochran did not get on with Wingate; they had little in common except courage and a remarkable war record. Cochran was full of fun and never took himself seriously whereas Wingate was a very serious, studious man who seldom smiled and who appeared to be a very lonely man and a deep thinker. During these months, Gill met Wingate many times and came to know him remarkably well. Wingate was a very determined single-minded man who did not suffer fools gladly. He knew little about the RAF or its tactics yet he controlled his columns in the jungle by wireless in a similar way an air commander would control his fighters by radio control in the air. Although he seldom smiled, Gill discovered that deep down, he had a keen sense of humour.

On 13 January, the Supreme Allied Commander, South-East Asia Command, Admiral Lord Louis Mountbatten, and General Wingate visited the Squadron by air at short notice. They were met by Sqn Ldr Gill, who introduced all the officers to them. After speaking to every officer, 'Lord Louie', as he was affectionately called, stood on two tool boxes (which he promptly fell off!) and addressed all the NCOs and airmen who had been formed up on the airfield. After the 'Supremo' had departed, General Wingate had tea in the Officers' Mess. He was later driven back to his Headquarters, which were in the Gwalior Hotel. Next evening, General Wingate visited the Squadron again at the invitation of the Squadron Commander and dined in the mess with the officers.

On 16 January, Gill was summoned to HQ SEAC for a conference with the AOC-in-C ACM Sir Richard Pierse, the Senior Air Staff Officer, Air Marshal John Baker and General Wingate concerning the Squadron's future role. Gill was informed that, when speaking to the Supreme Commander a few days earlier, General Wingate had specifically asked if 84 Squadron's re-equipment with the Mosquito could be postponed so that the Squadron could go into battle with the Special Forces when they flew into Burma. Gill's views were sought before the AOC-in-C finally decided. Gill made it clear that the Squadron was raring to have another go at the Japs and was quite happy to wait to re-arm with the Mosquito at some future date.

A few days later a letter was received by the Squadron Commander:

"I am writing to thank you for the excellent arrangements you made at such short notice for my visit to 84 Squadron.

Vengeance AP137 over Ratmalana in May 1943

I was so impressed by the bearing and enthusiasm of your officers and men and by your own desire to get back into action as soon as possible that I immediately took up the problem of your Squadron's future with the Air Commander-in-Chief. Bearing in mind that General Wingate had formed such a high opinion of 84 Squadron and was so anxious to have you with him, I pressed Sir Richard Pierse to let you go forward into the battle and I know that you will be glad to know that he has agreed. I appreciate that there will be some disappointment in losing your turn for re-equipment, but on the other hand you will get a really worth-while battle much earlier this way and you will always get on to a new type of aircraft a bit later on.

Personally I think that 84 Squadron is going to make history with the Long Range Penetration Brigades and I send you all my best wishes for success.

Signed, Louis Mountbatten.

So thanks to Major-General Orde Wingate DSO and two Bars, intervening at a crucial moment, 84 Squadron was able to take part in a vital battle against the Japanese forces in Burma, which proved to be a turning point in the long war against Japan.

AND THE ACTION

On 11 February 1944, No.84 Squadron arrived at Kumbhirgram in Assam and joined No.168 Wing, commanded by Group Captain E A 'Titch' Whiteley DFC. This new airfield had been hacked out of a tea plantation, using elephants and native labour to construct a 2,000-yard all-weather runway. Initially the Squadron was accommodated under canvas but new basha huts were completed soon after arrival and housed the Squadron officer's mess, sergeant's mess, airmen's mess and billets, as well as Station Headquarters, sick quarters, technical flights, equipment section and stores.

The Squadron was completely self-contained, with an establishment of 16 Vengeance II dive-bombers in two flights, 'A' Flight under the command of Flt Lt John Goldfinch RAAF and 'B' Flight under Flt Lt Dick Johns RNZAF. The Squadron Head-quarters was under the command of Flt Lt Bryan Lilly, the Adjutant, together with the intelligence and cypher sections. Fg Off John Ramsden, the Engineer Officer was responsible for all first- and second-line servicing, the Armament Flight and the MT Section. The Squadron had its own Signals Flight under Plt Off E J McKie and a large equipment section. In addition, the Squadron had its own Medical Officer, Flt Lt Geoffrey Cooper and medical

staff. The strength of the Squadron totalled some 450 personnel made up of seven nationalities. Counting the English, Welsh, Scots and Irish as one, the Squadron also had Australians, New Zealanders, Rhodesians, Canadians, French Canadians and an American.

The Squadron quickly settled in and was operational within days. On 14 February, Sqn Ldr Arthur Gill with his navigator, Flt Lt Jimmy Hawke RAAF, flew over the mountains and deep jungle which separated Assam from the fertile Imphal valley at Manipur, a flight which they were to do so many, many times during the next few months - to visit Headquarters No.221 Group at Imphal and call on the new Air Officer Commanding, Air Cdre Stanley F Vincent DFC AFC, who had taken over from that very odd AOC - Air Cdre H V Rowley on 7 February. Gill received a very warm welcome from the AOC, who had himself commanded 84 Squadron at Shaibah from 1933-35. Arthur Gill then visited the Headquarters of the 'Special Force', 3 Indian Division, at Imphal for a meeting with Orde Wingate to discuss his plan to fly the brigades deep into Burma behind enemy lines to attack the Japanese from the rear. General Wingate wanted Gill's assurance that his dive-bombers would be able to reach the furthest enemy targets.

The first operational mission took place on 16 February when 14 Vengeances dive-bombed Japanese positions in Burma. This was the start of 84 Squadron's most successful campaign in its long history and lasted without a break for over five months. During this period, operational missions were frequently undertaken two and sometimes three times a day. The number of aircraft flown on each mission was normally twelve Vengeances, with four held as reserves or being serviced. On occasions, six aircraft of one flight would attack one target while six aircraft of the other flight would bomb a different target. To destroy a bridge, it would be necessary to send only three aircraft, such was their accuracy. The type of formation used was invariably in 'Vics' of three aircraft stepped down, the second, third and fourth flights tucked in behind and under the one in front. This formation was reasonably easy to maintain and less tiring on long flights and gave the best protection from possible Japanese fighters.

Although each Vengeance could carry 2,000 lbs of bombs, the normal load consisted of two 500-lb carried internally and two 250-lb carried under the wings. The type of bomb carried on each mission varied according to the target being attacked. For example, against troop concentrations and Japanese-occupied villages, transport and airfields, the load would consist of two 500-lb high-explosive (HE) bombs and two 250-lb (HE) general purpose bombs, sometimes fitted with nose rods and instantaneous fuses. Against deep bunkers, the construction of which the Japanese were experts, delayed-action high explosive bombs would be used to achieve penetration. Against supply dumps and buildings containing stores, a mixed load of high explosive and incendiary bombs (250-lb and 30-lb clusters) would be used. Against bridges, instantaneous fused and long-delay fused bombs would be used, which would continue to explode up to seven days after the attack in order to make the task of rebuilding difficult. It would have been amusing to see the faces of the Japanese engineers who, having just completed the rebuilding of a bridge, would see it blow up again without a single aircraft in sight.

The sixth and twelfth aircraft carried F.24 cameras which were switched on by the pilot just before he peeled off into the dive and automatically recorded the leader's bomb strike and the accuracy of the other pilots, except for the last two aircraft. On returning to base, the photographers would rush the film to their mobile caravan and process the films in time for the de-briefing of the aircrews. Copies were then flown to No.221 Group Operations Room for analysis and recording and for a decision as to whether another strike would be necessary, depending on the type of target.

By careful attention to engine handling during the climb over the mountains en route to the target and during the cruise at 10,000-12,000 feet, 84 Squadron were able to accept targets deep into Burma almost half as far again as any of the other Vengeance squadrons. As a result, the Squadron was seldom given any fighter cover, even when sweeps by 40-plus Japanese 'Oscar' fighters were made to within 30 miles of Kumbhirgram. Some of 84 Squadron's missions in support of General Wingate's brigades were of over three hours duration and the Hurricanes and Spitfires had insufficient range, even when fitted with long-range fuel tanks. On these long flights, all pilots were briefed to check their fuel state as they approached the Imphal Plain on the return flight in order to divert to Tulihal or one of the other forward airfields to refuel, if necessary.

On 4 March, the Squadron suffered its first operational casualty. The Squadron was carrying out its second attack that day on a concealed Japanese camp in the jungle west of Kontha. Direct hits were made on the target but, during the 90-degree dive, the aircraft flown by Warrant Officer 'Curly' Keech, an American who had joined the RAF, with Warrant Officer E R Watkins as his navigator, was seen to explode. It was never established whether the aircraft was hit by anti-aircraft gun fire which was seen to be hosing up from the ground, or whether one of the 500-lb bombs failed to clear the aircraft as it was released during the dive. The internal bombs were thrown clear of the aircraft by two pronged forks or crutches fitted in the bomb-bay to which the bombs were attached. These swung out so that the bombs cleared the propeller when the aircraft was in a vertical dive.

The next day, 5 March, the first Chindits of 77 Brigade, one of General Wingate's Long Range Penetration Groups, were flown into Burma by glider from Lalaghat to 'Broadway', a jungle clearing to the west of the River Irrawaddy. At the last moment, just before take-off, it had been discovered from a last-minute photo-reconnaissance flight that 'Piccadilly', the main landing ground, had been covered with teak logs laid in rows by the Japanese. This turned out to be simply a logging operation and did not mean that the Japanese knew of the intended landing. "Operation Thursday", which Wingate had planned for so long, had begun. The first wave was followed by more brigades and, in six days, 9,052 men, 175 ponies and 1,183 mules and 509,082 lbs of stores were transported by air to 'Broadway', 'Aberdeen' and 'Chowringee' in Burma. In addition, another 2,000 men of 16 Brigade made their way on foot with their equipment through the jungle to join up with the others at 'Aberdeen'. No.84 Squadron was immediately switched from supporting units of the 14th Army to bombing Japanese targets in support of the Chindits.

Phase Two of General Hanayoa's massive Japanese land offensive began on 8 March 1944 when over 100,000 well-trained and well-equipped Japanese troops crossed the River Chindwin from Burma into India, with Delhi as their ultimate target. Two thrusts were made against Imphal, the Allies' advanced base for the central front, by the 15th Japanese Division under the command of Lieut-General Yamauchi and the 33rd Japanese Division under Lieut-General Yanagida, with their supporting mountain artillery, engineers, signals, transport, field hospitals etc. To the north, the 31st Japanese Division, commanded by Lieut-General Sato, moved quickly east and cut the vital British road communications between the railhead at Dimapur in Assam and Kohima, a small garrison town in the Naga hills, and Imphal, the HQ of the British 14th Army to the south of Manipur. Further south, the Imphal - Tiddim road was cut by the Japanese, trapping 17 Indian Division at Tiddim. To the north, Ukhrul had to be abandoned by 23 Indian

Division after a fierce and gallant action against stronger Japanese forces.

The Japanese Air Force was now very active and, on 8th and 9th March, 46 Japanese aircraft were destroyed in the air and on the ground by our fighters. On the 11th, another 31 was destroyed or damaged. Strikes were now being made by 84 Squadron once or twice a day against Japanese troop concentrations, occupied villages, road blocks, Japanese HQs, supply dumps, tanks and armoured fighting vehicles, supply lines and bridges. A secret cypher message was received by the Squadron from Nos. 2 and 3 Vic Force operations saying: "Sincere thanks to all personnel for prompt action and co-operation taken on all demands for support". This was the first of many 'strawberries' received by 84 Squadron during the next few months.

The Squadron had settled down to a strenuous, regular routine. The aircrew and duty groundcrews were awakened at 04.15 daily, followed by breakfast and briefing at 05.00 hours, in order that the aircraft could be off the ground on their first mission soon after dawn. As the formation would be flying east directly into the brilliant morning sun, the leader usually had to fly on instruments to maintain a steady course and not weave all over the sky, making it difficult for those behind him. After the first mission, lasting maybe two hours or longer, the aircraft would be re-armed and refuelled, which took less than an hour, and would be off again on another strike. On occasions this would be followed by a third mission. There would be no Sundays off-duty for the weeks and months that followed. The Squadron worked round the clock and seven days a week. Crews would be rested in rotation whenever possible, every third day or so. But they were all young and fit, despite the poor food, such as dehydrated cabbage and potatoes, powdered eggs and 'bully mutton' which could be poured out from the tin in the heat. Practically everything was tinned or dehydrated, except pumpkins and sausages made from soya flour! But there was plenty of tea, with powdered milk and the bars were well stocked! However the squadron did at least have enough to eat, unlike their brethren who had been left behind in the Far East and were now Japanese prisoners-of-war.

The big difference between this campaign and the last campaign in which 84 had fought in Sumatra and Java was that the Squadron had an AOC, Air Cdre Stanley Vincent, who was 'on the ball' and knew exactly what he was doing, alongside the Army Commander, General Sir William Slim. There were good communications between the Squadron, the Operations Room at No.221 Group and the Army, both at their HQ and on the ground in the field. The Squadron was flying a far superior aircraft, with better armament and a heavier bomb load. Although the targets were different and far more difficult to find, the navigators, especially Jimmy Hawke, the Navigation Leader, were highly skilled and were able to navigate the formations of aircraft right up to the target. The Squadron Commander seemed to develop a knack of memorising the target to be attacked by studying the topography of the area from maps and photo-reconnaissance photographs, when available, and he was able to pick out the tiny target from 10,000 or 12,000 feet during the few moments his aircraft had rolled on its back before entering the dive. Each pilot was then able to choose his own aiming point after following the leader down, thereby saturating the target with bombs.

Another very important factor in this war against the Japanese, compared with the earlier Far East fiasco, was that we had the outstandingly successful Supreme Commander who, because he was a showman, we all knew. Lord Louis (later to become Admiral Earl Mountbatten of Burma) inspired the 'Forgotten Army' - the 14th Army - with the will to win by proving that the Japanese was not the superman everyone had previously thought him to be. Lord Louis was a leader in every sense of the word and, by his understanding of the 'common soldier' and his problems, earned the respect and dedication of every man who served under him.

Back in Burma, during the first two weeks of March, 336 sorties were flown by Japanese fighters and bombers over the N Burma front. On 12 March, the Japanese bombed 84 Squadron's airfield for the second time in a sneak attack between 05.00 and 05.07, in an attempt to pre-empt the dive-bombers' early morning take-off. Three Japanese aircraft, believed to be "Sally" twin-engined bombers, came in from the south in a shallow dive from 10,000 feet. The weather was fine, with no cloud and a full moon. The aircraft dropped twelve 30-kg GP bombs, with one 50-kg bomb and nine 30-kg high-explosive bombs, killing six civilians and injuring another thirty-eight. One of 84's Vengeances was damaged by burning camouflage netting falling on to it in the dispersal pen and three aircraft of No.110 Squadron received minor damage.

Spitfire VC MA290 The Looker *used for reconnaissance by No. 84 Squadron at Kumbhirgram*

Two basha huts containing engine and airframe spares were completely destroyed. The AA guns opened fire but failed to hit the raiders. By the end of March, 119 enemy aircraft had been accounted for.

On 21 March, the following signal was received by 84 Squadron from the Brigade Major of 17 Division which was trapped in Tiddim: "Your bombing 300 yards from our own troops on smoke indicator [at] Mile 99 Tiddim Road excellent".

On 4 April, the Japanese besieged Kohima, where a small garrison of some 2,000 British and Indian second-line and administrative troops, including a battalion of the West Kents and personnel convalescing after malaria and other tropical diseases, were stationed. The Japanese quickly dug themselves into deep bunker positions in the commanding hillsides and over-ran part of the town. Very soon the defenders were at the limit of their endurance, short of water, food, ammunition and medical supplies. No. 84 Squadron dive-bombers were immediately switched into attacking the Japanese bunkers, roadblocks and supply columns, together with No. 34 Squadron's Hurricane fighter-bombers whilst No. 31 Squadron's Dakota transports were daily supplying the hard-pressed troops at Kohima with their necessities.

Whilst the Battle for Kohima was being fought, 84 Squadron was still expected to attack the enemy on other fronts, in such locations as Tiddim and Homalin, which the Japanese had occupied and where they had a large headquarters and supply dumps, in villages high up in the mountains at 8,000 feet, at Thangdut east of the River Chindwin and the Japanese occupied airfield at Tamu where they had a very large supply base.

It was during this very busy period that the Squadron received the news that General Wingate had been killed when the USAAF B-25 in which he was returning to base had flown into a mountain in bad weather. This was a great loss to the Allies and a personal loss to members of 84 Squadron, of whom the General had gained such a high regard. Major-General W D A Lentaigne assumed command of the Chindits.

The weather continued to deteriorate and difficulty was sometimes experienced in locating the targets. On one occasion, Arthur Gill remembers having to lead a formation of 12 dive-bombers through a 'tunnel' formed by a valley in the mountains covered by dense cloud, an eerie experience as it was so dark. Almost without exception the Squadron found its targets and was able to bomb successfully. It was for this reason that No. 84 was selected to lead the other dive-bomber squadrons whenever a 'maximum effort' strike was demanded.

It was during one of these difficult flights on 6 April that 'B' Flight, led by Flt Lt Dick Johns with Fg Off Ken Dicks as his

navigator, unwittingly flew into a large cumulo-nimbus thunder cloud with its tremendous up-currents. The flight of six aircraft were thrown all over the sky whilst still in cloud. Miraculously none of the aircraft collided but one of the gunners, Plt Off Ron Gabrielson, found himself half-way out of his cockpit, hanging upside-down. He was unable to climb back into the aircraft but just managed to reach the quick-release clip on his belt and fell away from the aircraft. Fortunately he had removed his chest parachute from the stowage rack and had clipped it on to his harness as the flight had been so turbulent. His parachute deployed immediately and, soon afterwards, he hit the ground in a valley with hills on either side and landed in a bamboo thicket. Naga head-hunters found him and led him back to their village. Here he was greeted by a heavily-armed Miss Ursula Bower, known to the Nagas as the 'White Princess', who manned a secret observation post in the hills reporting any Japanese movements in the area by wireless to British Intelligence. After being fed and given an escort, Ron Gabrielson set off on his long journey by foot and later by train and road back to the Squadron. Six days later, much to everyone's surprise, he walked into the CO's office at Kumbhirgram, saluted and said "Reporting for duty, Sir". Gabrielson was even more surprised to discover that his aircraft, flown by Plt Off B Finnie RCAF, and four of the others had returned safely to base. Unfortunately, Sgt F R Dyer's aircraft had crashed in the mountains. He had suffered head injuries and his gunner Flt Sgt Reg Russell had both his arms broken. Fortunately, both survived; it was their 22nd mission.

Sqn Ldr A M Gill in the cockpit of MA290

An urgent signal was received on 8 April from the LRPG's column at Mawlu on the River Irrawaddy. A strong Japanese force had dug itself in, in deep bunkers, overlooking the British landing ground and had pinned the Chindits down. Twelve Vengeances led by Gill flew the 450 miles and, after talking to the ground forces by radio, bombed their smoke indicators. 18,000 lbs of bombs were dropped, using .025- and 11-second delay fuses, slap on the target. On their arrival back at base, the Squadron Commander received a signal from the Chindit commander stating that the bunkers had been totally destroyed and 265 dead Japs had been counted. On 11 April, during the siege of Imphal in which No.84 was fully committed, Fg Off Ken Dicks completed his 100th operational sortie with 84 Squadron, having flown with Wg Cdr Bill Russell in Greece, in the Middle East, the Far East and now in Burma (having previously completed seven sorties over Europe with Bill Russell). That day, 20-plus Japanese 'Oscars' and medium bombers attacked the bridge over the river on the Imphal to Silchar track but failed to breach it.

Despite the appalling weather, with continuous heavy rain and low clouds, the Squadron attacked the Japanese besieging Kohima on numerous occasions, often bombing within yards of our own troops who were dug in inside the town. On the 15th, an urgent request for help from IV Corps to attack a large Japanese force dug in on a ridge south of Sagolmang, 10 miles NE of Imphal. Gill led 24 Vengeances from Nos.84 and 110 Squadrons which dropped 36,000 lb of HE bombs. A report was received next day stating that the Gurkhas went in immediately after the bombing and occupied the whole area with very little opposition. 450 dead Japs were counted and many more were never found.

Following a strike on the 17th, Sgt L T Hamlyn crashed on landing due to engine failure. He was unharmed but his navigator, Sgt R H Bovill received slight head injuries. That day a message was received from No.23 Air Support Control stated: "Your bombing this morning TOT (time over target) 09.40. Ground forces report your bombing a bull's eye. Bloody good show".

Back at Kohima, the battle was being fought fiercely, with no quarter being given on either side. Attack was succeeded by counter-attack and the fighting was intense and critical. On 20 April the troops in and around Kohima, worn out by continuous fighting, were relieved by units of 2 British Infantry Division which had been rushed in from 2,000 miles away. One by one, the Japanese defences in the centre of Kohima were destroyed. British endurance finally triumphed and by the night of 16 May 1944, the battle for Kohima had been won and the Japanese utterly defeated. During the months of gruelling fighting, the British and Indian casualties had been very heavy. Their bodies rest in a large military cemetery at Kohima. Not one of 84's dive-bombers was lost, despite the odds against them.

Admiral Mountbatten and Field Marshal Wavell both stated that the battle for Kohima will be seen as one of the greatest battles in history and a turning point in the war against Japan. No.84 Squadron is very proud to have played such a vital part in that battle and to have avenged in some small way the deaths of those members of the Squadron who were killed in Sumatra and Java. The name of their aircraft, 'Vengeance', was perhaps appropriate.

On 22 April, Gill led 24 Vengeances on a dive-bombing strike on a Japanese- occupied village of Ningthougnong, 16 miles SW of Imphal. 36,000 lbs of bombs all landed on the target and as the last aircraft pulled out of its dive, trucks and tanks carrying British and Gurkha troops were seen rushing south to attack the Japanese. The next day, the 23rd, 15 Vengeances of 84 Squadron were airborne at dawn for a three-hour flight to attack Chindit targets and to bomb petrol and supply dumps at Indaw airfield, north of Lake Indaw. The 450-mile flight was in thick haze with less than half-a-mile visibility, and nil in places. Despite this, the targets were found and bombed. Later, a signal was received from the Advance Headquarters 3 Indian Division (the Chindits) which read: "Secret: Commander Special Forces congratulates all ranks of 84 Squadron on excellent results obtained in bombing targets today".

So accurate had the Squadron's bombing become that, on one occasion, the target given to the Squadron had been the NE corner of a large house in a Japanese-occupied village in which the Japanese commander slept and used as his office! Needless to say that after the Squadron had bombed, not only the house but the entire village had disappeared in a cloud of smoke and flame.

A day later, on the 23rd, Flt Lt Alan Blackburn completed his 100th operational sortie with 84 Squadron, having previously operated over Europe with Bill Russell and Ken Dicks. The end of April saw the departure from No. 84 Squadron of Flt Lts John Goldfinch and Dick Johns. Flt Lt George Plumb and Flt Lt Ron Davies became the new flight commanders.

From a health point of view, 'Doc' Cooper kept a very close air on the aircrew to ensure that they were not suffering from the stress and physical strain of dive-bombing day after day with very little rest. But he also kept a tight watch on the health of the whole Squadron. By careful attention to hygiene, particularly in the kitchens and latrines, he was able to maintain a very high standard of health amongst all ranks. The incidence of malaria and dysentery were remarkably low and there were no cases of cholera, beri-beri or VD.

During the raid on the 26th to attack another Chindit target, the Squadron was diverted following a radio message from 221 Group Operations because 50-plus Japanese fighters were known to be in the area awaiting the Vengeances. On this rare occasion, the Squadron had been given an escort of Hurricanes of No.5 Squadron. Gill dived the Vengeances in tight formation down to 6,000 feet - the height of the mountains in the area - to prevent the enemy fighters from attacking from underneath. The Hurricanes were jumped by a large formation of Japanese 'Oscars' which damaged two of the Hurricanes but failed to destroy any of them.

Two and three full missions were flown every day as the fighting became even more fierce. The Army became more and more dependent on the Vengeances and the Hurricane fighter-bombers as the battle became more intense. On 7 May, 36 Vengeance led by Gill dropped 54,000 lbs of bombs on Japanese bunker positions at Potsangbam. Every bomb landed on the target. But not all the missions were so successful for next day 36 dive-bombers set course for Kalewa to bomb Japanese supply dumps in atrocious weather. No.110 Squadron RAF and No.7 Squadron Indian Air Force turned back; 84 Squadron pressed on and found the target. Despite heavy AA gunfire, the bombing was accurate and fires and a huge explosion resulted. Later the same day, Gill led another 36 Vengeance to the same target, another three-hour flight. Fires were still burning from the previous raid and again there was heavy ack-ack fire from 20 mm guns. Yet again the bombing was accurate and much damage was caused. It was becoming almost impossible to keep up with the Army's demand for support, despite undertaking two or three missions a day. After almost every strike on Japanese-occupied villages, the Army was able to make an immediate ground assault and rush in to capture the village. The Japanese losses were enormous. Worse still, they were not now able to receive badly-needed supplies of food and ammunition.

On 19 May, when Gill led the attack on a Japanese roadblock at Kanglatongbi only ten miles from Imphal, he completed his 100th personal operational sortie with 84 Squadron. He was to complete another 42 sorties before the end of the campaign.

On 22 May, the monsoon broke and 500 inches of rain were to fall in Assam during the wet season. (England receives less than 26 inches during the average year). From now on flying would become really difficult. It was like flying into a black wall of water and had been known to early aviators over the years as the 'Wall of Death'! It was impossible to fly over the solid banks of clouds as the Vengeance did not have a high enough ceiling and it was impossible to fly underneath it. The Squadron wasted valuable flying hours trying to reach their targets but being unable to find them.

With this in mind, Gill asked the AOC if he could be given a Spitfire which he or George Plumb, who had taken over as flight commander of 'B' Flight and who had flown a few hours on Spitfires, could fly out to the target area to check if the weather was suitable for the Vengeances to find the target and to bomb it. If so, a coded message could be signalled to base and the dive-bombers could immediately take-off. Thereby, hundreds of flying hours and fuel could be saved. The AOC agreed it was a good idea and 84 Squadron became the proud owner of a Spitfire Vc MA290, which the Squadron named 'The Looker'.

Sqn Ldr Gill flew the first of many 'weather recces' on 17 June to the Kabaw Valley. At the same time, 20 Japanese 'Oscars' carried out a sweep over Palel airfield in the Imphal Valley, whilst Japanese aircraft dropped urgent supplies to their troops on the ground. The Spitfire squadrons claimed six enemy aircraft destroyed, four probables and two damaged.

As a result of these weather reconnaissance flights over the target areas, the Vengeances were able to reach their targets whenever there was a break in the weather and successfully bomb the enemy. When the weather became very bad, the Squadron devised a new type of shallow dive-bombing from a much lower altitude, which proved to be very useful when the weather was too bad for vertical dive-bombing. On one of the first attacks of this kind, a flight of three aircraft destroyed the Ya-nan bridge which was vital to the Japanese to bring up reinforcements and supplies.

A Vengeance at Maharajpur, December 1943. Lined up are two unknown, Hamlyn, Bovill, Pedlar, Bruce, two unknown

The bridge was breached in two places and the centre collapsed. This attack was followed by many successful low-level raids after the other Vengeance squadrons had been pulled out of the theatre of operations and back to India to rest and re-equip.
only dive-bomber squadron still operating in Burma. The Squadron doggedly soldiered on, now mainly using its shallow dive technique. Being the only Vengeance squadron available to the 14th Army, it was in great demand.

On 22 June, 2 British Division, fighting down from Kohima in the north, and 5 Indian Division fighting up from the south, met 29 miles from Imphal. The road was open once more and the siege of Imphal had been lifted. A signal from No. 25 ASC was received by the Officer Commanding No. 84 Squadron:

"Following message from Commander 2 Division - Very many thanks for splendid air support today. Vengeance on target, Hurricanes were superb and gave exemplary air support to tanks".

Ken Lister, an ex-84 Squadron pilot, was by that time flying 34 Squadron's Hurri-bombers.

On 26 June, the Squadron, led by Flt Lt Ron Davies, with Fg Off Ken Dicks navigating, bombed the Japanese-occupied airfield at Tamu. When approaching the target, the cockpit of Vengeance III FD105 filled with white and grey 'smoke'. Expecting the aircraft to catch fire at any moment, Plt Off B Finnie RCAF ordered his gunner, Fg Off Jack Ellis, to stand-by to bale out. Ellis acknowledged, saying, "Ready when you are". But he must have misunderstood the pilot and disconnected his intercom when Finnie opened the front cockpit to try to clear the fumes (which were in fact caused by a burst hydraulic pipe). As Finnie pulled away from the formation and headed west, Ellis baled out. Fg Off Jack Prentice and Fg Off R F Poole flew low over the jungle and saw the parachute canopy draped over the trees but there was no sign of Ellis.

It was later reported that Jack Ellis had been captured by the Japanese, imprisoned and tortured and then executed as a spy. The fumes in the cockpit dispersed and Finnie, having now lost two gunners, returned to base. But his troubles were not yet over. He found that he had no hydraulic pressure so had to open the bomb-bay to jettison his bombs and then pump the wheels down, using the emergency system, before landing safely.

Aubrey Pedler, writing from his home in Australia, outlines what he calls 'one operation I shall never forget'.

"During my period of attachment to No.84 Squadron in WW.2, I flew a total of 99 operational sorties on Blenheim and Vengeance aircraft. There is only one which I remember in detail from beginning to end, which took place on the 29 June 1944 - 48 years ago.

Flying had been abandoned for the day because of bad weather. However, shortly after lunch, whilst I was in the Officers' Mess at Kumbhirgram, I received a phone call from the CO, Arthur Gill, that I was to report to the ops room with my crew immediately and bring Ron Davies and his crew with me as we were flying. We were briefed by the CO that a bridge over the River Yu, east of Tamu was being used constantly by Japanese troops and supply vehicles and it was vital that the bridge had to be destroyed.

The third Vengeance dive-bomber had difficulty starting up in the rain, so I took off in formation with the CO. On becoming airborne, Arthur Gill immediately turned east and headed for the mountains instead of doing the usual circuit of the airfield to gain height. As we approached the crest of the mountains, I felt that the leader had misjudged his height and, at the last second, I pulled my aircraft up. As I dropped back into position, the CO gave me a broad smile and a hand signal which required the use of only two fingers! Shortly after the third aircraft caught us up.

The dive-bombing achieved its object and we destroyed the bridge. The CO then climbed up through the dense clouds. Formation flying in cloud over Burma was always great 'fun'. We broke cloud at about 11,000 feet and we returned to base above the clouds. There we found a break in the clouds and the leader led us down through a hole at a steep angle. I noted an indicated airspeed of 450 mph between 9,000 and 10,000 feet, which gave a true speed in excess of 500 mph!

That evening, whilst socialising with the fighter pilots of a Spitfire squadron, I was approached by one of them who said 'I believe you were flying one of the Vengeances this afternoon'. He said his attention was first alerted by the extent of the noise of the aircraft and when he saw the speed and angle of the dive he had doubts as to whether the aircraft could pull out safely. He added that a Spitfire in the same situation would be in real trouble! I assured him, with my fingers crossed behind my back, that, for us, it was just a normal trip - to destroy yet another Jap bridge!".

The hazards of low-level attacks were shown on 5 July during a strike by 12 Vengeances against heavily-defended ammunition dumps and troops at Le-U. The formation attacked in flights of three and Flt Sgt W Natrass, who was flying as No. 3 to the CO, was caught directly from an up-blast from a huge explosion when the leader's 11-second delay fused bombs hit an ammunition or land-mine dump. The aircraft were severely damaged but Natrass nursed it back to base and, although shaken, neither he or his gunner were badly hurt. Almost invariably during these attacks, the leader fired long bursts of machine-gun fire from his four front wing guns to keep the Japs' head down. But during this attack, there was heavy 20 mm and 37 mm anti-aircraft fire.

Sqn Ldr Gill took off in the Squadron's Spitfire on 10 July on

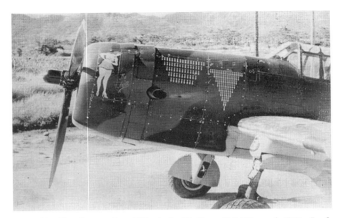

The Troll, *flown by FO Aub Pedlar RAAF and FO Jack Prentice RAAF, displays 140 raid symbols*

a weather recce of the Kalewa area. He was unable to reach Kalewa, the primary target for the Vengeances, due to 8/8ths cloud up to 15,000 feet or more south of the Imphal Valley. So he turned north-east until he came to a gap in the clouds at 10,000 feet. From there he turned due east and entered the Kabaw Valley, which means 'Death Valley', and dived through gaps in the cloud to 4,000 feet south of Tamu before turning north to see if the weather was suitable for the Vengeances to reach Humine, the alternative target. At that moment two Ki-43 fighters - 'Oscars' - passed over him flying in the opposite direction. Gill immediately turned starboard into cloud and climbed because he feared he would run into the mountains. When he came out of the cloud moments later one of the enemy aircraft was immediately ahead of him, slightly to port. He closed to within 100 - 200 yards and opened fire. 20 mm cannon shells were seen to hit the 'Oscar' and a large part fell off. The Japanese fighter rolled slowly on to its back and went down vertically. It was later confirmed by HQ 3rd Tactical Air Force at Comilla as definitely destroyed. The Air Officer Commanding No.221 Group was not pleased, as Gill had flown beyond the geographical limit laid down for weather recces and threatened to take the Spitfire away if Gill did it again!.

The final strike by 84 Squadron, in fact the final combat mission ever flown by an RAF Vengeance, took place on 16 July 1944. 12 aircraft led by Sqn Ldr Gill, with Alan Blackburn as navigator, in a Mk III (FB981 *The Queen of Shaibah VII*, carried out another low-level attack on Le-U. 8/8ths cloud persisted for most of the flight and covered the target area but the target was located and the bombing was accurate. In five short months, Gill had led 1,476 operational sorties.

The Squadron received the following secret cypher message from the AOC No. 221 Group;

Sqn Ldr Gill and two ground crew pose before Queen of Shaibah VII *after 121 operations*

"Thank you for your work in 221 Group. In five months you have carried out 1,800 sorties, an average of a full squadron mission every day, dropping over 900 tons of bombs. Good Luck at rest and in the future.

Signed Vincent".

The following letter was received by the Squadron Commander from General Lentaigne, Commander of the Chindits.

"Dear Gill,

I want to thank you, all your pilots and aircrew and your ground personnel for the first-class co-operation the Squadron gave to us, both before and during this year's operations. It was hoped originally that we would have been able to call on you for support far more often than has been the case. We fully appreciate the fact that we have not been able to do so is through no fault of yours. Our loss was the gain of the troops on the Imphal Front.

Your Squadron's co-operation during the training period in Gwalior was especially valuable in that it enabled us to work out a system which has proved its worth time and time again in operations.

I understand that you are being re-equipped and I hope that this will lead to renewed combined operations in the future. Please convey my best wishes to all.

Yours very sincerely,

W D Lentaigne

During one of my interviews with Wg Cdr Gill he told me: "Not one of 84's many successes in Burma would have been possible if it had not been for the very hard work of my ground crews who, under the skillful guidance of their Engineer Officer, John Ramsden, worked for long hours in appalling conditions of heat and sweat, choking dust followed by mud. It was their aircraft which fought the battle for Burma, and won. The "drivers, airframe" flew the aircraft, but it was the crews on the ground that

Brigadier General Orde Wingate

AN964 G being serviced at Kumbhirgram

kept the aircraft in the air, spending hours lovingly servicing, maintaining and polishing the aircraft. I will always remember the ground crew who came up to see me in the early days and asked me to take a certain pilot off their aircraft as he was ruining it. Without the dedication and the skill of the fitters, electricians, armourers and mechanics and all the other tradesmen - such as the carpenters, metal workers, instrument bashers, photographers etc, and not forgetting the cooks who fed us and who probably worked harder and for longer hours than any of us - the Battle for Burma could not have been won. As the Army Commander, General Sir William Slim said, "The men of the Fourteenth Army would have been doomed if it had not been for the men of the Air Force".

Although recommendations for awards were submitted after the campaign, not one airman's name appeared in subsequent honours list. None of the flight commanders who had shared the difficult job of leadership to find isolated targets in the mountains and valleys of Burma in appalling weather at times, was honoured. Only four DFCs were awarded" These went to Dicks and Blackburn who had flown well over 100 operational sorties in five campaigns, to Hawke the Navigation Leader and to Gill, the Squadron Commander.

The mention of the number of operational sorties flown by the Squadron means that as there were so few casualties, the majority of aircrews flew approximately the same number. The three log books I have had the privilege to study all show 90 or more missions flown.

From Kumbhirgram, the Squadron flew to Samungli in the North-West frontier of India on 27 July 1944 for a well-earned rest prior to re-equipping with the Mosquito FB.VI.

The ground staff travelled nearly 3,000 miles by train from Silchar to Quetta and then by road. George Isaacs, one of the Squadron's armourers, opened what he thought was a door to the lavatory on the troop train during the first night and woke up on the railway line! Having been in two hospitals en route, he eventually rejoined the Squadron two months later after being given up for lost.

At Samungli, to keep the aircrew in flying practice and to keep the groundcrew occupied, flights were made to Fort Chaman, Kohat, Chaklala, Peshawar and over the various mountain regions of the Afghan frontier. Gill's last flight with 84 was with Fg Off Ken Tonkin RAAF on 25 September 1944, when they flew Vengeance FB981 via Lahore to Palam (Delhi), escorted part of the way by the whole Squadron. After three years with 84, having joined the Squadron in Iraq 1941, Gill was posted back to Burma to join the staff of the Joint Headquarters of the 14th Army/No. 221 Group under Stanley Vincent, now an Air Vice-Marshal, as the Air Plans Staff Officer. He was to travel down through Burma, this time by road, as the Japanese forces were driven back and finally defeated.

In the Squadron's Christmas magazine for 1944, the Adjutant, Flt Lt Bryan Lilly wrote: "I met Arthur Gill for the first time on 5 November 1942 when I joined the Squadron and I am not ashamed to confess that I had a lump in my throat when I watched him leave us for the last time two years later. That day the Squadron lost a CO who perhaps had exerted a greater influence over its history than any of his predecessors. When he took over in the spring of 1942 he found himself in command of approximately 132 men - all that remained of the disastrous adventure in the Far East - without aircraft, without equipment and without hope. His first objective was to prevent the Squadron being disbanded, a fate which overtook others similarly placed at the time. Having succeeded, he set himself the task of rebuilding 84 to its former levels of prestige and efficiency. Despite many early difficulties and disappointments, the results of his labours have spoken for themselves in a variety of directions.

I had the opportunity of observing Arthur Gill at very close quarters. I saw an excellent pilot, a good leader and a very able administrator but the qualities which, from the very first moment I met him, harnessed my admiration, respect and loyalty, was his unselfish and unsparing interest in every man serving under his command. Few indeed realised the debt which the members of the squadron owed to him. He rarely gave an order. His personal example was sufficient to invest a request with a greater authority. He praised his subordinates in the hour of success and in less happy times readily accepted responsibility. He was one of the most considerate men I have ever known. Perhaps it was a fault that made him do so many trivial jobs instead of insisting on others doing more for him. Despite the enormous amount of work that he did he never refused to listen or shirk an issue.

As I write I learn that he has been awarded the Distinguished Flying Cross. I know that every man in the Squadron will join me in congratulations and best wishes that the future will hold even more glittering prizes than the command of this Squadron - prizes which we know he so richly deserves.

Signed BL.

Aircrew in front of Mosquito TE667 X; Wg Cdr M H Constable-Maxwell in centre of middle row

CHAPTER 15 - AT LAST, THE MOSQUITO

After Kumbhirgram and the heat of Burma, Samungli airfield near Quetta was a haven of rest for the Squadron personnel, particularly after the eight-day rail journey across the top of India with a change of trains at Sibi in the foothills leading up to Quetta. This necessitated unloading and reloading all of the Squadron's baggage and technical equipment due to a change of rail gauge.

Over the following weeks, many of the crews left the Squadron. Those that had come from the Dominions were given the choice of either transferring to fighter squadrons or returning home to train as flying instructors. Flt Lt Aubrey Pedler was given the opportunity to become a Thunderbolt pilot but turned this down in favour of returning to Australia whilst Flt Lt Colin Papps, later to become a wing commander in the RNZAF, saw service on a Spitfire PR Squadron over Burma. Fg Off Leo (Shooter) Burnett (an American citizen serving in the Royal Canadian Air Force) left the squadron to fly Thunderbolts in Burma, flying as wing-man to the late Neil Cameron, later to become MRAF Lord Cameron. Burnett returned to the United States in 1946 and was denied 'veteran's rights' because he had not served in the US forces. He later trekked north across the border and was granted 'veteran's rights' in Canada. He returned south with an engineering degree and a wife and found work with Piasecki Helicopters (later to become Boeing Helicopters) from which he has recently retired.

During September 1944, a dummy attack was made on the Quetta Staff College to celebrate Battle of Britain Day. Ten days later, on the 25th, Sqn Ldr A M Gill DFC left the Squadron to join No. 221 Group. During the few weeks between his departure and the arrival of Sqn Ldr I L B 'Badger' Aitkens as Commanding Officer, the acting squadron commander was Flt Lt George Ravencroft Plumb.

LAC Ken Wild joined the Squadron at Quetta. He well remembers his first impressions: "I wondered how anyone could exist, let alone work, on aircraft, in the conditions at Quetta. One of the climactic features on the NW frontier was the continuous strong wind. The fine particles of sand which covered the entire landscape, created a sandblast effect and one's skin became creased and parched very quickly. Being fair-skinned like most ginger-haired people, I was particularly badly affected but, thankfully,

Mepacrine tablets (anti-malaria drug) came to my aid and I very quickly assumed a very yellow appearance".

September brought a general reorganisation of the Squadron. 209 airmen were drafted to No.7084 Servicing Echelon. A servicing echelon consisted of a flight lieutenant engineer officer (now called the Technical Branch) in command and all the airmen and NCOs needed to service a squadron plus all the necessary ground equipment. Eleven others were sent home. This reduced the Squadron strength to 23 officers, 37 NCOs and 121 airmen.

By October 1944, the Squadron had disposed of all its Vengeances and on 31 October moved to Yelahanka near Bangalore to re-equip with the Mosquito FB.VI.

The rail journey took eight days and the usual problems with long hauls were experienced - cooking by the side of the line, ablutions under the water-towers, fending off the kite-hawks from dinner plates and coping with the everlasting heat and insects. The primitive lavatories always proved a challenge, especially at night when the cockroaches became increasingly active. The slatted wooden seats also made an impression on one's backside. The arrival at Bangalore Cantonment station was also unusual when large numbers of small monkeys which lived in the vicinity would drop from the trees overhanging the platforms on to the carriages beneath.

October saw the arrival of Flt Lts John Clyne and Ron Cameron and Fg Off E R Moxom, who had been Mosquito instructors in the UK. Their job was to convert the pilots on to twin-engined aircraft. At that time, no Mosquitoes were available and three Oxfords of No.1672 MCU were used for flying training. Replacement pilots Plt Offs R Shakeshaft and J Robertson joined the Squadron in early November. On 12 November, Wg Cdr R E Jay assumed command of the Squadron, Aitkens becoming 'A' Flight Commander. Further changes were the leaving for home of Flt Lt D J Hawke DFC RAAF who had been with 84 since November 1941 and Fg Off Jim Farrer RAAF. The flight commander vacancy was filled by Flt Lt G R Plumb who was promoted to acting squadron leader.

Advice was received that, owing to technical difficulties with the Mosquito, the Squadron would re-equip with Vengeance IIIs

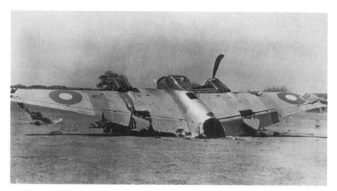

Flt Lt Cameron's crash at Yelahanka on 28 February 1945

and return to the forward area. A fortnight later, on 19 December, this order was cancelled owing to the lack of available Vengeances and the Squadron was instructed to continue the conversion on to the Mosquito. The hiatus over the Mosquito - back to Vengeance - then to Mosquitoes again was caused by the fact that the reserve Vengeance IIIs held in store at No.301 MU at Karachi had not had their rubber fuel tanks properly inhibited at the factory. As a result, when they were being prepared for issue it was found that, after refuelling, they leaked like sieves and there were insufficient spare fuel tanks available. However on 30 December, further orders were received stating that a Vengeance detachment was to be selected for operations in support of the 14th Army in Burma, consisting of two flights of nine complete aircrews under the command of Sqn Ldr G R Plumb. This order was again rescinded when word was received that the whole project was to be 'scrubbed' due to the fact that Mosquitoes would be forthcoming some weeks earlier than expected. At that particular time the aircraft on Squadron strength were four Vengeance IIIs, two IIs and a Harvard trainer. Gp Capt John Ramsden, the Engineer Officer from January 1944 - August 1946, commented in letters to the author: "The Vengeance IIs and IIIs which are recorded must have been the same ones we used at Kumbhirgram and re-issued to the Squadron".

A near disaster was averted on 11 January by the prompt action of Sqn Ldr Plumb and Fg Off P Downer. After landing from a local flight, the Vengeance was being refuelled when petrol ignited around the funnel, spreading to the hand-pipe on the bowser. After a short 'flap', Sqn Ldr Plumb brought a fire extinguisher to bear on the flames which were finally put out with the help of Downer and others who were nearby. No damage was caused, but the consequences could have been serious had the bowser not been driven away from the area and the flames attacked without delay.

On 26 January, Flt Lt D Wilkes, with Flt Sgt Wanstall as navigator, were returning late after ferrying crews to Poona in an Oxford, when they became lost and decided to do a 'belly landing' whilst they still had sufficient light to see a suitable field. Damage was done to the aircraft but there were no casualties.

In mid-February, the first Mosquito arrived. Ron Cameron in correspondence to the author writes: "My first familiarization flight was on 26 February with Flt Sgt Cox". Two days later, Cameron wrote off the aircraft. He continues: "My recollections of the accident are that I was doing practice take-offs and landings and I had to go around again. When opening up, both engines failed due to the fact that I was flying on the outer tanks when I should have been flying on the inner ones (as instructed in the manual). The aircraft stalled from about 20 feet above the runway, crashed and broke its back. Fortunately it did not burst into flames. I simply opened the escape hatch, stepped out on the wing and slid on to the ground, much to the obvious disgust of the Irish fire-tender corporal who was swinging a large axe. Eventually the invest-igating team decided it was pilot error and the endorsement in my log book read as follows: "This pilot failed to carry out the correct fuel tank drill thereby causing his engines to cut when making a dummy approach and causing damage to HM aircraft HR638 - CARELESSNESS' Signed by Gp Capt Commanding RAF Yelahanka".

A humorous result of Cameron's crash was that the aircraft finished up in front of the Flying Control. At that time an infant air service, possibly Tata Airways, was operating a service between Bangalore and Delhi using Lodestars. The passengers' waiting room was in the control tower and on this particular day were awaiting the arrival of their aircraft. When the runway had been

cleared, the civil aircraft arrived. On boarding one of the passengers (an Indian gentleman) was found to be missing. One of the other passengers explained that after witnessing the Cameron crash he had left the room muttering something about a train to catch!

Cameron went on to say: "A few days later I took off in company with WO E McMahon with a full load of fuel. On reaching 4-500 feet the port engine seized. McMahon had a busy time pumping down the undercarriage because the engine that failed worked the hydraulics. We landed safely, despite the CO's instructions from the tower to bale out. On landing I taxied into the correct space amongst the other 'Mossies'. Later it was found that no glycol had been put in the propeller feathering control at the last service. I received no endorsement for saving a Mosquito".

March began with a fatal accident. On the 5th, Fg Off F R Moxom with Sgt T Varker navigating crashed on the bombing range. They were buried at the Hosoor Road Cemetery, Bangalore. The same week Flt Sgt W Natrass landed after a routine flight, overtook an Oxford and hit it, causing damage to both aircraft. Flt Lt R H Davies, on his first night solo, made a rough landing with the result that the starboard undercarriage collapsed. A memo in the Squadron records states that it is obvious that many of the crews will not achieve their conversion on to the Mosquito.

Dummy attacks were carried out by eight aircraft led by the CO on the coast South of Cochin. The following day six aircraft led by Sqn Ldr G Plumb made a similar attack on the docks of the city. A further attack on 31 March was led by Flt Lt Milnes. These dummy attacks were good experience but night formation flying left much to be desired. A summary by Wg Cdr Jay states that the squadron strength at the end of March was twelve aircraft and the lack of replacements was hindering training considerably. Also, although the position of Flight Commander 'A' Flight was filled on paper by Sqn Ldr I L B Aitkens, it had in fact been vacant since 12 February when he left the Squadron. This has had an adverse affect on the morale of this flight.

The initial training programme was completed on 3 April. During the following week the delivery of aircraft improved and by the 10th the strength was up to 16 aircraft.

The next few paragraphs are attributed to John Ramsden. In correspondence he writes: "In early April 1945, George Plumb's fiancee, Kay, who was serving with the Red Cross, arrived in Delhi and George applied for permission from the CO to fly to Chharra via Delhi. As my sister was also stationed at Delhi, I thumbed a lift with George. We left Yelahanka on 18 April in Mosquito FB.VI HR617. At that time George Plumb had a bad attack of 'athlete's foot' and therefore flew in carpet slippers. Yelahanka to Delhi must be well over a thousand miles and I reckon we were pushing it a bit not to plan a refuelling stop. We flew up India with myself map reading all the way. (No dead reckoning about my navigation!) Somewhere south of Delhi, we experienced fuel problems and George feathered one engine and transferred the remaining fuel to the side of the good engine. Neither George Plumb nor myself had ever been to Delhi airfield but we knew the runway bearing. By now, George was having trouble keeping directional control due to the extra load on the rudder pedals caused by asymmetric flight and giving him great pain to his feet. He developed a 'must get down' syndrome.

"Approaching the city of Delhi we saw an airfield right on our nose with a runway of approximately the right bearing. 'That must be it' said George. 'I'm going in'. He called Delhi tower, declining an emergency and obtained clearance as No. 1 to land. Since we were approaching the airfield approximately into the wind which we reckoned existed, George lowered the undercarriage and went straight in. The approach was somewhat erratic as I remember, with George moaning with pain every time he had to make a rudder correction. After we touched down, George taxied off the runway and we sat still for a few minutes. Then we noticed that it was not only us that was still! It was as quiet as a churchyard. We taxied up to the control tower and I got out and wandered about, eventually finding a chowkidar (night watchman) armed with a lathi (an iron-clad bamboo stick). He approached us cautiously and I found that our aircraft was the first one he had ever seen. The airfield's name was Gurgaon and it later transpired that it was one of a series of unmanned airfields around Delhi built for the air defence of the capital".

"Back at the aircraft, George had been trying to raise Delhi Main on the radio but because we were on the ground could not do so, although he reported that there seemed to be a lot of traffic on all channels. 'We seemed to have landed in the middle of a flap' he said, not realising the cause of the flap was us! The chowkidar had gone off saying that he would try and get someone who could help.

Mosquito FB. VI TE604 at Kuala Lumpur in September 1946

George was unable to walk far so we settled ourselves on the wing in the sun to await events. We did not have long to wait. An L-5 light observation plane hove into sight, circled above us and eventually landed. We told the pilot our story and he told us he was part of a search force because a major emergency had been declared with a Mosquito crashing on its approach, having announced he was on finals and then disappearing. He said he would get airborne, call off the search and arrange for ground transport to pick us up. He offered to give one of us a lift back to Delhi Main but we elected to stay together. When we did get back to Delhi we were met in the control tower by a very irate group captain who seemed to think we had caused the flap deliberately".

Arrangements were made for a supply of fuel to be sent to the airfield next day, when George and I went back to the aircraft (now closely guarded by a very proud chowkidar clutching his stick and obviously feeling very proud, that, at last he had a proper job). We refuelled the aircraft by hand-pump from 40-gallon drums on the back of a truck and next day (20 April) flew the aircraft into Delhi Main. George then spent some time with his fiancee (and limping like a wounded veteran and something of a celebrity because the whole of the service population of Delhi had learnt by now of our escapade). Three days later we flew to Chharra to rejoin the Squadron".

On 23 April, the Squadron moved to Chharra, an airstrip near Calcutta, to await a move forward. Fighter affiliation exercises were held with Spitfires of No.615 Squadron daily. On one of these, John Clyne's aircraft was damaged when the dinghy released itself in mid-air, striking the fin. Another 'Mossie' suffered damage when taxying to dispersal, when the hinge pin of the tailwheel retracting jack sheared. The same thing happened on the following day to another Mosquito, with the result that all aircraft were grounded for checks.

The 8th of May 1945 brought 'Victory in Europe' and the rumours of another move, this time to Chakulia. After a station parade on the 9th, orders came to stand down. Later, the victory was celebrated by an issue of six bottles of beer to all ranks.

At 07.00 on the 14th, four aircraft of 'A' Flight led by Flt Lt R H Davies took off on a training flight over the Ranchi ranges. 15 minutes later HR628 F, was seen to break up in mid-air after entering a dive from 5,000 feet. Flt Sgt W Natrass and his observer WO Vetters were killed instantly. The funeral, held at Ranchi cemetery, was attended by all of the aircrew.

After the advance party had left for the Squadron's new base at Chakulia, orders came that the move was postponed because of the shortage of transport. Three days later the advance party returned.

On 25 May, Wg Cdr R E Jay left the Squadron to take over the post of Wing Commander Training at No.228 Group. On the same day, Flt Lt G H Cooper left for home. He had been the Medical Officer with the Squadron for two years and five months. His parting gesture was to donate a challenge trophy for the inter-section football competition, the Zaccheus Cup.

June 2nd brought another mishap when, after landing from a test flight, Sqn Ldr Plumb swung on touching down and, to avoid hitting native labourers, over-corrected, swung violently and ground-looped. Further mishaps occurred over the next few weeks. A Mosquito flown by Flt Lt P Downer brushed a tree on landing and WO H Budd hit a kitehawk, slight damage being caused to both "aircraft".

A summary in the records states that although training was proceeding smoothly, the continual shortage of aircraft was worrying. In the first half of the month, only three aircraft from each flight were serviceable. Replacements were not forthcoming and the total strength was down to nine aircraft when de Havilland representatives condemned three - except for straight and level flying - owing to the deterioration of the wing surfaces.

On 14 June, Wg Cdr M H Constable-Maxwell DSO DFC was appointed Commanding Officer. (Constable-Maxwell was believed to be distantly related to the Royal family. Later, it was rumoured, that when the Squadron was in danger of being disbanded, he wrote, addressing the letter to "Dear George" hoping for the King's support). Commenting on this statement, John Ramsden writes: "The rumour about Michael Constable-Maxwell's letter to HM King George VI is entirely fictitious. It is true that Michael was related to both Lord Lovat and the Duke of Norfolk and that the family can show a line of descent from King Edward III. The story about the letter arose out of the fact that Michael managed to have the decision to disband the Squadron turned round by a personal signal to the late Air Chief Marshal Sir Leslie Hollinghurst, a member of the Air Council. Sir Leslie, himself ex-84, was a personal friend of Michael's family, having served in 1918 under Michael's brother Gerald in No.56 Squadron.

Constable-Maxwell brought with him Flt Lt John Quinton DFC. John Quinton was killed several years after the war when he handed his parachute to an Air Training Corps cadet when the aircraft in which they were flying was in difficulties and subsequently crashed.

At the end of June, the Squadron moved to St Thomas Mount, Madras, with a detachment moving to Guindy. On 16 July, a traditional Squadron initiation ceremony was held at Guindy as decreed by the Mayor and Mayoress of Shaibah.

Criticism has been levelled at Maxwell's insistence on dive-

A group of sullen Japanese POWs labouring on Tengah airfield, November 1945

Kuala Lumpur airfield

bombing with the Mosquito. One letter states that the thought of dive-bombing without dive brakes was hair-raising to say the least. It was later to have dire consequences when flights participated in practice dives over the ranges. The Squadron's third fatal accident occurred on 22 July when Flt Sgt Kirby, with LAC Tildsley as passenger, made an error of judgment and hit the water almost on the shore-line, the aircraft bouncing on to the shore and immediately bursting into flames. It was believed to have been caused by a high-speed stall. Both occupants were killed and on the same day they were buried at the cemetery of St. Thomas Mount. Their deaths brought an end to dive-bombing with the Mosquito.

The ranges in the Madras area were under the command of West African troops who constantly disregarded the red flag; fortunately no one was ever injured.

On 18 July, the AOC BAFSEA, Air Marshal L N Hollinghurst CB OBE DFC as he was then, accompanied by Gp Capt F Aitkens AFC, made a tour of inspection. After being introduced to the officers, a discussion on bombing methods took place. Two days later, the AOC No.224 Group, AVM The Earl of Bandon CBE DSO (known to all and sundry as 'The abandoned Earl), visited the Squadron.

The end of July heralded a change of personnel for 84 Squadron. Five complete aircrews were posted to swell the ranks of No. 45 Squadron. Sqn Ldrs Aitken and Plumb and Flt Lt Milnes all left the Squadron and to replace them came Flt Lts B G Slip, G E Pettitt and Fg Off R V Chasney.

At the end of July 1945, the Supreme Allied Commander in South-East Asia, Vice-Admiral Lord Louis Mountbatten, was recalled to London. On the 15th, he was told that from that date his command area included the Dutch East Indies and French Indo-China, an area about 800,000 sq kms with around 90 million people, of which 750,000 were Japanese, approximately 80,000 POWs in 250 camps and an unknown number of internees.

August 8th brought the news that the first atomic bomb had been dropped on Japan. Two days later, Russia declared war on Japan. It was noticeable that everyone on the Squadron was now anticipating an early end to hostilities. On the 15th, Japan accepted the surrender terms. It was followed on the 16th by a Thanksgiving Service in the cathedral at Madras. A cricket match was hastily arranged between the officers and NCOs playing the airmen. This was followed by a fancy dress soccer match and a special dinner with all ranks sitting together. At the Victory parade in Madras on the 20th, 40 groundcrew under Flt Lt R L Morris took part as No.84's contribution. The fly-past later in the day included six aircraft from each of Nos.45, 82, 84 and 211 Squadrons, plus detachments of Corsairs, Hellcats and Spitfires from visiting carriers. Three Catalinas and three Sunderlands completed the fly-past.

Two days after Japan had surrendered on 17 August, an independent state of Indonesia was declared. This was with the help of the Japanese, who had handed over their weapons to the natives. It was little realised at the time what problems this was to cause over the following months.

A few days later, Flt Lt R H Davies and Fg Off F V Bird left the Squadron. Both had been with it for over two years. Others to leave in the next few weeks included Flt Lts P Downer, P C Thorns, D D Wilkes, Fg Off G Paterson and Plt Off T A Davies.

Following a visit to the station by the AOC-in-C SEAC, ACM Sir Keith Park KCB KBE MC DFC, it was heard later that the Squadron had been taken off 'Operation Zipper'. Instead, they

were to go to Singapore with the occupying forces. Two days later it was learnt that 18 aircraft were to proceed to Baigachi on 1 September. On that day, only 12 aircraft left, led by Wg Cdr Constable-Maxwell. A further five led by Sqn Ldr J R Brain followed on the 2nd. Ten days later, 17 aircraft left Baigachi to fly to Hmawbi (due north of Rangoon). On landing Flt Lt John Clyne became bogged down whilst taxying, while Flt Lt Keith Miles swung off the runway, both aircraft damaging their undercarriage. Ron Cameron comments: "The overnight stay at Hmawbi will always be remembered. After bedding down under canvas, we were awakened by Japanese troops rushing through the camp firing guns and throwing grenades. Fortunately none of the crews were injured!

On the 12th, 16 aircraft took off to fly to Kallang, three diverting to Penang to refuel. On the 22nd, the Squadron moved to Seletar. Whilst there, priority was given to finding ex-84 Squadron members from the many Japanese POW camps and taking them back to the station, a remarkably compassionate gesture by any standards. Amongst those who were found was Barry Paterson, who has been mentioned in previous chapters. On the 29th, Flt Lt Ramsden with two other officers and half the squadron personnel embarked on the SS *Talma*, a coal-burning vessel which had been converted into a troopship. Conditions were grim, with 800 airmen sharing six showers, 12 hand basins and 15 WCs. Sleeping, in most cases, was on deck. The only high spot was the food which was plentiful. They arrived at Singapore on 4 October.

The same day, Flt Lt Wilson landed heavily, wrecking the undercarriage and immediately bursting into flames. Fortunately, the crew escaped but the aircraft was a write-off. Three days later two aircraft were detailed to search for a Liberator which was missing on a flight from the Cocos Islands to Singapore. Although searches were made over several days, nothing was found.

Amongst the duties carried out by No.84 Squadron was the transportation of visitors. Two incidents stand out, the first proving fatal. WO H G Budd and his observer Flt Sgt Harris were detailed to fly Miss Marjorie Benn of the YWCA Welfare to Bangkok. They crashed a mile-and-a-half off the coast near Kampong Jambu. The aircraft was seen to dive out of cloud with the base less than 1,000 feet. Two bodies were found by local fishermen but the body of Miss Benn was never found.

Wg Cdr M H Constable-Maxwell and Flt Lt John Ramsden went to the scene of the crash. They were flown there in a Sunderland of No.230 Squadron, where they were met by Lt Col F S Chapman, Commander of Force 136 in the area. Force 136 consisted of British officers working with Chinese communist guerrillas behind the Japanese lines and, until a civilian administration could be set up, had come out of the jungle at the end of the war and were in temporary control of the country. From there they travelled up the east coast from one Force 136 post to another until they reached Kota Trengganu where they were looked after by the headman. After visiting the crash site, they made sure that the bodies were buried properly and the graves well marked. They then interviewed eye-witnesses, rewarded the villagers and collected the personal effects which had been recovered from the bodies. From there they made their way to Kuala Lumpur, where Flt Lt Ferguson picked them up.

A few days later, Flt Lt Ron Cameron and WO G McMahon took a high-ranking lady of the French Red Cross to Saigon. During the flight the passenger always sat at the navigator's feet. They had been instructed to fly at 12,000 feet and after about 30 minutes flying it was noticed that the lady had passed out due to

Kemajoran Airfield Java, 1946

breathing difficulties. McMahon obligingly gave her his oxygen mask and they reduced height. After a few moments she came to her senses and titivated herself for her arrival in Saigon, seemingly none the worst for her experience.

When the Squadron was ferrying Red Cross and RAPWI (Repatriation of Allied Prisoners of War and Internees) personnel around South-East Asia, single passengers flew in the crew department in front of the navigator, sitting either on the floor or on a camp stool which was pushed under their bottoms by the groundcrew before the hatch was closed. Alternatively if there were more than one passenger, a second person could be carried in the 'Black Hole' - the compartment in the rear fuselage, just aft of the bomb-bay which housed the batteries and other electrical gear and the oxygen bottles. A very unpopular place for passengers!

On the return flight, problems were experienced with the aviation fuel. Evidently the Japanese fuel had been stored in aluminium drums and the filters on the 'Merlin' engines were clogged up with the scum which had accumulated in the bottom of the drums. It was well known that Japanese aviation fuel was of a lower octane content. Cameron returned to Saigon where the filters were thoroughly cleaned. They resumed their flight to Seletar, only to run into a monsoon storm. Flying in cloud all of the time, they finally reduced height to about 200 feet as they neared the Malay coast within ten minutes of their ETA. It was later found that, by flying through the storm, the leading edge of the aircraft's wing had worn to half its normal thickness. The aircraft was immediately written-off and used for spares.

All aircraft were grounded pending an investigation into the fuel consignment. On 30 October the remainder of the Squadron arrived from Madras aboard the SS *Prince Albert*.

Meanwhile the situation in Java was becoming serious. It was estimated that, at the end of hostilities, there were on the islands of Sumatra and Java some 630,000 armed Japanese and 123,000 POWs and internees. Clearly the most important task was to release the latter from the appalling conditions under which most of them were being held. Many of the ships which were to form the backbone of Operation "Zipper", the plan to recapture Malaya and Singapore, were loaded, filling the ports on the east coast of India.

No.224 Group RAF was deployed and ready to support the assault on the west coast of Malaya. From this force, No.904 Wing was ordered to proceed to Java in support of 23 and 5 (Indian) Divisions which were to take over from the Japanese and release the prisoners known to be held there. What No.904 Wing had not been told was that the Japanese had handed over their weapons to the Indonesians and had encouraged them to set up a government before the Allied forces arrived.

They arrived at the port of Tanjong Priok to find complete devastation. An ammunition ship had blown up several months earlier and had wrecked the port. They were ordered to take over the airfield at Kemajoram and immediately improvements were made to the runways. Soon after, 24 Dakotas from No.31 Squadron arrived to begin the task of moving the prisoners.

Disembarking from LST 3035 at Batavia, January 1946

Flt Lt John Clyne recalls the position: "During the latter days of September, I was flown in with a Major from the Royal Artillery who was required to find all the ack-ack and artillery emplacements. On driving into Batavia from the airfield, a considerable number of kamikaze aircraft could be seen and, if peace had not been declared, Operation "Zipper" would have been a very hazardous and difficult operation".

On 1 October, a detachment of eight Mosquitoes from No.84 Squadron together with six from No.110 Squadron flew to Batavia. Its first operational flight was made on 1 November when Flt Lt D Tissington and Fg Off E C Childs made a tactical reconnaissance over the Magelang area. It was noticed that the Indonesian flag was flying over many of the buildings and that the words 'Japs here' were marked out on the ground.

Two days later, 'recces' made by Flt Lt Clyne and later by WO C V Thomas showed trains moving, loaded with troops. In Djakarta, a procession of about 2,000 people were seen moving towards the railway station. No weapons could be seen but some streets had been blocked off by fallen trees.

It was clear that British forces could not possibly occupy the entire island. So bridgeheads were formed around Batavia and its port Tanjong Priok, Semarang airfield and a third at Soerabaya. It was hoped that, from these points, all of the prisoners and internees could be evacuated. The landing at Soerabaya was bitterly opposed by well-armed Indonesian troops and it was not until 9 November that Thunderbolts of No.60 Squadron plus a detachment of Mosquitoes from Nos.84 and 110 Squadrons were able to move on to its airfield. Until the taking of Soerabaya airfield, flights of nearly 900 miles were necessary with only 30 minutes over the target area.

The first operation from Soerabaya was flown on 10 November by Fg Off R Chasney and Flt Lt G E Pettitt, the target being the Government buildings and also to strafe areas in the immediate vicinity. Unfortunately the results were not encouraging with the first 500-lb bomb falling short of its target whilst the second, although a direct hit, did not explode. Two days later Wg Cdr M H Constable-Maxwell with Flt Lt John Quinton navigating, made three separate sorties over Soerabaya. On the first two occasions, the bombs failed to explode. On the third run an attack was made on the Hotel Brunet using a 40-degree bombing approach but once again accuracy was poor.

On the 13th, raids on the marshalling yards at Sidotopo were carried out. Orders came through that all traffic leaving and arriving at Batavia was to be strafed. Sqn Ldr J R Brain carried out a leaflet-dropping raid over the towns of Pamekasan and Singeradja. Unfortunately some of the leaflets lodged in the starboard radiator, causing the engine to overheat and necessitating the aircraft's return on one engine. Two Mosquitoes attacked railway installations at Soerabaya, both being hit by accurate ack-ack fire. TA497 X was struck by two shells, one entering the main spar inside the starboard nacelle. Flt Lt Bob Cherry commented in the report made on the 19th: "During my first run over the marshalling yards south of Soerabaya, little flak was seen. But, on the second run, continuous ack-ack was encountered. It was becoming increasingly accurate both for height and direction".

Strikes and tactical reconnaissance flights continued throughout November. The Squadron's first casualties occurred on 1 December when Sqn Ldr B G Slip and Flt Lt T Andrews were killed. They had been detailed to strafe road transport. At 1400, wreckage was seen amongst burning cars and houses. It was learnt later that the bodies of the two crew members had been taken to the hospital at Tjirandjang. A week later on the 8th, the Squadron lost Flt Lt J D Taylor DFC and Flt Sgt E Hale (110 Sqn) in the Batavia area. A report was received from flying control that an aircraft had crashed. Two Thunderbolts from 60 Squadron were sent up to locate and orbit the crash. Later an armoured column was seen operating in the area. Later it was seen to push forward across the river towards the scene of the crash where the bodies were recovered and taken back to the airfield.

As the Army pushed forward to relieve Bandoeng, Java's second city and its commercial centre, attempts were made to use the railway to ferry troops in and bring internees out. Unfortunately, due to continuous ambushes along the route, this did not prove practicable. On one occasion, a train was ambushed and many of its Gurkha guards murdered. It was therefore necessary for No.31 Squadron's Dakotas to continue flying in supplies, and bringing out ex-POWs and internees. In December, No.904 Wing suffered its biggest loss when a Dakota returning from Semerang with 19 Indian troops on board was compelled to force-land only five miles from Kemajoram after an engine failure.

All on board were seen to evacuate the aircraft but when a rescue party arrived there was no sign of the occupants. Later troops were sent to comb the area and, in the village of Bekasi, it was found that the entire crew and their passengers had been murdered and buried on a river bank. The village was later razed to the ground. Road convoys were escorted by Mosquitoes and Thunderbolts. On one occasion the RAF officer and his wireless operator who were controlling the air support were both killed in their Air Contact jeep. Later curfews were introduced in an attempt to curtail the nightly activities.

All Mosquitoes were grounded at the end of December, pending an inspection of the main spar. Of the eleven aircraft checked, eight were declared unserviceable. From the flying point of view, late December and the whole of January was unsatisfactory. Most of the flying time was taken up by ferrying aircraft to Seletar for inspections. Repairs were taking longer than expected owing to the shortage of plywood while fresh stocks were taking weeks to arrive.

In January 1946, the remainder of the Squadron moved to Batavia, its ground crews and equipment travelling in LST 3035. During the voyage the 'Crossing the Line' ceremony took place. Up to this point, there was only a detachment of essential groundcrews at Batavia. John Ramsden recalls that his duties included flying between Singapore, Batavia and Soerabaya keeping an eye on things. On reaching Batavia, it was found that the huts allocated to the Squadron were unfit as quarters. To remedy this, all work was stopped for four days and the airmen were given time to clean and repair the accommodation. In spite of every effort made by No.904 Wing, conditions were very bad. The period was made more difficult owing to disturbances on many RAF stations in the Far East. The spirit of No.84 Squadron, however, remained as high as ever and was summed up by one airman who said: "We could never strike, it would have spoilt the good name of 'Eighty Four'".

The New Year brought a gradual improvement. Relations improved and it was agreed with Soekarno that two Dakotas a day could fly into the interior to evacuate prisoners. Over the following months, many thousands of POWs and internees were released and evacuated. On average 140 a day were flown from the interior, many of whom were on stretchers. Children were often so emaciated that several could be bundled together under one seat belt.

Cpl James Bush, the Squadron photographer, was one of those who came from Seletar on LST 3035. In his letters he recalls that it was rumoured that extra pay would be paid, which was an incentive for a mere NCO. During the occupation, the Japanese had banned the Dutch guilder, the island's pre-war currency, and had introduced 'banana money' - rupiahs. When the British arrived, the locals, encouraged by their ex-masters, refused to take the Dutch guilder. Meanwhile the Army had unearthed the printing presses which the Japs had used and started to print rupiahs. Every UK serviceman in the Dutch East Indies received a free weekly issue of Rupiahs as extra pay. They would buy a meal at any of the local restaurants and also goods from the markets and street traders and there was plenty of loot for sale. So much phoney money slushing around could not have done any good to the new Indonesian economy! Bush continues by saying: "The talk given by the CO before leaving Seletar emphasised that we should not take sides in the Indonesian fight for independence but no mention was made of any restrictions in fraternising with the population. Even if there had been, I doubt if it could have been enforced as most of the men easily succumbed to the natural hospitality of the Javanese once the initial mistrust had been overcome. The children, as always, made the first advances and quickly learned that members of No.84 Squadron were a good source of sweets and chocolate. In contrast to the 'Amsterdam Yanks', as the Dutch forces were called because they were kitted out in American uniform, we never carried arms other than on sentry duty whilst the Dutch seemed to be laden with every type of weapon they could lay their hands on".

"The "Amsterdam Yanks" were Dutch marines who had been trained in the United States. They had been landed at Tanjong Priok 'by accident' as Dutch troops were not allowed on the islands of Java and Sumatra at that time. It was soon appreciated where our sympathies lay and many of us bought copies of the Merdaka magazine and accepted tracts prepared by the Indonesian support groups. The NCOs and airmen were billeted in a road now known as Jalan Bunga Besar. On a recent visit to the area, I was able to locate the house where I spent those few months and was surprised to find that it is now occupied by two retired Indonesian Air Force men".

At that time, terrorists were still in control of areas around

Japanese seaplanes at Seletar and a trainer at Kemajoran.
Top: *Aichi E13A1 three-seater, code-name "Jake"*
Centre: *Mitsubishi F1M2 two-seater, code-name "Pete"*
Bottom: *Yokosuka K5Y1, code-name "Willow"*

Batavia and were using every weapon they could lay their hands on. In several incidents, POWs and internees were killed.

Flt Sgt Keith Rimmer also joined the Squadron in January 1946. He writes: "After ferrying out a Mosquito from England to Madras, I was sent to the transit camp at Bhopal to await a posting to an active squadron. This resulted in my joining 84 at Seletar at the end of December 1945. A few days after joining the Squadron, my navigator, Flt Sgt F Searles and myself were summoned before the CO and asked if we wished to volunteer for detachment to Batavia. Apparently all aircrews were given this option. My log book is littered with names I have long since forgotten, Soekaboemi, Poentjak Pass and other indecipherable towns. Instructions were that roadblocks and signs of rebel activities were to be logged. The rebels had a few Bofors guns (probably Jap ack-ack), which they popped off at us regularly but our instructions were not to fire back until we had radioed HQ to obtain approval, which never seemed to be granted".

He remembers that someone in the Sergeant's Mess had acquired stocks of Pacific ration packs and that a rota of members used to take turns in going to the local market and exchanging them for fresh food, including crates of chickens. At the time, they had Korean ex-prisoners working in the mess and, at first, they took it as natural to pluck the chickens alive before killing and cooking them!

February was another disappointing month. The Mosquitoes remained grounded the whole time for comprehensive inspections. Seven aircraft failed to pass and were flown to No.390 MU for

repair. Meanwhile Fg Off Shakeshaft had travelled to Allahabad to collect a new Mosquito. Out of 99 Mosquitoes there, only one was passed fit for flying and even this aircraft was found to need a new leading edge when it arrived at Seletar. During February, the detachment of crews serving at Soerabaya was pulled out, leaving behind Flt Lt J G Ferguson and Flt Lt K Brown to look after one Mosquito which had been deemed repairable. It was not until the 20th that these two officers were able to rejoin the Squadron at Kemajoram.

In February, Flt Lt M N Brownrigg and Ron Cameron left the Squadron. Flt Lt John Clyne followed in early March. It saw the arrival of Sqn Ldr 'Dizzy' Addicott on attachment from No. 110 Squadron pending a posting as flight commander on No.84 Squadron.

The first operational sortie since 20 January was flown by Fg Off W S Matta and Flt Sgt D Fraser on 15 March. Taking off at 16.30, they relieved a section of No.81 Squadron's Thunderbolts on convoy patrol over the mountains between Buitenzorg and Tjiandjoer. Over the next few days, further sorties were flown looking for suspected concentrations of Indonesian terrorists. For the first 14 days of March, 84 Squadron flew operational sorties in conjunction with No. 81 Squadron's Thunderbolts. They consisted mainly of flying patrols over army transport convoys between Batavia and Bandoeng. Two tactical reconnaissances were flown over areas south of Bandoeng and a photographic flight over Tjilatjap.

No.84 Squadron was noted for its characters and one of these was Sgt Jack Steele. Sqn Ldr Addicott writes that: "Steele had a chequered history but was extremely keen. He endeared himself to everyone when he acquired an immaculate Lincoln Zephyr V12 from somewhere in Batavia. (It was later commandeered by Gp Capt Hughie Edwards VC DSO). Later, he acquired a 600cc BMW motor-cycle which had been removed from a German submarine which had been refuelling at Tanjong Priok. He spent weeks rebuilding this, until it was taken over by the MPs".

On 18 March 1946, the aircraft were again grounded operationally pending a further inspection of the main spar. It is stated in the records that the Squadron had more confidence in its own carpenters and asked for permission to inspect the aircraft on the spot. Headquarters, Netherlands East Indies, were unwilling to alter the ACSEA decision and had not even bothered to find out what was the nature of the inspection, saying that the higher formation must have good reasons. As a result of backing by Gp Capt D Lee, the Station Commander, Wg Cdr Constable-Maxwell, obtained permission to visit HQ ACSEA. On 31 March, Constable-Maxwell accompanied by Ramsden the Engineer Officer, flew RF960 from Kemajoram to Singapore. On arrival they flew very low and very fast along the waterfront in full view of the Cathay Building which housed the HQ, doing tight turns and slow rolls to demonstrate to the AOC-in-C and his chairborne warriors the complete faith they had in their aircraft. After Constable-Maxwell had stated his case, Headquarters agreed to let the Squadron carry on flying operationally and to do the inspections themselves. As a result, the Squadron did not miss a day's operational flying and also completed the inspections in a third of the estimated time given by the MU. Constable-Maxwell put on record the sterling work done by Sgt Tom Dyer and his team of carpenters.

April continued with convoy cover patrols. On the 9th, a superhuman effort resulted in 12 aircraft taking off to escort the AOC-in-C, Sir Keith Park, into Batavia. On the 15th, five aircraft took off to look for an overdue Sea Otter but were recalled after 15 minutes. the Sea Otter having landed due to a fuel problem. It was followed a day later by an airborne pilgrimage to Tjilatjap by the CO and Flt Lt John Ramsden. It was flown as a gesture of respect to those members of No.84 Squadron who had escaped from Java just over four years previously. During the month, 50 operational sorties were flown totalling 139 flying hours.

It was becoming obvious to Soekarno and others in the Indonesian Government that it was essential for some of the Dutch to remain on the islands. By early May, negotiations were in progress between the two countries. May also saw 84's participation in the Java campaign come to an end. By the 13th, all of the aircraft had been flown to Kuala Lumpur. Four days later, the CO, ten officers and 140 airmen left Batavia by sea on board the SS *Johann de Witt* sailing to Singapore. On the 21st, the boat party arrived at Kuala Lumpur. The airmen were billeted in a girls' school whilst the officers and NCOs were quartered in houses alongside the racecourse. The change of diet from Pacific rations was welcomed by all!.

During the month of June, no operational flying was done by the Squadron. Formation flying practice flights were carried out

View from the cockpit during a formation flight over Singapore. Note the size of the code letters used. Idnetifiable are RF656 PY-U and TE667 PY-X

and the Squadron flew flypasts over the Victory Parade in Kuala Lumpur and over the King's Birthday Parade in Singapore. On the 10th, the airmen were moved from the girls' school to bashas near the airfield. Unfortunately the majority of them leaked, which did not improve tempers!.

In July the Squadron rapidly increased its flying hours, mainly in the form of navigational trips and formation flying. Twelve aircraft took part in a search for a Transport Command Dakota which had last been heard of over the Cameron Highlands. Due to the nature of the ground and the usual cloudy weather in the area, nothing was seen. Three new crews joined the Squadron whilst five other crews left on temporary duty, flying to Allahabad to ferry five Mosquito PR.34s to Singapore for No.684 Squadron. On the 22nd, the Squadron lost one of its senior NCOs, when Sgt Pratt died from scrub typhus.

On 21 July, the Squadron was reduced to a half-squadron. The establishment of 16 aircraft plus three reserves was reduced to eight plus two. A few men left at the beginning of the month and on the 26th a further 48 were posted. The aircraft were checked for spar trouble and Sgt Dyer rejected five out of the 17 aircraft.

On 1 August, Flt Lt John Ramsden, the engineer officer, completed his tour overseas. He had served throughout the Burma campaign and the conversion to the Mosquito. His knowledge of the Squadron history helped enormously to uphold the continuity of the Squadron tradition and his oft repeated phrase "Get some in, mate" was well known to all who made inaccurate statements about the Squadron.

The same day, a signal from Group Headquarters stated that the Squadron was to be disbanded on the 15th and that all flying was to stop. The CO visited the acting C-in-C and appealed to him to make recommendations to the Air Ministry to keep the Squadron in being, no matter how small it might have to be. The airmen were informed of the news and the whole Squadron was in a state of gloom. On the 8th, a signal arrived cancelling the earlier one and stated that 84 would remain in being on the basis of one flight with eight aircraft plus two in reserve. Criticism was levelled at AHQ on account of its lack of consideration to the Squadron. It was fully appreciated that any squadron may have to disband, but such a callous and sudden order and amended it a week later, was something not appreciated by its members.

The gloom was not dispelled when on the 9th Fg Off Jock Anderson and his navigator Fg Off Doug Wright were killed. They met their deaths at Mingaladon airfield, Rangoon, when the Mosquito PR.34 which they were flying in from India swung on take-off, hitting a monsoon ditch. The cause of the swing was not known. A few days later, Sgt Steele and Fg Off Tippell force-landed in the Gulf of Siam. Steele made a superb landing in the sea near an island just off the coast of French Indo-China. The Mosquito stood up to it well and was washed on and off the island on three successive tides. They were fed by native fishermen and, after three days, were sighted by Flt Lt R Chasney and Fg Off Jenkins. Supplies were dropped by a Beaufighter and they were finally picked up by a Thai seaplane flown in for the purpose.

The reduction of manpower was such that on 1 June the strength was 284. By 1 September the numbers were down to 156. These figures included all ranks, ground personnel and aircrew.

During the month a number of tactical recces were flown over the Grik and Perak areas in support of the Army. Malaya

Command stated the presence of Mosquitoes raised the morale of our own troops whilst lowering that of the communist guerrillas. On 29 August, two aircraft led by Constable-Maxwell took off on instruments from AHQ to investigate a dinghy. After searching the area designated nothing was sighted. It was later learned that the W/T message had been incorrectly read. The message being "Floated mine sighted" and not "Floated men sighted". They landed after dark when the new flare-path was tried out for the first time.

Early September brought an increase to the Squadron of five navigators from recently disbanded No.22 Squadron. This was countered immediately by three crews being seconded to No.45 Squadron, which was down to one serviceable pilot and a CO with a broken arm.

The 4th was 'D' Day for Operation 'Mudlark', an operation designed to clean up the bandit activities in the islands and marshes west of Lumut. At the same time they provided cover for an Indian Division which had landed. It was not a great success but prisoners were taken and the British prestige improved accordingly. The operation continued over the following days.

A day later, nine Mosquitoes led by the CO took off to escort a York aircraft bringing in the AOC-in-C, Air Marshal Sir George Pirie. They rendezvoused with a York over Port Swettenham and escorted it to Singapore. It was not until it landed that it was realised that there were five Yorks in the circuit and they had escorted the wrong one! Nevertheless the AOC-in-C was treated to a flypast of nine aircraft when he landed later. The same day the Squadron started its move to Seletar and by the 13th the move was completed. On the 14th, a parade was held on Changi airfield to commemorate the 'Battle of Britain'. No.84's contribution was a flight of six Mosquitoes led by the CO which flew over the field at a height of 200 feet. Flt Sgt K Rimmer, flying as No.2, commented in his letters that "The CO's enthusiasm to get as low as possible resulted in parts of the parade scattering!"

The move to Seletar was appreciated by all ranks, the accommodation being a considerable improvement on the bashas. Liberty buses were laid on for transport into Singapore every evening.

On 6 October, 84 Squadron's Mosquitoes took part in a search for a York which was overdue on a flight from Calcutta to Changi. The wreckage was eventually found by a Sunderland which had come down in the sea with engine trouble and was taxying back to base. Rimmer and Searles left the Squadron on the 8th, flying home a Mosquito PR.34 which had arrived only a few days previous. Incidentally, their flying time for the journey from Karachi to St Mawgan was 21 hours 35 minutes in just over two days, a record at the time.

Later in the month, Operation 'Coconut' was devised as a training programme. The Squadron was detailed to find and attack HMS *Venerable* believed to have been in the area of the Anamba Islands. Eight Mosquitoes were airborne by 0715 and set course for Mubur Island. At 0800 the CO returned with engine trouble escorted by Fg Off Howse. The remaining six aircraft continued their flight, located the carrier and succeeded in pressing home the 'attack'. During the month, 30 operational sorties were flown totalling 87 flying hours. It was also learned that, because of continual problems with glue fatigue and separation of the mainspar, the Squadron were at last to lose their Mosquitoes and re-equip with the Bristol Beaufighter TF.X.

During November, a series of practice 'operations' were flown against carriers in the area. On Operation 'Brandy', eight Mosquitoes took off to attack HMS *Venerable* which put up four Fireflies and eight Seafires in her defence. The Mosquitoes went in two waves, the main attack force of six aircraft at low-level whilst two decoys flew at high level, which were scheduled to attack in a dive immediately after the main force. Owing to an early sighting by a patrolling Firefly, the attack lost its synchronisation but was nevertheless considered to be successful. It was followed a few days later by Operation 'Ginger Ale'. During these practice operations, visits were made to the *Venerable* by eight officers and 30 airmen.

On 1 December, Wg Cdr F Gomersall OBE arrived to take over the command of the Squadron from Wg Cdr M H Constable-Maxwell DSO DFC. Two days later three aircraft took off to carry out a strike against HMS *Belfast*. Four attacks were made in waves of three and also singly from bow to stern. After returning to base at 1530, the Squadron was inspected by the AOC Malaya, AVM Breakey. The following day the Chief of Air Staff, Marshal of the Royal Air Force Lord Tedder, visited the Squadron and spent some time chatting informally to the officers and men. His sympathetic approach to the problems of release and extended service created a

The scrap yard at Seletar in November 1946 full of Mosquitoes, including No.84's PY-B in the foreground

very good impression on all ranks.

The first of the Squadron's Beaufighters (RD804) arrived at base on the 6th, being test-flown by Wg Cdr M H Constable-Maxwell before he departed. Operation 'Allen' and Operation 'Nervo' were flown during the early days of December, both of these being practice strikes on HMS *Glory*.

On the 13th, a signal came from AHQ ACFE that all aircraft were to be inspected for water seepage of the inboard flap. Corrosion of the securing bolts meant that four of the Mosquitoes were immediately grounded while another five were to undergo a more thorough inspection. So ended the Mosquito's service with No.84 Squadron. As Sqn Ldr D Addicott comments in letters: "The Mosquitoes were excellent aircraft but were never designed for tropical climes. In extreme heat the wood would shrink and when the heavy rains came, the rivets would pop out from everywhere". Nevertheless, with all its drawbacks, No.84 Squadron could be proud of the fact that, by sheer hard work, it kept them flying for the two years they were equipped with them.

The following paragraphs give the reader an indication of the problems encountered by the engineering staff of the Squadron to keep the Mosquitoes flying.

The Mosquito had scarf joints in their main spar just outboard of the engines, glued with casein cement under pressure during manufacture. As with other joints in the aircraft, a loss of adhesion occurred on some aircraft in tropical conditions. The Mosquito was manufactured at a number of places in the UK, some by the major furniture manufacturers and aircraft from a couple of these sources were particularly prone to glued joint deterioration. The inspection of this joint necessitated trepanning a hole about 1" **check** diameter with a rose cutter in the plywood facing to the spar at a precise position on the spar. It had to be expertly done so that the spruce of the spar boom was not damaged. The cutter had only to penetrate the thickness of the plywood. When the scarf was revealed, one could measure with feelers if any separation had taken place. A tolerance was given both to the depth of separation and the percentage of the length of scarf that was affected. It was up to the engineer officer to ensure that these tolerances were adhered to. According to the condition of the joint the aircraft was either written-off or given further finite life. After the inspection, serviceable aircraft were recovered by gluing and pinning an accurately cut disc of plywood into the trepanned hole and doping a fabric cover over the insert. An inspection hole had to be cut in the leading edge to get at the spar and to complete the recovery process a flush patch had to be applied to the leading edge. It could be that silver dope was used to apply the fabric over the repair disc in the spar to give the mistaken impression that the trepanned hole had

been filled with lead.

There were other areas of the aircraft which at some time or another in late 1945 or 1946 had to be inspected for glue separation after such conditions had been found by other users. One of these areas were the leading edges. A PR Mosquito crashed at Singapore because a large portion of the leading edge became detached, which was followed by the wing ripping off. The inspection consisted of a careful examination of the joint of the leading skin at the top and bottom of the main spar and by tapping along the line of the leading edge ribs to see if the pinned and glued joint of the skin to the rib was sound. Deteriorating adhesion produced a hollow sound. Damaged leading edges could be repaired, within the limits laid down in the Repair Manual, by flush patches. If the damaged areas were excessive, sections of the leading edges could be replaced if spare sections were available. Some damage, such as that caused by hail in tropical storms, necessitated the aircraft undergoing 3rd line repair.

There were also problems experienced with the rigging of the aileron controls in the early days but this was, in many cases, due to lack of experience. John Ramsden's log book shows that he flew on three air tests in HR634 between 15 March and 6 April with Flt Lt Milnes as pilot to get the aileron adjustment right, the first of which was described as 'dicey'. John Ramsden closes by saying that "There were also instances of recurring trouble with certain fuel system components. But I do not think the aircraft caused much trouble generally. She really was a 'Beaut' on the ground and in the air".

The float from an Aichi E13A1 is modified to a seven-seater canoe

A group photograph of No. 84 Squadron in front of Beaufighter A at Tengah in 1947

CHAPTER 16 - WAS THE BEAUFIGHTER THE ANSWER?

Conversion to the Bristol Beaufighter had been scheduled to begin in January 1947, but the grounding of many of the Mosquitoes on 13 December precipitated matters and training started on the 14th when Flt Lt Chasney 'solo-ed' after a dual flight with Flt Lt Parker DFC. The same month, Parker returned to 'Blighty' for his 'demob'. Chasney took over the role of instructor and by the end of December, six pilots had solo-ed.

During the month, the Squadron lost many of its aircrew and started the New Year with nine pilots and six navigators. In addition the impact of the release scheme had been harder than expected and many of the valuable tradesmen had left for 'Civvy Street'. Fortunately, the Squadron's technical efficiency had been maintained. The timing and conversion to Beaufighters was said to depend on the availability of spares and equipment at No.389 MU. Although the Squadron Engineer Officer was confident, the MU was not prepared to commit itself because they had not had time to sort out the crates!

By the end of December, spares were beginning to arrive but the flow was not expected to reach full scale until the end of January. Meanwhile, conversion on to the Beaufighter was maintained, despite the usual moans that the controls were heavy compared with the Mosquito. The aircrew tempered this with the comment that the 'Beau' seemed to have few vices.

During January, a number of practice cross-country flights took place. Two aircraft of the Squadron co-operated with the Lancasters of No.7 Squadron in a formation flight over the island and on the 24th, Flt Lt Ross and Fg Off Tippell assisted in Operation 'Red Lion II', by ensuring that the target area, Perak Island, was clear. A memo in the records state that the accuracy of the bombing was pathetic, with the abundant bird life being only slightly disturbed.

The following day, 84 Squadron lost one of its crews when Fg Off Loman and Flt Sgt Grayston were killed when the Beaufighter they were flying crashed on take-off at Poona. They were on detachment to No.45 Squadron for ferrying duties. Four days later, another fatality occurred when Fg Off Maltese who was demonstrating the aircraft to Fg Off Belsham, crashed. Belsham had a miraculous escape, suffering cuts and bruises with 3rd degree burns but Maltese died from his injuries. He was buried on the 30th at Kranji Military Cemetery.

Mike Verschoyle, one of the Squadron's navigators, wrote in letters to the author that: "Regarding Maltese's crash, Fg Off Belsham, the second pilot, was standing behind Maltese when he crashed into coconut trees on an island in the Straits of Johore. Belsham was thrown clear and was taken across to the mainland by native boat, remembering nothing until he found himself standing in the road trying to thumb a lift into Singapore". Verschoyle continues by saying that "He spent a few days in hospital with minor burns but later declined to return to flying".

The conversion programme received something of a set-back with this accident. Although not mentioned at the Court of Enquiry, doubts were put forward as to the ability of the Beaufighter to maintain height on one engine. These were confirmed by a signal from AHQ Malaya forbidding single-engine flying until the result of the Court of Enquiry was known. However, before the signal was received, two demonstrations had been carried out, showing convincingly that a 'Beau' could climb on one engine at certain heights.

Coupled with this set-back was the fact that there was a great deal of minor unserviceability. This appeared to be traceable to the fact that the Beaufighters which were being issued, although comparatively new, had been stored under poor conditions for long periods, with inevitable deterioration. In addition, the spares which the Squadron were receiving were suffering in the same way. Of 15 magnetos which were issued by No.389 MU, all were faulty to some degree.

Verschoyle continues by saying that "As I was the Squadron Navigation Officer, I deemed it my duty to fly with all the pilots during their Beaufighter conversion. Continual problems with engine failure was experienced (mainly due to the aircraft being 'mothballed' in India for some years) and, although additional aircraft were flown in, the troubles persisted. I myself experienced two engine failures, including an aborted landing and going around again on one engine".

Due to the shortage of personnel on the Squadron, sporting activities were effectively curtailed but rugby and football teams were formed with No.81 Squadron calling themselves the 'Beauquitoes'.

Serviceability improved during February, with the result that several mock operations were carried out with the Royal Navy. On the 4th, three aircraft led by Wg Cdr F Gomersall attacked HMS *Aeneas* (code name Operation 'Iliad'). The second called Operation 'Dotage' was against the carrier HMS *Venerable* and the third (Operation 'Baptism Phase I') was against HMS *Ocean* and her attendant destroyers, *Contest* and *Finisterre*. At the end of the month, a search was organised for a missing Dakota from No.48 Squadron but, after nearly 22 hours flying, the search was abandoned with nothing seen of the aircraft or any survivors.

During the month, Flt Lt Dave Ross and Fg Off Mike Verschoyle were sent to Bangkok to retrieve an abandoned Beaufighter which all the other crews in the area had refused to fly. On examining it, they found a large cobweb filling the cockpit (so much for daily inspections!); also the navigator's cupola was missing. After a 'night on the town', they took off the following morning. The radio 'packed up' at the end of the runway, but they continued without clearance and headed out over the China Sea. The engines ran like sewing machines and, after a flight of four hours and ten minutes, they landed safely at Seletar. They were met by the Squadron engineer officer who told them to taxi the aircraft over to the dump and leave it there!

Because of the shortage of officers on the station, Verschoyle's duties included a stint on flying control, relief Civil Administrative Officer (in charge of 3,000 native coolies and 800 Japanese POWs), Visual Liaison Control Officer with the Army and finally Jungle Survival Instructor for South-East Asia. Not a bad coverage for a mere FO! The last post allowed him the use of a jeep without a driver. He had it painted with yellow and black squares for easy visibility. He also acquired a three-ton truck which he had equipped with W/T, VHF and a night fighter Mark X AI radar set which had been removed from a 'butchered' Mosquito. Thus equipped, the Squadron were able to bring in supplies to the jungle with their very own aircraft directional radar control, a totally unknown facility in those days!

The aircrew at that time included a Frenchman, Jacques Lenthall, who earlier, had been bitten by the Squadron dog. As a result, he had to suffer repeated injections in case he developed rabies. There were also four pilots from the first post-war course at Cranwell, W C 'Flush' Kendall, E F Budworth, Billy Wells, and Graham Brie, son of a helicopter specialist, whose idea of amusement was to fly very low and blow the junks over on their sides. This was only curbed when Verschoyle threatened to report him, having been reduced to a nervous wreck!

Practice cross-country flights continued throughout early March and the Squadron's part in Operation 'Lady' had to be cancelled due to bad weather conditions. Fg Off Graham Brie flying on an air test on the 15th had the port engine fail on take-off but managed to do a successful circuit before landing on one; for this he was awarded a 'green' endorsement. On the 25th, WO Jock Makin and Cpl Mellor were killed when the 'Beau' they had been testing spun in on the approach to land at Sembawang. As a result of this accident, all of the Squadron's aircraft were grounded pending a full investigation. The Squadron were also sickened to learn that Fg Off Joe Colvin, a navigator who was on detachment to fly a Mosquito to New Zealand with Wg Cdr Hoare, had been reported missing over the Gulf of Carpentaria. A search was made by Dutch Dakotas and, on 5 April, the Squadron received the official confirmation of the death of Joe Colvin. He was an extremely popular officer and was sorely missed.

Confidence in the Beaufighter had sunk to a very low level with the two accidents, the cause of the problem being put down to engine sleeve seizure.

The Squadron strength took another dive during March. Coupled with the three fatalities, six officers were posted, whilst the groundcrew decreased from 111 in February to 90 in March.

It was not until 11 April that the first of the Beaufighters were ready for an air test. During the fortnight they had been grounded, all of the cylinder heads had been removed and cleaned in an effort to check the sleeve failures. A certain amount of flying had been done using No.209 Squadron's Harvard trainer.

By the 14th, two more were ready for their air test. The following day, Sqn Ldr Butler of the Empire Flying School visited the Squadron to fly the Beaufighter to 'keep his hand in', having not flown one for over a year or two. His asymmetric landings and overshoots were an excellent demonstration of what could be done with the Beaufighter and were witnessed by ground and aircrews alike. The next day he took up Flt Lt Ross, Fg Offs Kendall, Wells and Budworth on demonstration flights. All were greatly impressed and learnt many new tips on how to get the best out off the 'Beau'.

On the 25th, a search was ordered for the ship *Sir Harvey*

Adamson of the British India Steam Navigation Company, carrying 250 passengers, which went missing somewhere between Penang and Victoria Point. Unfortunately, the two aircraft allocated for the search went u/s after the first flight.

The following days were spent practising formation flying, preparing for the King's Birthday Flypast at Kuching. A photo-recce flight was carried out over the Phuket area and anti-piracy patrols were flown over the Malacca Straits. On 6 May, the jib of a crane working on the airfield, fell across the rear fuselage of a Beaufighter, causing considerable damage and rendering the aircraft u/s for some time.

The visit to Changi of Lincoln *Thor II* of the Empire Air Armament School brought considerable interest and the majority of the Squadron turned out to see it.

From the maintenance angle, the months of April and May were disappointing. Two aircraft were grounded for the greater part awaiting spares. Three exhaust rings were changed and a new engine on its first test flight became u/s because of moisture in the magnetos. There were also other engine failures which necessitated a lot of work to find the cause.

After nearly five weeks training in the art of formation flying, the King's Birthday Flypast was flown over Kuching as it was the first occasion the King's birthday had been celebrated in this colony, only recently ceded to Great Britain. Unfortunately, of the five aircraft of No.84 Squadron to lead the flypast, one had to drop out due to unserviceability. However, three runs had to be made over the town of Kuching to coincide with the military parade. Later a letter was received from the Governor of Sarawak thanking the Squadron and all concerned for their efforts.

On their return from Kuching, Flt Lt Ross experienced engine failure. He was compelled to feather the starboard propeller but landed without further mishap.

On the 17th, the first air-to-ground cannon-firing sorties were carried out, chiefly to give the armourers practice in loading and arming the aircraft. The sorties were not very successful as, in each case, the guns stopped after firing a few rounds. Another problem to be sorted out! The same afternoon Fg Off 'Flush' Kendall and Sgt Byrne were airborne on a low-level cross country when a urgent signal was received from Labuan for anti-rabies serum for six villagers who had been bitten by a mad dog. The nearest place where the serum could be obtained was Kuala Lumpur and Kendall was contacted by radio and diverted to collect it; from there it was flown to Seletar where a Mosquito of No.81 Squadron carried it on to Labuan. It was later reported that the serum had been successful and that the villagers had recovered.

During the month, Sqn Ldr M J Gloster DFC arrived to take over the duties of flight commander, taking over from Flt Lt Ross. On 2 July, Wg Cdr Bird-Wilson DSO DFC AFC visited the Squadron in a Gloster Meteor IV. After showing a film and giving a lecture on jet propulsion, he showed its capabilities with a flying display. This was of particular interest as it was the first time many of those present had seen the Meteor, and certainly at such close quarters.

Over the following days, the four serviceable aircraft on the Squadron carried out mock attacks on HMS *Belfast*. Whilst one was despatched just before the main force to decoy the fighter cover, the other three carried out a simulated rocket and torpedo attack on the cruiser. In the middle of the month, an aircraft carried out an interception exercise on the *Empire Trooper* which was outward bound from Singapore to the UK. A couple of days later, at the request of the Straits Steamship Company, a search was made for the motor vessel *Sedenak*. It was feared that it had been requisitioned by the Indonesians in preparation for their struggle against the Dutch but it was later reported that it had arrived safely at Singapore.

On 21 July, Wg Cdr F Gomersall and Sqn Ldr M J Gloster DFC paid a visit to AHQ Malaya, the object being to discover if they could expect any replacement flying personnel and to acquaint Air Staff with the seriousness of the situation. The Squadron was at that time reduced to the Commanding Officer, one flight commander and two flying officers.

The first fortnight of August was noted for its total lack of flying by the Beaufighters; 22 hours were flown on the Harvard. This was due to the fact that the Base Servicing Wing had been told to work on the Mosquitoes of No.81 Squadron at the expense of the Beaufighters. On the 14th the CO went on leave, with the result that there were now only Sqn Ldr Gloster and Fg Off J Wells left as pilots. Fortunately, the return of Flt Lt D Ross and Fg Off G Brie from detachment enabled the Squadron to take part in a mock attack on the sloop HMS *Black Swan* on the 28th. Although the exercise was considered a great success from 84's point of view, a

Beaufighter TF.X RD826 at Tengah (J D Rawlings)

breakdown of communications between the ship and its Spitfire defenders led to questions being asked by the Air Staff and by officers of *Black Swan*.

It was followed on the 30th by a mock torpedo attack on HMS *Glory*. After being shadowed by a single Beaufighter, three aircraft attacked when the carrier was 270 miles south-east of Singapore. The main striking force had delivered its first torpedo and was reforming for a pseudo rocket attack before the flight was intercepted.

September started favourably with 10 hours 40 minutes being flown on the first two days of the month. Unfortunately, it was not maintained and by the end of September a total of 56 sorties had been flown totalling 56 hours 15 minutes. The reduction in flying was made due to the fact that three of the Squadron's Beaufighters were awaiting spares while the others were on minor inspections.

In addition, the move to Changi caused a certain amount of diversion when the groundcrew had to spend much of their time packing the Squadron stores and aircraft spares. 'Battle of Britain Day' was celebrated on 15 September when the Squadron was inspected by the AOC, AVM J D Breakey CB DFC. The day was declared a holiday and the Squadron stood down.

With effect from the 15th, a major change took place on the Squadron. The post of commanding officer had been reduced to that of a squadron leader and that of flight commander to a flight lieutenant. Sqn Ldr M H Gloster DFC assumed command from Wg Cdr F Gomersall OBE who was posted.

The following day, Fg Off Budworth and Flt Sgt Handley took part in Operation 'Manxman'. The exercise was designed to give practice to the *Manxman's* fighter direction officer by directing Spitfires of No.60 Squadron to intercept the Beaufighter. Fg Off Budworth made two runs over the minelayer. On each occasion he started from a point on a circle of 70 miles radius of the ship. On neither occasion was he intercepted although, after the first attack, he saw two Spitfires over the ship setting course for home. After the second run he was asked by the ship to make a series of attacks in order to exercise her guns and fire direction equipment.

The move to Changi was completed on 26 September. This meant sharing the station with five other squadrons and an AOP flight. It also meant that the Squadron found itself very short of office accommodation.

Unserviceability problems were once more the name of the game in October. During the latter half of the month, no fewer than four of the Squadron's seven aircraft were u/s, the result being that the three remaining aircraft were being flown much more often and were rapidly approaching their minor inspections.

On 10 October two of the remaining aircraft, flown by Fg Off Wells and WO K Dillon, took part in Operation 'Theseus'. After a rendezvous with a Sunderland of No.209 Squadron, they were homed on to the carrier HMS *Theseus* where they were directed to attack its attendant destroyer HMS *Cockade*. After the attack they returned to Changi, being airborne for 3.45 hours. A night exercise was carried out with HMS *Manxman* on the 23rd when flares were dropped, allowing the aircraft to make successful mock attacks.

With the return of RD774 on the 29th, it was hoped that there would be an improvement, but it was not to be. After being air-tested on the 31st, it was discovered that the starboard engine had developed an oil leak from its carburettor. The unit was changed and the aircraft re-tested on 8 November. On this occasion, it was found that the magneto on each engine was breaking down in the air. The result was that all the magnetos were returned to Seletar for checking. It was found that the magnetos were arcing at high revs, so the points were cleaned, the magnetos re-tested and replaced. On assembly in the aircraft, the engines were run up, but the mag-drop remained as before. It was therefore decided to take the magnetos known to be serviceable out of RD801 which was on a 'major' and fit them to RD774. This rectified the problem in the starboard engine but the port engine was still giving trouble. The aircraft was test-flown in this condition, in the hope that continuous running at high power might clear up the trouble and, although they were run continuously for over one hour, the same symptoms occurred. It was then decided that it was a case of the entire harness breaking down at high power. In the end, the aircraft was returned to 'R and I' for a complete harness change and the fitting of Simms magnetos in place of the BTH mags previously used.

This was typical of the luck which had dogged No.84. Squadron since being equipped with the Beaufighter. Another cause of prolonged unserviceability was the difficulty of keeping the BLG charging unit for the tail oleos serviceable. Leaks were a continual problem. Any alteration would have meant that the aircraft would have become more difficult to handle on the ground as it became directionally unstable.

It was rumoured that about this time the groundcrew should be encouraged to fly with the pilots on air tests to ensure that they took a greater pride in their work. Some letters confirm that the standard of maintenance improved after this was introduced.

Because of No.18 (Burma) Squadron's disbandment, the Squadron took over its 'Pampa' sorties (Meteorological reconnaissance flights). This not only resulted in extra flying time but an increase in flying personnel, including a new Commanding Officer, Sqn Ldr D R Turley-George DFC, who replaced Sqn Ldr M J Gloster DFC, who was posted to No.390 Maintenance Unit.

With No.18 disbanding, four of its aircrews joined No.84 Squadron. Group Captain Hugh Tudor writes: "I joined 84 Squadron on 1 November 1947 and left the Squadron on 26 May 1948. About the time I was posted I was engaged on a prolonged ferry flight, collecting a Mosquito from Karachi which had had an engine fire whilst being ferried out to the Royal New Zealand Air

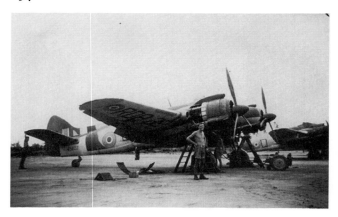

RD822 with LAC 'Taff' Whale

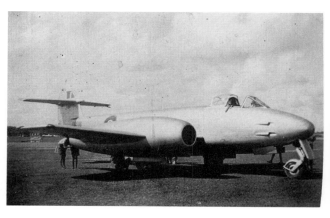

Meteor F.IV visiting Seletar in February 1947

station increased its station duties. At the time, there was no mention of the Squadron taking part in the campaign.

John Guthrie also comments on the shortage of ground personnel whilst at Tengah. "During my stay at Tengah I carried out the duties of NCO i/c Orderly Room as well as my flying duties; another time Fg Off Jacquest and myself were told to help other aircrew assemble rockets. One odd duty was the checking of tyres before take-off. The navigator had to get out at the end of the runway with a screwdriver to dig out the stones in the tread. I still have the chit signed by Flt Lt G Vaulknes stating that Nav II Guthrie has been examined by me and is in my opinion competent to check aircraft tyres for serviceability."

The first week of August saw five complete aircrews leave for the UK for a conversion course on the Bristol Brigand. These included Flt Lt D Ross, Fg Offs Jacquest, Kendall and Smith and PI Perkins. Ross and Jacquest became tour-expired and their places on the course were later taken by Sqn Ldr S G Nunn and WO K Dillon.

At 2000 hours on 9 August, orders were received that two aircraft, fully armed, were to take off for Kuala Lumpur at dawn on the following morning. A further two were to be on stand-by at 0800. This entailed the groundcrew working throughout the night. On the 10th, Sqn Ldr S G Nunn and Fg Off Budworth left Tengah at first light on detachment to the RAF Task Force at Kuala Lumpur. At Kuala Lumpur it was found that no bomb winch was available and a signal was sent to Tengah for the Harvard to fly one up. Later in the day it was discovered that RD786, the aircraft that the CO had flown, was u/s and Budworth flew it back to Tengah, exchanging it for RD858.

From Kuala Lumpur, the two Beaufighters flew to Kota Bharu where they were met by the British Adviser to Kelantan. In the evening the two pilots attended a briefing when it was decided to attack an old gold mine which was inhabited by insurgents. On the 12th, the two Beaufighters took off, each carrying two 500-lb bombs and eight 60-lb rockets. Despite the difficulty of the terrain, which necessitated attacking over a ridge and down the steep side of a valley, direct hits were made on a large bungalow and several outbuildings. Later it was learnt that 30 insurgents had been killed together with one elephant.

Another strike followed on the 13th when a rocket attack was mounted against bashas south of Triang which was believed to house a communist training camp. Spitfires of No.28 Squadron joined in the strafing and also took photographs. The 16th brought 84's most successful strike when an area south of Tapah, which was known to be occupied by insurgents, was strafed. It was planned that immediately after the strafing, the local police would go in and 'mop up'. Many bashas were hit by the Beaufighters, either collapsing them or setting them alight. On his first attack, Sqn Ldr S G Nunn's aircraft was struck by the debris of his exploding rockets. One spinner was severely dented, whilst numerous small holes appeared in the aircraft and the whole covered in mud, completely obscuring the view through the front windscreen. By reaching out through the clear-vision panel, Nunn managed to clear the windscreen sufficiently to follow up his attack. It is thought that he hit a store of ammunition, this being substantiated by the police finding large pieces of ammunition amongst the bashas. Later it was discovered that the target was one of the headquarters of the MPABA (Malay Peoples Anti-British Army).

The 17th was the Squadron's last strike of the detachment. Troops were to attack a jungle area south of Bentong and a RAF

strike was required for a morale effect on any insurgents in the area. Fg Off Budworth opened the attack, carrying two 500-lb bombs and eight 60-lb rockets. There were no actual targets but all missiles were placed in the designated areas. After the attack a 'flag waving' low-level run was carried out along the valley from Karak to Bentong. Beaufighters from No.45 Squadron and Spitfires from No.60 Squadron completed the strike.

The detachment returned to Tengah on the 18th. For the following few days four aircraft were on stand-by to replace any of 45 Squadron's Beaufighters. Later in the month, Sqn Ldr Nunn left for the conversion course on the Brigand. With effect from 1 September, the Squadron became temporarily non-operational so very little flying was done.

Over the following weeks, most of the Squadron's Beaus were handed over to No.45 Squadron. October saw the departure of No.84 Squadron from Singapore, having served in Air Command, Far East since 1946, during which time it had been stationed at Batavia, Kuala Lumpur, Seletar, Changi and Tengah.

At 0715 on 11 September 1948, the Squadron left Tengah by road for Singapore Docks. There the Squadron paraded on the quayside and, in the presence of the majority of the officers from RAF Tengah, Group Captain Casey OBE, deputising for AVM Sanderson, AOC Malaya, delivered his parting address and wished the Squadron 'God Speed' and good wishes for the future. He then took the salute as the Squadron marched past, headed by the Band of the RAF (Malay) Regt. Embarking on the HMT *Empire Trooper* at 0900, it sailed for the Middle East at 1500 hours.

After a pleasant voyage from Singapore, the Squadron personnel disembarked in the Middle East on 1 November and proceeded to the transit camp at El Hambra where they were to stay for several weeks until air transport could be arranged to fly them to Habbaniya. The first party arrived there on the 28th.

The Commanding Officer, Sqn Ldr S G Nunn DFC, arrived at Habbaniya on 16 November from the United Kingdom to prepare for the arrival of the ground crews and administrative personnel. Meanwhile, in the UK, five aircrews continued their conversion course. It was during this period that the Squadron suffered the first of a number of set-backs. Firstly the aircraft required certain modifications which delayed their departure to the Middle East. It was then found that the spares provisioned for stations on route had not been despatched. This was rectified and

Discussion group, probably deciding whether P was serviceable

Beaufighter A on a sortie from Tengah in 1946

the departure was expected to take place in the immediate future. Another slip-up occurred when the spares were despatched to the Far East by mistake. By the time this was known and rectified several more weeks had elapsed.

If anyone reading this should think, 'the same old shambles all over again' I can promise that there are many more to come. With hindsight both the allocation of the Mosquito and the Beaufighter were nothing more than getting rid of surplus aircraft to squadrons in the Far East where little thought was given as to the suitability of the aircraft or in many ways the safety of the aircrews. Reading back through the Beaufighter chapter, it seems astonishing that the

Squadron could be operational for weeks on end without one aircraft available. You can understand now why I headed the chapter 'Was the Beaufighter the answer?'.

Throughout the month of December, the remainder of the ground crews were airlifted from El Hambra to Habbaniya and a great effort was made to have all the personnel on the new station for Christmas. Unfortunately the Christmas dinner was not up to standard but it was partially made up for by the abundance of beer at the bars. Nevertheless, morale at that time was low, with no aircraft and little to look forward to!

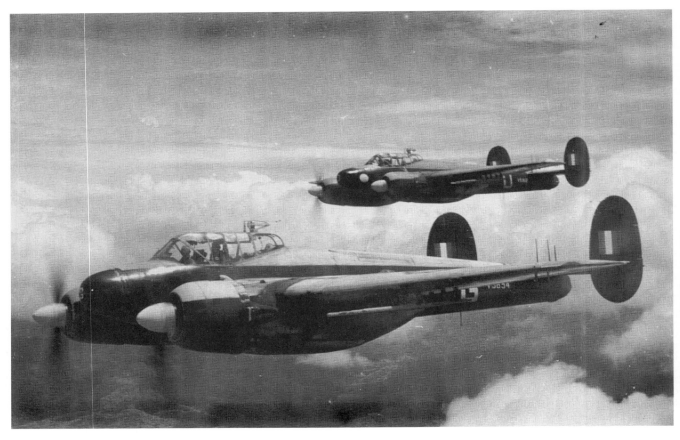

Brigands VS854 G and VS812 D on a strike over the Malayan jungle (Sqn Ldr P Elton)

CHAPTER 17 - LIFE WITH THE LAST TRAM FROM PATCHWAY

The first Bristol Brigands were expected to arrive at Habbaniya at the end of January 1949. Their delay could hardly worsen the planned operational role of the Squadron as the ground equipment and spares were still in the pipeline. However, the ground crew who had been attached to other units on the station had been assembled in No.84 Squadron's offices and hangars in readiness. Space at that time was rather cramped but would ease when No.249 (Tempest) Squadron moved to its new base in Egypt.

On 27 January, it was learnt that the first seven aircraft allotted to the Squadron had flown from St. Athan to Manston. On 5 February, the first two, RH817 crewed by Fg Off D W Smith, Flt Lt R S Wrigglesworth and Sgt C Sharkey and RH818 crewed by Fg Off W C Kendall, Flt Lt G Ottea and Sgt O'Brien, took off on their flight to Habbaniya. Two days later, RH810 (Fg Off J W Hedges, Flt Lt D E Breed and Sgt Mason) and RH812 with a ferry crew followed. On the 7th, RH817 and RH818 arrived over Habbaniya escorted by three Tempests of No.249 Squadron. They were met at dispersal by the Station Commander, Group Captain D W Lane and the OC No.84 Squadron, Squadron Leader S G Nunn DFC. By 20 February, three more aircraft had arrived, RH809, RH813 and RH815.

The Bristol Brigand had originally been designed as a torpedo-fighter and was intended for issue to Nos.36 and 42 Squadrons in 1946. By that time, the requirement for a strike aircraft in Coastal Command no longer existed and they were retained at Filton for conversion to light bombers suitable for tropical duty in the Far East. Their conversion consisted of the removal of the torpedo-carrying facility and the installation of bomb racks for two 1,000-lb bombs. In addition, external bomb racks and rocket rails were to be placed outboard of the engines. The four cannon were retained but the rear gun was omitted. Of the 147 aircraft built, only three squadrons were to receive them, No.8 at Khormaksar, No.84 at Habbaniya and, a year later, by No.45 at Kuala Lumpur.

On 24 February, Sqn Ldr Nunn flew to Shaibah to collect the Squadron silver which had remained at the MU in Iraq since 84 left its 'ancestral' home in 1940.

The first few days of February were spent trying to beg, borrow or sometimes steal items of equipment which had not yet arrived. The arrival of the aircraft did much to raise the deteriorating morale of the groundcrew. Even then there was a restriction on the Brigands to the number of hours flown. It seems astonishing that a squadron scheduled to become operational in October 1948 should have received only 50% of its 'pack-up' by March 1949. Of this percentage, no items of urgently needed requirements such as mainwheels, tyres, tubes and starter batteries had been received. Even harder to believe was the fact that no items of hydraulic equipment had been provisioned for.

By March, the Squadron was almost back on its feet. The final Brigand had been ferried in, bringing the total to eight. Still handicapped by lack of equipment and spares, 88 hours were flown by the three crews. During the month two successful searches were carried out, the first on the 14th when a Tempest crash-landed after its engine failed. The second, at the request of the British Embassy, was for a motor boat that was adrift on Lake Bahi el Milth after a tropical rainstorm. Night-flying sorties were carried out and two communication flights made, one to Mafraq, the other to Fayid.

No armament training could be undertaken due to the lack of rocket rails, practice bombs and 20 mm cannon ammunition. Furthermore, the lack of cameras in the aircraft prevented any simulated attacks. The lack of hydraulic spares had already been felt as five hydraulic pumps had become unserviceable. The lack of cartridges for the emergency undercarriage-lowering system had prevented an otherwise serviceable aircraft from flying. It was also found that, as the first aircraft received was given its minor inspection, it would become unserviceable for some time due to the fouling of the fuel tanks.

Comments in the CO's notes stressed the fact that the Squadron was still drastically under strength with only five pilots, four navigators and five signallers. It pointed out that achieving a pre-arranged flying programme was very difficult owing to the number of station duties which had to be carried out. It was also possible that some officers might have to take their turn on air traffic control duties.

On 29 March, No.249 Squadron moved to its new base at Deversoir, just south of Ismailia in Egypt. This considerably eased the office accommodation. Another benefit was that the ground-crew were able to move to quarters near the Flying Wing, with an improvement in their living and messing facilities.

The lowest point came on 14 April, when not one aircraft was serviceable. Inspection had revealed that all hydraulic high-pressure lines showed signs of perishing although later it was decided that some were fit for limited flying. It was then heard that the Squadron would be receiving a Harvard trainer, and later a Bristol Buckmaster with which to continue instrument flying training. The problem of spares had been temporarily overcome by stripping one of the aircraft. By the end of the month, that aircraft was short of 18 major components including a propeller, two hydraulic pumps and a complete nose unit. Finally, a halt had been made in the case of this aircraft but comments state that other aircraft would suffer the same fate if spares in quantity were not soon provided.

There had been no improvement in the armament situation; 4,000 rounds of 20 mm ammunition had been flown in to bridge the gap but, of this, 3,500 were 'black listed'. It was announced that practice bombs and rockets would be arriving by sea but the RP rails and external bomb racks were being returned to the UK for modifications.

May was noticeable for several events. On the 2nd, Fg Off Derek Smith took off in RH809 'F' to take part in a realistically-planned desert rescue exercise. A vehicle representing a crashed aircraft was found and the information passed from the aircraft to enable groundcrew to locate the crash. It was made more difficult by a dust storm which varied in intensity throughout the exercise. On the 6th, four Brigands took off at 0800 for an hour's concentrated formation flying whilst later two aircraft flew a low-level navigation exercise. Two days later a Brigand took off at 0300 to fly to Sharjah and drop supplies to a French Dakota which had made a forced landing near Jask.

Cpl David Baxter, a clerk on the station, remembers a couple of flights he made at this time. "The first was on a low-level exercise when we scattered and chased a herd of camels much to the annoyance of the Arab who visibly shook his fist at us. We were that low! The second occurred on our return from a training flight; the radio had 'packed-up' and when we arrived over Habbaniya we found that a sandstorm was obliterating the airfield. The pilot could not see the runway and our fuel was running low. To my horror, I was assured that a parachute drop was a 'piece of cake' (even without practice). Fortunately the pilot saw a bit of the runway and I was relieved when he was able to make a successful landing."

Problems arose on the 10th when severe wrinkling of the inner and outer mainplane closing strips were found. It was suspected to have been caused by steep turns exceeding 3+G. On the 11th, cannon-firing exercises were carried out for the first time. During the following days over 5,000 rounds were expended in trials designed to test the gun installations and to check the stoppage incidence. Starting on the 14th, 26 flying hours were logged in the search for a missing Morane-Saulnier flown by Mme Dupeyron. By refuelling at Sharjah, the area being searched was extended. On the afternoon of the 15th came the news that the Morane, together with its pilot, had been found 50 miles north of the area searched. As a result of the Squadron's efforts, the AOC received a letter of appreciation from the French Ambassador in Baghdad.

At the end of the month, the Squadron was shocked to hear of the death of WO Edmunds, who had served with the Squadron until his recent transfer to the Repair and Inspection section. He was found drowned in the airmen's swimming pool.

With the arrival of new aircrews, the Squadron was able to put six Brigands into the air on 1 June in a demonstration of formation flying before visiting members of the Iraqi Staff College. During the following days, a 'show the flag' exercise was flown over towns and villages of the Trucial States. The six days of intensive flying were marked by the failure of no less than ten hydraulic pumps, which provided overwhelming evidence of the inadequacy of the 'Integral' pumps which were fitted on the Brigands by order of the Ministry of Supply.

John Guthrie, in correspondence, writes: "The 'show the flag' exercises were a major operation. As Flt Lt 'Tubby' Marshall's navigator, the first leg was to fly to Sharjah on 13 June and the following two days involved flying sorties, one lasting 5.05 hours. Alas, good old RH815 could not make it home to Habbaniya, being left at Sharjah for repairs. The crew returned to Habbaniya by courtesy of a Communications Flight Dakota KJ880."

On 16 June a search was instigated for a missing Devon aircraft lost between Aqaba and Habbaniya. A day later, news came through on the 'bush telegraph' that the crew of the Devon were safe in a village 90 miles south-west of Habbaniya called Nu Kheib. The following day, the AOC in his personal Devon flew down to collect the crew. Other aircraft which took part in the search included Lincolns of No.617 Squadron based at Shallufa, Dakotas from No.205 Group at Kabrit and a solitary Lancastrian which was on a visit from EFS.

On 24 June, an all-ranks Squadron party took place in a room adjoining the Airmens' Mess. During the evening, Flt Sgt Shepard presented the CO, Sqn Ldr S G Nunn with a wedding present from the NCOs and airmen of the Squadron. Two days later, the wedding took place between Sqn Ldr S G Nunn and Flt Off Chadwick WRAF. The following day, a Brigand flown by the CO flew to Cyprus for the honeymoon. In addition to the crew of three the aircraft carried Flt Off Nunn, Flt Lt D E Breed to attend a course and Fg Off 'Flush' Kendall to fly the aircraft back to Habbaniya. It was mentioned that in future RH813 'H' will be known as 'The Bridal Brigand'.

During July, only 66 hours 20 minutes were flown. The first practice bombing sorties were flown on the 8th when two aircraft flew four sorties carrying eight 11-lb practice bombs. 30-degree dive-bombing was practised but the results achieved tended to be very much a question of trial and error. It was found that the bottom ring in the gyro-gunsight was useless with undershoots of 300 yards. Later, the pilots discovered that the only datum point which could be used for aiming was the windscreen de-icer delivery nozzle! This was used for 20-degree dives. If the cloud level was low, straight and level bombing had to be employed. The pilot would then allow the target to go under the nose, count three and release. The height of sophistication! By the end of the month the entire stock of practice bombs held by No.115 MU had been used, 34 in all.

Chaos was caused in the servicing section when a signal received from AHQ quoted the wrong reference number, causing all the Brigands to be grounded because they were fitted with the wrong type of compressor. Calm descended two hours later when it was discovered that the reference number quoted in the signal referred to the correct compressor instead of vice-versa. On the 19th it was found that there were only sufficient centrifuges to equip three Brigands. In addition, six propellers became unserviceable and spares were still awaited. It was once again a case of 'robbing Peter to keep Paul flying'.

Not one Brigand was serviceable at the end of July, leaking flap-jacks causing faults in three of the aircraft. The position was not greatly improved during August. Eight centrifuges arrived during the month but were virtually useless due to the lack of suitable propellers. In all, only three aircraft were serviceable of which RH818 'G' completed 27 hours of a total of 41 flown in the month.

On the 16th, the Squadron's Buckmaster arrived, flown by Flt Lt Massey of the Overseas Ferry Unit. As the port engine was giving trouble, the aircraft was immediately made unserviceable. The 24th brought further problems when Sqn Ldr Nunn took-off on a cross-country flight. During the climb to 8,000 feet the starboard engine failed necessitating a return to base. On examination, it was found that the cylinder sleeve assembly had seized, the con rod had snapped and the lower end had penetrated the crankcase. Three days later, the CO took-off on a 15 minute flight test. Just as he became airborne the starboard tyre burst and the aircraft swung violently, coming to rest 300 yards off the runway. The impact of the unserviceable wheel caused the fire extinguisher switch to operate and both engines cut due to the injection of CO2 into the air intakes. No one was injured.

There was a marked improvement in the Squadron's fortunes in September, although it could have resulted in a serious accident. After aborting a low-level cross country flight because of a faulty starter motor, Flt Lt D W Smith's ground-crew were trying to diagnose the fault and when turning the propeller over, the motor fired. Fortunately, no one was hurt but there were some very pale-faced airmen about for the next hour or two. On the 15th of the month, 14 long-awaited metal propellers arrived and two new aircraft, RH826 J and RH828 K. Good Luck was not to last, Fg Off Don Baker flying RH828, was carrying out a low-level flight over the River Tigris when the aircraft touched the water, resulting in both props having their tips bent back approximately two feet. Despite the damage, Baker flew the aircraft back to base, a distance of some 200 miles.

On the 16 September, Sqn Ldr George Unwin DFM took over the command of the Squadron from Sqn Ldr S G Nunn who was

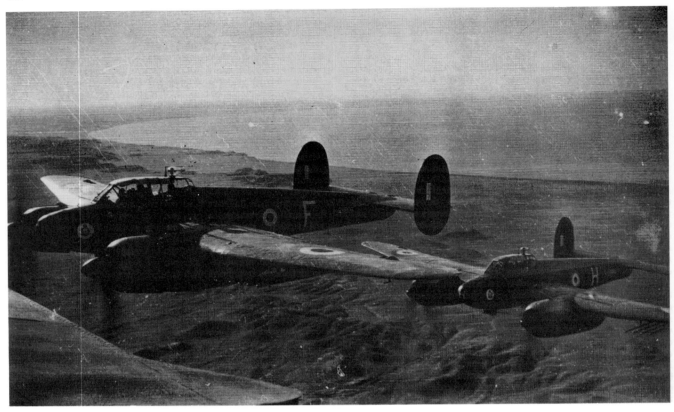

RH809 F and RH814 H over Iraq, Summer 1949

tour-expired.

A tactical exercise was carried out in co-operation with No.2 Armoured Car Company on the 23 September. A simulated ACC 'attack' on Habbaniya by a 'foreign force' was planned. No.2 ACC requested air support; four Brigands took off carrying practice bombs and 880 rounds of ammunition. For the first time 100 flying hours had been logged in a month. A marked improvement!

Armament training with rocket projectiles continued in November. Unfortunately, after one sortie, two aircraft were found to be unserviceable with cracks in the skin on the underside of the mainplanes and wrinkles on the upper surfaces.

During the month the Squadron was put on a two hour stand-by by AHQ for a possible movement to Aden to support other squadrons in the event of trouble arising in Somaliland. Later the possibility of trouble receded and the two-hour stand-by was extended to 48 hours.

The structural faults which had developed in the Brigand drastically curtailed the armament training programme. Following the cracking and the wrinkling of the mainplane surfaces, a minimum amount of 'G' had to be imposed, preventing dive-bombing. Rocket and cannon-firing continued but were carried out carefully to avoid unnecessary stresses on the aircraft. Fortunately, low-level bombing was allowed to continue with improved results.

On the 18th, RH818 and RH826, the two aircraft with surface wrinkling, left to fly to the UK for inspection by BAC. While on the ferry flight RH818, flown by Flt Sgt Hickson, extensively damaged the tail unit after the pilot had successfully landed at Fayid with a port engine failure. Referring to this flight, John Guthrie writes: "I was the navigator on RH818 and we had been briefed before take-off for Fayid about the cracks in the wings which had been pasted over with brown paper. In the event of this tearing we were to ground the aircraft. As it happened, we reached Fayid without trouble and were due for an early take-off next morning to land at Luqa in Malta before 5.00 pm local time as the airfield would be closed to allow HRH Princess Elizabeth, who was visiting her husband, the Duke of Edinburgh, to land there".

"On the pre-flight rev-up, we developed engine trouble and thought of sand in the fuel. We shut down and the groundcrew did a check and pronounced the engines OK. As laid down at that time, Signaller Dai Rees stepped down to allow the engine fitter to board for the air test. Pilot PII Hickson had an engine failure on take-off and immediately called 'May-day, May-day', at which the flying control sent us round again. Pilot PII Hickson had to keep the

airspeed up with a full load of fuel aboard with the result that when we did eventually get down, we ran out of runway.

So much for a mid-trip tour to the UK. It was back to Habbaniya with the help of a Dakota of Communications Flight".

Towards the end of the month, the Squadron played host to 24 students from the Iraqi Staff College. An air support exercise was staged for their benefit with the help of No 2.ACC. Another visitor to the Squadron was Air Chief Marshal Sir John Slessor GCB DSO MC, the inspection and flypast being most impressive. No exercises were carried out in December, although limited flying was allowed, due to restrictions on all aircraft showing signs of wrinkling on their upper surfaces to straight and level flying. Those with cracking on their under-surfaces were immediately grounded. At the end of the month, these restrictions were lifted and aircraft were limited to a maximum of 300 knots and 2G.

On 22 and 23 December, cross-country navigation flights were flown and Christmas cards to neighbouring squadrons were dropped through the flare-chute. The following day, judging began for the best and most original 'Christmas Bar' competition. The airmen's mess with a replica of the SS *Tora Peachy* were the easy winners.

During the early part of January 1950, representatives arrived from BAC to inform the aircrew and technical ground-staff the results of the tests carried out on RH826. They found that the defects were not too serious and that it was possible to repair the aircraft on the station should it occur in the future. Modifications to the elevators were suggested and also the fitting of accelerometers as near as possible over the C of G where they could be read by the navigators.

On 11 January, Fg Off Jimmy Hedges had the misfortune to fly into a flock of birds over the lake near Jabal Abatah. Inspection showed 32 large dents in the airframe which necessitated considerable repair work. The same day four aircrews were detailed to prepare for an attachment to Mogadishu to provide air support for troops and personnel based there. All other squadron aircrews were put on stand-by because of a possible emergency in Kuwait. Four days later the Sheikh His Highness Sir Ahmed al Jabir Al Sabah died, but no signs of trouble resulted.

On 4 February, Flt Lt Derek Smith suffered a few anxious moments when the port propeller of RH809 over-sped during an air test resulting in an emergency landing. On the 15th, the Squadron was ordered to prepare for the flight to Mogadishu to support No.8 Squadron in the event of disturbances. Groundcrew departed in three Dakotas which left prior to the Brigands.

During the month the Squadron football team won the Station League Division II and the League Cup. This was indeed an achievement because the Squadron last won the trophy in 1934-35.

Air Marshal Sir John Baker KCB MC DFC AOC-in-C, MEAF accompanied by AVM J N Boothman DFC AFC AOC Iraq, paid an informal visit to the station, where they met the remaining aircrew and ground personnel.

The four Brigands, under the command of Flt Lt D W Smith, landed at Mogadishu on 2 March to take part in Operation 'Caesar', the withdrawal of British troops from the area. Flt Lt Smith takes up the story: "On 9 March, whilst on a flag showing trip to the north of the country, I had a hydraulic pump failure and had to return to base. On arrival I could not get the undercarriage to lock down by using the hand pump. We cut a hole in the hydraulic tank using the escape axe, poured in water (and other self-generated fluid) but all to no avail. The best we could do was to get one mainwheel locked down, with the other one down but not locked. The groundcrew did not want me to use the explosive system as we had neither the equipment or the time to carry this out before we had to leave for Habbaniya. In the end, there was no other option but to use it, the wheel that was locked down came up and the one that was down still refused to lock. I was left with no option but to do a belly-landing.

This also had its moments; on my first approach just before touchdown I decided to jettison the canopy so that we could get out quickly in case of fire. It did not come off! So I decided to go round again, whereupon, shortly after full power was on and we were beginning to climb away, the canopy flew off. It was a pretty draughty ride for the navigator and signaller but the eventual touch down was reasonably smooth and we all left the aircraft hurriedly but unharmed. Had we been at Habbaniya the aircraft could have been repaired because it was not badly damaged. Without the proper engineering support, however, we could do nothing other than take off what removable items we could recover and then set fire to poor old RH817 which I had first taken out to Habbaniya in February 1949. The cause of the failure of the explosive system was that a valve had been assembled the wrong way round on its original manufacture".

With four Brigands from No. 8 Squadron, the three remaining aircraft took part in 'Exercise Blue Boy' on the 13th, a tactical communication exercise with the Royal Navy. The handing back of the territory to Italy took place without incident. By the 18th, preparations began for the withdrawal of all forces from Somalia. On the 22nd and 23rd the three aircraft returned to Habbaniya. Taking part in the exercise were 10 officers, 14 NCOs and 53 groundcrew.

On their return to Habbaniya they were told that the Squadron had been ordered to Tengah on Singapore Island.

THE FAR EAST

The Malayan emergency, which lasted on and off for ten years, began with an attempt by the Chinese Communists to overthrow the British Colonial Government then in power. Strangely, many of the leaders of the so-called Malayan Peoples Anti-British Army learnt their trade as jungle fighters with the British Force 136. One, Lau Yew, had led the Malay delegation to London for the Victory Parade. Many of the camps used by the Communist terrorists were originally built by members of Force 136 during WW.2. The weapons they used were British weapons which had been parachuted in during the war and secreted in special hide-outs. It was estimated that their strength was about 5,000 men and women. They considered that by the inflicting of terror, a well-organised minority could conquer a nation.

On 16 June 1948, the British managers of three rubber plantations were murdered. This was the start of years of terror for many. In July a state of emergency was declared followed, a few days later, by the shooting of Lau Yew, Chin Peng's military adviser. In the coming months, Sir Edward Gent was relieved of his position as High Commissioner and replaced by Sir Henry Gurney. One of Sir Henry's first jobs was to resettle 600,000 Chinese squatters who lived on the jungle fringe. By resettling them in new villages under guard, he immediately deprived Chin Peng of thousands of willing and unwilling workers. Strikes and ambushes were still common and acts of terrorism against native workers assured the authorities that the CT were still very active.

1949 was a very bad year for the security forces. Many of them had no training in jungle warfare and, over the year, 344 civilians had been killed with a further 160 missing. The security forces suffered 229 killed and 247 injured. Against these figures,

619 CT had been killed, 337 captured and 251 surrendered to the authorities.

Morale in Malaya reached a low ebb in January 1950 when it was heard that the Labour government under Clement Attlee had recognised Mao Tse Tung as the official Chinese leader, the very man who was supplying the CT with its needs. Fortunately, the British civilian population were determined in their efforts to rid themselves of the communist threat and means were gradually being introduced to lessen it.

This was the scene when No.84 Squadron arrived at Tengah in April 1950, led by Sqn Ldr George Unwin DFM. The first flight which was routed through Sharjah, Mauripur, Palam, Dum Dum and Don Muang, arrived on 8 April and was met by the AOC-in-C, Air Marshal F J Fogarty CB DFC AFC and the AOC Malaya, AVM F J W Mellersh CBE AFC, both 84 Squadron 'old boys'.

The period of attachment was to be for a minimum of three months. It turned out to be nearly three years.

Six days after their arrival, the first strike against the insurgents were carried out in the Broga area by six aircraft each carrying four 500-lb bombs, six 60-lb rocket projectiles and 800 rounds of ammunition. Over the following days, strikes were made against targets in the Broga and Temerloh areas and the main railway line between Mentakab and Gamas. Later in the month, selected targets in the Kuantan area was attacked. The first attack using 1,000-lb bombs was flown on the 27th by Flt Lt D C Marshall and Fg Off J H Hedges. In 17 days, aircraft of the Squadron had flown 156 hours 55 minutes on operations. During these operations, 151,000 lbs of bombs had been dropped, 390 60-lb rockets fired and 475,375 rounds of 20 mm ammunition had been expended.

The attacks on the Klawang area continued on 1 May with 18,000 lbs of bombs being dropped. Convoy patrols were carried out daily and, on one occasion, a convoy was escorted for 26 miles. During a lull in the bombing, two aircraft were detailed to carry out a cross country navigation exercise. An interception exercise with the USS *Boxer* was also flown.

On the 24th, three aircraft attacked targets in the Rawang area, and, in a ten-minute attack dropped 9,000 lbs of bombs and fired 17 RPs (one hung up). Strafing runs followed on a small hill in an area of jungle. On the 30th, a message of congratulations was received from the Gurkha Rifles for a strike in their support. 61 sorties were carried out during May and 141,000 lbs of bombs were dropped.

Flt Lt Marshall took off at 0755 on 1 June and soon established radio contact with a road convoy proceeding towards Kluang. It was then escorted to Rengam without incident. After a reconnaissance by the Brigand, the convoy continued to its destination. Two hours later, Brigands led by Sqn Ldr George Unwin, attacked targets in the Labis area. The next day, Flt Lt Smith and Sgt Hickson attacked targets along a ridge, followed on the 3rd by further strikes on Ampang, barely six miles north of Kuala Lumpur. On the 4th, a series of attacks was made on targets in the Sepang area, a large expanse of marshy jungle. Later in the day, two aircraft bombed encampments on the fringe of the Lothien Rubber Estate.

Despite continual strikes, training proceeded for the King's Birthday Flypast which was to be held on 8 June. On the day, six Brigands took part in the flypast. Witnesses comment that it could not have been bettered. It was to be the last flight with the squadron of Flt Lts Derek Smith and George Ottea and Fg Off Don Baker prior to their return to the UK.

On the 7th, AVM McCauley RAAF, AOC Eastern Command visited the Squadron. He later accompanied Sqn Ldr George Unwin on a flight over the target areas.

One interesting exercise was flown on 9 June by Flt Lt Marshall and Sgt Limbert, when Spitfires of No.60 Squadron made simulated attacks on the Brigands. Attacks on targets continued throughout the month, only interrupted on the 26th by the Squadron's participation in Exercise 'Blue Road', an exercise spread over three days with an Indian naval squadron and units of the Royal Navy. At 1500 on the same afternoon, a formation of six Brigands (three from No.45 and three from No.84) and six Spitfires from No.60 Squadron joined forces in carrying out dummy attacks on the cruisers. The final exercise with the combined naval squadrons took place on the 28th, when live RP and cannon attacks were made on a towed target. During this exercise the dive-brakes were used on manoeuvres to decrease the speed and increase the angle of attack. On Limbert's aircraft the port side one collapsed and only quick thinking and great skill on the part of the pilot prevented the aircraft from meeting a watery end. It was found that the fabric on the dive-brakes was subject to

RH817 A belly-landed at Mogadishu, Somaliland, March 1950

wear and porosity in the humid conditions and as from July 1950 they were disconnected.

The fact that the Squadron was only attached to FEAF caused unnecessary administrative problems, both from the manning position (replacements had to come from MEAF) and from the married aspect. Airmen were not eligible to take their place on Tengah's waiting list for married quarters, although they were on the top of Habbaniya's waiting list.

In July, the Squadron continued its attacks on rebel strongholds in the Songei Siput areas. Later examination by ground forces discovered they had not been inhabited for several months. The continual movement of the rebel forces became more frequent as they were forced to withdraw under pressure from bombing.

On 7 July, a Brigand from No.45 Squadron crashed into the jungle and burnt itself out. Shortly afterwards Brigand RH815, crewed by Flt Lt D Marshall, Flt Lt R S Wrigglesworth and Sgt Blakey, crashed whilst escorting a convoy of school children from their school in the Cameron Highlands to Tapah. The cause was never officially known but extreme weather conditions over the road, which was very tortuous through the mountainous area, was put forward. The two officers had been with the Squadron since its reorganisation in Iraq.

A further problem arose when it was found that the aircraft skin was splitting around the housing for the bomb hoist hook. Up to then, two 1,000-lb bombs had been carried, but this now was restricted to one 1,000-lb and one 500-lb bomb. During July a total of 178 hours were flown on 73 offensive patrols. A further 60 hours were flown in converting two new pilots, Plt Offs K J Fullager and I S McPherson. The good news for the month was the award of the British Empire Medal to Flt Sgt Shepard who had been with the Squadron since 1947.

No less than four aircraft were unserviceable at the beginning of August, all awaiting the delivery of hydraulic pumps. The situation was worsened on the 9th when Fg Off Fullager was unable to lower the undercarriage of RH823 and had to crash-land at Seletar, where it was discovered that a selector valve had jammed. Gp Capt R Whittam, writes: "I was at Seletar that day and saw the wheels-up landing. It was a good landing but the starboard prop bent over in the shape of a plough and a stream of turf landed on the signaller. He was not amused."

Three days later, Sgt Hickson piloting RH816 attempted to overshoot but he raised his undercarriage and flaps too soon, causing the aircraft to sink and make an unintentional belly-landing. Fortunately the crew was unhurt but the aircraft was a write-off.

The arrival on the Squadron of RH831 lasted only briefly.

After one sortie, the selector valve failed making it unserviceable. Despite these problems, strikes were flown on most days by one or two aircraft. On the 31st, Flt Lt A P Norman arrived from No.45 Squadron as a replacement to Flt Lt Marshall.

As a result of Tempests of No.33 Squadron observing movements of insurgents near Ipoh, a strike was laid on by two Brigands of 84 followed by two from 45 Squadron. The attack was marred by a 20-lb bomb falling from a Tempest on to a school, injuring a teacher and several children.

RH832 was delivered to the Squadron on 21 September, but further problems with RH809 and 810 caused the number of hours flown to drop to 150 hours 40 minutes spread over 72 sorties. Sqn Ldr George Unwin commented: "Personally I was convinced it is due to the inferior quality of the rubber in the piston halves of the undercarriage jacks. They were disintegrating after a very short life and particles were finding their way into the selectors, causing seizure. I warned, that if continued, more crash-landings could be expected.

On the 26th, Sgt Plt Alan Limbert took off in company with two Brigands from No.45 Squadron to fly to the opening of Kuching Airport in North Borneo. Unfortunately, on arrival the aircraft were marshalled into a very small dispersal area and Limbert's aircraft became bogged down, preventing him from taking part in the flypast. This mishap was followed on the 27th by Fg Off J H Hedges ground-looping the Squadron's Harvard, necessitating a new wing and port oleo.

In early October, Brigands of 45 and 84 Squadrons joined Lincolns in bombing targets in the Durian Tipus area. Reports said that the bombing was extremely accurate and that captured terrorists appeared to be stunned by the ferocity of the attack. Comments from captured CT tended to show that the morale of the rebels was suffering from the continuous bombing. A few days later the attack was repeated when it became known that terrorists had re-infiltrated the area.

On 4 November, RAF Tengah was visited by Under-Secretary of State Aiden Crawley, in company with the AOC, Air Vice Marshal Sir Francis Mellersh. A week later, the one millionth pound of bomb were dropped. On the 24th, news came through that the administration of the Squadron had now officially been taken over by FEAF from MEAF. The effect of this was the administration of the Squadron would be considerably improved as, being manned from 4,000 miles away was proving difficult when it came to replacements. A day later, some of the groundcrew had a half-day off when 15 were guests of the Archipelago Brewery where Anchor beer was brewed. A further nine were hosted by the Tiger Brewery; reports say that a good time was had by all!

Flt Ltd D W Smith and FO 'Flosh' Kendall getting some hours in on Harvard KF350

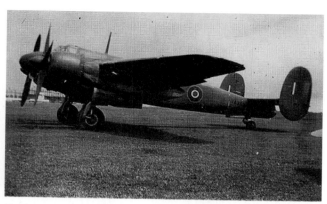

Buckmaster T.1 VA363, a side-by-side trainer version of the Brigand, at Seletar in 1951

On the 28th, a first joint-reunion was held, one in London for the 'old boys' of 84. The same evening, officers of the Squadron dined out in Singapore.

Two more of the Squadron's original Brigands were written-off in November. The CO's aircraft, RH828 *The Queen of Shaibah*, carried out a flapless landing on the 9th, the pilot swinging off the runway hoping that the long grass would act as a brake. Unfortunately the aircraft run into a hidden ditch and one of the oleos went up through the wing. The second incident occurred on the 20th when Sqn Ldr George Unwin was lifting off on a strike in RH809. His 1,000-lb bomb dropped off on passing Learoyd barrack block. The bomb bounced off the runway and hit the underside of the fuselage just forward of the tailplane. The damage, which was considerable, resulted in the aircraft being classified as category 4. LAC Reg Powell, who was watching from his window in the barrack block wrote: "As you can see from the enclosed photograph, the window is only about 150 yards from the runway and I remember seeing the bomb drop off, I just stood there and stared as it bounced down the runway".

During the month, the squadron co-operated with the 2nd Scots Guards and the 4th Malay Regt in locating targets. In all, a total of 75 sorties were flown against 34 separate targets. Having only seven Brigands on strength limited the number of sorties to 46 during December. Since the Squadron had commenced anti-bandit operations in April, a total of 565 sorties had been flown, well over a million pounds of bombs dropped, 3,167 rockets had been fired and nearly a quarter of a million 20 mm rounds has been expended. It is difficult to say what percentage of bombs exploded. Out of 16 dropped on 16 December, only six exploded.

On 9 December, six aircraft took part in the Kallang Air Display. Three days later, riots broke out in Singapore over the Maria Hertzog affair; all ranks being confined to the station until 19 December. January 1951 was noted for its spell of exceptionally bad weather. Over 24 inches of rain fell, the third highest recorded. The month brought an increase in bandit activity in the Kuala Langit forest reserve and terrorists were held responsible for a number of incidents. Troops were occupied elsewhere and the police had insufficient jungle-trained squads. With this in mind Nos.45 and 84 Squadrons were asked to attack seven selected targets to harass the bandits and to raise the morale of the local populace.

In January 1951, there is a note in the Operational Record Book: "Undercarriage selectors are still giving trouble, as are the hydraulic pumps. However, by taking a page out of Heath Robinson's book, there is every confidence in being able to lower the undercarriage in such emergencies". Gp Capt Ron Whittam explained by saying: "What the writer meant was that each aircraft would carry a five-gallon can of hydraulic oil and two large spanners. A Brigand crew could always be recognised by what they carried to the aircraft, besides the spanners and the hydraulic oil, an axe was a necessity plus a decent supply of drinking liquid to refresh the crew! The axe was to sever the appropriate hydraulic line to the selector, thus allowing the undercarriage to come down; the hydraulic fluid to top up the system and the spanners is a sophisticated method of doing the same thing but only if one knew which line to open, then shut. If a pilot was seen going out to the aircraft without an axe, it could only have been the CO, George Unwin, as only he understood the system".

"The one easy thing about the Brigand was taking off; that is if you remembered to switch on the tail wheel lock. If not, the

waltz down the runway had to be seen to be believed! Taking off with the flaps down was a near impossibility and not to be recommended. It was essential before take-off to check that the pilot's seat was locked, otherwise the pilot, as he opened the throttles, was pulled backwards and flat, looking up to the sky as he screeched to his navigator to push the seat back upright. Exhilarating stuff but not to be recommended to budding staff officers!

February brought a new problem for the Brigand when a 45 Squadron aircraft was lost due to cannon shells pre-exploding in the blast tube. Hereafter, only ball cartridge ammunition was carried. During the month, RH823 was returned to the Squadron after its accident in August. After only three sorties, the aircraft was again unserviceable due to hydraulic failure.

Operation 'Stymie' was mounted on 3 February and started with a series of air strikes accompanied by extensive ground patrols. In an early engagement, twelve bandits were killed and four captured, whilst other contacts brought the number killed up to twenty. The initial attack was by Lincolns of the Royal Australian Air Force, followed by attacks from Brigands from 45 and 84 Squadrons. Over the next few days, strikes were continued against targets in the Kota Tingii areas. On 27 February, AVM T C Traill CB OBE DFC visited the station and chatted to the crews. Over the next four days, strikes were flown in co-operation with the Green Howards, Gurkhas and Scots Guards.

After the previous month's record number of operations, April was disappointing with only 21 strikes. It was thought that the bandits were building up for a May Day operation and were temporarily lying low. Continuation training was carried on and 200 hours flown. Two new aircraft arrived (RH786 and VS869). However, May Day passed quietly with little need for increased activity.

During May, the station sports day was held but the Squadron was unable to repeat last year's performance by winning the trophy, losing to Technical Wing in the field sports. In a cricket match against No.1 Squadron RAAF, the Aussies were far too strong and disposed of the Squadron in the same way as they did with the MCC 'down under'.

On the 16th, the two millionth pound of bombs was dropped on the fringe of the Glendale estate. At the end of the month, four of the original crew members, Flt Lts D W Breed and P W Harle, Fg Off J Hedges and Sgt D Rees became tour-expired and returned to the UK.

June 1951 was a tragic month for the Brigand squadrons. On the 1st, VS869 crashed on a routine training flight killing its pilot, Fg Off K J Fullager and the crew of two, Flt Sgts H L Gregory and C Sharkey. When making a practice single-engine approach, the aircraft crashed in the undershoot area and caught fire. Two weeks later, an aircraft from No.45 Squadron took off on a routine check flight. On the downwind leg, the pilot increased the revs and an engine fell off, the aircraft crashing into Kranji Creek. The pilot escaped through the front of the aircraft which was upside down in the water; the navigator, Sgt Bowen was trapped under the mainspar and died. The signaller, Sgt Weston, was able to release himself from the back. On examination, the outline of a small nut was found two-thirds from the tip of one prop blade and the blade had sheared off at this point. The resulting vibration had caused the engine to tear away from the mountings.

Four days later, RH811 was coming back from an operation in support of the 2/6 Gurkha Rifles in the Segamat district. Piloted

RH798 after undercarriage failure while flown by Flt Lt Dicky Tuffin

by Fg Off I S Macpherson with Fg Off R Matthews as navigator, the aircraft joined the circuit at Tengah. The same thing occurred and, as Macpherson increased the revs, an engine tore itself from its mountings. Fg Off Macpherson was able to escape from the aircraft and land by parachute but the navigator was killed. This time the ring which held the blade on to the prop mechanism sheared in half; as a result the whole blade came off resulting in severe vibration. As a result, all Brigands were grounded and propellers and engines were restricted in the number of hours they could be used, 400 hours in the case of the props.

Sgt Terry Stringer writes: "Instead of a three-man crew (pilot, navigator and signaller) we were restricted to a crew of two from this period. The navigators were fitted with the paratroop back parachute instead of the clip-on type which was fitted on the front in an emergency. The new 'chute' was rather large, bulky and when you moved around the cockpit sometimes deployed and you ended up with the whole canopy on the floor, a dreadful set-up!

On 16 June, Operation 'Warbler' was mounted by army units in the State of Johore in an effort to rid South Malaya of the terrorists. Seven strikes were carried out against targets in the Muar, Kota Tingii and Rengam areas. During the following days, continuous strikes were flown which were only halted by the grounding of the Brigands. In spite of the shock of three Brigands crashing with fatalities in 19 days, morale of the aircrew remained high. By 7 July, the first Brigand had been fitted with new propellers and engine bearers and, by the end of the month, all modifications had been completed. On the 12th, the first sortie was flown since the grounding of the aircraft and three weeks later the number of strikes had risen to 41. On the 31st, a spinner was seen to break up in flight and only prompt action by the pilot in feathering the engine prevented another accident. Landing at Butterworth, the airscrew was changed and the aircraft returned to Tengah the following day.

In August the CO, Sqn Ldr George Unwin, was admitted to hospital after breaking his leg playing football. The Squadron team lost the match to the station armoury (must be a story there!). Flt Lt A P Norman was given the acting rank of squadron leader whilst George Unwin returned to the UK for medical checks. On the 5th, VS865 flew on a strike. Over the target, a violent explosion was felt under the aircraft. It was later found that the blast tube of the port outer gun had burst as the gun was fired. Since then the use of cannons were banned. Apart from Operation 'Warbler', which was still being flown, a new attack was mounted

in the Sitiawan area. Aircraft of Nos.45 and 84 Squadrons were joined by Hornets of No.33 and Vampires from No.60 Squadron. According to ground reports, the attack was impressive and most of the targets were demolished.

As cannons could not now be fired, the Brigand's carrying capacity had been reduced to four 500-lb bombs and six rockets. The firing of the rockets had also brought their problems. The pigtails were not plugged in until just before take-off. Groundcrew have told of the tendency for the rockets to fall off, breaking just aft of the warhead.

September 1951 was the worst month since the Squadron moved to Malaya; only 13 strikes were made consisting of 38 sorties. During the month, four complete crews moved to Butterworth under Flt Lt G V Wadams. Only two strikes were made from there but much use was made of the Butterworth rocket ranges. On the 14th, the Squadron took part in a 'Battle of Britain' flypast over Singapore and the RAF stations of Tengah, Seletar and Changi. In the same month, it was announced that Sgt R Benn had been Mentioned in Despatches for services to the Squadron in Malaya. October brought a considerable increase in the number of sorties flown and in the amount of armaments dropped and fired. For all that, the three Buckmasters which were on the station were still proving troublesome. This meant that instrument flying training and asymmetric landings had to be done on the Brigands which were not a satisfactory substitute for a dual-control aircraft.

Operation 'Rebel' was mounted on 1 October in co-operation with Hornets of No.33 Squadron and the Royal Marines of 45 Commando. Terrorists, who had been very active in the Broga areas, were attacked and scattered. Six days later, Sir Henry Gurney, the High Commissioner, was ambushed and murdered whilst he was travelling up to Fraser's Hill. Two days later, two policemen were killed in an ambush by the same gang which was estimated to be 40 strong. On the 5th, arrangements had been made for an air/sea exercise with the carrier HMS *Glory*. Unfortunately the exercise, which was finally flown on the 8th, was not a great success as the Brigands were intercepted by *Glory's* Sea Furies 30 miles from the carrier. With the approval of AHQ, a series of long range navigation exercises was flown. The first of these on the 12th was a flight to Labuan, where the crew stayed overnight before returning.

During November, Operation 'Pursuit' was carried out, over 900 rockets being fired. Two more of the Squadron's long serving members left, when Sgt G E Hickson and Flt Sgt R S Walters were

No. 84 Squadron, Kuala Lumpur, 2 May 1952
Left to right: Mike Alden, Terry Stringer, Willy Williamson, Roy Bowring, Keith Abberstein, Jordy Cartwright, Cliff Powell, Al Rand, Jim Duncan, Dicky Tuffin, Jock Fraser, Bill Banks DFC, Sqn Ldr A P Norman, Jeff Wadams, Peter Elton, Joe Bohan, Basil Cochrane, Jock Bradshaw, Jock Armstrong, George Taylor, Les Whiteside

posted home. In their place came Fg Off P J Elton, Plt Offs J C Duncan and B A Cochrane and Sgts Abberstein, Armstrong and Hughes. Cochrane and Armstrong were immediately despatched to No.45 Squadron.

Further bombing trials were carried out on the Butterworth ranges during the early part of December. Operation 'Springtide' was mounted on the 3rd in the State of Perak. 'A' Flight under Flt Lt W Banks left on detachment to Kuala Lumpur on 4 December. A day later, the last of the original Brigand crews left when Flt Sgt Alan Limbert left for home. Limbert, who had joined the Squadron in September 1949, had flown over 150 sorties, a large proportion of which, he had led.

On Christmas Day 1951, the Squadron was visited by one of its old commanding Officers, Air Marshal Sir Francis Fogarty KCB CB DFC AFC, who was then AOC-in-C FEAF.

Of the three Buckmasters which were on the station's strength, two had effectively been written-off due to their continued unserviceability. The number of strikes flown during January 1952 lessened because of extensive flooding in the central lowlands at the start of the month which curtailed ground movement. On the 15th, six aircraft, together with one from 45 Squadron, took part in Operation 'Bank Holiday', a naval exercise with the French carrier *Arromanches* and the British sloop *Amethyst*. During the month, honours came to two members of the squadron rugby team when chosen to play in a Selected XV against the Royal Navy and for the Combined Services XV against Singapore and Perak.

February proved to be a successful month. On the 7th, seven aircraft were sent on detachment to Kuala Lumpur, where they took part in Operation 'Helsby'. The area chosen was just south of the Perak-Thailand border. All escape routes had been blocked off and 54 paratroops were dropped from three Dakotas. The Brigand sorties were flown on the 'cab rank' principle over the valley whilst the paras secured the DZ. A second operation was undertaken on the 22nd, when reports came through that large numbers of terrorists were seen in the jungle area. The next four days were spent bombing and strafing the area in company with No.1 Squadron RAAF Lincolns. During the month Fg Off I S Macpherson created a Squadron record for asymmetric flying when he was forced to fly three hours with one prop feathered. On landing an electrical fault was found. Peter Elton commenting on his feat writes: "It was made all the more impressive because the flight was almost all over the sea and Mac was very short, which meant that he had great difficulty reaching the pedals and in applying sufficient rudder to correct the yaw".

"One other incident I recall happened on 8 February 1952. On a detachment to Kuala Lumpur, Peter Norman organised a dinner. All the officers gathered in secret above a restaurant to have a feast of roast suckling pig. At the time, it was illegal to kill suckling pigs and this made a remarkable meal all the more interesting. It was in total contrast to the food served at the armament practice camps where the food was awful, the accommodation rough and the trips to Penang in the evenings the only thing of note".

His comments about the Brigand are also worth recording: "The main fault of the Brigand was the folding wing trick, caused by pulling too much 'G' in turns and dives. 'G' meters were fitted but often not noticed. It was a point of Squadron efficiency and pilot skill to see how quickly four aircraft could unload their armaments and clear the area. Furthermore we had a minimum safety height above which we had to be when the bombs exploded. So it was prudent to climb fast after releasing the bombs in a 45-degree dive. The Brigand at that time had the highest wing loading of any aircraft serving in the RAF. So, all in all, we spent our time diligently trying to kill ourselves! The aircraft were fitted with dive-brakes which were activated by filling bellows with air from the airstream. But the bellows were made of fabric which rotted in the tropics, so we could not use them. It also had a dodgy hydraulic system and we carried drums of hydraulic fluid to top up the system in the event of a leak. The final (official) instruction was to pee into the system if all else failed. It was not an aircraft on which to build one's confidence in its last years of service. Life was still cheap seven years after the war."

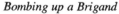

Bombing up a Brigand

VS854 G armed with bombs and rockets for a strike

"Many strikes were scheduled to attack targets at dawn. This meant a night take-off when the runway was illuminated with tins of paraffin into which was stuck a piece of rag; these were known as 'goose neck' flares and were used extensively in the RAF. The trouble was that the natives used to nip out of the jungle, pull out the lighted wick and pour the paraffin into a bucket, replace the wick and return to the jungle. By the time we came to line up for take-off the flares began to go out and the departure was made through a rapidly disappearing flare-path. The return to base, if caught by bad weather was equally interesting; fly down the coast to Port Swettenham, follow the railway line to Kuala Lumpur for a few miles and then, when it turned sharp right, we knew when to close our throttles and settle on to the runway a few hundred yards ahead. This approach was taught us by a pilot flying the *Straits Times* Anson."

Increased terrorist activity in March led to 86 sorties being flown against 26 separate targets. At the beginning of the month, the Squadron was divided into two flights; 'A' Flt commanded by Flt Lt W Banks and 'B' Flt under Flt Lt 'Curly' Wadams, rotating between Tengah and Kuala Lumpur. It was interrupted by an accident to Wadams and Sgt Bowring. Whilst flying in an Auster, the aircraft stalled on the approach to the airfield, Bowring suffering from spinal injuries which kept him in hospital for several weeks. Wadams, fortunately was not injured. During the month the Squadron was pleased to hear of the award of the DSO to Sqn Ldr G C Unwin for his service to the Squadron in Malaya.

78 operational sorties were flown during April with over 78,000 lb of bombs dropped. On the 29th, the first night sortie was flown when three aircraft dropped 50 flares along the length of railway line to deter rebel activity. Operation 'Biterbit' was laid on in preparation for terrorist activity on May Day. This entailed two Brigands maintaining a patrol over Kuala Lumpur with R/T from dusk to dawn. A further two aircraft were kept at immediate readiness and the remainder on stand-by. It was not a great success as the increase in terrorism did not materialise. However, it did prove, as an exercise, to be practicable.

On 3 May, the Squadron lost Fg Off Basil Cochrane and Sgt J B Armstrong on a strike near Chenderoh Lake in Perak. It was made harder by the fact that the accident was never explained. Witnesses say that the aircraft, which was carrying a crew of two and an airman who went along for the flight, after releasing its rockets over the target, they saw a flash under the starboard wing and all of the outer section fell away. The aircraft, RH755, rolled over, crashed into the jungle and immediately burst into flames. Fg Off Basil Cochrane and Sgt J B Armstrong had only recently returned from attachment to No.45 Squadron. It was not possible to retrieve the wing to find the cause and the discovery of the bodies took five days. A second incident occurred on the 25th when, after

carrying out a training flight in RH796, Flt Lt Dicky Tuffin experienced extreme vibration in the starboard engine and immediately feathered the propeller. A normal single-engine landing was carried out but, after touching down, the aircraft swung violently to starboard towards a line of aircraft. In an effort to avoid the parked aircraft the undercarriage was strained and collapsed.

June proved to be a disappointment as to the number of strikes flown. On the 7th, 'A' Flt returned from detachment at Kuala Lumpur, being relieved by the Hornets of No.45 squadron. A fortnight later, 'B' Flt proceeded to Butterworth to carry out the first armament practice camp allotted to the Squadron, returning on 4 July. Only 16 strikes were carried out, the lowest number since the Squadron moved to Malaya in April 1950. During the month, Sqn Ldr L L Johnston assumed command from Sqn Ldr A P Norman. from 1 August, all the Brigands were grounded, when a signal from HQ FEAF ordered all aircraft to be checked for 'possible shearing of rivets holding angle attachment and web of front mainspar'. Five days later the check was completed and the aircraft resumed flying.

Further awards to the Squadron was announced in the London Gazette during August. The Distinguished Flying Cross was awarded to Sqn Ldr A P Norman and Flt Lt W Banks and the Distinguished Flying Medal to Sgt Alan Limbert.

Due to the run-down of experienced groundcrews, serviceability suffered and all aircraft were grounded whilst checks were made on No.1 fuel tank bays. After these checks were completed, an improvement came in September when 94 sorties were flown and the total weight of bombs dropped approached 150,000 lbs with over 240 rockets fired. At the end of the month the detachment to KL returned to its base at Tengah.

During October, a series of exercises were flown with the cruiser *Ceylon*, destroyer *Cockade* and frigate *Possum*. On the 31st, a reliable report came through that high-ranking members of the MRLA were having a meeting in the Kluang area. Strikes by five Brigands were carried out followed by attacks by Australian Lincolns.

On the same month, the Squadron had the honour of providing an escort to the Duchess of Kent and her son, both at the arrival at and departure from Kuala Lumpur before they flew on to Hong Kong.

Operation 'Gangway' was mounted on the 7 November in the Plentong area; its aim being to eliminate all elements of the MRLA in the area. Later, reports from captured terrorists stated that their morale was very low because of repeated instances of officers of the rebel army finding refuge in Thailand. By the end of the month, the number of strikes were reduced, only 38 being flown. On 25 November, Peter Elton led five strikes, each lasting only 15

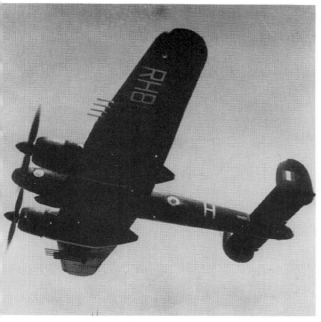

RH813 H fitted with rocket rails

Briefing for a strike;
left to right: Peter Norman, Jimmy Duncan, two unknown,
Bill Banks, Anon Dog, unknown, Ian Macpherson, Sgt
Bradshaw

o 20 minutes in support of the army fighting in the hills
overlooking Kuala Lumpur.

On 5 December, the Squadron said farewell to Flt Lt W
Banks and Fg Off I S Macpherson. Both had been with the
squadron for two-and-a-half years. Sgt Terry Stringer writes: "My
ast flight on Brigands was early in December 1952. from 23 June
1950, when I joined No.84 Squadron, my log book shows that I
flew 218 operational sorties culminating in a strike on the Kolai
area of Johore on 2 December".

Training continued, but the end came when RH823, crewed
by Flt Lt B Massey and Sgt E C Powell, crashed on 20 December.
As the aircraft started to pull out from a shallow dive, the starboard
wing was seen to break away. The aircraft crashed and burst into
flames. Flt Lt Peter Elton writes that the suspected cause of the
crash was crystalization of the main spar. The crash was the
prelude to No.84 Squadron's activities in the Far East.

As Ron Whittam concludes: " To be fair, the beast did pack a
considerable punch when fully armed. Large areas of jungle were
laid to waste and, no doubt, many terrorists were killed. Nevertheless, any aircraft which could shoot itself down with its own
guns and could shed airscrew blades with ease has to be unique but
lethal. When the wings fell off, it was time to call it a day! As a
light bomber, it was a tram and best forgotten.

Rumours were rife that the Squadron was to be disbanded or
to be reduced to a cadre in the UK. On 16 January 1953, a parade
was held at Tengah when the AOC-in-C FEAF, Air Marshal A C
Sanderson KBE CB inspected the Squadron and addressed the men.

In the afternoon a more poignant ceremony was held in the
squadron dispersal area when a model Brigand was burnt on a
funeral pyre. It was accompanied by a farewell speech by the
'Mayor of Shaibah'. The day closed with the traditional 84
hospitality when beer and other refreshments were handed out to
anyone who liked to attend. On 26 January 1953, Sqn Ldr L L
Johnston departed to become a liaison officer with the RAAF,
leaving Flt Lt W Macleod in charge for the final days.

Closing down parade; Air Marhsal A C Sanderson KBE, CB,
inspecting the squadron

The closing down ceremony with a model Brigand being
cremated. The Mayor, with Mayoress and Aldermen, reads
the address on the right, 16 January 1953

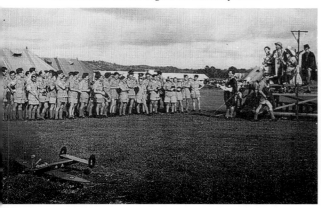

Led by FO E F Budworth, No.84 Squadron marches out of
Singapore

Valetta C.1 VW196 at Mahfid, Aden Protectorate (via A S Thomas)

CHAPTER 18 - THE CHANGE TO TRANSPORT

It seems probable that No.84 Squadron had a powerful friend in high places - none other than ACM Sir Francis Fogarty, because three short weeks after the Squadron had disbanded at Tengah, it re-emerged at Fayid in the Canal Zone, Egypt, having taken over No.204 Squadron's numberplate, aircraft, aircrew and duties.

For the previous six years, No.204 Squadron had been equipped with first the Dakota and then, from May 1949, with the Valetta as a medium range transport squadron. It had served with distinction from 1929, flying a variety of large flying boats culminating in the Short Sunderland V in 1945. It was an appropriate change of numberplates as No.84 Squadron had had interests in the Middle East since 1920 and Coastal Command wanted its numberplate back to equip a new squadron with the Shackleton MR.2.

The Vickers Valetta, powered by two 2,000 hp Bristol Hercules engines, had already replaced the Dakota in many of the squadrons and the same type of work was expected from it. Its requirement was for an aircraft which could be used for troop-carrying, military freighting, paratrooping, ambulance and supply-dropping. Later, search and rescue was added to its duties. it had a strengthened floor and a large door fitted in the side of the fuselage for easy loading. The double door had a smaller exit fitted into it for personnel access and for paratroop dropping.

There were no changes of personnel and Sqn Ldr H H Jenkins remarked that at one moment he was CO of No.204 Squadron and the next he has changed his allegiance to No.84 Squadron. It was as quick as that! The strength of the Squadron at that time was eight aircraft, 15 officers, 21 SNCOs and 43 airmen.

Its routine schedules included Khormaksar, Port Sudan, Mafraq, Habbaniya, Nicosia, El Adem, Benina, Idris, Luqa, Wadi Halfa, Khartoum, Juba, Eastleigh and Aqaba.

Supply dropping continued and air-supply drops of petrol were made to Army units engaged in Exercise 'Longbow'. On 5 March, Exercise 'Pegasus II' was mounted, led by Flt Lt F Mulkern, a night paratroop exercise which involved five of the squadron's aircraft, one acting as pathfinder, the other four making two sorties each to the DZ at Qassassin. Overall, a total of 180 troops were despatched. Due to a misunderstanding, 40 of them were dropped from a height of less than 800 feet. Fortunately no

injuries resulted but a Court of Inquiry was held into the affair. Surprisingly, 527 hours were flown during the month, 411 of these on airborne support.

Records state that during March, No.84 Squadron's property arrived, which included the Squadron silver (valued at £873), a book of photographs, a VC citation (Proctor's?), a communist flag, two communist caps and three articles of ladies underwear. It continues by saying that all the latter articles were trophies presented to the Squadron during the anti-bandit campaign in Malaya!

During April, Exercise 'Snowdrop' began, an Army support exercise employing the whole wing and included the dropping of the 16th Independent Parachute Brigade on a DZ in Cyprus. The exercise was in two phases, a night drop on the 29th followed by a day drop on the 30th. Five aircraft of the Squadron took part, led by Sqn Ldr Bert Jenkins. In all, 200 troops were despatched by the Squadron and the exercise was considered a great success by both the Army and the Air Force. 13 routine flights were flown including the movement of No.14 Squadron RNZAF ground personnel from Abu Sueir to Nicosia. During the exercise, one of No.84's captains was congratulated. After becoming airborne his port engine fire-warning light came on. He landed and took over the spare aircraft, complete with his load and was airborne again in just over ten minutes.

In May, the astonishing number of 535 hours were flown made up of routine flights and continuation training. Two aircraft were flown to Nicosia to pick up No.14 Squadron RNZAF and take them to Dar-es-Salaam and Entebbe for the Colonial Coronation displays.

The Coronation Parade was held on 2 June 1953. On that day there was to be held a Coronation Air Race at Deversoir. Amongst the entrants for this handicap race was a Meteor NF.13 from No.39 Squadron stationed at Kabrit, a PR Meteor from No. 13 Squadron, Vampires from Nos.6 and 73 Squadrons, a Hastings and an Auster from some obscure Army unit. No.84 Squadron had entered VW818, its best aircraft. Over the weeks, Sqn Ldr Jenkins had had it polished down to the bare metal. On its rehearsals on 28th and 30th May, it behaved impeccably and Jenkins had great hopes of winning the trophy. Unfortunately, on the day, the port

Sqn Ldr H H Jenkins, Sgt N Belchamber, unknown, Flt Lt Ken Styan, unknown. Taken on a flight to Istanbul to deliver medical supplies after an earthquake

tyre went flat as he was taxying out for take-off, with the result that 84 had to scratch. The race was won by Flt Lt Kevin O'Sullivan flying a Meteor WM315 with Flt·Lt David Carrington navigating. Rumour has it that Sqn Ldr Bert Jenkins swore that the aircraft had been 'nobbled' and by all accounts, he was in a bad mood for weeks afterwards.

Whilst landing at Deversoir after a routine flight from Nicosia, the stern frame of WD157 collapsed, causing considerable damage. Later the aircraft was temporarily repaired and flown to No.109 MU. Later in the month, VW821 arrived as a replacement. All the Squadron's aircraft were due for a 2,000- hour overhaul, but this was later extended to 2,400. Sqn Ldr Jenkins' rather sardonic comments in the notes reads: "Hope they last that long".

July was the first month for over a year when the allotted flying hours were not met. This was due, primarily, to the need for 'spit and polish' for the forthcoming inspection by the AOC MEAF Transport Force at the end of the month. Amongst the special flights made was the moving of a contingent of East African Pioneer Corps from Fayid to Nairobi. Other flights involved the transporting of No.8 Squadron's groundcrews from Khormaksar to Nicosia and the personnel of No.6 Squadron from Nicosia to Habbaniya. One aircraft was detailed to stand by at Khartoum while the Queen Mother and the Princess Margaret proceeded to Rhodesia for the Centenary Exhibition.

The rest period after the AOC's inspection was short-lived and the Squadron once more exceeded its flying target in August. It also flew more hours than any of the other four squadrons in the wing. Unit movements included the transporting of Marine commandos from Malta to Fayid and Aden Levies from Aden to Sharjah. Two replacement aircraft (VW202 C and VW821 D) were delivered to the Squadron which kept the strength to eight aircraft.

During September, one aircraft took part in Exercise 'Candlelight', a clandestine supply-dropping exercise in Cyprus. Six paratroop-dropping sorties were carried out. Over the month, 409 flying hours were logged of which 322 were flown on routine schedules. Amongst the flights were trips to Aqaba, Port Sudan and Mafraq. There was an increase of hours flown during October reaching 489 of which routine flights accounted for 371 hours. Of interest were the moving of No.19 Squadron personnel from Nicosia to Habbaniya and No.78 Squadron RAAF from Takali to Idris. Meanwhile, one aircraft flew to Nicosia on stand-by for the England - New Zealand Air Race.

During November, the groundcrew of a Lincoln squadron were flown to Eastleigh for operations against the Mau Mau. At the end of the month, five sorties were flown totalling 36 hours in the paratroop Exercise 'Crusader'. It continued into December when a further 17 hours were flown. On 11 December a second visit to the station was made by the AOC Transport Force, Air Cdre W K Beisiegel OBE. Flt Lt Ken Styan fills in the details: "The AOC's inspection was quite a story. He was irreverently known as 'The Bike' and he decided that his initial visit to Fayid (his only station) was unsatisfactory so he called for an individual inspection of each squadron on different days. It was No.84's chance to shine. When he reached 'B' Flight he approached our sole tractor driver standing beside our only tractor (fully bulled up). "Start it up" ordered the AOC, confident that it would not go. The lad leapt into the driver's seat and pressed the starter button, whereupon it burst into life, much to the chagrin of the AOC and the delight of the Squadron. Air Cdre W K Beisiegel was later transferred to Kenya

for the Mau Mau campaign.

Immediately after the inspection, the CO, Sqn Ldr H Jenkins, prepared to take off in VW818 for the UK for aircraft reconditioning. Before leaving Fayid the port starter motor was found to be malfunctioning. Fortunately Flt Sgt Barr, NCO i/c Servicing, was one of the passengers and the offending unit was changed in record time. Must have been the call of the UK.

On the 23rd of the month, the usual Christmas party was held, which was a marked success considering the absence of many of the aircrew. The following day, four Squadron aircraft converged on Fayid from the four cardinal points, returning from Nicosia, Khartoum, Habbaniya and Luqa.

Ken Styan writes: "It was late in 1953 that I reached top of the points table and was allocated a married quarter. Unfortunately, it was located about 100 yards from the Squadron dispersal. The sound of two Hercules being run up in the small hours ready for an early take-off took a bit of getting used to. Since the early morning was the best time for flying, this was not a rare occurrence".

He goes on to say: "Fayid was not a good shopping centre and trips to Nicosia were highly prized. Anybody (including families) could apply for an indulgence flight and my wife went over a couple of times to do her Christmas shopping. Normally there were empty seats. But once she went to stay for a couple of days with one of the Cyprus wives and then found the return flight full. This happened again a few days later and by then she was getting a bit panicky. The same thing happened on the third occasion. She was eventually brought back as a supernumary crew member sitting in the 2nd pilot's seat by a sergeant pilot of No. 114 Squadron. Fortunately, the Wg Cdr Flying on the station turned a blind eye to it when he met the aircraft".

In February 1954, the Squadron took part in a para-drop of the 16th Independent Parachute Brigade in Jordan. The Operation 'Lionheart II' was watched by King Hussein and Colonel Glubb Pasha. In the same month, rioting broke out in the Sudan and one aircraft was detailed to fly to Khartoum, from there to El Obeid where it took on troops of the Sudan Defence Force to return to Khartoum to deal with the problem. In March a search and rescue mission was flown to search for missing ~Vampire WL574 of No.213 Squadron. The wreckage was found ten miles ENE of El Ballah and the pilot was killed in the crash. Ken Styan, writing about the Valetta as a SAR aircraft, comments: "The aircraft was not ideally suited for the ASR role but it was the only large aircraft permanently available in the MEAF. One aircraft was always on stand-by at Fayid, fitted with Lindholme gear, and with a crew available. There were no bomb aimer's panel or turret to assist with visual searches and the view from the cockpit was not very good for detailed observation straight down".

In letters written to the late Owen Greenwood, the President of No.84 Squadron Association, dated 2 March 1954, Sqn Ldr Jenkins refers to a replacement set of ladies' underwear. He writes: "As for Jane's Panties Mk II, these were obtained through a piece of good luck. When I was taking an aircraft across to Cyprus some months ago, one of the passengers was a Group Captain. (Alas, I cannot remember his name). We were talking about 84 Squadron and I happened to mention Mrs Jane Newman (née Jane Smith) and the story of her 'panties'. I explained that the original set had been lost in the Western Desert in January 1942 and we were unable to contact Mrs Newman and ask for replacements. By a remarkable piece of luck, he knew her address which he gladly gave me. I immediately sent a letter to Mrs Newman telling her of our plight and she very kindly obliged us by sending the Mk. II replacements, which we received in September suitably autographed". This letter makes one wonder whose were the three articles which he received in April 1953.

Sqn Ldr John Smith in a recent interview recalled that on the 3-5 April he flew 20.25 hours in four sorties in a search for Valetta VW205 of 216 Squadron which was missing from a flood relief flight to Baghdad. During the search, the squadron provided five aircraft which flew 22 sorties totalling 104 flying hours. The longest being 6.20 which as Smith recalled "was pushing it a bit for a Valetta". The aircraft was eventually found by bedouin several days after the search had been abandoned, 70 miles south of Aqaba in mountains at 8,000 feet. There were no survivors and it was later found that the wreckage could not be seen from the air. In all, 370 hours were flown by the five Valetta squadrons employed in the search.

John Smith recalled another flight on 9 April in connection with the search for Comet G-ALYY. His log book records a flight in VW826 from Fayid to El Adem to search and, later, a direct return flight to Fayid.

In May, Exercise 'Quick Return' was flown. It involved a

Sqn Ldr H H Jenkins and VX506 on the tarmac at Tabora, Rhodesia, May 1954

route trip to Cape Town, with the CO captaining VX506. It is thought to be the first time a Valetta had flown to the Cape from Fayid. Routed through Rhodesia, the crew received tremendous hospitality from the Royal Rhodesian Air Force. On its return VX506 left for the UK for reconditioning.

During June, the Squadron won the coveted Vickers trophy awarded annually to the MEAF Valetta squadron adjudged to have shown the greatest all-round efficiency. Ken Styan comments: "The trophy was given by Vickers during 1952 and though the touting for gifts was frowned upon, Vickers came up with a beautifully mounted silver model of a Valetta". Air Marshal Sir Claude Pelly, AOC-in-C MEAF, presented the trophy during a ceremonial parade on 14 June 1954. An entry in the records state that "a party held in the evening suitably washed the Squadron in and washed most of the Squadron out".

During July, the shortage of new and reconditioned Valetta C.1 aircraft led to the T.3 version being sent to MEAF. These were intended for navigation training and were fitted with five astrodomes and other navigation equipment. Although unsuitable for carrying troops and freight, they were used primarily for continuation training, thus relieving the C.1s for operational work. When the Squadron received WG257, amongst the comments made was: "The aircraft was quite pleasant to fly but had a very poor asymmetric performance". Later the aircraft were stripped of all the navigation equipment, which enabled them to fly lightweight spares and other suitable small freight.

It was about this time that LAC Gordon Musson was posted to 84 Squadron after serving for nine months on nearby No.109 MU. In correspondence he writes: "I shall always remember a 48-hour pass spent at Aqaba; 35 of us were able to spend a break sunning ourselves and swimming in the Red Sea. When the time came to return, we all piled aboard and Fg Off Jimmy Hedges said "How about a beat-up of the airfield"'. After taking off, he banked the aircraft and flew at zero feet, 'hedge-hopping' over the tents and generally creating a stir. Over the sea again he again banked steeply and I can swear that if anyone had been on the wingtip, he could have touched the water. From there he flew close to the steep mountains until we reached a comparatively safe height. I have never seen so many white and green-faced passengers before. Needless to say, word got around and low flying was banned over Aqaba from then on".

Musson comments: "I often flew as a fourth member of the crew acting as steward or any other odd job. When carrying mail, the procedure was that if only one bag was to be delivered, it was thrown out rather than bother to land. Quite often, notices would be put on the notice-board at Fayid, saying that if anyone was corresponding with someone stationed at Aqaba, would they note that the last mail drop finished in the Red Sea and was lost". Another instance of bad supply-dropping was when a team tipped a wicker basket of stores out and hit the tailplane, causing the pilot to 'blow his top'.

On 14 July 1954, Flt Sgt Eddy Tutt arrived to join the Squadron. He writes: "The first problem was that there was no accommodation available in the Sergeants' Mess, as the Canal Zone was in the early stages of closing down. Families were being sent home and the Mess was having to accommodate ex-living out members. I found myself with a bed and a mosquito net under a veranda with my few possessions stuffed in my kit-bag. At the time, the standard of food in the Mess had hit an all-time low, mainly savoury mince or corned beef with powdered potatoes, plus a salt tablet. I recall that many of the airmen went 'on strike' over the standard of food and conditions. There was little choice and the only place for a change of diet was the 'Arizona' rest house which was just outside the main gate. I can still taste the goat's meat sandwiches which were a speciality of the house".

"On 19 July, I flew to El Adem in VW162 with Fg Off Jimmy Hedges at the controls. The flight served as my check out for a 'D' category 'Freight Only' air signaller on six months probation. Another signaller on the station was Sgt George Pettitt and he was scheduled to fly to Habbaniya on a night-stop freight only run, Fayid - Mafraq - Habbaniya. His problem was that he had an offer of a 'Leave UK - Free Air Passage - 28 days'. He asked me if I would volunteer and as I was very inexperienced (only nine hours flying), I said "OK". It was a flight I was unlikely to forget, arriving back at the station on 22 August, several days after George Pettitt had returned from leave".

"We took off at 0515 on the morning of 23 July. The crew for the Habbaniya flight was Fg Off Wicksteed as captain, Fg Off Pete Lord as navigator, myself as signaller and a National Service SAC who had come along for air experience. The aircraft was VW826, carrying general cargo and a replacement Hercules engine. The trip was fated from the start. On take-off I called out "No airspeed indicating" as the air signaller doubled as the pilot's assistant on take-off and landing. The pilot aborted the take-off, turned around so as to hide the rear door from the control tower and told me to nip out and remove the pitot-head cover which he had forgotten to remove! On our take-off the tower remarked that the starboard engine was smoking badly. As all seemed well on instruments, we pressed on".

"The trip to Mafraq took just over two hours. There we refuelled and attempted to take-off again. By now the engine was banging and spluttering and each time we ended up by swinging around crating a dust storm. It was to be the 29th when we eventually left Mafraq after awaiting spares and other equipment. Whilst there I suffered from 'Gyppo Gut' after drinking ice-cold Stellar beer. We had no sooner set course for Habbaniya when the engine started misbehaving again. We were left with no alternative but to land again, this time at H4, one of the small strips laid down alongside the pipeline. In addition to the airstrip, there was a Jordanian Customs post and a small fort nearby to provide shelter for the border patrols and their camels. The SAC and myself were allocated a place in a small hut, which turned out to be an overnight stop for the Arab long-distance drivers. By the time the RAF servicing teams had arrived from Mafraq, it was to be 9 August before we attempted to resume our flight. We were now down to a crew of three, the SAC having returned to base with the RAF servicing team".

"Half-way down the runway, the engine again failed to respond and Wicksteed shouted: "Crash landing, brace yourselves". Luck was with us as the runway had a gentle slope from which we were able to lift off and gain flying speed sufficient to do a gentle turn and land back at H4. This time a Coles crane came out from Mafraq carrying a new engine and accompanied by a full repair team. After a further eleven days, we were ready for an air test. On 21 August at 1315, we finally took off for Habbaniya, arriving early evening just in time for the Sergeant's Mess dinner of roast beef". Tutt closes by writing: "On the day prior to leaving H4, I was invited to share a bottle of Booth's gin. Returning to the fort I flaked out. Fortunately I was found by one of the repair team and transported to the rest room. There was no doctor available and the only medical man was a vet who looked after the camels of the Jordanian border patrol. He was persuaded to come and look at me. After giving me an injection to lower my heart beat, he gave me a medicant to clear the gin from my system. I could probably claim to be the only squadron member to have his life saved by a camel vet". Even after 35 years, Eddy Tutt still can't look a gin in the face and still says "The old service saying still holds good; never volunteer for anything!"

In July a flight of 30 minutes duration was a search for an Anson which was returning to Fayid on one engine. The aircraft was in radio contact with the search Valetta flown by Sqn Ldr H Jenkins and was seen to force-land just north of Abu Sueir.

In addition to the search and rescue flights, three aircraft were provided to convey officials to Almaza to participate in the negotiations with the Egyptian authorities on the proposed Anglo-Egyptian agreement which, it was hoped, would bring an end to the anti-British troubles in Egypt. There were many such flights and it is recorded that, despite the ill-feeling of the Egyptians generally towards the British, the Egyptians were very hospitable to the Valetta crews whenever they visited Almaza.

During August, No.78 Squadron was disbanded, with most of their personnel posted to 84. In September, Sqn Ldr H H Jenkins became tour-expired and Sqn Ldr J H Dunn assumed command on 31 October 1954.

The beginning of the run-down of British Forces in the Canal Zone became apparent in November when, during the third week, the Squadron assisted in moving equipment of HQ MEAF from Ismailia to Nicosia. Further unit moves took place in December when part of GHQ Land Forces was transported to Cyprus in two double shuttles. This airlift included the first contingent of WRAC to be posted to Cyprus.

In May 1955, an aircraft flying a familiarisation flight crashed when, after practising asymmetric flying with the port engine feathered, the starboard engine fire warning light came on. Unfortunately the pilot feathered the starboard engine before the port engine restarted, with the result that the aircraft 'pancaked'. No one was injured.

The Congo rebellion blew up in June 1955 and aircraft and crews were detached to Accra to assist in the evacuation of civilians from Leopoldville and other trouble spots.

Rumours of disbandment, which had been circulating for some time, came to a head in June when it was announced that the Squadron would disband at the end of October. It was also announced that the Squadron Standard was ready for presentation. It was hoped that the presentation would take place at the beginning of October before the Squadron disbanded.

A month later, the endless troubles caused mainly by pro-Yemeni tribesmen in the Aden Protectorate flared up once again and eight aircraft took part in ferrying troops and equipment to Aden. During August, a Valetta was detailed to search for a crashed Auster. After a five-hour search the crash was located and supplies were dropped to an Army detachment in the area.

In September, the CO, Sqn Ldr J H Dunn, stated that he had received information that the Squadron would not now disband in October, as originally planned, but would continue for a further period as a medium-range transport squadron. The strength of both air and ground personnel would be reduced due to the dearth of replacements from the UK. He also stated that it was becoming increasingly difficult to fly and maintain the aircraft, the situation being aggravated by the shortage of spares.

During the same month, Flt Lt 'Mac' McLean was posted to the Squadron from the Iraq Communications Flight at Habbaniya. In correspondence he writes: "After my initial acceptance checks, my first flight with 84 Squadron was a 27.45 hour flight to Eastleigh and back. At Port Sudan, after refuelling, we panicked when the aircraft fire alarm started sounding. Fortunately it was a vehicle quite close to the aircraft which had burst into flames. All was well and we flew on to Khormaksar where we made a night stop. From there to Hargeisa in British Somaliland where the landing was made on a strip reminding one of the beach at Brighton". John Smith, on the facilities at Hargeisa, told me: "Refuelling at Hargeisa was from a 250-gallon hand pump bowser. A succession of 'locals' would take it in turn to pump ten gallons each - a lengthy and exhausting process when temperatures would be well over 100 degrees". Mac continues: "On to Eastleigh we flew at a reasonable height so that my 20 or so passengers could see the larger animals. All of a sudden the aircraft was difficult to hold straight and level, a little right wing low. All of my passengers had moved over to the right side of the aircraft and were looking up at Mt. Kilimanjaro, all 19,300 feet of it! We pressed on and started the climb into Eastleigh airport".

"A day off at Eastleigh gave me a chance to make contact with my old rear gunner from my Wellington days. He had become chief brewer at the local brewery and was only too willing to show me the sights. I had promised to take some pineapples back for the crews at Fayid and each time I mentioned it to him, he replied: "The old lady down the road has some". I eventually discovered that it was his mother he was referring to - because just behind their home there were acres and acres of pineapples. The flight back to Fayid was uneventful thanks to my navigator, Fg Off Pomford, and my signaller, Sgt Lancaster. The other 'milk run' in those days was the trip to Masirah via Riyan and Salalah. It was on one of those flights that the officer in charge of a party of one sergeant and 20 airmen on the small strip asked us not to spend too much time in the mess as the beer was running short, because the supply boat had not arrived".

In late October, the CO announced that the Squadron should have been presented with its new Standard on the 21st but, due to operational commitments, the date had been deferred until early in the New Year. As the Squadron had been due to disband at the end of October it had been greatly run down. Nevertheless, morale continued at a high level. November brought increased activity in moving personnel and equipment from the Canal Zone to Nicosia. This consisted of the movement of the main party of the second-line aircraft servicing flight from Fayid to Nicosia and also No.56 Motor Flight from the Canal Zone to Amman. The latter half of November was spent in packing up in readiness for the Squadron move to Abu Sueir early in December. During the month, 16 aircrew were posted to the Squadron, mainly from Nos.70 and 216 Squadrons which were being reformed with Hastings and Comets respectively. This was one indication to support the current rumour that No.84 Squadron would continue for some time as part of the MEAF Transport Force.

'Mac' McLean recalls one particular flight on 1 November 1955. "The CO of the Aden Communication Squadron asked us to make a trip to Thamoud. He said "It is not on the map but this is an operational necessity". When asked "How do we find it?", he replied "Fly to Riyan, take an overhead course of 015 degrees for umpteen miles and it should be right on the nose". With Fg Off Pete Tuke navigating and Sgt Pettitt checking the drift recorder, it was a case of 'left one degree' and again 'left one degree'. All that for 01.35 hours and there was the fort *voila* at Thamoud, just where he said it would be. The strip was marked by white painted stones and the sand was soft and deep. By now the cargo was

VW821 D at Habbaniya in 1954 (R C B Ashworth)

beginning to smell a little; it turned out to be shark meat. When we arrived back at Khormaksar, the Squadron Commander congratulated us by saying: "Not many of the lads can find the place first time".

On 5 December 1955, the Station at Fayid closed down. It was decided that as a farewell gesture, the Squadron would indulge in a formation flight over the Station. Mac McLean writes: "No-one could say that the Valetta was an ideal aircraft for formation flying but, on this occasion, the eight Valettas flew overhead in impeccable formation ending in a stream landing. I, as No.3, touched down when the two ahead of me were still on the runway, not bad for a transport aircraft". He continues: "At that time Abu Sueir was being used by No.208 Squadron with Gloster Meteor FR.9s. They were very impressed by our arrival and really the Christmas celebrations started from that first landing on 5 December. Whilst there, I had several flights in a Meteor and, in return, gave the Meteor boys flights in a Valetta. Night flying was of especial interest to them, witnessing St Elmo's Fire for the first time. After this display, one of them told his fellows not to take the 'Micky' out of the PIG transport types".

On 5 January 1956, Fg Off D M Remnant, as Standard bearer, received the coveted Squadron Standard from ACM Sir Francis Fogarty KCB KBE DFC AFC at the presentation ceremony. Mac McLean writes: "I was just the insignificant parade adjutant, but it gave me a chance to go with 'Sir Joe' to the Airmens' Mess that night for a sing-song. Shaibah Blues and all the old songs were sung but when we reached 'Salome' there was only Sir Joe, one other officer and myself who knew the words. By that time, it was getting rather quiet".

In March 1956, Abu Sueir closed down and the Squadron moved to Nicosia. Little had changed with the 'milk runs' except that they were now all longer flights. Instead of starting from Abu Sueir, the Squadron made it the first stop on all flights to Eastleigh, Entebbe, Khormaksar and Bahrein.

Until the repeal of the Anglo-Egyptian Treaty of 1954, the Egyptian Air Force had been organised entirely on RAF lines and supplied principally with British equipment. After Nasser's *coup d'état*, it was planned to build up the Egyptian aircraft industry with Russian aircraft and engines built under licence. 1955 saw the signing of a three-year trade pact with Czechoslovakia involving the supply of £80 million pounds worth of Eastern Bloc military equipment. Equally important was the arrival of large numbers of Russian and Czech technicians. The first swept-wing fighters to arrive were MiG-15s towards the end of 1955 (between 100 and 150) plus approximately 35 Il-28 twin-jet bombers. Shortage of experienced crews, however, minimised their usefulness, although they were used against Israeli targets. Thanks to the previous British occupation, the RAF had some superb airfields along the Western banks of the Suez Canal, amongst them Deversoir, Fayid and Shallufa.

Nicosia provided a much-needed rest to the Squadron; although the same number of hours were being flown, the increased number of married quarters allowed many more families to take up residence. At that time Group Captain A A Case, later to become an AVM, was the Station Commander. He was a wonderful character who had made up his mind to fly every type of aircraft based at Nicosia. He especially wanted his Transport category on the Valetta. Mac McLean writes: "He flew with me several times over various routes. On one trip to Malta we timed it so that he could get in as many night-flying hours as possible. Dawn broke as we were on the approach to El Adem so he pulled his 'scrambled egg' hat down over his eyes and said 'Will this count?' On return to Nicosia on the Sunday, he was still about an hour short of his required night hours. So we circled Nicosia for an hour, much to the air traffic controller's annoyance".

Flt Sgt Eddy Tutt writes: "Looking through my log book I noticed that I was on the aircraft that took AVM Boyce (CO of No.84 Sqn in 1942) on his farewell flight around his stations and we stopped for lunch with the Egyptian station commander at Abu Sueir. Just prior to our departure for Nicosia, the Egyptian CO came over and shook us all by hand saying "Goodbye, I don't suppose we shall meet again". At the time it seemed a strange thing to say as our aircraft were always calling in to refuel. The date was 26 July 1956 and we departed Abu Sueir with its MiG-15 fighters lined up on the runway, at 13.05 local time. Later that afternoon, Nasser sent his troops in to take over the Suez Canal. So AVM Boyce must have been the last RAF officer to leave the Canal Zone before we went to war with Egypt".

In the summer of 1956, Britain and the USA announced their withdrawal of financial support for Egypt's Aswan Dam project, so Nasser nationalised the Suez Canal, claiming that the revenue received from traffic would pay for the dam. Pending the

Conference of 23 Nations, including Russia and Egypt, on 16 August 1956 and as an outcome of talks held in London between the UK, France and the United States, Canberras were flown to Cyprus and leave was cancelled on the Canberra stations in the UK. Meanwhile the carriers *Bulwark* and *Theseus* left their stations for the Eastern Mediterranean. Demands by the UK and France that Egypt should withdraw its troops to a distance of ten miles from the Canal Zone were rejected and, on 31 October, Operation 'Musketeer' was mounted.

An air operation involving both land and carrier-based aircraft against military targets in Egypt began at dusk on the 31st. Canberras and Valiants based in Cyprus and Malta bombed the airfields at Almaza, Abu Sueir and Kabrit with the intention of destroying the Egyptian Air Force. The Allied Air Task Force Commander was Air Marshal D H Barnett - former AOC No.205 Group in the Canal Zone and also ex-CO of No.64 Squadron at Shaibah.

On the first three days of November, strikes were made against airfields in Egypt. On 4 November, leaflets were dropped by Hastings aircraft urging the local population to accept the Allies' proposals. The following day, several thousand paratroops were dropped on to Gamil airfield by RAF Hastings and Valettas and French Noratlas aircraft over Port Said. It was to be the biggest airborne operation since the war. At the same time seaborne troops of the Royal Tank Regiment and the 3rd Commando Brigade were coming ashore at Casino Pier. On 6 November, the fighting ceased and Allied troops occupied the Canal Zone until the arrival of UN troops. The action was said to have achieved the object of stopping a major war in the Middle East 'before the Egyptian Air Force, organised by Russia, ran amok'. Unfortunately, history shows that the action was in reality a shambles, and achieved exactly the opposite to what Eden had anticipated! The Egyptians sank several ships in the canal, rendering it useless! Not only were several British ships trapped, but pumping stations on the Iraq - Lebanon pipeline were destroyed. It had effectively cut the short cut to British possessions in the Far East and may well have proved to be the turning point in the ending of the British Empire.

No.84 Squadron's part in the six-day war can be summed up by Mac McLean. "During the briefing, the Colonel of the Paras said that his intelligence report covering Gamil airfield spoke of oil drums with wire stretched between and over them. He turned to Brigadier Butler and said 'Keep your legs together or you could be ruined for life'. Gp Capt Adrian Case volunteered to fly as 'second dickie' with me on the Suez drop. The rest of the crew was Flt Lt Wilkinson and Sgt Brown. Case, popularly known as 'Uncle', used the second pilot's seat but was having difficulties, what with the parachute harness, Mae West, Sutton harness and his 22 stone, his straps would not go around him. In the end he threw the harness over the back of the seat and said "This was definitely was not built for me". We were No.6 in the formation and, at the briefing, we were told to break off as soon as the paras had left the aircraft and not to fly over the town of Port Said. We had despatched all of our paratroops but No.5 kept on flying straight and level. So Case shouts 'Come on, Mac, break off'. I side-slipped under No.5 and, as I did so another paratrooper jumped out. I shall never know to this day how I missed him".

A week or two after the campaign, a lunch was organised at the Dome Hotel, Kyrenia. All the pilots who took part in the drop were there and, by chance, I sat next to the paratroop officer who was in No.5 Valetta. I asked him what delayed the paratrooper who I had nearly hit. It turned out that he was a very young member of the paras and had tripped over the main spar. He was nearly in tears because he thought that he would miss the action - so we threw him out!"

The weeks after Suez were chaotic, not knowing who was the potential enemy. No.84 had a Valetta at Bahrein, awaiting an engine change and McLean was detailed to go as passenger and bring the aircraft back. Because of the situation we were told 'No-lite' over Syria. We were not allowed to overfly that country but, to cut corners, we used to cheat. This time my pilot left changing course a few minutes late. I was trying to sleep in the back and was roused by the change of engine note as we dived to clear the area. It did not take many seconds to get the signal, "Don't do that again!" My return flight was routed through Habbaniya and Elazig in Turkey. Landing was a problem, even though we had clearance. No one spoke English and eventually using my schoolboy French, I managed to obtain sufficient petrol for the trip to Nicosia. I did not dare risk trying to ask for the right grade of oil!

Fg Off Les Coyle and I had just returned from that trip and we were expecting a quiet week-end when the station 'Wingco' came in and said that an emergency had arisen and that an Army surgeon had to fly to El Adem to perform an operation. The trip to El Adem was smooth and, after we landed, the colonel got into a waiting jeep and was driven off into the desert. Meanwhile the crew bedded down in the aircraft awaiting his return. Next morning at flight planning, there was a signal from the colonel requesting an air lift from Derna. I sent a signal to Nicosia telling them of the change of plans and said 'Will return soonest'. They expected us back by midday to do another trip. We found Derna on the map NW of El Adem and realised that the colonel had motored there. Derna was an old wartime airfield and had probably not been used since. Its surface was terrible and it surprised me that we did not get a puncture. Nevertheless, when we landed, we found the ambulance with the patient awaiting us. The stretcher case was carried on board and a saline bottle was attached from the roof to the patient. How the saline bottle remained attached after the bumpiest take-off I have ever done was nothing short of a miracle".

"An Army ambulance was waiting for us at Nicosia and the colonel went on his way after thanking us. Only the duty flight met us as if we were returning from a routine flight. I later realised that as the flight was only verbally authorised and, consequently was not written up on an authorisation sheet, the trip was never entered in my log book".

"Another meeting of interest was after landing at Habbaniya one afternoon when we went into the transit mess. Only one person was in there and he shouted, "Come in, lads, and join me". It was the Station Commander, Group Captain Hughie Edwards VC DSO DFC, who was waiting for the Australian and New Zealand holders of the Victoria Cross to arrive. They were flying to meet the Queen at the Centenary of the Victoria Cross celebrations at Buckingham Palace. That evening, I sat next to Captain Upham VC and bar and his wife for dinner, not many of those about!"

Mac concludes by saying: "During my service with No.84 Squadron from September 1955 until 3 January 1957, I flew over 700 hours. I would like to think it trouble-free and it nearly was apart from the one tragedy. A sad ending, but if history is to be written it must be mentioned".

On the 26 September, Sqn Ldr J H Dunn became tour-expired and command of the Squadron was assumed by Sqn Ldr F L Spencer. He was to be CO for only three months for, at the end of December 1956, No.84 Squadron was disbanded.

PIGS IN ADEN

Wg Cdr Ken Bowhill writes: "You may know that No.84 Squadron was disbanded in Cyprus in late 1956 and the number-plate, silver and Standard was transferred to Aden where it was presented to the Command's transport squadron, which gloried under the name Aden Protectorate Communications and Support Squadron (APCSS). I had been commanding APCSS since April 1956 and at the time of inheriting No.84 Squadron's numberplate, it had three flights, one Valetta, one Pembroke and a helicopter flight. As far as I can recall, Flt Lt Dennis Stoten commanded the Valetta Flight with an establishment of 18 aircraft, Flt Lt N E Pash, the Pembroke flight with five aircraft and Flt Lt C S Bamberger DFC the two Sycamore helicopters.

The Valettas had a scheduled and a non-scheduled function. The scheduled routes included regular runs to Cyprus, Nairobi, Karachi (Mauripur) and to Bahrein via the Gulf stations. There were also shorter regular runs to Riyan, Salalah, Masirah and Sharjah. In addition, to these there were the daily supply runs to the up-country strips such as Beihan, Ataq, Mukeiras and odd flights to Lodar and Mahfid where either RAF Regiment, Army or Government guards were stationed.

It is also of interest that at these up-country strips, a jeep with a couple of fire extinguishers represented the total airfield services. At more obscure strips such as Lodar, notice had to be given to friendly forces so that the surrounding hills could be cleared of dissident tribesmen likely to take a shot or two at you.

As to the Pembrokes, they were used in lighter transport roles and would fly supplies and personnel into the smaller strips, such as Dhala and Mudia. When the occasion arose they would be used for casualty evacuation, as were the Sycamores. Both the Pembrokes and the Sycamores were transferred to No.78 Squadron (Pioneers) based at Khormaksar in the spring of 1957.

One of the few flights that stand out was on 18 April when I flew a Valetta to Lodar with two senior political officers on board. They were there to mediate between two tribes on a water dispute. A stream had been diverted, which resulted in the taking of hostages, and a tribal battle was about to break out unless the officers could solve the dispute. This was typical of many tribal rivalries that prevailed in the interior of the Protectorate".

VW184 H forcelanded 15 miles from Riyan, May 1957

Flt Lt Jack Babbington arrived in Aden during January 1957. In correspondence he writes: "The role of the Squadron at that time was primarily to protect the UK's oil interests in the whole of Aden and in Oman. In addition, we provided a line of communication to a crumbling Empire with regular flights to Nairobi. This was considered to be a Squadron 'perk' as the crew had a full 24 hours in which to relax. Coupled with this it was possible to 'indulge' the wife and family".

Commenting on the airstrips he states: "The terrain in our operating area, generally north-east of Aden, consisted of the gently rising desert merging into some quite astonishing mountain peaks. One such was known as 'Sugar Loaf' mountain which had seemingly perpendicular sides with a village filling every square inch of the peak with terraced fields for the crops. Soon after passing the 'Sugar Loaf', the escarpment came into view with Mukeiras strip at 4,000 ft asl. Immediately below Mukeiras was Lodar at 2,500 ft which had a built-in cross wind. Both of these were approximately 30 minutes flying time from Khormaksar. The next two strips, Beihan and Ataq were about one hour away from base. All were served on a daily basis, the larger strips having, on occasion, three flights a day. On one occasion, as a result of increased Yemeni threats, the Squadron put a Valetta into Wadi Ayn, which was just around the corner from Beihan, every 30 minutes. This allowed 20 minutes for the turn round and ten minutes for the dust to settle. Mukeiras presented frequent problems owing to its proximity to the Yemen border. Generally a left-hand circuit would be flown, but following a bullet embedding itself in the head cushion of the captain's seat of an Aden Airways aircraft, it was felt that right hand circuits might be wiser.

Navigation within the Protectorate was of a rudimentary nature with absolutely nothing by way of ground aids. The crew of a Valetta included a W/op, who acted as co-pilot on take-off and landing and a navigator but as most navigating was done by map-reading, they were not strictly necessary. It took some time but after a while one came to know the desert terrain like the back of one's hand.

The three bases along the coast, Riyan, Salalah and Masirah were regularly serviced twice a week. Fresh meat was always a problem as there was no facilities for refrigeration aboard the aircraft. The first two usually received their quota in fairly good shape but after eight hours flying to reach Masirah it would be ready to leave the aircraft unaided. Bahrein and Sharjah were also visited twice weekly with a refuelling stop at Salalah. The flights to Nairobi could not be flown without a stop at Hargeisa in British

Somaliland. Generally speaking, this trip created few difficulties yet, on one occasion, one of the crews missed it on the return trip and finished up at Berbera in Somaliland. They had to refuel the aircraft from five-gallon drums through chamois leather filters!

At the end of April 1957, Sqn Ldr Ken Bowhill returned to the UK and command of the Squadron was assumed by Sqn Ldr Bill Talbot. Sqn Ldr Talbot writes: "I went to Aden at the end of April and left in April 1959. I took over a squadron of grounded Valettas as a result of one shedding a wing through main spar failure. (This aircraft was not one of 84's). The grounding gave the 'tech boys' a chance to clean up the aircraft. However the situation was too good to last and in May the grounding was lifted and the aircraft were released for flying at a reduced payload and eventually cleared in full".

It was said that every strip in the Protectorate had a crashed 'pig' except Beihan. This seemed to be so since it was more difficult and the pilots had to concentrate more. It retained that record until 12 June 1957. Jack Babbington writes "My log book records Valetta VW165 Khormaksar - Beihan, with no return flight. As they say 'I remember it well'. Since many of the strips were limited in length, the speed over the boundary was critical. I seem to recall it was 90 knots and then 'three point' it just inside the markers. At about 30 feet and all set to land, the aircraft gave an almighty shudder and began to fall. The application of power did nothing and the aircraft struck the ground just on the edge of the runway. It showed a marked reluctance to continue to roll and I had to apply considerable power to get to the end of the strip. A burst tail wheel I figured. Having reached the end of the strip, I stopped the engines and, turning in my seat, I found that I could not see two feet down the cabin. Sand in suspension obscured everything. Groping my way aft, I found my sole passenger fit but puzzled. On opening the rear door I was confronted by an officer of the Cameronians holding aloft a Valetta tail wheel and who asked, 'I say, old boy, does this belong to you?' It was unusual to read on the Form 700 a comment by a certain Fg Off Joy 'this aircraft stalled at an unusually high airspeed'. Any aircraft damaged on a strip was written-off. The engines, radio and instruments were removed and brought back to base. The rest of the aircraft gradually disappeared into various villages and were put to good use as water channels, etc. The cause of the accident was eventually put down to the fact that when clearing the strip of large boulders, a large heap had been left right on the centre line of the runway at the end of the strip. It was the exact spot where the tail wheel had struck".

The cockpit of a Valetta

"Later, I had a tail wheel which failed to lock down causing considerable damage whilst landing at Khormaksar. Thereafter I was known as 'Tail wheel Jack'".

Having mentioned the difficulty in finding some of the airstrips, there was a second Valetta loss during 1957. This aircraft, piloted by Fg Off Harry (Tank) Martin, was on a relief flight to Habarut which was under siege. On the return flight the port engine failed due to 'oil gulping'. Unable to gain height to clear the mountains Martin set course for the beach which would add approximately 400 miles to the flight. He eventually ran out of fuel 15 miles from Riyan, 3 miles east of Shihr and within sight of the runway. Even then Harry's problems were far from over, because of a large Wadi between him and Riyan, rescue crews had to make a 150-mile detour. Fortunately there were no casualties but, later Fg Off Martin's nickname was changed to 'Empty tank'. Another incident of note was when Flt Lt John Meakin had the misfortune to clip the tailwheel at Mukeiras. Once again there were no casualties and the dismantled Valetta provided sufficient piping and tankage for a super hot-and-cold water supply for the resident political agent's house.

On 23 September 1957, the Squadron provided two aircraft in support of Col Sir Hugh Boustead, an influential political officer. His job was to recover a large number of school children from Riyan to Aden. The children had been rescued by the colonel who, single-handed, had arranged a cease-fire between two warring tribes and thus enabled the children to return to school in Aden. The sight of the colonel marching down the Wadi at the head of hordes of children would have outdone the Pied Piper.

Flt Lt Reg Ponting, who served with No.84 Squadron during the 1957-58 period, writes: "During my spell with No.84 I had an eight-month stint in charge of Riyan. For company I had 30 airmen and 50 locally-recruited levies and a dump of thousands of 44-gallon drums of aviation fuel".

"More popular was the weekly flight to Nairobi where the abundance of fresh vegetables, fruit and milk in Tetrapacks which we brought back made us very welcome in Aden. It was not the purpose of the flight, of course! We used to land at Mogadishu to refuel because, at certain times of the year, the weather was inclined to turn violent and there were few navigation aids. On the more regular runs to Beihan, I remember being ticked off for saying 'Good Morning' to some willowy type in a silk dressing gown. Evidently it was the mark of a 'peasant' to speak to a 'Blue and Royal' before breakfast!

"Another of our duties was supply dropping to the SAS who were engaged in a war in support of the Sultan of Oman against rebels who were trying to take over the country. The country was 'hellish bleak' and mountainous with isolated, surprisingly fertile valleys. the rebels were well supplied with light ack-ack guns and various other weapons which were attacked by RAF Vampire fighters firing on these mountain top positions. We in No. 84 Squadron were fortunate that no losses occurred during these drops but I recall that at least one Vampire was brought down. It was impossible to recover the body of the pilot but one of the Squadron

Valetta's flew out a padre and a photographer, and wreaths were dropped at the site of the wreckage".

Fg Off Peter Rover says: "My memories of 84 are predominantly of the discomforts of life in Aden. Khormaksar in those days did not enjoy the blessing of air-conditioning so it was always a relief to get airborne. I do recall landing at Beihan through a swarm of locusts and having to disembark from the aircraft in the thick of them! When we finally left the oasis had been stripped bare".

He also comments on his spell as CO of Masirah Island. "The satellites of Riyan, Salalah and Masirah Island were each manned by personnel from Khormaksar for six months at a time. The COs were Flying Officers from either No.8 or No.84 Squadron; they alternated. Masirah was supplied by sea periodically and the CO had to arrange for Arab dhows and local labour to transship the stores from the supply ship anchored in the channel to the shallow water jetty on the island. There was train system on the island which used to, mainly, carry the 44-gallon fuel drums to the fuel compound. The CO was the only person authorised to drive the train since the locomotive was a slightly different gauge to the track and had to be driven very cautiously otherwise it would have come off the rails. It weighed seven and a half tons so getting it back on the rails was a considerable chore!

Peter Rover returned to the UK in November 1957 having flown 1,252 hours with APCS and 84 Squadron. His career later is also of considerable interest. Leaving the RAF in 1961 he joined the Royal Navy and became a helicopter pilot. His original intention of joining BEA later on with the Fairey Rotodyne fleet. This, of course never entered service and Peter Rover remained in the Navy. Later, he served with Nos.814, 705, 706 and 826 Squadrons aboard HMS *Hermes*, *Victorious*, *Albion* and *Eagle*. Afterwards he became a Naval Staff Officer at the NATO School at Oberammergau and finally as Commander Flying School Training at Culdrose.

All of the aircrew commented on the inability to converse with many of the passengers. Most crew knew 'Mahfeish cigaren' (no smoking prior to take-off). Notwithstanding, one crew member wandered aft to find his Arab passengers having a 'brew-up' over a kerosene burner in the cabin. Oddly enough, no aircraft were lost through fire or explosion.

Another incident which, although it is nothing to do with No.84 Squadron, is worth recording. It happened to a Beverley which had come into Aden on a proving flight. It had operated into Beihan and on its departure an engine had failed. For some reason the pilot decided to return to Beihan instead of landing at a strip such as Ataq, 30 minutes away. Following a good touchdown, the three remaining engines were put into reverse pitch to reduce the landing run. Unfortunately the aircraft swung off the runway and into the dunes. The nose buried itself and the boom broke aft of the main fuselage arching across the cockpit. Looking at photographs of the wreckage, it was a miracle that anyone survived. In the event only the W/op died and this was the result of swallowing his dentures!

During 1958, the Squadron Commander, Sqn Ldr E W Talbot was awarded a bar to his DFC, a rare decoration in peacetime. Fg Off Harry Bray was awarded the AFC. The event leading up to these awards was an unusually daring incursion of Yemeni forces as far as a ridge overlooking the airstrip at Dhala. The strip was so short and difficult that only the Pembrokes could operate from it. With hostile forces overlooking it, there could be no flights at all. In order to reach this point, the hostile troops had passed around and isolated one of the many forts that existed in the Protectorate. Since Dhala had no ground forces of any size, it became necessary to bring up a column from Aden, which during the day and the following night carried out a most daring assault. Using local guides, the Cameronians climbed the almost perpendicular cliff using goat trails. After a short engagement, they secured a foothold. It was at this point that No.84 Squadron joined in. All available crews and aircraft were used. The DZ was literally just over the edge of the ridge, which involved overshooting the enemy with high ground to the left and right. 'Guard dogs' in the shape of No.8 Squadron Venoms timed their firing on the enemy positions at the moment of our overshoot.

The citation for Sqn Ldr Talbot's award reads: "In late April 1958, a large force of Yemeni troops crossed the border in the Dhala area, occupied the heights, and surrounded the fort at As Sarir. This fort was occupied by Government Guards and a British Political Officer. All attempts to reach the fort by ground troops proved unsuccessful and the occupants were in dire need of food, water and ammunition. Air drop of these supplies was the only method that could be used. No.84 Squadron immediately responded

Valetta C.1 VW141 at Khormaksar

and carried out six supply drops under continuous fire from rifles and automatic weapons. Although fighter cover was provided, the Valetta aircraft flying at 100 feet above the ground came under heavy fire. Nevertheless, the repeated runs, up to 13 per sortie, were carried out to ensure the accurate delivery of, and to prevent the enemy capturing, these essential supplies. All supplies fell either on the fort or within 100 yards and were retrieved by the defenders. With the fort supplied, and a major attack in progress to relieve the fort by ground forces, it was found that the only method of re-supply to advance elements on top of the hills was by air supply. A further eight sorties were flown and supplies dropped to advance troops while the aircraft were under heavy fire.

A total of fourteen sorties were flown totalling 22 hours flying time. 64,000 lbs of supplies were dropped and 90% were recovered and serviceable for use.

Sqn Ldr Talbot, as OC No.84 Squadron, led each of the major dropping sorties carrying out the first flights into each area. Unperturbed by enemy fire, he carried out his deliveries accurately and successfully and set an example which all his crews immediately followed. He made four sorties and, in addition, put in outstanding personal effort to ensure aircraft serviceability and availability.

The relief of the fort at As Sarir and its continued resistance was mainly accomplished by the efforts of No.84 Squadron and through the outstanding example and accuracy under fire of the Squadron Commander, Sqn Ldr E W Talbot. I have no hesitation in recommending Sqn Ldr E W Talbot for a bar to the DFC".

In May 1958 the arrival of the first two Beverley's on the station meant a gradual decline of the Valetta flights. Sqn Ldr Bill Talbot DFC and bar writes: "The position of Harry Guile and myself as 'joint' COs was grey to say the least. The unfortunate thing was that the Beverleys did not get going for some months due to persistent engine problems. The future of the Valettas was chewed over until it was finally decided to extend their lives in Aden. We were more or less regarded as No.84 Squadron 'A' and 'B' Flights and the situation was finally resolved by the reforming of No.233 Squadron with 84's flight of Valettas, which were eventually retired in 1964 when No.233 Squadron was disbanded.

VW140 with supply canisters under the fuselage

FO Jim Jinman, FO Ian Macdonald, Sgt Eddie Tutt with VW851 at Fayid

Beverley C.1 XL149 of No.84 Squadron (via Jack Meaden)

CHAPTER 19 - WITH THE BEVERLEY IN ADEN

A brief history of the first two years of the Squadron's service with the Blackburn Beverley was written by Fg Off D R Jones. It gives a very light-hearted look as to how the Beverley arrived at No.84 Squadron.

"The stage set; the hub of the old boy's network at MOD. Two senior RAF 'types' were chatting. "But what on earth can we do with them" says Fred. "I honestly can't think" replied Mac. "I have already worn out three pairs of shoes trying to flog them to the airlines. I can always sell part-worn crews to Silver City or Skyways, but even they won't consider buying these brutes". "My dear chap" commiserated Fred. "I do sympathise but we cannot have them clutter up our green and pleasant land. They are so enormous, they even have four engines; four each, that is".

By now, one will have realised that the 'Bev' was the aircraft they were talking about. There was just no comparison with the Vickers Valetta which the Squadron had been using since April 1953. Wing span alone was 162 feet and the aircraft weighed in at about 135,000 lbs. Powered by four 2,850 hp Bristol Centaurus engines, it had a payload of over 50,000 lbs over comparatively short distances. With a light load, it had an excellent take-off and landing performance; with a full fuel load it was capable of remaining airborne for 15 hours.

The variety of loads carried included a radar scanner 46 ft long and 9 ft wide; a bulldozer weighing about seven tons; one Whirlwind or two Sycamore helicopters; a Hunter fighter; a complete field hospital with all its equipment and staff; or a couple of signals caravans each weighing about 19,000 lbs.

Used in the passenger role, it could carry 92 seated passengers, but fewer were normally carried to allow for priority freight. When used in the aero-medical role, it carried 48 stretcher cases on the lower deck and 30 sitting in the boom.

With low pressure tyres fitted to its eight main wheels and two nose wheels, a loaded Beverley actually exerted less pounds per square inch than a loaded Valetta. This, together with its ability to 'land short' with the aid of propeller braking, made it the ideal aircraft for landing on the up-country strips of the Aden Protectorate.

The Beverley was already in service with Nos.47 and 53

Squadrons at RAF Abingdon, pioneering routes to Germany and the Near East, and being used operationally in November 1956 after the Suez crisis. In April 1957, the Beverley was issued to No. 30 Squadron and to No.242 Operational Conversion Unit at Dishforth

During the early months of 1958, Yemeni forces had crossed the frontier into the Emirate of Dhala and occupied the heights of Djebel Jehaf. As the situation worsened, a state of emergency was declared. At the same time, British military activity increased and sufficient aircrew were assembled for the formation of a new squadron at Abingdon. The unit chosen to receive the Beverley was No.84 Squadron which was already at Khormaksar flying the Valetta. The new type would be no stranger to Aden as No.30 Squadron had had a detachment of two aircraft based there since February 1957.

During the next few days, XM108 and XM109 were ferried in from No.27 Maintenance Unit at Shawbury to Abingdon. Originally the scheduled date of departure was to be the middle of June. It soon became apparent that an earlier date was desirable and the training of the first crews were given priority. Most of the members of the Squadron had already had their embarkation leave and, as soon as the crews were classified, they were ready to leave.

On 28 May, the two aircraft left Abingdon on their three-day flight to Khormaksar. In each were three pilots to ease the flying. Flying XM108 was Fg Off R Livermore AFM with Fg Off P M Youll and Fg Off H C Farmer. In XM109 Fg Off A E Herbert was captain with Fg Offs A D Pryde and R B Lamb as co-pilots.

In addition to the crews, twenty ground staff were carried, plus a quantity of aircraft equipment, spares and personal kit. There were no incidents on the flight and the pair arrived at Khormaksar on the afternoon of 30 May to be greeted by the Valetta crews who were already based there.

Sqn Ldr E W Talbot, OC No.84 Squadron, greeted the new arrivals and offered them a few days break before their official operations began. During this period a tour of the up-country strips was flown under the guidance of Flt Lt R W Dye, the Wing pilot.

Meanwhile, back at Abingdon, the remaining crews continued their training and on 18 June, XM106 and XM107 took off for Aden.The first aircraft was flown by Flt Lts K Webster and R H

Pitman DSO as joint captains, with Fg Offs B W West and C W Ellis as co-pilots. In XM107, Sqn Ldr H W Guile (CO) and Flt Lt N J Adams (captains) with Fg Off W R Oatey co-piloting. Again a number of groundcrew travelled as passengers.

Over the following weeks, Fg Off D R Jones tells of the conditions: "Perhaps the biggest problem was how to get our knees brown without sunburn. We had arrived in the middle of Aden's hot season and the climate took a bit of getting used to. Temperatures in the upper 90s coupled with high humidity which persists even at night, proved a strain on the body and no less the trouser pocket. Very soon we all got to know the Aden colony very well. We sampled the delights of the swimming clubs and wandered in and out of the many bars at Steamer Point and Crater, where we learned how to bargain with the local traders. We learnt the meaning of 'baksheesh', 'imshi' and other Arabic words in common use. We found that the camel, the creature described by Fg Off Herbert as "a horse built to Air Ministry Works Dept specifications" possessed the most incredible smell imaginable and we were also told that, although the Arab men walked around holding hands, it was just 'something they did'.

Once in Aden, the Beverleys formed a separate flight alongside the Valettas which were not due to end their assoc-iation with the Squadron until August 1960. All of this time, they operated as a separate unit under the command of Sqn Ldr H W Guile. What was unusual was that for the first time the Squadron had two Commanding Officers sharing the same small office. Sqn Ldr Bill Talbot DFC remained in charge of the Valettas until April 1959 when they were handed over to No.233 Squadron. Accom-modation had always been in short supply at Khormaksar and for some months the crews shared the same offices and crew rooms. It was not ideal, but fortunately both flights managed as well as they could. Coupled with these problems was the fact that the tour was to become a two-year posting. The number of airmen on the station soon created an outcry in parliament over the living conditions and building was put in hand almost immediately to remedy this state of affairs. Priority was given to married quarters at Khormaksar and Steamer Point, while extra barrack blocks were built for single officers and airmen. All of the furniture needed would have to be imported from as far afield as Singapore and Hong Kong. For the first eighteen months, Khormaksar was nothing more than a large building site.

At this time, the Beverleys were decorated with their celebrated scorpion on the nose of the aircraft and the card symbol on the fin. Flt Lt Ken Webster became Flt Commander (Air) and Flt Lt Jim Adams Flt Commander (Ground). Later in 1958, Flt Lt Mayall took over the second appointment. Flt Lt Ken Brown was appointed Navigation Leader and Master Signaller Palmer became Signal Leader.

The crews were to find that flying was divided into two completely different types; short-haul supply runs into up-country strips like Mukeiras, Beihan and Ataq or route flying to the stations along the Arabian coast - Riyan, Salalah, Masirah and into the Persian Gulf to Azaiba, Sharjah and Bahrein. Flights to Eastleigh (Nairobi) were also becoming more frequent.

Already, serviceability problems were beginning to show themselves; the combination of heat, humidity and sand did not do the aircraft any good at all. The spares situation was often critical and engine changes numerous. Nevertheless, in spite of what were minimal working conditions for the groundcrews, the job went on.

On 14 July 1958, Sqn Ldr H W Guile received an urgent message telling him to report to the War Room at Headquarters, Steamer Point. There he learnt that King Feisal of Iraq had been murdered in a *coup d'état* in Baghdad and that the British forces in the Middle East were to take certain precautions against possible future unrest in the area. Two Beverleys left for Nairobi on 15 July and returned the following day loaded with soldiers. For the next few days, 84's Beverleys were ranging all over the area of the command, from Entebbe to Bahrein, carrying troops and military equipment and for several weeks a detachment was based at Bahrein. Several crews rotated on a fortnight's stand-by, either training or, in most cases, sheltering from the excessive heat.

Fg Off D R Jones wrote: "Khormaksar at that particular time was a most uncomfortable place. To add to the discomforts, many more personnel were moving in, in connection with the emergency and the overcrowding made life almost intolerable".

Two squadrons of Vampires of the Royal Rhodesian Air Force arrived to assist. One Beverley, flown by Sqn Ldr Harry Guile, flew to Mogadishu in Italian Somaliland to take the equipment necessary for them to stage through the airfield. In September, he returned to Mogadishu to collect the equipment when the Vampires of the Royal Rhodesian Air Force returned

home. At the same time Flt Lt Pitman and his crew flew to Harra Meda in Ethiopia to assist those who travelled a different route. Whilst there, Flt Lt Pitman were honoured by a visit from the Emperor of Ethiopia, His Imperial Majesty Haile Selassie. During the two days spent in Ethiopia, the crew were entertained by various Ethiopian families and officials.

In August 1958, one of the squadron's groundcrew lost his life when he was accidentally electrocuted whilst working on his car. The same month the Squadron took part in Exercise 'Beggar's Opera' designed as a rehearsal for the rapid movement of air transported forces. It took place on Kamaran Island in the Red Sea, some 300 miles from Aden. Of the three Beverleys which were used, two carried 88 fully-armed soldiers, whilst the third carried a further 36 troops and several Landrovers. The aircraft took off from Khormaksar and set course for Kamaran Island at 300 ft above sea level, escorted by fighters. For the last 200 miles the Beverleys dropped to 200 ft, made a direct approach to the airfield at Kamaran and taxied to their positions, 37 seconds behind schedules. It was a great success.

Routine work followed with regular trips to the Protectorate's garrisons, with occasional flights to Masirah and Salalah. However the last week of October showed the Beverley's capabilities when the Squadron became involved in moving troops from Aqaba in Jordan to Kenya. The men were brought by ship to Aden, from there they were airlifted to Nairobi. The task occupied a week and during that time 1,000 troops were flown the 1,000 miles to Nairobi.

In October, the last two aircraft arrived with three new crews. The captains being Flt Lt L S Alden, P V Mayall And D R Molloy. At the same time the crews were increased by the inclusion of a flight engineer, a job which up to then had been done by the second pilot.

At the beginning of November, Aden was plagued by a series of riots believed to have been caused by the Yemeni influence in the colony. No Europeans were hurt but several of the service personnel had their cars overturned and set on fire. By the end of the month, over 300 of the trouble makers had been rounded up and deported.

December 1958 started badly when Fg Off Denis Mayoux, a second pilot on detachment from No.30 Squadron, was killed when he fell from the tail boom whilst carrying out a pre-flight inspection. Wg Cdr Harry Guile wrote in the Beverley Association magazine 'Mag-Drop':

"To get to the tail section where the powered flying control units were placed, one had to go through the toilet doors. If, at the same time, someone opened the boom floor parachute doors, you would then open the toilet doors on your return and the momentum would carry you through the open para doors some 30 feet to the concrete below. A simple solution involved the toilet doors having locking-pins and, to make sure these were visible, the doors were trimmed. Unfortunately, the 'Mod' was given the classification that amounted to 'do it when you have time'. Needless to say that when I took over the Squadron, I presumed that the mod had gone through. As a result, when Flt Lt Andy Andrusikiewicz brought a new aircraft in on detachment, and knowing his ability, I did not worry unduly. Next morning at first light, whilst Mayoux was doing his pre-flight checks, the groundcrew had need to adjust the number of seats in the boom and had opened the boom parachute doors. Fg Off D A Mayoux fell through and died later that day".

At the beginning of the New Year, the Valetta flight moved from the main Squadron building to offices and crew rooms elsewhere on the station. This eased the overcrowding considerably for both air and groundcrews. The groundcrew, up to then, had been situated in a broken-down caravan and an equally decrepit tent at the side of the dispersal area.

During the month Flt Lt Webster, on landing at Salalah, had found a bullet hole in his starboard wing. It was later thought that some trigger-happy Arab had shot at the aircraft on its approach to the airfield. Fortunately, it was not serious and the aircraft was able to return to Khormaksar where repairs were carried out. On 23 January 1959, the station was visited by the retiring Chief of Air Staff, MRAF Sir Dermot Boyle, who was carrying out a farewell tour of all RAF overseas establishments.

The day he arrived, the heavens opened and for three days it poured. As there was no drainage, the water just stayed where it fell and large areas of the airfield were flooded. Some up-country flights to Mukeiras were cancelled because of low cloud over the airstrip, hitherto quite unheard of!

In February, Fg Off Oatey left the Squadron to join No. 78 Squadron flying Twin Pioneers. At about the same time the aircrew were increased by the arrival of Flt Lt F L Swales and Fg Offs A R

Beverley XM103 V unloading at an up-country airstrip

Weet and A J Bosley. That month gave the Beverley a further chance to show off its ability when, during the final weeks of the Jebel Akhdar campaign, it carried out numerous flights into short airstrips and also air-dropping large loads.

During April the Squadron was honoured by a visit from ACM Sir Phillip Joubert de la Ferté. At that time he was collecting material for a series of radio talks on famous RAF Squadrons. In the three days of his visit, he was given a tour of the up-country landing strips and witnessed 84 Squadron's new role in the Middle East.

By that time many of the wives and families had arrived and were beginning to take advantage of the 'Nyali Leave Scheme'. Service families were transported at public expense to Mombasa by DC-3s of Aden Airways, to spend two weeks at the Nyali Leave Centre just outside Mombasa. During the same period, the Squadron had begun to fly their aircraft to the UK for major servicing. These trips proved a blessing for the crews who flew them home.

In the first week of June, a courtesy visit was made to the Imperial Ethiopian Air Force at Harra Meda by the Venoms of No.8 Squadron. Two of 84's Beverleys went along in support. Similar support flights were carried out later in June and in early July, when No.208 Squadron, based at Eastleigh, were invited to visit Salisbury, Rhodesia, for an exercise.

One day in August, SAC Boardman (alias Gurking) found himself having a day off. Accompanied by his mate (not from 84) they wandered around the town in search of entertainment. Later, they took a boat trip out to the Russian-owned, Italian- crewed passenger ship SS *Fair Sky* which was anchored off Steamer Point. They were received on board and joined the inevitable party. After no doubt sampling the liquid hospitality they found a quiet corner to sleep. They awoke to find the ship was just entering the Red Sea, bound for England.

In a letter written to his mate, SAC 'Svengali' Civelli, Boardman writes: "We had a marvellous Mediterranean cruise and were treated as passengers for 14 days. The only thing wrong was the captain's insistence that we were to be in bed by 10 o'clock but, of course, we hid amongst the passengers. The last time we did this, we were kept locked up for three days. When we docked at Southampton we were taken to West Drayton where we were locked up for a further 24 hours. After questioning they treated it as a big joke and sent us off for seven days leave.

Well, Sven, I'll see you on the 26th of this month. We are flying back by Comet"

Signed: Gurking.

Recently Wg Cdr Harry Guile told the author that, although the incident warranted a black mark in Boardman's records, little was done about it!

The Battle of Britain celebrations on 19 September 1959 included a flypast over Aden and Government House by four Beverleys and one Valetta. The fact that four Beverley's were used in the flypast, in addition to the squadron's normal routine flights, reflected great credit to the groundcrews. The Squadron received congratulations from many sources on their formation flying; the groundcrew, in their turn, earning crates of beer from a grateful CO.

During September, LAC Ross-Skedd, one of the engine fitters, took a fortnight's leave to go on a fishing expedition. Hitching a lift, he eventually reached the Arab town of Mukalla, where he spent a few days getting tips from the locals. In his own words he wrote:

"We went out in a motor-boat and I had just hooked a small shark. The line was let out and I waited. Suddenly I hooked another, and I am convinced that, had I not been wearing game harness, I would have left the seat and the boat. The rod bent under the strain, the line hissed like it was alive and all I could do was hang on and try and stop the monster's run for freedom. After two hours, the fish slowly gave up its fight and we pulled it alongside. It was three-quarters the length of the boat and all I could do was to watch the others tie the catch alongside. On our return to Mukalla, we had to cut the fish up to weigh it and, in spite of the weight lost in cutting it up, it weighed 450 lbs. It was the heaviest fish I had ever seen, let alone caught. I was never satisfied with the smaller ones after that!"

In early October, Flt Lt Molloy left the Squadron to join 30 Squadron at Eastleigh and Flt Lt Timilty left for his captain's course at Dishforth. A visitor to the Squadron was ACM Sir Hubert Patch who had recently took up the post as C-in-C British Forces Arabian Peninsula.

During October two crews flew a Beverley to Changi to deliver a replacement engine for a Britannia which was unserviceable. The crews spent an enjoyable four days before returning to Aden.

After 15 months in operation, a total of just over 3,000 hours, covering 1,600 sorties, had been flown. During that time the Squadron had carried over 2,500 tons of freight, a creditable effort considering the high degree of unserviceability, caused mainly by the harsh climate. During November, visitors to the Squadron included one of its old COs, Air Marshal Sir Denis Barnett, AOC Transport Command. Others included the Chief of Air Staff, ACM Sir Thomas Pike and the Chaplain in Chief to the RAF, the Reverend A V Cooks. One of the more interesting flights occurred when a **Beverley** accompanied two Shackletons of No.37 Squadron to Pakistan to take part in an exercise with the host nation and the Americans. The Beverley, captained by Sqn Ldr Harry Guile, transported their equipment to Mauripur near Karachi. The following month, Flt Lt Mayall flew there to help bring '37' home.

Christmas came and went, during which time there was a 15-day strike by local labourers which fortunately ended on Christmas Day. January 1960 brought new life to the Squadron. The majority of the existing staff were going on to pastures new and posting notices began to appear on the notice boards. The AOC's Annual Inspection took place on the 21st of the month with the Squadron Standard paraded before the AOC. Fg Off Youll had the honour of carrying it, escorted by Flt Sgts Biddiscombe and Edwards and Master Signaller Palmer. The highlight was the debut of the station band with Flt Lt Jim Adams of No.84 Squadron at the helm.

During the first three months of 1960, 400 sorties were flown carrying 3,500 passengers. In February, Beverley XB266 was flown to Khormaksar to bring the Squadron strength up to seven aircraft. Members of the Hadrami Bedouin League were flown from Riyan to Thamoud, an area noted for its waterless vastness. It was noted that the one hour's flight was equivalent to five days overland travel. Operation 'Outpost' was mounted against dissident tribesmen in the Awdillah hills; a contingent of Aden levies was airlifted into Mayfah for the two day operation. In May, Flt Lt Bob Pitman had a 'hairy' experience when an engine failed over Somalia, necessitating the jettisoning of four tons of freight to enable height to be maintained. The same month, No.84 Squadron won the 'Lord Trophy' for the most efficient medium range transport squadron in the RAF. This was the first year the trophy had been open to overseas based squadrons and 84's winning team had been captained by Flt Lt P V Mayall.

Trouble in Kenya and Uganda led to six aircraft being put on standby to ferry troops to any of the trouble spots. It meant that only one aircraft was available for up-country support. During August, an eighth Beverley was flown in, XL151 being transferred from Abingdon. Its stay with the Squadron was short because, on the night of 11 October, it crashed when it was diverted to make a low-level search for a Beechcraft C-45 of the Somali Republic missing on a flight from Hargeisa to Khormaksar. In moonless conditions, the Beverley hit the top of a sand dune, killing all five of its crew.

During September, the Commanding Officer, Sqn Ldr Harry Guile was replaced by Sqn Ldr K H Perry DSO AFC.

In November 1960, two aircraft were detailed to fly to Bahrein where trouble was brewing in the Persian Gulf. Known as Operation 'Stunsail', it was to be the first of a series of detachments to the Gulf area which were to last until 1964. Operation 'Grout' was mounted on 18 December due to an attempted coup in Ethiopia. in the event, no air support was requested. Exercise 'Warden' involved a 60-hour task, airlifting troops and equipment from Bahrein and Sharjah. This was followed by Exercise 'Placard' which involved a mobility scheme mounted at Sharjah and lasting the second half of January and all of February. In March 1961, the Squadron joined No.30 Squadron in Exercise 'Roulade', a combined services exercise with the Royal Marines from HMS' *Bulwark* undertaking an amphibious landing.

The same month, Flt Lt Madden flew a medical team to Kamaran Island in the Red Sea. This was a regular visit made every six months. The following month, Madden and his crew flew out two replacement engines for a Pembroke which had force-landed at El Fasher in the Sudan. In June 1961, a detachment of two aircraft, XM106 and XM107 flown by Flt Lts Charman and Madden, flew to Eastleigh to assist No.30 Squadron and to take part in Operation 'Cheetah'. This involved moving troops of 24 Independent Brigade to Nakuru, an airstrip NE of Eastleigh. The Kenya detachments were always looked upon as a pleasant change from the heat of Khormaksar. The countryside was pleasant, the social life was good and the temperature at 5,000 feet was a welcome relief. Whilst there the two aircraft assisted in flood relief work.

1961 saw the beginning of improvements to the runway and dispersal areas at Khormaksar. The introductions of other squadrons to the airfield necessitated large areas of land being tarmac-ed and concreted. Adding to the RAF's troubles was the expansion of the civil airport at the eastern end of the airfield. Unlike some cities, space prohibited the building of a separate civil airport and the RAF Squadron's were gradually being squeezed down the runway by the civilian authorities. During the course of 1960 and 1961, the whole of the southern side of the 3,000-yard runway was converted into hard-standing for both civil and military aircraft. The hangarage also created problems and only major

servicing was undertaken under cover. The introduction of the trolley-mounted hydraulic jack meant that the Beverleys could be taken into the hangar with a little care. It was designed to cradle the nose-wheels and lift the front of the aircraft, the result being that the fins and rudders were sufficiently depressed to allow them to pass on either side of the roof beams. Later, a fresh water washing plant was built in an effort to keep corrosion to a minimum.

It was fortunate that, during this period of expansion, there was little in the way of crises to interrupt the building. Training continued but, at the end of June 1961, Operation 'Vantage' was mounted when the Sheikhdom of Kuwait was threatened by its neighbour, Iraq. A treaty signed by Britain and Kuwait enabled the ruler of Kuwait to call upon Britain's assistance should his country ever be threatened by an aggressor. At this time, Iraq took the opportunity to claim sovereignty over Kuwait and threatened invasion. Britain's immediate response was to send a strong military force to counter the Iraqi display of force along its border.

The whole of No.84 Squadron was placed on a four-hour stand-by. On the 29 June 1961, Beverley XM110, flown by Flt Lt F A Madden took off to fly to Bahrein carrying a spare crew plus servicing personnel for No.8 Squadron's Hunters. A second Beverley followed carrying ground equipment for 84 Squadron. The next two days were spent ferrying troops of 45 Commando Royal Marines from Aden to Kuwait, after which the Beverleys settled down to fly a daily supply mission. The display of force had the desired effect on the Iraqis but both Nos.30 and 84 Squadrons stood by appraising the situation until the end of the month when they were withdrawn. The crisis in Kuwait may have ended but there was still a threat to British forces elsewhere in the Gulf. The first occurred on 22 September when XL131 (on short-term loan from No.30 Squadron) was flown by Flt Lt Ron Sneller AFC from Kuwait to Muharraq. A small bomb, thought to be plastic explosive with an acid fuse, had been placed aboard by one of the many civilian workers. It exploded blowing a large hole in the side of the fuselage. Fortunately, the aircraft, which was carrying rockets for No.8 Squadron's Hunters, landed safely. A fortnight later on 6 October, XM110 V was severely damaged when a time-bomb exploded in the freight whilst after returning from Kuwait. At the time it was parked at Muharraq. Although there was a prompt response from the Bahrein fire service, the aircraft was a write-off. It was later used for training by the Parachute Regiment. An immediate security clamp banned all civilian loaders. Troops of the 3rd Battalion the Parachute Regiment took over the task on a temporary basis.

Two lifts of note were flown during 1961; a 5,000 gallon fuel tank was flown into the 850-yard strip at Dhala during March and a 20,000-lb gravel crusher was flown into Beihan for a new runway during August.

In November, XB266 flew to Kenya to drop supplies and animal foodstuffs to villagers marooned in a flood disaster. In the New Year, the 84 Squadron detachment flew back to its base at Khormaksar after it was relieved by aircraft of No.53 Squadron. The return of the Squadron brought about the renewal of operations in the Western Aden Protectorate when occasional shots were fired at aircraft landing on the up-country strips. The end of February saw the capitulation of tribes who were creating trouble.

By March 1962, the total strength of the station had been increased to over 3,000 men, making Khormaksar one of the largest and most complex stations in the Royal Air Force. It also saw the near completion of the building of new barrack blocks and married quarters, the 1,000th being completed that month. Operationally, there were over 5,000 movements a month from the airfield, carrying large numbers of passengers and huge quantities of freight. In June 1962, five Argosies of No.105 Squadron arrived to take the strain off the Beverleys. It also enabled the Squadron to return the aircraft one at a time to the UK for major overhaul. Corrosion was considerable on the mainplanes and major surfaces needed re-skinning.

In May 1962, the first-ever 'Oryx' air lift operation was carried out by Beverley XB263 crewed by Flt Lt Ron Sneller, Bob White and Ron Duncan. After landing at Riyan to refuel, they flew to Thamoud where they unloaded a freight-bay full of supplies for the Aden Protectorate Levies. From there they flew into the middle of the 'empty quarter'. It was the sort of place where one could use any of the 360 different runways. Here they found Ian Grimwood, the leader of the expedition, who appeared very relieved by their arrival. He announced that the animals were already in their crates, so loading could start immediat-ely. That night the crew slept under the stars, taking off for Khormaksar at first light and arriving there three hours later.

Conditions at advanced airstrips were difficult. Here at Thumier, a Beverley disappears in a cloud of dust after using reverse thrust on landing

On 3 July 1962, Sqn Ldr Perry and Flt Lt Madden flew XM107 to Gan in the Indian Ocean. With a flight time of 13.10 hours it was the longest flight yet flown by a Beverley. The record was only to last a day, the return flight taking ten minutes longer. Later that month Sqn Ldr Perry flew the Sultan of Socotra from Ouisah on the mainland to his summer residence on the island of Socotra.

During September, Sqn Ldr Ken Parfit took over as Squadron Commander from Sqn Ldr K Perry. Flt Lt Andy Andrusikiewicz, who had recently joined the Squadron wrote: "Sqn Ldr Ken Parfit, a wartime pathfinder, was on the staff at the Air Ministry prior to taking over the Squadron. As a navigator, he was one of the first to obtain the command of a Squadron. The story was that, whilst still at the Air Ministry and knowing his next posting, he had a hand in selecting quite a number of the aircrews he wanted for his squadron, having known them from his days as a flight commander on No.53 Squadron at Abingdon. I was one of the fortunate ones being posted from wing pilot duties at Abingdon to operations officer, training officer and pilot leader on an operational squadron".

The Western Aden Protectorate continued to be fairly quiet until September 1962 when the ruler of the Yemen died. He was succeeded by his son Muhammad-al-Badr. A week later he was overthrown by Egyptian-inspired revolutionary forces and the Republic of Yemen was formed under the Presidency of General Sallal. Immediately, hostile propaganda was broadcast against the British influence in the area. On 22 October, unidentified aircraft crossed the borders and fired rockets at villages in the WAP. To counter this invasion of air space, Hunters of Nos.8 and 208 Squadrons mounted daily patrols over the borders. It was followed on 9 November by a speech made by the Yemen President decrying the British and advocating all of the southern area to join in a battle against 'colonialism'. The situation was partially resolved on 13 November when it was decided that Britain would not recognise the republican regime in Yemen but would continue to support the Federation of Southern Arabia and the plans to incorporate Aden into it. This eventually came about in January 1963.

During September, Fg Off J Young dropped a load of supplies to the detachment stationed on the island of Kamaran. It was brought about by the breakdown of the ship which normally supplied the island and was carried out in full view of the Yemeni on the mainland.

During October, the Aden Protectorate Levies had become part of the Federated Regular Army and, at the end of the month, a battalion was airlifted into Beihan together with armoured vehicles and other equipment. This operation was master-minded by Major Inglis, the Army liaison officer on the station. Due to the tense border situation, it had to be completed in one day. At that time, all up-country flights were carried out in daylight but this time the number of aircraft loads necessitated rotation well into the night. The programme involved taking off from Khormaksar to land at the up-country strip at first light, returning and then handing the aircraft over to the second shift and so on.

In the same month the Squadron airlifted large complex loads into Mukeiras for the building of a radar station. In November the first Beverley landing was made at Wadi Ayn, a small roughly triangular piece of ground between two outcrops of rock in the mountain range, which formed the border between pro-British Beihan and the Yemen. It was open towards the Yemen and only a solitary footpath provided access from Beihan. There was also a small strip on a lower slope which was used with some caution by the Twin Pioneers.

Andy Andrusikiewicz continued: "At the same time, border skirmishes with the Yemeni greatly escalated and British troops were in continual need of heavier equipment. I was sent aboard a Twin Pioneer to look the place over and, if all was well, I would fly in a loaded Beverley from Khormaksar later in the day. There was, however, a slight hitch in the plan; the Twin Pin lost an engine just as it was returning through the gap in the mountains and had to put down at Beihan. Khormaksar was informed of the situation and, in response, Flt Lt Barry Lambert flew the already loaded Beverley into Beihan. I took it over and, with daylight soon coming to a close, decided that after off-loading at Wadi Ayn, I would return direct to Khormaksar. This brought a plea from the Twin Pin crew and its passengers not to be left at Beihan. So we all crowded on to the Beverley.

Having seen the place, there was no problem. After going through the gap, I made a descending approach avoiding the Yemen border and possible ground-fire. Landing up the slope, the Beverley soon stopped. The Army Corps were overjoyed and, having been assured of future bulk supplies, asked, 'What could be done to improve the strip?' All I could think of was to move some of the larger stones from the turn-round area. The slope was so pronounced that I asked my handful of passengers to remain in the freight bay until I moved up for take-off. I was afraid that if they were in their seats in the boom, the aircraft would tip up on its tail. Fortunately, the take-off went smoothly and, after climbing in an unfinished '8' towards the gap, we waggled our wings over Beihan and set course for Khormaksar".

During November, Flt Lt Barry Lambert and his crew were

Watched by a guard from the Hadrami Bedouin Legion, a Sycamore helicopter is loaded on to a Beverley

detached to Sharjah for five days for the colonel-in-charge to use as required. On one occasion he was detailed to take a load of goats to Buraimi oasis as a 'softener to the local friendlies'. In correspondence, Barry Lambert wrote: "The job, as usual, had to be done yesterday! We, the crew, spent the next two hours sellotaping the Movements Section's entire supply of plastic bags around the goats genitalia. The goats were not pleased and were anything but co-operative. The pilot officer i/c Movements went berserk and did not want to have anything to do with the loading. Further indignities were heaped on the unfortunate goats by the crew taping their legs on one side of the wallbars. Apparently, according to the loadmaster, the sight in the hold had to be seen to be believed when Lambert started up. When they untethered and debagged the goats at Buraimi, they took off into the Bunda with their intended owners (dhotis in the midriff position) in hot pursuit. We saw no more of either. On our return to Sharjah, we found that the colonel was a little peeved that I had not obtained a receipt. Fg Off Jimmy Young (later with British Airways) was the co-pilot and Plt Off Robin Geath the navigator".

In December 1962, Flt Lt Barry Lambert and his crew were sent in the scheduled Comet to help No.34 Squadron during the Brunei revolt. From Singapore they flew by Hastings to Labuan. Lambert continues: "The five Beverleys just about took up the entire dispersal area at Labuan and the duty crews were forever taxying the Beverleys to a remote spot, then back for loading when a sortie came up. During that time duty crews remained at the top of the rota for six hours, to either fly a sortie or to shift one's aircraft. Then they went to the bottom of the rota to work their way up to the top again. One particular sortie stands out. We had to take a party of Gurkhas to recapture a strip at Sebbu, just south of Kuchni. The plan was that when the aircraft came to a standstill, the Gurkhas would charge out from the lower doors and fan out firing as they spread into the surrounding jungle. "Don't fly over. Go straight in" I was told. I hung on the props for a very short landing as the strip was only a few hundred yards long. In the event, I had no trouble stopping as both wing tips were clipping the trees on both sides of the airstrip. The disembarkation went according to plan, although it was a bit unnerving hearing the rattle of machine gun fire above the noise of the engines when one's nose was only a few yards from the action. We then had the problem of

taking off again. There was no turning circle so I had to back up the entire length of the strip with the AQM hanging out the rear door with such instructions as, "left hand down a bit, Captain". We also managed to catch a few saplings which we missed on landing. Returning to Labuan we received a rocket from 'Chiefy' who was not very pleased to see shrubbery littering his aircraft's wing-tips. In all, 16 sorties were flown supporting the Gurkhas and the Queen's Own Highlanders".

"During the 12 days of our detachment, the Labuan Hotel where we were based never once ran out of beer, thanks to No.48 Squadron's Hastings. The detachment over, we returned to Khormaksar just in time for Christmas".

Back at Aden, Flt Lt Palliser displayed a high standard of airmanship when landing at Ataq when the nose wheel steering failed. By skillful use of the reverse thrust, he kept the aircraft on a straight course on the very narrow airstrip, thus avoiding the possibility of an accident.

On 20 December, Flt Lt Andrusikiewicz, with Sqn Ldr Ken Parfit navigating, flew to Qas Karma on the island of Socotra carrying AVM Rosier and his party. The airstrip was a small wartime airfield which was used by Wellingtons for anti-submarine patrols. Since then, the runways had had numerous deep channels cut across them caused by tropical rains and filled in by waist-high bushes. This was no problem for the Beverley. It was later learnt that the two Landrovers which were taken to transport the party to the seat of local government on the north coast, could not deal with the state of the roads and the journey had to be completed by camel, much to everyone's disgust.

Christmas and the New Year brought the usual number of parties with Flt Lt Sweatman performing his 'Tarzan act' and Plt Off McGilchrist playing the bagpipes and leading the 'conga' around the married quarters.

In January 1963, a spate of engine failures cast doubt on the reliability of the recently introduced Centaurus 175 engines. Seven failures occurred at Khormaksar, two in the Persian Gulf and one at Riyan. The latter, on 17 February, necessitated a three-engined return flight to Khormaksar, because the engine technicians were so hard-pressed that neither men nor equipment were available to undertake engine changes elsewhere.

Operation 'Sandflight' was mounted in February 1963 to assist the ferrying of two No.26 Squadron Belvederes from El Adem to Khormaksar. Commanded by Sqn Ldr Ken Parfit and skippered by Flt Lt 'Bunny' Warren, the flight was made in XM107 to provide navigational assistance for the helicopters and to carry the groundcrews, equipment and fuel. The first leg was flown from El Adem to LG.53 in Libya, the Beverley landing first and then homing the 'choppers' in on RT. After refuelling, the Belvederes took off, followed by the Beverley for Jebel Uneiwat, a 6,500 feet mountain on the Sudanese-Libyan border. After the Suez campaign, it became known as Nasser's Corner". From there they set course for Wadi Haifa. After spending the night there, feeding on compo rations and cans of beer, they flew to Port Sudan and on to Massawa. Here the Beverley had to refuel with two-gallon cans and a length of rope. Even then the flight was not completed, for the last leg was flown against strong headwinds which forced the Belvederes to land at Perim Island, an hours flying time from Khormaksar. In all, a total of 2,600 miles were logged.

In the same month, Britain was ordered to close its mission in Taiz, Yemen, thus severing any diplomatic relations between the two countries. Shortly after, a party of all ranks from HQ Middle East became lost whilst on an adventure training course. The party, which included members of the Women's Services, inadvertently crossed the border and were fired on, four being killed and two wounded; 18 escaped back into Federal territory and 21 were captured. The casualties and prisoners were escorted back to Taiz by Egyptian officers and were later released after 12 days of diplomatic pressure.

During these months, a number of trips were flown to airstrips near the Yemeni border where 169 royalist refugees were airlifted out. Supplies were flown into Mayfar, Zamakh and Lodar. Wadi Ayn and Negub were also visited and eight sorties flown to Dhala and Beihan. A further 24 flights were made to Ataq and Mukeiras. One such clandestine flight occurred during May when Flt Lt Barry Lambert was detailed to fly a load of metal to a map reference in the Bunda and were assured that a Beverley could land there. It was well-known that the metal was gold but Movements had to manifest it correctly. Flt Lt Lambert wrote: "We landed in this God-forsaken spot where the Bunda stretched to the horizon. Nothing was in sight and we just sat there, with the navigator checking to see if we were in the right place. Eventually a cloud of dust was spotted and, from this emerged a gaudy clapped-out truck.

On 21 June 1967, Flt Lt Pat Manley taxied over a land mine at Habilayn, causing an undercarriage leg to collapse. Because of the difficulty of recovery from this airstrip, XM106 was stripped of parts and abandoned

From it came a fearsome looking band and I thought 'Do I or don't I hand it over to these jokers!' Suddenly the most sophisticated public school accent boomed out from beneath a burnous and atop a neat shaggy beard! Captain So and So of the 9th/12th Lancers (or was it the Hussars) at your service. This time I received a receipt and the truck roared off into the distance.

Now came the problem. The Beverley was up to its axles in sand. Out got the crew with the exception of myself with the one and only shovel and anything else suitable for making a ramp for the aircraft to run up. I briefed the lads that when I revved up the Centauruses, if she became clear they were to scrabble aboard before she sank again. After an agonising rocking to and fro, she popped out like a cork. With all aboard and after the longest run, she unstuck, enabling us to return to Khormaksar".

The late Andy Andrusikiewicz provided a feast of anecdotes from his own period with No. 84 Squadron. They are well worth a paragraph each. The first details the multitude of parties held by Sqn Ldr and Mrs Ken Parfit. "During one of the many barbecues, Parfit had the misfortune to step barefooted on to the hot grill. It was even more unfortunate that a big station parade was due with a march past of all the squadrons with Standards flying and bayonets fixed. Parfit proposed that I should lead the Squadron but that was vetoed by the Station Commander, Gp Capt Blythe. The result was that the station doctor had to pump Parfit full of pain-killing drugs for the occasion whilst I reverted to taking part in the flying display".

Andy also mentioned that the motor cycle was the favourite method of transport for most of the bachelor members of the squadron. Once, a co-pilot riding towards the main gate saw one with a pillion passenger approaching from the opposite direction. They played 'chicken' with the result that a head-on crash occurred and three co-pilots were unfit for flying for some considerable time. The rest had to work overtime.

Another story tells of an exercise which included drops on DZs in the Oman. One keen co-pilot decided to record the results on his cine-camera from the Beverley's freight bay. With the back doors removed, it offered an unrestricted view. His captain tried to help and did a low flypast with a 'beat-up' of the place. Due to rapidly changing 'G' forces, our photographer found himself lying prone on the roller conveyor accelerating towards that gaping hole at the back. Somehow he managed to save himself at the last minute, at the cost of several fingernails.

One of the many problems which occurred on the smaller airstrips was refuelling. Fuel in barrels and a fuel pump borrowed from Aden Airways were pre-positioned on the strip. All went like clockwork until they landed for refuelling. One thing the planners had overlooked was the difference in height between a Dakota and the Beverley. The pump provided could not raise a head of fuel to

such a height and eventually packed up. Refuelling a Beverley with jerry-cans was not everyone's idea of a pleasant job, especially as it involved pouring fuel from the barrels into cans, then carrying these up two ladders through the freight bay up to the flight deck. Then along to the after flight deck and finally through the hatch to the wing. It was a job where all the crew had to 'muck-in'. It was noticed that there seemed to be little progress made. In the end, it was decided to throw the book of rules, about mandatory minimum fuel to be carried, out of the window.

On 11 June 1963, Operation 'Alfred' was mounted when the Squadron was called to readiness and ordered to move all available aircraft to Salisbury in Rhodesia. From there they flew to Marsapa in Swaziland where a general strike had been declared and which threatened the economy of the country. Four Beverleys (XB266, XM106, XM109 and XL121) with six captains (Flt Lts Bower, Gould, Smyth, Andrusikiewicz, Hayward and Lambert) took part. During the following week, the aircraft airlifted a battalion of Gordon Highlanders into the area. With this show of strength, the strike fell through and the detachment returned to Khormaksar on 23 June.

Throughout June, July and August, the engine failures continued, seven in July alone. During September 1963, Operation 'Tusk' was planned to bring under administrative control an area east of the Federation and troops of the Hadrami Bedouin League were positioned at Thumier and Al Ghayda. In all, 20 sorties were flown in 29 hours. This operation continued into the New Year. In November, supplies were taken into Murait and Sanau; the dropping of one ton containers indicated the increase in terrorist activities. Detachments were flown to Bahrein, where para-training was undertaken in the Jebel Ali and Al Khatt regions and to Eastleigh where support was given to troops in the Northern Frontier district of Kenya engaged on anti-shifta operations.

On 10 December, an incident occurred which finally brought drastic action from the British forces. a large official party had gathered at Khormaksar to bid farewell to the High Commissioner, Sir Kennedy Trevaskis. As they stood talking before boarding the aircraft, a grenade was rolled across the tarmac into the assembled party. In the split second before it exploded, the Commissioners assistant, George Henderson, pushed Trevaskis aside and took the full force of the grenade. Henderson died from multiple wounds several days later, One other, an Indian lady, was killed and 53 people were injured.

The response was immediate. A State of Emergency was officially declared throughout South Arabia, the frontier with Yemen was closed and 280 Yemeni were deported. It was the start of what was to become the Radfan campaign. The mounting of Operation 'Nutcracker' on 4 January 1964 was to carry out a demonstration of force in the area of Radfan and convince the terrorists that the government had the ability and the will to enter the area as and when it felt inclined.

Unfortunately, over the following months the presence of troops in the Radfan area was of short-term value only. By March 1964, it had become evident that the Federation's resources were being strained and that it could not cover this as well as police the border against Yemeni incursions. During this time No. 84 Squadron flew 14 sorties in 30 hours into Dhala, Mukeiras and Lodar. Over 450 tons of freight were airlifted together with one ton of mail.

In early January, two of No.84's Beverleys and crews were despatched to Eastleigh. Andy Andrusikiewicz takes up the story: "On 21 January at the time of the rebellions in the recently independent East African countries, 84's crews were being briefed for a possible assault landing at Entebbe. Royal Marines, based at nearby Mombasa, had commandeered a civilian airliner and ordered its pilot to fly to Entebbe. At the same time, the AOC East Africa, aboard an Argosy serving as an airborne command post and carrying a contingent of the RAF Regiment, was determined that the RAF was going to be the first on the scene. Whilst the civilian airliner was on its final approach, the AOC ordered the Argosy captain to land from the opposite direction. Fortunately, the airliner overshot, allowing the Argosy to burn its brakes out on its run downwind. I had the easy job of stream landing when we realised that there were to be no 'fireworks'. After spending the night in the reception area of the airport, we returned to Eastleigh the next day. For the next few days the Beverleys flew trooping flights in between Eastleigh, Dar- es-Salaam and Tabora to ensure restoration of order in the different areas".

During February 1964, Flt Lt Tony Myers arrived at Khormaksar to replace Flt Lt John King. He wrote: "After four-and-a-half years on PR Valiants, it was a nasty shock to be sent to Khormaksar". His first week on the station took him to Salalah and Bahrein. On his return he was detailed to navigate to Nairobi. His comment was "Andy did not believe the new boys hanging around".

On 2 March, Flt Lt Andrusikiewicz was on detachment to Bahrein. "In the wake of some exceptionally bad weather, causing flooding on the Oman coast, I was ordered to do a 'recce' and, if possible, land supplies at Tarif emergency airstrip which was marked only by a series of oil drums. As it turned out it was quite luxurious compared with some of the strips. Some strips were checked by an Army lorry driving along them at top speed. If it did not get stuck, then it was safe to land. On the following detachment, the Beverley was used on a search and rescue mission for a small boat with three passengers. It was later found some distance inland where the high tide had beached it".

A flight to Hadibo on the island of Socotra provided a few problems. It was laid on to take a party headed by AVM J E Johnson CBE DSO DFC, AOC Middle East, to give a presentation sword to the local Sultan. Unfortunately, his overworked ADC had forgotten to take it with them and all records were broken to fly back and collect it. To avoid the island's camel transport, a new strip had been constructed on the north of the island. For a change, two AQMs were provided for the VIPs on their overnight stop-over. A shower was even installed with the help of numerous pulleys and buckets.

A further instance of using the Beverley as a search and rescue aircraft occurred on 19 April 1964 when the two aircraft on detachment to Muharraq flew search missions off the coast of Dhahran following the crash of a Middle East Airlines Caravelle two days earlier. On the night of the 30th, Flt Lt Catcheside made a night supply drop at Thumier delivering medical supplies, rations and ammunition to an SAS patrol which had become isolated during a skirmish with the terrorists. Further trouble in the Radfan necessitated the lengthening of the runway at Thumier which, up to then, had been suitable for only the Twin Pioneers. Photographs show that the problem with Thumier, just as it was with the majority of the up-country strips, was the ingestion of sand. The use of reverse pitch to bring the Beverley to a halt only worsened the situation, effectively cutting forward vision to a minimum. Sand and the increasing corrosion made the groundcrew's job a nightmare.

Flt Lt Myers, on his first visit to Firq in April, wrote: "This was the strip where the captain of the local Trucial Scouts used to come down from the mountains with a mule train to haul away his supplies. The local air traffic instructions were, 'Straighten up over the crashed Valetta and land straight ahead, stopping short of the abandoned steam roller'. The roller had been flown in to build the strip and never recovered. To say this place was a desert strip was an understatement. On one occasion, about five minutes after we

had landed, the 'Works and Bricks man' who had come along for the ride, shot out of the aircraft, shouting 'Have we crashed?' To which I replied that it was the norm for Flt Lt P J Kemp', last heard of as Air Attaché Oslo.

On 5 June, the first flight was made into Thumier (later to be known as Habilayn), Although only 25 minutes flying time from Khormaksar (about 63 nm) the alternative was a four-and-a-half hour journey by truck down a 3,000 feet slope reputedly littered with land-mines. With the Station Commander, Gp Capt Blythe in the co-pilot's seat, the landing was well photographed and publicised. The strip itself presented no problems. On one occasion a Beverley did a 'windmill' start when the starter packed up on take-off.

A tour of the British territories in Southern Africa by AVM and Mrs J E Johnson began on 14 June. With Sqn Ldr Ken Parfit as aircraft commander, the Beverley was piloted by Flt Lt Andy Andrusikiewicz, co-pilot Fg off Cassells, navigator Flt Lt Weir, and signaller Flt Lt Nuttall plus three AQMs. The route taken Khormaksar - Eastleigh - New Sarum - Pretoria - Lobatsi - Gaberones - Khanzi-Maun - Serowe - Francistown - Matsapa - Bloemfontein - Maseu - New Sarum - Eastleigh to Khormaksar. The aircraft was loaded with two Land Rovers and a assortment of servicing equipment to ensure self-sufficiency. The passenger boom was divided into compartments and partially equipped with standard married quarters furniture from station stores to provide Lady Johnson with some degree of comfort. Thanks to the distinguished passengers, local hospitality often extended to the crew, which compensated in many ways for an exacting schedule. Most of the legs were flown at low level to allow the passengers to enjoy the views. I was told that on one flight they were 'attacked' by two eagles which thought that the Beverley was invading their air-space. It was rather amusing to see them apply their air-brakes when they realised how much bigger the Beverley was than themselves. They returned to Khormaksar on 29 June.

During June, the Air Force Cross was presented to Flt Lt A H Bower, the Queen's Commendation to Flt Lt Catcheside and the AOC's Commendation to Master Engineer Binfield, WO Venables, J T Aitken and SAC Bills. In spite of continual engine failures, the Squadron moved more than one million pounds of freight, 3,000 passengers and nine casevacs over the last few months. Sixteen tonnes were flown into Thumier alone.

The end of June brought the cessation of the Radfan campaign, after which No. 84 Squadron reverted to its normal operations in the increasingly unsettled Protectorate. The month of July continued with a further 28 sorties into Thumier, whilst six supply drops were made to the Royal Marines at Jebel Wadina and Yas island. Jebel Wadina was a difficult drop, being on a small plateau at 5,500 feet. Regular runs were made to Bahrein, Salalah and Masirah.

During July, XM108 returned to the UK for attention by 32 MU. It took with it the De Havilland D.H.51 Miss Kenya for delivery to Hatfield for restoration and eventual display at Old Warden by the Shuttleworth Trust.

Over the following months, the Beverleys lost their silver paint and were camouflaged in a two-tone sand and earth scheme with black undersides. At the same time the cockpit roof was painted in gloss white to reflect as much heat as possible.

The month of August was noted for the flying of a large airlift of men and equipment into a new strip at Ahwar. Flt Lt Myers wrote: "On the 20th, Barry Lambert flew a gun-run into Ahwar. On landing, he put the aircraft into reverse, the desert went up in the air and fell back all over us. We opened up the back and within seconds a truck appeared and we started unloading. At that moment, over the nearest sand dune came what looked like the touring cast of the 'Desert Song'. They started breaking open the boxes and trotted back over the dunes with a couple of guns each. 'Thanks, chaps' say's a rather scruffy 'type' and promptly disappeared, leaving nothing but a pile a scrap wood, the Beverley and its crew".

In addition to Ahwar, the strip at Mukmuq was opened. Four aircraft were sent on detachment to Matsapa; at that time there was a battalion based in Swaziland. Flt Lt Barry Lambert, one of the captains wrote: "I think that Ken Parfit was the only one who knew why we were on stand-by, as we did not fly at all during the four-day stay. It rapidly became a social detachment. As soon as we arrived at the local hotel (the landlord was rubbing his hands with glee at so many bods there at the Queen's expense), I borrowed a spare room and with the aid of the wardrobe doors turned it in to a small bar (sold on sale or return). Then, with the landlord's co-operation, Ken Parfit was able to issue cocktail invitations to such locals who were recommended by mine host. It was a full house

XM107 at Matsapa, Swaziland, February 1965

and certainly broke the ice for the rest of our stay. Incidentally the bill was split between 30 of us and it made everyone blink when it went on until the small hours. After which, Flt Lt Fred Pennycott decided that everyone should go for a dip in the local pool. As a result of this party, various members were invited to see the agriculture and forestation projects in hand for the country's economy. This detachment finished in October, except for one aircraft and its crew who remained at Eastleigh".

Familiarisation flights were still being made by new crews during these months and numerous sorties were flown over Wajir, Garrisa and Moyale to supply the garrisons of the Kenya Army who were still having problems with the Shifta in the Northern Frontier District.

On 14 October 1964 Sqn Ldr R J Barnden assumed command of the Squadron from Sqn Ldr K Parfit. On the 23rd, he was flown around the up-country strips by Flt Lt Lambert.

It was mid-November that the Belgian Congo hit the head-lines, when rebel troops attempted to take the town of Stanleyville from Government forces. Already rumours of murder of European residents had filtered through and Belgian troops had been flown in to restore order. At the same time, it was decided that a Beverley of No.84 Squadron and an Argosy from No.105 should fly to the Congo with a field ambulance and help in the evacuation of British subjects. XH121, with a crew consisting of Flt Lt R Livermore (his second tour), Fg Offs Mallinder and Ponder, Sgts Hartley and Meaney, two AQMs and two groundcrew, took off from Aden to fly the seven-and-a-half hour flight to Nairobi. After landing, it was loaded with five tons of equipment made up of two Land Rovers and trailers of 24 Field Ambulance under Major David Finlay. Food and medical supplies made up the load.

Approaching Stanleyville, the aircraft made a very steep descent to the runway with the idea of keeping out of the way of small-arms fire. The system worked well because neither the Argosy nor the Beverley suffered hits. On the ground, contact was made with a member of the British Embassy. His instructions were that the crew should come under the control of the European official who was organising the airlift. The refugees were in the hangar and were to be loaded as and when airlift capacity became available. Both aircraft were to fly with the maximum permissible load. With the assistance of a RAF Mobile Air Movements team, which had flown in on the Argosy, the Beverley was unloaded and with 100 minutes of its arrival had taken off with 84 refugees on board to fly to Leopoldville. The following morning, the 26th, orders came that the aircraft were to return to Stanleyville with supplies consisting of biscuits, rice and milk. Though the flight was uneventful, it was noticed that there were bodies of the rebel army

lying inside the confines of the airfield. It was obvious on landing that most of the refugees had gone and the crew were told that they could return to Nairobi. The mission involved a total flying time of 26 hours.

On 6 December 1964, a Beverley took off to fly a party of scientists to Socotra. As members of the International Geophysical Society, they were to spend a year there studying the conditions. Five days later, a Beverley was used as a flying ambulance, when on a flight to Nelfah about 200 miles NE of Aden. With a nursing orderly from Khormaksar and a supply of oxygen, the aircraft picked up two villagers in need of urgent medical attention. The first, a man whose injured arm had turned gangrenous and the other, a woman who was suffering from internal bleeding. Both were taken to the Queen Elizabeth hospital at RAF Khormaksar.

The same day Flt Lt Al Rankin was detailed to take a JCB bulldozer to a map reference called Nisab. The only signs of life was a Land Rover with a small pennant showing the wind direction. The crew had been assured that a driver would be there to help unload the JCB. Instead, the only volunteer available was a local Arab who intimated that he was able to drive. Clambering up on to the vehicle he started it up only to get it wedged across the freight bay. It was to be another four hours before a second Beverley appeared carrying an Army staff sergeant who had been dragged out of his billet to come and move the JCB. With a couple of quick movements of the wheel he had unloaded it and was demanding a quick return to Khormaksar. Unfortunately, it was now dark and a makeshift flarepath had to be made. Leaving Rankin in the aircraft, the crew spread oil over thorn bushes for a thousand yards, finally igniting them before dashing back to the aircraft to scramble aboard as Rankin edged forward to take off. Rankin was told later that the Army did not appreciate his buzzing the Land Rover placed at the end of the runway. They were not to know that the starboard outer engine had packed up just as the aircraft lifted off. Rankin later admitted: "It was not one of the easier trips".

New arrivals to the Squadron needed continuation training and checking into marginal airstrips. During the month, ten sorties were flown into Thumier. At the same time Operation 'Stab' was mounted which involved the moving of troops into Lodar, Beihan and Mukeiras. In January 1965, the Beverleys of 30 Squadron were moved from Eastleigh to Muharraq. This brought a detachment of two of 84's Beverleys to Eastleigh, with Flt Lt Pat Kemp as detachment commander. He was later joined by Flt Lt Fred Pennycott as detachment adjutant/operations officer. Their main role was in flying to strips at Wajir, Mandera and Garissa, the latter two being on the Kenyan/Ethiopian/Somali borders. The strips at that time were on a war footing with sporadic guerrilla sniping from roving Somali bandits. It seems odd that, in Aden, small arms were not issued to aircrew, yet in Kenya the crews were offered a choice of revolvers, .303, Sten, Bren or riot guns. February was marked by a search and rescue sortie flown by Flt Lt R W Wright in XB266, looking for three British Army mountaineers reported missing on Mt. Kenya.

The search by the Beverley was unsuccessful but a Kenyan Police light aircraft located the bodies on the Darwin glacier at 14,000 feet. A ground party was immediately sent with the intentions of bringing the bodies back. This proved impossible and it was decided to bury the bodies where they were. Later a funeral service was read by a retired RAF chaplain living in the area, a Beverley flown by Fg Off Hamish Raynham overflying and acting as an airborne pulpit.

As 1965 continued, terrorism in Aden worsened, mainly grenade throwing and sniping which caused an ever-increasing number of casualties. Fortunately women and children were not the main targets but their presence was worrying to the authorities. During the previous Christmas, a grenade had been lobbed through a bungalow window, killing the 16-year-old daughter of Air Commodore Sidley and wounding four other youngsters. It was becoming increasingly clear that the future looked bleak for the British and that a long struggle lay ahead to combat terrorism.

In March, Flt Lt Lambert and Fg Off Ferguson flew XM106 back to Britain for a complete overhaul. They returned in XL149. During the same month, several trips were made to the airstrip on Perim Island in the Red Sea. The nearness of the Yemeni border meant that it was under constant threat. Men and supplies were ferried in, in case a take-over by the rebels was attempted.

On 19 April, a Beverley crewed by a mixed 30/84 crew, provided air transport for the duty battalion in Swaziland for security duties in the coming election in Basutoland (Lesotho). Whilst there, the crew relaxed in a small hotel at Manzini. In the event, there were no disturbances and, apart from one short flight which was at the request of the OC Lancashire Regt to show the King of Swaziland's wife and family around Swazi, it proved to be a holiday. The Queen (believe it or not) was known as the "Great She Elephant" and was accompanied by a large number of junior wives and dozens of children.

In May the Squadron were delighted to hear that Flt Lt Andy Andrusikiewicz DFC had been awarded the AFC for outstanding service during the Radfan campaign.

During May 1969, air-landing sorties were flown, an average of three a day, each sortie averaging 53 minutes, which was excellent considering the high rate of engine failures. In early June, Sqn Ldr Barnden skippered XH121 to help in the withdrawal of the 1st Battalion of the Lancashire Regt from Matsapa. He was followed by Flt Lts Corbin, Kemp and Fg Off Ferguson flying XB266, XM103 and XH121 to undertake the changeover of troops stationed there.

Even the hot period of 1965 did not stop the activities of the terrorists, with the result that the High Commissioner introduced emergency measures. Terrorism continued to escalate with incidents too numerous too mention, for example the complete destruction of an RAF Dakota standing on the apron of the civil airport at Khormaksar. In August a British Superintendent of Police was shot in the Crater district, followed a month later by the assassination of Sir Arthur Charles, the British Speaker of the Aden State Council. Even these acts of violence did not bring condemnation by the Aden Chief Minister and it came as no surprise when HMG issued instructions for him to be removed from his post. HMG dissolved the Aden Government and took over its responsibilities.

The curfew was extended from just the Crater area to cover the whole of Aden. The effect of this was far-reaching as personnel were unable to go out in the cool of the evening. Schools and places of entertainment were closed because of the fear of casualties from bombs or grenades. Large numbers of airmen were needed to supplement the Army and RAF Regiment on guard duties. This forcing the already overworked groundcrews to limit their servicing to Khormaksar alone.

In August, one aircraft and two crews were detached to Riyan to fly reinforcements to Sanau, Al Ghayda and Thumier. Night stopping was out of the question. At Dhala, Flt Lts R Livermore and L G Corbin were both faced with this possibility. To avoid it, Livermore flew out with a partially repaired engine whilst Corbin, who had had starter motor trouble, made a successful 'windmill' start. In efforts to help the natives, detachments of Royal Engineers were helping in the building of roads, schools and wells. In October Flt Lt W Howell dropped eight one-ton containers of

cement. It was later realised that this was a complete waste of time; for apart from the likelihood of casualties, the terrorists were knocking things down just as soon as they had been built.

On 23 November, a Beverley took off for Nairobi carrying a load of liquid oxygen. Little is known about this operation except for the quote 'Hairy' alongside it in the records. Flt Lt Al Rankin, flying XM109 into Beihan on 7 December, had a particularly difficult experience when, after taking off on the return flight, his No. 2 engine exploded and caught fire. After climbing away, he was able to extinguish the fire, notifying Khormaksar after reaching the coast. He then lost No. 3 engine with dropping oil pressure. Again calling Khormaksar, the air traffic controller asked if he required assistance. Rankin replied that apart from a straight-in approach, there was little they could do! He commented "Landed safely but rather sweaty".

December also brought an end to the Kenya detachment. The newly-formed Kenyan Air Force had acquired some D.H. Caribous from Canada and so released the Beverleys from their duties. For the first time No.84 Squadron were able to have all six aircraft at its base at Khormaksar. The same month saw a further increase in terrorism and several RAF personnel were killed during their off-duty spells. Mortar shells were occasionally fired on to the airfield and protective pens of water-filled oil drums were constructed.

No sooner had the detachment returned to Khormaksar when it found itself back in Africa, this time in response to the Rhodesia Declaration of Independence. The Beverley's job was to support the Javelins of No.29 Squadron which were being deployed from their base at Akrotiri to N'dola and Lusaka in Zambia. The support aircraft, XH121, XL149, XM103 and XM107, spent over a week shuttling supplies and fuel from Eastleigh to Lusaka. This detachment were to stay in support of the Javelins until their withdrawal in September 1966.

In the New Year 1966, the number of sorties into the up-country strips increased, with Dhala receiving 27 loads, whilst two sorties were flown to Perim Island in a massive build up of the garrison. Six months later the island was evacuated and Perim Island was left to the Yemeni. No longer was it trigger-happy tribesmen but well-armed guerrilla forces supported by FLOSY (Front for the Liberation of S Yemen) which was demanding the withdrawal of British forces.

In February, Flt Lt Tony Myers completed his two-year tour. He commented: "My total flying hours during the tour were 800 day and 50 hours night. Probably as far as job satisfaction went, it was my most productive tour in my service. Looking back, I wouldn't have missed it but I do not think I would want to do it again".

In the same month, HMG announced that the British intended to withdraw its forces. The shock to the Federation rulers was such that they found themselves with an independence they could not maintain. The atmosphere brought increased acts of terrorism and casualties mounted. Not only did the incidents occur more often but weaponry became more sophisticated. Mortars were used in ever increasing numbers.

In May 1966, XH121 left Aden for a complete refurbishment with the Hong Kong Aircraft Co. The flight took six days and the crew arrived back in Khormaksar in early October. During June and July, over 160 sorties were made to the up-country strips. The Perim Island garrison was evacuated and aircraft were flown to Wadi Ayn to assist the withdrawal from such a vulnerable position.

Colin Scarth arrived at Khormaksar as a very new AQM. He writes: "I remember a detachment to Riyan that I was on. It was primarily to move the Hadrami Bedouin Legion around their forts. The job used to be a five or six day effort and, as Riyan was a very small station, we took provisions for in-flight rations. On this particular occasion, we asked for sufficient tins of soup and I suspect that one variety was difficult to move on as we spent the whole detachment consuming tins of mulligatawney! Whilst there, the headman approached the captain, Flt Lt John Craig and asked if he would mind transporting his goats. He rather unwittingly agreed and told the two AQMs to expect two goats. Next morning, the headman turned up with 30. We had to set to and make a series of pens out of cargo nets, with old tents on the floor.

Later on I was asked to take the Thursday schedule up country to re-supply the local defence force. The load consisted of a 25-pounder field gun and a quantity of ammunition. Arriving at our destination, the gun was handed over to the British Army sergeant on secondment to the defence force. Imagine my surprise when, on the following Sunday morning, I was called out to do a run to the same destination with the same load. I asked the Army loading team if war had broken out and they suggested that I should not ask that question when we reached our airstrip. On arrival, we were

A Landrover is loaded through the clam-shell doors of a Beverley

met by a rather subdued sergeant and I asked him, 'What was so important to get me out of bed on a Sunday morning?' After his explosion, he was able to speak and he said that the gun was to replace the one which had been brought up a few days previously. 'Oh, is it u/s then?' I remarked. 'I bloody well hope so. It was nicked last night'. I continued 'How can you lose anything so big and so well dug in. Do you have any idea where it has gone? I know exactly where it is' he said, 'It's on that hill over there overlooking your aircraft'. At that point the conversation ceased and a new record was made for unloading a Beverley".

In July, a near international incident occurred when XM106 en route for Matsapa was impounded by the Congolese Army whilst staging through Lumambashi. The ill-disciplined Congolese troops broke open cargo containers, desert survival packs, and emergency water containers with complete disregard for the invaluable lifesaving equipment. After intervention by the British consul, the aircraft and crew were released some five hours later and took off in disgust for N'dola before proceeding to Matsapa. The object of the flight was to support the Royal Irish Fusiliers in efforts to bring law and order to Basutoland prior to its independence. Things quickly returned to normal and on 12 July the aircraft returned to Khormaksar.

At the end of August, Operation 'Aloe' was mounted to withdraw the Javelins from Zambia. A detachment of four Beverleys under Sqn Ldr Bob Barnden flew to Lusaka, staging through Mombasa in order to take on maximum fuel for the long leg to Lusaka. It was followed a month later by a further detachment to Matsapa to provide air mobility for the 1st Battalion of the Royal Irish Fusiliers during the independence celebrations in Bechuanaland and Basutoland. During the detachment, Flt Lt Ferguson and his crew flew an emergency casevac to take an airman who was seriously injured to hospital in Pretoria. On the 14th, the same crew flew two sorties from Matsapa to Lourenco Marques taking troops to catch a charter flight to the UK. This was the only known occasion in which a Beverley visited Lourenco Marques.

In a recent copy of 'Mag-drop', Sgt John Meaney describes one trip in a Beverley, a near fatal one. "Our aircraft, piloted by John Craig, was on a routine flight for a supply drop on Mukeiras. As was usual in the hot season, we were flying with the flight deck windows slightly opened and the overwing hatches removed. These were forward of the main spar where the aileron hydro-boosters were situated. This particular aircraft had a history of leaks in the starboard wing and I had been requested to take a look at it during the flight. It was necessary to adopt the crouching position but, for some obscure reason, I stood upright under the open hatch. I was now half-way out of the aircraft and had a magnificent view of acres of flexible shining metal. The noise was indescribable as my helmet, goggles and oxygen mask were torn off and I was flailing my legs to stop myself being sucked out. Although it could not have been more than a few seconds, it seemed an eternity. I made my was back to the flight deck to be greeted with 'Where the hell have you been?' followed by roars of laughter when I told them. The annoying part was that I had to pay for the lost equipment when we returned to base.

In October 1966, Sqn Ldr S Hitchens assumed command of the Squadron from Sqn Ldr R Barnden. The same month saw the highest number of terrorist incidents so far - 84 in all - and the future looked grim. In November it was decided that no more families would come to Aden and the evacuation would start in March 1967. Fortunately there had been very few casualties amongst the Service families, but the restrictions on their mobility made life difficult.

The number of sorties to the up-country strips lessened monthly, only 38 in November and 43 in December, It was a clear indication that the authorities realised that the South Arabian campaign was a lost cause and were intent on running down the garrison before leaving them to FLOSY. The New Year continued in the same way, with only 30 sorties being flown in January. These were becoming increasingly dangerous with aircraft often coming back to base showing signs of ground fire. XL149 flown by Fg Off J C Craig suffered bullet strikes after taking off from Dhala, one soldier being injured.

In December 1966, XB266 now operating with 30 Squadron, was found to have fatigue cracks around the fuselage/ wing spar joint. Although in this case the damage was repairable, a check on XM107 (84 Sqn) and XH119 (30 Sqn) resulted in them being certified 'Category 5' fit for flying as far as the MU prior to scrapping. It should be realised that many of these aircraft had amassed between 4,000 to 5,000 flying hours in some of the worst conditions imaginable. The first aircraft, XM107, piloted by Fg Off M Westwood, was flown back to the UK, arriving at Shawbury on 23 March 1967.

On 1 January 1967, there were nearly 9,300 dependents in Aden. When repatriation started in May, the number was down to 6,500, after which they left at the rate of about 200 a day. By the middle of July, the civilian departures had been completed.

A record was claimed in February when XM103 was flown for a one-ton container drop to Francistown in Botswana, the entire trip (4,500 miles) being made in the door-off configuration. The Squadron's fiftieth anniversary was celebrated on 23 February and marked nearly 47 years of unbroken overseas service, of which most had been spent in the Middle East. At the anniversary celebration, the Squadron silver and other trophies were displayed, together with a presentation sword and a bound copy of the memoirs of MRAF Lord Douglas of Kirtleside, a former commander of the Squadron. The sword and memoirs had been presented to the Squadron at an Old Scorpions' dinner in London.

By March, terrorism had spread to Socotra and the dissidents were said to be plotting the overthrow of the Sultan and his government. Operation 'Snaffle' was mounted and four Beverleys, two from No.30 and two from No. 84, were despatched to Riyan. From there they flew a large contingent of the Hadrami Bedouin Forces to Socotra, where they quickly dealt with the rebels. Colin Scarth commented: "We made a surprise landing at dawn (or as big a surprise as one can get flying a Beverley) off-loaded the troops and took-off again to orbit the area, awaiting a call from our troops. To our amazement, the call came quicker than we expected and we were requested to land and pick up the prisoners. We landed and loaded the freight bay with the prisoners who had been tied up, along with some rather edgy-looking guards. I was more concerned with them shooting holes in the aircraft, rather than keeping an eye on the prisoners".

On 22 September 1961, a small bomb exploded in the hold of XL131, on loan from No.30 Squadron

A badge being presented to No. 84 Squadron by the Saudi Arabian Army in appreciation for the Squadron's support to the Army in upcountry Saudi Arabia. Left to right: Gp Capt D F Browne, Station Commander, Khormaksar, Col Dick Lawson SAA, Flt Lt R Coutts, Sqn Ldr S Hitchin, Brigadier J Dye, SAA. Taken inside a Beverley on the last support flight, taking a Saladin from Khormaksar to Beihan.

Due to a general strike in Aden, the fuel situation reached a critical point during June, both Avgas for the piston-engined aircraft and Avtur for the jets. XH121 was modified to carry 2,500 gallons of Avtur in four of its eight fuel tanks and began a shuttle service from Djibouti to Khormaksar. The Avtur was then pumped into the airfield fuel tanks.

The same month, two Beverleys under the command of Sqn Ldr Stan Hitchen were despatched to Nairobi at the request of the Kenyan Government to help distribute supplies to areas which were suffering from serious flooding. With the Beverleys ability to carry enormous loads, the famine relief situation was soon completed and the aircraft returned to Khormaksar. These were the last Beverley flights into Kenya.

On 21 June, XM106, flown by Flt Lt Pat Manley, taxied over a land-mine which had been planted by the terrorists at Habilayn. The starboard undercarriage was blown off and the starboard wing collapsed on to the ground. Pat Manley had the foresight to feather the props before the wing hit the ground. The crew, who were unhurt, abandoned the aircraft through the front door. I was told that the navigator, having been warned about the possibility of other landmines, instead of taking more care, proceeded to clear the area by taking even longer strides! After salvaging as much as possible, the aircraft was dragged off the strip and the remains were left for the Arabs. Apart from one visit to the UK for a complete overhaul, XM106 had spent its entire life with No. 84 Squadron.

In July, Flt Lt Craig flew the AOC to Kamaran Island, from where they picked up the entire British garrison and returned to Aden. The island was occupied by the Yemeni the next day. It is noted that during June, the Squadron acquired a Dakota which was used for some of the up-country trips. The airlift of fuel continued until 19 July when storage at Djibouti became exhausted. Later, further supplies were flown in from Assab. By August, it was noticeable that Britain was prepared to complete the evacuation from Aden earlier than the proposed date of 1 January 1968. Only 17 flights to the up-country strips were made during August. Three of the Squadron's Beverleys completed the withdrawal from Riyan on 2 September and all training flights were suspended due to the possibility of small arms fire from overlooking properties.

Later that month the Squadron Standard, silver and other trophies were flown to their new home at Sharjah. Preparations were already in hand to fly the Beverleys back to the UK for disposal. Due to the Arab/Israeli conflict, it was not considered wise to overfly Egypt. A alternative route through Turkey was considered, but height restrictions for the old Beverleys meant that it was unlikely that they could reach 16,000 feet. However, on 18 September 1967, XH121, XH120 and XB284 took off from Khormaksar for the last time to fly to the UK via Iran and Turkey.

Over the last few weeks, the three remaining aircraft amassed a further 309 flying hours. Flights were made to the Persian Gulf and to up-country airstrips. Few of the latter were flown without a Hunter escort. The end came on 29 October when a formation of three Beverleys and one Dakota flew a flypast in front of the Senior Air Staff officer, AVM Andrew Humphrey.

The route to the UK was changed by courtesy of President Nasser, and the aircraft were allowed to overfly Egypt. The aircraft, XM111, XM103 and XL130, were captained by Sqn Ldr S Hitchen and Flt Lts Barton and Coutts. All were flown at their near capacity, Sqn Ldr Hitchen remarked that he did not intend to leave anything behind for the FLOSY. Aircraft were decorated with the usual graffiti, aircraft 'U' suffixed with an added 'K and/or bust'! They left Khormaksar on 2 November at 15-minute intervals, Sqn Ldr Hitchen being the last to take-off.

First away was Flt Lt John Coutts flying XM111, the co-pilot was Fg Off Parker and the navigator Fg Off Jeremy Collins, possibly better known as the author of articles in the 'Flypast' magazine. He wrote: "After passing over Jeddah we settled on the long haul to El Adem. Suddenly we were in the midst of a hailstorm with stones the size of golf balls. The noise was tremendous. Diving through cloud, we levelled out at 6,000 feet to see the damage. The over windscreen had been smashed as had the astrodome and AQM Menzies reported that the nose was like a colander. Fortunately the Beverley was still flying and after 11 hours 35 minutes we touched down at El Adem". Ground checks found 147 dents or holes in the Beverley's skin. After numerous patches had been added, XM111 continued on its flight to the UK, arriving at Abingdon on 9 November.

Flt Lt Barton piloting XM103 suffered a double engine failure over the Gulf and diverted to Jeddah. Sqn Ldr Hitchen also diverted to give assistance; but was told to fly on at gun point. Later, an engine was flown into Jeddah by an Argosy, XM103 reaching Abingdon on 15 November.

After being forced to take off from Jeddah, Sqn Ldr Hitchen set course for Ras Babas on the Egyptian coast. When approaching, Flt Sgt Hankes reported that a couple of MiGs were formating on the starboard side. One of them fired its rockets, followed by cannon fire, across the nose of the Beverley. After hurried communications with the Egyptians, the MiGs were called off, much to the relief of the crew. The Beverley's radio transmissions were intercepted by an Argosy in the Persian Gulf with the result that London was informed of this near international incident. Landing at El Adem, Sqn Ldr Hitchen underwent an intense debriefing before he was allowed to continue. He took off the next day for the UK which he reached without further trouble.

During the nine-and-a-half years No. 84 Squadron had been operating with the Beverley, 27,000 flying hours had been logged. Nearly 43,000 tons of freight had been moved and 123,000 passengers had been carried. It is perhaps a little sad that the only Beverley in existence is XB259, one never used by No. 84 Squadron. It stands at the Museum of Army Transport at Beverley, Humberside, as a reminder to all those that served in Aden, Borneo, Kenya and other exotic outposts that the Beverley more than did its share over the years.

XM111 D, with heart on tail and scorpion on nose, rests at Bicester after returning from the Middle East

Andover XS645 E touches down on a typical gravel up-country airstrip

CHAPTER 20 - THE AFFAIR WITH THE ANDOVER

After nine years at Khormaksar, flying Army support missions in the Beverley C.1 transport, in and out of dust-laden country airstrips, 'B' Flight of No.84 Squadron was formed at Sharjah to re-equip with the Andover C. Mk.I. The military Andover was a heavier and more powerful version of the civil Hawker-Siddeley 748, which had been redesigned with an upswept tail and rear loading doors. It also had the advantages of a widened centre section, which increased the span by three feet, a reinforced floor for the use of wheeled vehicles and, so that the rear ramp could be brought level with the tail-boards of the lorries, a kneeling undercarriage. It could also be adapted for the STOL support role to carry 30 paratroopers, 44 fully-equipped troops or 18 casualty stretchers, five sitting casualties and three medical orderlies. Alternatively, 14,000lbs of freight, including vehicles up to 10,500 lbs could be carried.

The first Andover (XS642) to leave Abingdon on 31 August 1967 was flown by Flt Lt Malcolm Harris, co-piloted by Fg Off Mac Sibbald and navigated by the Squadron's CO, Sqn Ldr Tony Radnor. Later the same day, XS641 left with Flt Lt John Wells, Fg Off Trevor Cockarill and Plt Off Derek Halton. Arriving at Sharjah on 3 September, the two aircraft formed the beginnings of 'B' Flight of No.84 Squadron, whilst the remainder of 84 Beverley Squadron was to remain at Khormaksar for another two months.

Malcolm Harris later wrote: "My first impressions of Sharjah were firstly the heat and the humidity and, secondly that we had landed on a very large and dusty building site. Up to that time, Sharjah had only been a staging post with a resident Wessex helicopter squadron. Now, a new dispersal pan was being laid with numerous buildings being erected to accommodate the greatly enlarged station".

Four days later, the Squadron's third aircraft (XS643) arrived, flown by Flt Lt John Luby. By 10 September 'B' Flight was allocated a disused hangar. On the 21st, Fg Off Peter Miles and Sgt Dave Kimber arrived in a Britannia, followed a day later by Flt Lt Roy Headland who arrived in a VC.10. During the first month, flights were made to the Gulf States, stopping at Masirah, Salalah and Khormaksar. Nevertheless, flying time amounted to nearly 208 hours.

In October, the hours flown increased to 318, which included the evacuation from Khormaksar of personnel from No.8 Squadron. They also had the pleasure of flying the members of a variety concert which included Mike and Bernie Winters, Dickie Henderson and 'plenty of lovely girls' from Muharraq to their venues around the Middle and Near East. Two more Andovers

arrived on 6 November, flown by Flt Lts Al Brindle and John Craig. Alan Brindle was another of the characters who coloured 84's history. He had spent the years between 1951 and 1958 as an instructor on fighters, ending as an instrument rating instructor on Meteors at West Raynham. He had then joined No. 111 Squadron, the famous 'Black Arrows' Hunter aerobatic team which appeared at Farnborough and elsewhere in 1958, 1959 and 1960. At the end of 1960, he was again posted to the fighter training world, but 1962 saw him back at Farnborough with No.92 Squadron. In mid-1963 he left the fighter scene and was posted to a Far East Communications Squadron, flying Hastings, before reaching 84 in late 1967.

It is noted that on 14 November the Squadron had an unexpected birth. The groundcrew had found a goat calmly chewing the tyres of XS642. So they promptly impounded it and tied it up outside the Squadron offices, where it was fed and given a drink. Having devoured its lunch with obvious relish and taken a long swig at the water, it rolled contentedly on to its side and started to pass wind. Before action could be taken to remove the animal, it gave a plaintive 'Baa..aa', rolled its eyes and delivered a black and white kid on the front steps. Later the goat and its kid were claimed by one of the native labourers. As one of the crew said: "On its own, nobody wanted the goat but, with a kid, there was no shortage of owners".

At the end of the month, Flt Lt Roy Headland and Sgt D Kimber returned to the UK to collect the Squadron's sixth and final Andover. They arrived back at Sharjah on 6 December, together with co-pilot Les Rockel and navigator Dave Crombie. The same day, a section of the Royal Fusiliers arrived on the station, many of them suffering from air sickness after their cross-country flight. Later, on the 14th, a flight was arranged to carry senior Army officers to Yas Island to watch demonstrations of the latest type of anti-tank missile.

Christmas was celebrated in the usual way with the officers serving the airmen on the evening of 23 December. On Christmas Eve, at an Officers' Mess dining-in night, attempts were made to sing the 'Shaibah Blues'. Unfortunately, John Craig was the only one who knew the words but, as he could not sing a note, the whole thing went rather flat! On Christmas Day a football match was arranged between the officers and NCOs versus the rest, followed by a Station Donkey Derby in which Mac Sibbald came second on 'Fully Feathered', the prize being a food mixer!

So ended another year for 'Scorpion Airways'. During the month, they had logged 256 hours and carried 134,500 lbs of

XS645 E at Saiq, 14 November 1970

freight.

Squadron records state the personnel were all new to the area and at no time was there a transition period for the old hands to pass on the customs to the new. Despite this, the 'Sign of the Scorpion' had gathered under it as big a bunch of ugly, debauched, yet highly professional rogues one would expect to find anywhere who were to become a credit to one of the finest squadrons in the Royal Air Force. This was typified by the sight of Al Brindle standing on his head at the dispersal waving farewell with his legs to two of his friends who were leaving the station.

During the middle two weeks of January there was a demonstration of Army Air Corps operations and 84 Squadron co-operation which became known as 'The case of the Manana Oil Drums'. The Army, in all its wisdom, wanted fuel to be flown to Manana to refuel some of its Austers. Having phoned 'Operations', the Squadron arranged that an Andover should do the runs with twenty 44-gallon drums of fuel. The Army representative came and discussed the task at length with the crew and arrangements were made for the Andover to be loaded before take-off some three days later. When the crew arrived, they found the aircraft empty. "Where's the load?" said Pete Miles. "Oh, did we have to order the fuel?" said the Army. The next thing to happen was that BP could not find enough 44-gallon drums and, when they eventually obtained them, they filled them with the wrong fuel. After a fortnight, the whole show was called off!

In January, damage was done to XS595 when one of the service policemen backed a three-ton vehicle into its wing fillet. In February, Flt Lt Tony Ross arrived from No.47 Squadron. During the month, flights were made to Manana and Tarif taking senior members of the Army to view manoeuvres. On the 22nd, the Squadron played host to the Sheikhs of Dubai and Sharjah, plus a host of other dignitaries. The display was labelled 'non-aggressive' so the Hunters of No.8 Squadron and the Shackletons of No.201 Squadron could not take part. XS642 was loaded with two Land Rovers and their crews and, at the appointed time, did a short landing in front of the crowd, taxied in and after kneeling towards Mecca, discharged its Jeeps and took on 30 fully armed troops. After a spot of reverse taxying, Flt Lt John Wells made a short take-off and 'hung on the props' up to 2,500 feet. A most impressive display!

Up to then, the Squadron had been remarkably accident-free but on the 14th, Tony Ross suffered a hydraulic failure when carrying a load of ammunition. Apparently the nitrogen pressure in the system was too high and forced the hydraulic fluid out through its overflows. After circling, Ross landed safely at Sharjah. On the 22nd, Mal Harris burst his third set of main wheel tyres. This was followed two days later by Roy Headland; when 60 miles out from Sharjah with a load of VIPs, his starboard fire warning light started flashing. After using both extinguishers, he carried out an asymmetric landing back at Sharjah. During the month, 312 flying hours were logged, and 172,485 lbs of freight were carried including 4,467 lbs of mail.

In March, there was a decline in hours flown, with only 220 hours logged. Starting on the 7th, the Squadron participated in Exercise 'Gold Leaf'. The exercise stretched from New Sohar on the East coast, through Wadi Jezi to Buraimi. 22 SAS were the 'baddies' and the Royal Fusiliers were the 'goodies'! As the odds were approximately 22 to 3,000, the Squadron was not unduly surprised when the 'Goodies' won.

April was highlighted by the visit of AVM S B Grant DFC to the Squadron. He was taken for a flight in an Andover and the aircraft's capabilities were demonstrated by Flt Lt Derek Ikin. Lack of Army tasks cut the number of hours flown and a shortage of parachute instructors curtailed some paratrooping exercises.

Over the previous months the Squadron had been raising money to finance a trip to the UK for the Civil Labour Officer's 12-year-old son who was suffering from a hole in the heart. Unfortunately, the boy did not survive the operation and on 5 June his body was returned to Sharjah via Muharraq.

On a lighter note, the Squadron enjoyed their first route training flight when two crews flew an Andover to Rawalpindi via Karachi and Peshawar. Whilst flying the middle leg at 15,000 feet, the starboard sliding window split across the middle. The aircraft was de-pressurised and descended. Comments to the nervous pilot who hastily strapped himself in a bit tighter included: "Have you ever thought of being sucked out of a side window at 15,000 feet and being shredded through a 14 ft 6 in. Dowty Rotol prop going round like a bee on heat?" After landing at Rawalpindi, the crews were driven to Islamabad where hospitality was given by the British residents.

During the first week of July, 22 members of the SAS arrived at the station for another series of death-defying exercises and amazed the aircrew by leaping out into space over the mountains or into the sea, night and day with apparent complete disregard for their own safety. During the time the SAS were at Masirah, a night drop was made for them by Flt Lt John Wells. Later, Flt Lt Mal Harris flew down and picked them up. He found to his amazement that part of their return luggage was a 300 lb turtle. Apparently the SAS boys were quite upset when Harris refused to have it on his aircraft.

XS641 B kneeling with its ramp down. The squadron motif is on the fin

In the middle of the month the Squadron had a visit from Mr Merlyn Rees, Parliamentary Under Secretary for Defence. It is said that he spent much of his time wandering around the station asking various members of the Squadron what they thought of Sharjah.

The Squadron lost the first of its 'old boys', Plt Off Derek Halton, at the end of July. He had been one of the first to arrive on the station, having been thrown in the deep end to become adjutant. Soon after Sqn Ldr Tony Radnor left to take up a posting to the Staff College, Bracknell. He was replaced by Sqn Ldr D S Gates who assumed command on 4 September.

During September, the Squadron took part in a nine-day exercise with the Queen's Regiment called 'Autumn Chase'. It involved a thrice daily run to Dibba. At the same time good news reached the Squadron that the route training flights were to be extended, with many trips to Akrotiri, Rawalpindi and to Addis Ababa.

In early October, two of the replacement crews returned to the UK, Colin Stephens on medical grounds and Jim Gatherer on compassionate. To replace them came Flt Lt Don Start and Flt Sgt Dave Carroll. A large proportion of the month's work was taken up by supporting the Grenadier Guards, 16 flights were made to Fujeira, seven to Tarif, three to Buraimi and a first-timer to Ibri. Two cases of fuel leaks led to asymmetric landings. On each occasion a safe return was made to Sharjah. Six flights were made to Shiraz in support of the MRDT who were there on CENTO exercises. On the 12th the first of the new route trainers took off on a five-day trip to Rawalpindi via Karachi and Peshawar. During the month, Wg Cdr Ken Parfit, CO from 1962-64, visited the Squadron.

In November, a further six of the original crew members left in an exchange with members of No.46 Squadron. Amidst all this crew transit, the routine work of the squadron continued. During November, there was a visit to the station by MRAF Sir Charles Elworthy and his staff. Whilst he was paying his visit, two of the aircrews and the Station Commander were on a route liaison flight to No.52 Squadron at Seletar. This was a 10-day flight with two night stops at Bangkok and two in Calcutta with Delhi and Bombay thrown in for good measure.

The busiest operational period in December occurred between the 7th and the 16th, when the Squadron too part in Exercise 'Pall Mall'. This involved low-level flights to Manana and Fujeira. Ferry tank trials were begun with some success. The first trip involved a diversion to Masirah due to a fuel leak in the starboard wing which was initially diagnosed as in-flight condensation. However, on touchdown at Masirah, the groundcrew informed the captain that there were in fact two leaks, one in the port wing as well.

The start of the New Year will long be remembered as the 'Night of the Big Storm'. To say that January started off with a bang would be an understatement because, on the fateful 7th at approximately 0700, a patch of unsettled weather (to quote the met forecasters) hit the camp with such force that sheer pandemonium ensued for just under an hour. Wind speeds of up to 80 knots were recorded, huge hailstones battered the camp violently and torrential rain fell (over 1 inch in 50 minutes). After the storm had subsided, the full extent of the damage was realised. Roofs were lifted off buildings and windows torn out, many rooms were flooded and the electricity was cut off. The effect on the Squadron was equally dramatic. Five aircraft suffered extensive damage to their top wing surfaces and trim tabs while XS641 was also hit by a falling crane which damaged its port aileron and wing tip. The only aircraft to escape damage was XS642 which was undergoing a routine servicing.

After inspecting this unexpected damage, all five aircraft were declared 'Cat 3' and a signal was sent to the UK requesting the immediate dispatch of a Hawker-Siddeley representative. In the meantime, XS642 became the Squadron workhorse and endeavoured to complete as many tasks as possible. In fact the only programme casualty was a route training flight to Addis Ababa. Seven days later, the HS representative arrived and declared that all the aircraft could be made serviceable after the trim tabs had been replaced. The nuisance value of the storm was alleviated briefly by the sight of the Inspector-General of the RAF, Sir Reginald Emson, wearing a pair of wellingtons, sitting, with coffee in hand, completely at home and seemingly enjoying the relaxed atmosphere of 84's crew room.

During the month, night landings were practised at Buraimi and one training flight was made to Akrotiri. Even this flight had its problems when the airfield at Jeddah was found to be flooded, causing the aircraft to divert to Muharraq.

February began with a series of unserviceability problems, in particular, unco-operative props and their attendant lights and indicators. However, the latter two weeks saw a decided improvement in flying hours which included three route training flights. The 'bread and butter' flying for the month consisted mainly in supporting the Grenadier Guards, with one-ton drops at Wadi Sifuni and also an exercise transporting their No.3 Company to that well-known hot-spot Manana. Of more operational interest was a first visit to Qusaiwara in the Liwa Hollows to deliver a Landrover engine. An airstrip recce was flown to Saiq (height 6,500 feet asl, length of strip 2,400 feet and 80 feet wide). Route

XS641 B fitted with a Sky-shout system installed on the ramp, Sharjah, 13 December 1970

trips flown include visits to Pakistan and Akrotiri, although on the Teheran - Ankara leg, a diversion had to be made to the Turkish base at Diyarbakir.

Workwise, March started with a bang, with the positioning and retrieving of the 105 mm howitzers of 13 Light Battery RA from Yas Island, and further landings at Buraimi and Abu Dhabi. Following closely was Exercise 'Athlete's Foot' which involved flying the Cheshires to Fujeira and Dibba, and Exercise 'Haploid' which started at the end of March and finished in the second week of April. This involved the positioning, resupplying and recovering units of the Grenadier Guards from areas around Buraimi. Two route trainers were flown, the first to Akrotiri and, the second to Addis Ababa from where Flt Lts Chris Alcock and John Tate returned carrying an extraordinary collection of wood carvings, shields and weird musical instruments. At the end of the month, a visit was made to the station by Air Chief Marshal Sir John Grandy, Chief of Air Staff.

During April, the entire range of support operations was performed, including both free-fall and static-line paratroop dropping. After 'Haploid' came Exercise 'Face' entailing a combined services assault around the Sohar area and resulted in the Squadron making several sorties to Sohar airstrip and supply drops to Al Liwa just north of the strip. Apparently the exercise not only to be a theoretical and practical success but it also aided in the killing and capture of real-life terrorists by the local population! Later in the month, Flt Lt Tony Hoyle and his crew pioneered two new low-level drops. The first flight lasted three hours and was routed via the southern coast of the Gulf, overflying Tarif, Mirfa and Jebel Dhana, and eventually reaching the Hafira DZ on Bahrein Island. Unfortunately for the paras, someone had put the DZ identification letters too close to the beach, with the result that the first drop landed in the 'drink'.

May started with a courtesy call to the base by Mr Edward Heath MP whilst doing a tour of the Gulf States. Later in the month news was received that the Squadron was to participate in Exercise 'Olympic Express'. On the 26th, 12 aircrew and 12 groundcrew took off on a flight which took them via Teheran and Ankara to Thessalonika. Flying took place over a 12-day period starting on 29 May. Although somewhat underworked, flights included troops and supply landings, one-ton drops both by night and day and an occasional casualty evacuation to Cyprus. Trips seldom lasted longer than one hour, but it made a change for the aircrews to have airfields like Sedes, Serrai and Kavalla in the log-books. By having one crew on stand-by, several members of the Squadron were able to see something of the Greek countryside.

Over the preceding months, there had been many cases of minor servicing problems and in July the Squadron aircraft had to operate on reduced power settings, which precluded operating from the STOL strips. In fact, the majority of July's hours were flown on various route training flights. On the 6th, Flt Lt Brian Love and his crew made their first visit to Nairobi. Despite a unserviceable doppler, faltering ground beacon and a lot of cloud cover, they reached Eastleigh with stops at Bahrein, Jeddah and Addis Ababa. The same day an aircraft left for Singapore (13 found an excuse for going) via Karachi, Delhi, Calcutta, Rangoon and Bangkok. At the end of the month, Flt Lt Dave Austin flew to Akrotiri via the Jeddah route, On his return he was obliged to follow the CENTO route due to the flare-up of the Arab-Israeli conflict.

During September 1969, 37 sorties were flown to Manana on Exercise 'Desert Song' and a further 13 to Muharraq. In September there was a major change of personnel with the majority of groundcrew being tour-expired.

During October, an exercise in the Dibba area resulted in eleven sorties being carried out. Strangely, during this exercise eight casualties were evacuated, six with appendicitis. Three route training flights were flown, one to Cyprus and two to Pakistan. Back at Sharjah the Squadron enjoyed a visit from 16 Parachute Brigade and the instructors of No.1 Parachute Training School who were training to become free-fall experts. Two trips were flown when their Hercules aircraft became unserviceable. On the 17th, The Minister for Defence, Mr Roy Hattersley, paid a visit to the station accompanied by AVM Pringle. By far the most important happening during the month was the change of CO, Sqn Ldr Des Gates departing for Benson to become a flight commander on No.114 Squadron Argosies. Replacing him came Sqn Ldr T G Chalmers straight from Staff College.

A total of 245 hours were flown during November; considering the poor overall serviceability it showed what a good job the groundcrews were doing by keeping the serviceable aircraft flying both day and night. Flt Lt John Tate took an aircraft to Pakistan and included Risalpur en route by way of a change. Not satisfied with the flight to Pakistan, he also flew to Jask to pick up members of the Special Boat Service which had landed from HMS *Nubian*.

The December flight to Pakistan was flown by Flt Lt Dave Carter and his crew. A second flight to the sub-continent was flown by Flt Lt Dave Orringe. The visit to Coimbatore, some 400 miles south of Bombay was highlighted by the fact that the Indian authorities had not been notified they were coming and so the Customs and Immigration people spent a long time deliberating on what to do with them. Eventually a note came from the Air Attaché, by which time the Indian Air Force was showing Orringe and his crew what the local hospitality was like.

A minor exercise in Manana, plus the re-supplying of the Royal Scots on a tour of Muscat, kept the Squadron in touch with the Army. An aircraft and crew were sent to Bahrein to take part in 'December Jump', a para exercise at Hafira. In December, Flt Lt John Tate departed to become a Britannia captain and Flt Lt Tony Hoyle became a flight commander at Abingdon.

In January and February, the serviceability levels improved. During these months the flights to Buraimi lessened, to be replaced by increased flights to Yas Island. Two exercises ran concurrently, 'Last Shot' and 'Shark Skin' involving the 3rd Light Battery and the Scots Guards. In early March, the withdrawal of the Scots Guards from Yas Island made further trips unnecessary. It also meant that ammunition stored there had to be rendered unserviceable. In March, Flt Lt Ian Mason feathered a perfectly good engine and returned to Sharjah only to find that the oil temperature gauge was u/s. At Muharraq, Flt Lt Pat Plunkett after take-off, found he had only limited aileron control but with considerable skill, he returned to make a safe landing. A recurrence of this problem was experienced by Flt Lt Dave Carter early in April, and again the skill of the pilot got the aircraft down safely.

During April a series of flights was made to Saiq and, although normally considered too short for the Andover, Flt Lt Chris Blake landed successfully. At the end of April, Exercise 'Burst Balloon' started but after three days, had to be terminated due to a further recurrence of aileron problems. Later it was found that the aileron gust locks were at fault.

Over the previous months, it had been the policy of the Squadron to have an aircraft and his crew on a 24 hour stand-by to transport medical patient and compassionate cases to Bahrein. When it was realised that the flight time to Bahrein was 1.35 hours, it is surprising to find that in some months up to 37 hours had been flown on these flights. On the night of 7 March, Flt Lt Graham and

XS642 C being serviced at Sharjah

his duty crew took off at 2335 for Bahrein to connect with the 0230 Qantas flight departure for Masirah. While he was away, another emergency occurred at Masirah when a soldier on detachment was taken seriously ill. Flt Lt Burnett and his crew immediately left Sharjah at 0455, collected the soldier and flew him to Bahrein, arriving back at Sharjah at 1345.

In June 1970, the Squadron aircraft were grounded with aileron problems. After an air test on the 10th, further faults were found on XS643 necessitating continued grounding until the 16th. On 23 June, Flt Lt John Douglas left for Khartoum carrying a replacement wheel and jack for a Shackleton with a burst tyre. Thirty minutes out of Bahrein, the Andover developed an electrical fault and the restricted landing times at Khartoum meant a return and a night stop at Bahrein. The next day Douglas resumed his flight to the Sudan where the Shackleton crews were waiting to unload the wheel and jack. Returning on the 26th, they refuelled at Jeddah by torchlight (an electrical storm had cut the power supply) before continuing to Bahrein. They arrived overhead at Bahrein just in time to see a Shackleton abort its take-off with burst tyres at the end of the runway with the result that Douglas and his crew had to circle for 30 minutes before the runway was cleared. It was ironic that the only jack on the station was in the Andover circling above!

From the 7th to the 13th July, the Andovers took part in Exercise 'Gazala Gallop', which involved a great deal of supply-dropping and air-landing flights to Buraimi. Because of the extreme temperatures, a large number of casualties was expected and, in order to be ready, the CO decided to fly some STOL trips to Manana. Over the month, three call-out flights were flown, a compassionate trip from Muharraq, a medevac from Masirah and a special flight to fix the position of the freighter *Varick Trader* which had caught fire. A demonstration was put on for a visiting medical officer, with the pilot collapsing over the control column at a height of 200 feet, with the result that the co-pilot Dave Eastmond gained a few more grey hairs before the pilot was lifted from his seat and he took over control.

During August, four medevacs were flown including one of the Sultan's troops who had been accidentally shot. In September, the Squadron took part in Exercise 'Jebel Bash' with a number of Hercules. A series of one-ton drops were made at Tayibah and supply drops at Manana. A route training flight was flown to Akrotiri by Flt Lt John Douglas. This eventually turned out to be a five-day stay (Records state that there was a wine festival on at the time!) To make a complete change, an Army Beaver had hit a tree whilst landing at the Eastern Trucial Station at Sohar; XS 639 was given the job of picking up the pieces.

Exercise 'Shiraz Sahara' was flown in early October. One aircraft and two crews were kept busy in an exercise involving the SAS and the Iran Special Forces. A visit was made to Sharjah by Mr Antony Lambton MP, Under-Secretary for Defence. At the same time the members of Air Support Command Examining Unit kept the Squadron on its toes. During November one aircraft was used as a VIP transport. The Ruler of Sharjah, His Highness Sheikh Khalid bin Mohammed al Qasami, was participating in oil talks with his near neighbour the ruler of Abu Dhabi. On that occasion the Squadron ran out the red carpet. The result was that the hospitality and comfort on board the aircraft prompted the Sheikh to remark "How much I regret not having availed myself of the facilities sooner". The captain for the flight was Flt Lt Pat Plunkett with the Commanding Officer, Sqn Ldr Ian Chalmers navigating.

In November and December, a double change of commanding officers occurred. Sqn Ldr Ian Chalmers was replaced by Sqn Ldr A B Stephens, only to be replaced a month later by an 'old boy' from the early Andover years, Sqn Ldr Derek Ikin on 20 December.

It is of interest that from its move to Sharjah in August 1967 to Christmas 1970, the number of air miles flown by No.84 Squadron amounted to 1,753,270. Over 18,000 passengers were carried and 6,727,740 lbs of freight including 64,000 lbs of mail was airlifted into various stations.

Experiments had been made by installing a 'Skyshout' system on the ramp door of XS643 and, although successful, the use of Rolling Stones tapes were prohibited.

On 30 December, the Squadron moved from Sharjah to Muharraq on the island of Bahrein.

During February 1971, Sqn Ldr E Sharples and Flt Lt W Tait represented the Squadron at the Ethiopian Navy Day. The same month brought a major change in personnel, the majority of the groundcrew being tour-expired. Flt Lt John Douglas left the Squadron to join No.46 Squadron and was replaced by Flt Lt John Daniels. In early March a visit was made to the Station by the Commander of the RAF Regiment in company with General Sir John Mogg. A few weeks later, on 4 April, HRH Prince Philip visited the Squadron whilst on a tour of the Gulf States.

Rumours of the Squadron disbanding were becoming commonplace during April. The number of route training flights were developing into four or five day tours to Akrotiri or Karachi. The area of operations was extended to the Jebel Akhdar area, the green mountain of Oman, using airstrips that were little more than flattened strips of gravel. On training flights south of the Buraimi oasis, the Andover crews would fly at a height of 500 feet along a

The fuselage of an Army Air Corps Beaver being loaded aboard an Andover

70-mile valley with cliffs towering to 4,000 feet on either side, the rising heat causing severe turbulence which called for a high degree of flying skill. During May an aircraft flown by Flt Lt Bill Tait and Fg Off John Boardman carried members of British and Central Forces, Gulf on a liaison visit to Teheran. On his return to Muharraq, Tait left for the UK to be replaced by Flt Lt John Adams.

The use of one Andover on a 24-hour stand-by was now known as the Desert Rescue Service and it was called into use on two occasions during June. An Air-India Boeing 747 was diverted from Kuwait to Bahrein to pick up a compassionate case. The same month a flight was made to Dhahran, Taif and Riyadh for casevac. On 2 July an Andover of the Desert Rescue Service went u/s at Rostaq with a fractured hydraulic pipe. The enforced stay proved very interesting and the crew were given a tour of the area by members of the Sultan's Armed Forces. At the same time a chartered Dakota en route from Muscat to Salalah force-landed 45 west of Masirah. A Skyvan from the Muscat Air Force was used to collect the passengers but it was left to the relief aircraft from No.84 Squadron to collect the crew.

In August, the rumour that No.84 Squadron was to disband at the end of September became a reality and a gentle run-down began. Three of 84's aircraft were to return to the UK, the rest were to go to Masirah to form a detachment of No.46 Squadron. The last flights made by 84 Squadron were to drop fuel to the Staffords who were on patrol in the area. So ended the three and a half years of 'Scorpion Airways'.

In a closing memo from the AOC Middle East, Air Commodore G A Mason DFC to the Squadron Commander, Sqn Ldr D Ikin, he wrote:

A is for Andover, sleek as a cat
B is for Bahrein, which is where you've been at
C is for cargoes you've carried with care
D is for dramas you've met in the air
E is for excellence in all you have done
F for your Farewell and thanks for the fun!

XS641 en route to Saiq over typically mountainous Arabian terrain, 14 November 1970

XK976 P of B Flight over the buffer zone. Squadron logo on nose and club symbol on fin

CHAPTER 21 - TO AKROTIRI WITH THE WHIRLWIND

The old adage that one cannot keep a good man down also applies to No.84 Squadron. After the disbandment of the Squadron at Muharraq in September 1971, it was reformed at RAF Akrotiri in Cyprus, from No.1563 Flight and a detachment of No.230 Squadron, on 17 January 1972. The Squadron was equipped with Westland Whirlwind HAR.10s, with the Headquarters and 'A' Flight at Akrotiri and 'B' Flight at Nicosia. In command was Sqn Ldr George Puddy with responsibilities for Search and Rescue and later in supporting the United Nations Force in Cyprus (UNFICYP).

The Westland Whirlwind HAR.10s were used as a short-range tactical transport and for ground support and search and rescue facilities, with accommodation for three crew and eight passengers. Powered by a 1,050 shp Bristol-Siddeley Gnome turboshaft engine, it offered considerably better performance, reliability and an improved safety factor than the earlier Whirlwinds powered by the Leonides Major radial engine. It saw service in Coastal and Flying Training Commands, in Germany and in the Far East.

'A' Flight's aircraft, with their primary role of Search and Rescue, were painted yellow overall with black lettering, its scorpion logo being portrayed on the door whilst its card symbol decorated the fin.

One of the earliest incidents was a joint search with a Hercules from No.70 Squadron for two seamen washed overboard from a Lebanese freighter. In the same period, a walker who had fallen off a cliff was airlifted to hospital. This was followed by the rescue of two drivers in the Cyprus International Rally whose car had gone off the road. This rescue was achieved by the light of the car headlights.

On 2 August 1972, a Whirlwind crewed by Flt Lt Mike Chapple (later the CO of RAF Hullavington) and Flt Sgt B Taylor took off from Akrotiri to intercept the SS *Ithaca* and winch aboard the wife of a Luton accountant who was suffering from acute appendicitis.

Early in 1973, Air Commodore D B Craig presented Flt Lt P Chadwick with a framed copy of a 'green endorsement'.

Chadwick was flying XP345 when, at a height of about 1,000 feet, the engine lost power without warning. He immediately initiated auto-rotation and turned his aircraft away. Diagnosing fuel computer failure and selecting manual throttle he recovered successfully and landed safely.

During April 1974, Sqn Ldr L Banham assumed command of the Squadron from Sqn Ldr George Puddy.

In July 1974, a military coup to dispose of the President of Cyprus, Archbishop Makarios, was followed by the Turkish invasion. At the beginning of the month the Squadron accommodated many of the male personnel with families in the married quarters, others had made arrangements for their families to live around Limassol. On the 14th, after a further Turkish advance, the decision was made to return the families who lived outside the airfield to the UK. By the 18th, all of the families had left the island with the exception of those fortunate enough to be in married quarters at the time. When it became apparent that Limsassol was reasonably calm, trips into the Town to collect personal belongings were undertaken and soon one of the hangars resembled a Pickford's Depository.

On 18 September 1974, the Squadron was asked to search for two soldiers who were missing in a boat off Larnaca. After an unsuccessful search by Army Sioux helicopters, Flt Lt Phil Course and his navigator Dave Short were alerted to search. One of the soldiers was found almost immediately. The other was found by the relief crew, Flt Lt Tim Wood and his navigator Garry Cooper, nearly nine hours later. The soldier was found swimming strongly towards the Lebanon when he was spotted and winched aboard; a million to one chance.

On 27 January, Flt Lt Malcolm Pledger was piloting XR454 three miles north-east of Troodos, when the aircraft suffered an engine failure which caused him to force-land in difficult terrain. Fortunately, of his crew and the five passengers he was carrying, only two suffered superficial injuries. These were later winched aboard a Whirlwind flown by Flt Lt K Smith whilst the remaining passengers and crew were rescued by an Army Puma.

A Whirlwind hovers over the stranded Greek freighter Achaios *off Akrotiri*

During April 1975, the Squadron was honoured by a visit from HM Queen Elizabeth The Queen Mother.

In the same month, the six crewmen of the 1,000 ton Lebanese coaster *Samik* were winched aboard after the ship was disabled in high seas. In early March 1976, the crew of the Libyan coaster *Farag* were snatched to safety by a Whirlwind flown by Flt Lts Phil Course and Robin Hammond-Doutre. Taking off from Akrotiri at first light and, after a refuelling stop at Dhekelia, they followed the coast north to Cape Andreas where they found the coaster hard aground 50 yards from the cliffs. In 12 separate winch descents MALM Jeff Longmuir succeeded in airlifting the crew to the nearby monastery of Apostolos Andreas. On the 11 March a letter of congratulations and thanks was received from the Libyan Embassy.

Later in the month a fly-past of No.84 Squadron Whirlwind helicopters plus Nimrods of No.203 Squadron and Canberras of No.13 Squadron based at Luqa, Malta took part in the disbanding ceremony of the Near East Air Force with Air Marshal Sir John Aiken taking the salute. During April, the AOC, AVM R Austin-Smith came to Cyprus to complete his six monthly life-raft drill. After the drill had been completed he exchanged places with MALM Jeff Longmuir and became the rescuer.

During the same month, Flt Lt Tim Wood, Flt Lt Dave Holmyard and Flt Sgt Ian Brinton searched for several hours for a small boat in which the husband and son of Dr Vivien Edwards were missing. Unfortunately the search was unsuccessful; but, as a gesture of appreciation, Dr Edwards presented the Squadron with an engraved rose bowl.

On 3 December 1976, a Whirlwind flown by Flt Lts Graham Dainty and Robin Hammond-Doutre picked up nine men from the 2,500 ton Cypriot cargo vessel *Archios* which had grounded on rocks on the Akrotiri peninsula. As rough seas battered the ship, much of the ship's deck cargo of timber was washed on to the foreshore. The ship's hulk can still be seen from the road leading to the station. On the 16th of the month, Sqn Ldr Banham returned to the UK and was replaced by Sqn Ldr S M St C Collins.

A report was received on 12 July 1977 by the rescue co-ordinator via the Cypriot police that a small boat seemed to be in difficulties off 'Ladies Mile' beach. Investigations revealed that a dinghy had capsized. Later it was reported that a man had been seen righting his dinghy. On the 16th a red flare was seen out to sea south of Cape Gata and the No.10 Port Squadron work boat from the Royal Corps of Signals was sent out. It was found to be a Cypriot yacht which had suffered an engine failure and become becalmed. It was towed into Limassol by the work boat.

On 15 July the Squadron's Standard Bearer Party departed for the UK to participate in the Queen's Jubilee review of the Royal Air Force at RAF Finningley. The review was unique in that all six Queen's Colours of the RAF and 68 Squadron Standards were on parade together for the first time. It was the first time that the Squadron Standard had returned to the UK since it had been presented in January 1956, The members of the Standard party were Flt Lt Jon Plenbry, WO Jeff Longmuir and Sgts Peter Thompson and Neil Turner.

During October the Chief of Air Staff, ACM Sir Michael Beetham GCB CBE DFC AFC ADC paid the station a visit. On 12 November 1977, four of the Squadron's Whirlwinds winched 125 passengers and crew from the pitching deck of a Turkish ferry boat in distress. Buffeted by a Force 8 gale they hovered over the deck of the 150-ton vessel *Erturk* before flying the 200 yards to the safety of the ancient walls of Kyrenia Castle. The ferry's main engine had failed and it was feared that the ship would begin to break up. The women passengers were the first to be airlifted, followed by the male civilians. Finally 87 Turkish soldiers who were returning to Turkey were taken off. The rescue lasted more than three hours and no casualties were reported, although several of the older passengers were taken to hospital suffering from severe sea-sickness and shock. The request for British assistance had come from the Turkish Cypriot leader, Mr Rauf Dentkash. Later, General Saltik of the Turkish forces, who watched the rescue said that "The Turkish Authorities very much appreciated the quick response by the UN and British authorities". It was noted that the Turkish helicopters stationed in their zone had no facilities for winching.

On 8 August 1978, a letter of thanks was received by the Squadron from members of the Cyprus Aero Club whose Cessna 150 had crashed in the Alaminos area. Although in difficult terrain, the crew was winched out successfully. Three months later, a Whirlwind, piloted by Flt Lt Dave Rigby and crewed by Flt Lt Dave Haslam-Eley and Sgt Graham Goosey picked an American lady, Mrs Victor Romaro, and her 13-month-old child from a small boat adrift in the Mediterranean and were taken to hospital suffering from exposure. She had left Larnaca with her husband, the child and a friend in a 30-foot power-boat. After the boat failed to return, there was growing concern for their safety. A day-and-a-half later, the boat was spotted adrift 44 miles SSW of Larnaca

23 October 1980. A new Standard is presented to the Squadron by ACM Sir Keith Williamson KCB AFC, AOC Strike Command

The old Standard is handed over to the Vicar of Beaulieu Abbey Church, the Rev Kenneth Davis, by Sqn Ldr N R W Hibberd

The woman's husband and the owner of the boat decided to stay with the boat until rescue arrived from Larnaca to tow the boat into port.

On 17 November an American F-4 Phantom crashed in the Cape Andreas area. The Whirlwind which rescued the pilot found that he had broken both his legs in the crash. It was learnt later that the three crew members involved in the pilot's rescue were to receive citations from the American authorities.

January 1979 started with a SOS being received from a Greek coaster MV *Georgios V* when the lives of the ship's crew were threatened by heavy seas breaking over the vessel. Two Whirlwinds stood by and hovered over the ship which was 37 miles due east of Famagusta. One helicopter went in to rescue the crew but the master chose to stay aboard due to improving weather conditions. The ship was monitored closely over the next few hours and she finally limped into Larnaca harbour.

On the 26th of the month, Sqn Ldr Mike Chapple returned to the Squadron to assume command from Sqn Ldr Collins.

In May 1979, ACM Sir David Evans, AOC-in-C Strike Command on his Farewell visit to the Station, congratulated Sqn Ldr Mike Chapple on completing 2,000 flying hours on the Whirlwind. The following July, the Squadron played part-host to 21 children between the ages of 10 and 14. They were part of an organised 'Holiday of a Lifetime' for under-privileged children.

The speed which distress calls were answered was high-lighted when a 'Mayday' was received from the pilot of Lightning XR723 of No. 56 Squadron who had ejected 15 miles south of Akrotiri on 18 September. Within ten minutes he had been found and was being winched out of the water by winchman Graham Goosey. After another ten minutes, he was in the hands of the medical team waiting on the helipad of the hospital. Later in the year, Flt Lt Steve Garrod, flying XD184, delivered 'Father Christmas' to St Lucia's School for handicapped children at Polemidhia.

In February 1980, a visit to the station was made by HRH The Princess Anne. A month later, a couple of casevac operations resulted in the driver of a Land Rover being rescued after it had tipped over, the second on the 28th, a five-year-old girl was picked up from her home and rushed to hospital with severe head injuries after falling from overhanging branches. In May a cliff rescue

proved successful when two walkers were winched to safety after slipping off a well-worn cliff path.

On 26 August 1980, Sqn Ldr Nick Hibberd assumed command of the Squadron from Sqn Ldr Mike Chapple.

On Thursday, 23 October 1980, a new Squadron Standard was presented to No.84 Squadron by ACM Sir Keith Williamson KCB AFC, the AOC-in-C, Strike Command. The Parade Commander was Sqn Ldr N R W Hibberd, Officer Commanding No. 84 Squadron. The two flights were commanded by Flt Lts N G Trott and R M Wilson. The Standard Bearers were Flt Lts S Carlton and K D Thomas, the Standard Warrant Officers were Master Air Loadmasters P Lane and E W Ainslie and the escorts were Sergeants H R Patel, D S Lawrence, B K Farrer and G Guest. In attendance were the Administrator, AVM R L Davis, the DCBFC, Air Cdre M R Williams ADC, the Commander Land Forces Cyprus, Col G E V Rochfort-Rae, The Chaplain-in-Chief, the Venerable H J Stuart and the following 'old boys' who had flown out from England on the 21st in a VC.10, together with the RAF College Band, ACM Sir Denis Barnett (CO in 1938), ACM Sir Walter Dawson (Sqn Pilot 1926), Air Cdre Angus A Nicholson (pilot in Greek campaign), Wg Cdr A M Gill (CO in 1942-44), Wg Cdr Peter Norman (CO 1951-52), Sqn Ldr H H Jenkins (CO 1953-55) and Owen Greenwood (1940-42). Doug Jeans (Arthur Gill's engine fitter flew to Cyprus from Australia to attend the ceremony). The old Standard was later laid up in Beaulieu Abbey Church for safe keeping, where it still hangs today.

The next rescue of note took place on 15 January 1981 when XP398 flown by Flt Lts Thomas and Trott and winchman Graham Goosey winched aboard five Syrians from the coaster *Forat Star* which had gone aground at Limassol. On the 29th, Flt Sgt G Goosey (still serving with 84 Sqn in 1992) was awarded the AOC's commendation by the Commander British Forces Cyprus.

Mention was made that 'B' Flight might be moved to Akrotiri, but this had still to be decided three months later. Sqn Ldr Hibberd commented: "The Squadron's future is still in doubt but hopefully this will be resolved within the next few weeks. Meanwhile the last two months have been very quiet".

During May, the Squadron took part in Exercise 'Short Switch', an island wide internal security operation. Sorties were being flown approximately one a day, 34 in April, 39 in May and

XD184 preserved as gate guardian to Akrotiri

Ldr Wedge and Flt Sgt J Lowther were awarded the personal commendation of the AOC-IN-C Strike Command.

On 26 June, a search was carried out for an Army Alouette helicopter which had force-landed after an engine failure. Later, both the aircraft and its pilot were airlifted to safety. The following day, 38 VIPs visited the station. It was recorded that 'lots of bull' were put in for this visit. At the same time the overworked groundcrew changed four engines and a main rotor gearbox.

On 12 July the Annual SNCOs Summer Ball was held at the Nicosia Hilton, followed a week later by the airmens' bi-annual dinner at the same venue. An air reconnaissance was flown on the 22nd when it was suspected that Turkish forces were attempting to advance a few miles west of Nicosia. Three days later, the wife of a detachment engineer officer was rushed to hospital in Akrotiri with labour pains. A baby boy was delivered 53 minutes later. In August, 105 hours were flown, the highest number since August 1974. During the month a Danish soldier was winched to safety from a speedboat off Famagusta.

Reduced flying hours in September (67) helped to avoid serious servicing problems. The fact that many of the Whirlwinds on strength were now nearly ten years old and, even after numerous engine changes, age was beginning to tell. On the 24th, an antennae was replaced on the top of a 50 ft tower at SWEDCON Larnaca. The same day Major-General W R Taylor visited the Squadron to say Farewell on his posting. Other visitors included the Austrian Chief of General Staff and the Canadian Minister of Defence, Mr G La Montaigne. On the 30th the wife of Sgt Flowers was flown to hospital where she gave birth to a son. No sooner had the helicopter returned to Nicosia than another pregnant woman had to be taken to Akrotiri.

In early November, Sgt Risdale was presented with the Long Service and Good Conduct Medal by Air Cdre Williams, the Deputy Commander British Forces Cyprus. This was a particularly busy month with two new pilots arriving for extensive training (one being Flt Lt M Faulkner, later to become the Squadron Commander).

It was learnt that as from 1 January 1981, the United Nations was to cut the Aviation Support budget by £250,000 and reduce the flying hours to 85 per month. On the 26th XP345 made a precautionary landing in a field when the pilot experienced severe vibration. It resulted in an engine change on site with the deployment of military police and guards. The engine change was successfully carried out with all the parts, including the replacement engine arriving by air. The aircraft returned to base 28 hours after the initial landing.

Over the next few months, the following hours were flown: February 37 hours, March 48, April 43.5 which included flying the wife of Flt Lt Mike Faulkner to hospital. It is noted that Mrs Elizabeth Faulkner gave birth to their third son, Christopher, on 7 May. On the 29th, two helicopters were brought to readiness when the call came to rescue six windsurfers who were being blown out to sea. In the event, they were rescued by a Turkish patrol boat. During May a new role was found for the Whirlwind when it was adapted for spraying mosquitoes which had gathered around a ruptured sewage pipe in the middle of a minefield next to the Nicosia's HQ. It proved to be 100% effective.

Two fire-fighting sorties were flown during June when the hot, dry weather caused a fire in scrubland between the two communities. In July it was learnt that a decision had been made to disband 'B' Flight based at Nicosia on 1 March 1982. On 1 August, the AOC awarded Cpl Munton a 'Good Show' award for spotting a fuel leak whilst marshalling an aircraft at night. Tragically on the 4 September, Cpl Munton suffered a cardiac arrest and died very suddenly. A memorial service was held on the 18th which the majority of the flight attended.

During November, XP329 made a precautionary landing when a fire warning light suddenly lit up. It was later found to be a faulty fuse. On the 12th, the UNFICYP Chief of Staff, Air Marshal D W Atkinson, and his party arrived on an informal visit. On Boxing Day, for the first and only time, a woman, who was being flown to TPMH with severe labour pains, gave birth aboard XK396 whilst flying at 1,000 feet above Limassol. The baby was delivered by Lt Col A S B Dixon, the UNFICYP Chief Medical Officer.

What was hoped was going to be a quiet period turned out to be far busier than usual. The problems associated with the introduction of the Wessex coupled with the continued servicing on the Whirlwind added to the groundcrews workload. XK970, which had given excellent service over the years, was flown back to Akrotiri for eventual disposal. During December and January preparations for disbandment were carried out, with buildings and equipment being made ready for handing over. On 2 February 1982, a Whirlwind was scrambled to rescue two Austrians who were in difficulties whilst wind surfing. They were eventually picked up by a Turkish patrol vessel.

On 19 February, a farewell party was held at 'B' Flight with about 100 guests attending, including the Commander of British Forces Cyprus, AVM R Davies and SWEDCON Force Commander Major-General G G Greindle. After farewell speeches, the Force Commander was presented with a 1/32nd scale model of the Westland Whirlwind helicopter. The guests then watched a short flying display by two Whirlwinds and two Wessexes, after which the aircrew were piped in by Cpl C Kirkbride. Seven days later the detachment left Nicosia for the last time. Three aircraft in formation were flown along the entire length of the buffer zone before returning to Akrotiri.

Wessex XS498, fitted with long range tanks, during winching practice

CHAPTER 22 - THE CHANGE TO THE WESSEX

To comply with a Royal Air Force requirement for a general duties helicopter to include the transportation of troops and equipment, casualty evacuation and occasionally for ground attack, Westland Aircraft radically redesigned the original Wessex airframe and replaced the single Gazelle engine with two coupled 1,350 shp Gnome turboshafts in a nose mounting. This effectively doubled the operational capabilities, provided additional safety with one engine out of action and could still maintain cruising performance whilst carrying 16 fully-armed troops.

The original Wessex HC.2s were ordered in 1961, which gives a clear indication just how old 84's 'choppers' were. In fact, XR522, one of the first delivered to the Squadron in December 1982, was built in late 1963 having served with Nos.72 and 78 Squadrons. It had nearly 6,000 flying hours to its credit. Of those which were still being flown by the Squadron, both XT463 and XT479 were amongst a batch built for the Royal Navy in the late sixties.

On 18 December 1981, the first Wessex arrived at Akrotiri. They were flown out from the UK by members of No.72 Squadron led by Wg Cdr A E Ryle. Unfortunately, the planned celebrations were cut short by the news that No.72 Squadron had to return to the UK the same night. During the next few months, Sqn Ldr A J Cann remained with the Squadron supervising conversion and familiarisation courses.

During February, the fifth 'green' Wessex, XV719, was painted bright yellow to match the others. At the same time the playing card symbols were painted on the fins (XR522 Ace of Clubs, XT606 Diamonds, XT675 Spades, XV721 Hearts, XV719 The Joker).

In March, with the need for economy, the two flights were officially amalgamated and based at Akrotiri. The duties of 'B' Flight were taken over by the newly-expanded 'A' flight.

With increases in the workload in support of the UN forces and in the casevac/medevac role, the new look squadron was, with the larger and faster helicopter, able to provide the whole of Cyprus with search and rescue cover.

During the first few months of its service, over 50 calls were made for Medevacs. Whilst a large number of these were from our own military medical branch, the Squadron received calls from both the Greek and Turkish civil authorities.

The Squadron's charter also provided SAR facilities for visiting fighter squadrons, transiting aircraft, the Sovereign Base coastline, the resident British personnel and the civil authorities, as neither the Greeks or the Turks had any facilities of their own.

Amongst the civilian incidents attended were snake bites, scorpion stings, appendicitis, heart and liver cases, divers with 'bends', multiple fractures and poisonings. This does not include the numerous pregnant women who were airlifted to hospital.

An example of the fast and efficient service provided by the Squadron came when the crew of a Canberra abandoned their aircraft. The two-man crew spent a wet three minutes in the Mediterranean before being plucked from the sea. They were in hospital beds eleven minutes after ejection.

A further example was when the Squadron was asked by the civil authorities to answer a 'Mayday' call from the Lebanese coaster *Sirocco*. The crew were abandoning their vessel after the engines failed to maintain the pumps as the old ship was taking on water. As the 15-man crew took to the lifeboats 30 miles west of Paphos, two aircraft of the Squadron arrived overhead and rescued them.

138

Another delivery - but not by stork. Newly-born Leah Hillhouse is ferried to a clinic in Tel Aviv

To round off the year's duties, mention must be made of the VIP role. Over the years, the Squadron had airlifted Archbishop Makarios and Earl Mountbatten of Burma. During 1982, Countess Mountbatten, when visiting the Royal Canadian Horse Artillery, and HRH the Duke of Gloucester, were added to the list of distinguished passengers.

On 24 December 1982, the SS *Uganda* was welcomed into Cyprus waters by a three-helicopter formation of No.84 Squadron. The formation was led by Sqn Ldr Bertie Cann. The second aircraft was flown by Flt Lt Steve Carlton with the Rev Sqn Ldr Lucas, the Church of England padre for Akrotiri as passenger. He had been the padre on the *Uganda* since 1975 and was delighted with his first airborne view of his 'parish'.

1983 proved to be the busiest year since the Turkish invasion in 1974. On 26 February, Sqn Ldr Bob King assumed command of the Squadron from Sqn Ldr N R W Hibberd. His personal comments included: "It was bitterly cold with hail and sleet. Not at all what I expected!".

The Squadron's role with the United Nations Peacekeeping Force was maintained by thrice-weekly flights to the Danish observation posts with food and water and to effect the change-over of personnel every fortnight. Although there were patrol tracks in the very mountainous area, they were often rough and dangerous, especially in winter, necessitating the flying-in of all supplies. During 1983, the Squadron delivered 577,000 lbs of food and water and carried over 1,040 Danish troops. Coupled with these flights, the helicopters carried out troop training exercises with all of the UN contingents. From along the entire buffer zone, the Squadron flew out 18 medical evacuations of UN personnel or their dependents. This did not include the movements of VIPs who were constantly visiting their respective areas.

On 7 September 1963, No.84 Squadron proved to be the 'Pathfinder' by providing the first helicopters to fly in support of the British forces in Lebanon (BRITFORLEB) who were part of the multi-national peacekeeping force. Numerous members of the British Embassy staff in Beirut were evacuated by the two Wessexes on the return leg of that mission. Although a detachment of Chinook helicopters were sent to Akrotiri, 84's Wessexes were the first into Beirut. After the bombing of the American Marine HQ in Beirut which resulted in several hundred deaths, two members of No.84 Squadron were flown into the midst of the fighting where they assisted in the treatment and evacuation of the injured troops.

At the end of the year, on 31 December, 27 sorties were flown in support of BRITFORLEB. Many of these included operations from ships of the Royal Navy, the US Fleet and the French carrier *Foch*. In addition to the normal stand-by commitments by the Squadron, further crews maintained a 24-hour, seven-days-a-week state of readiness.

Other incidents of note during 1983 were the presentation of the Queen's Commendation for Valuable Service in the Air to Sqn Ldr A J Cann for the work he did throughout his tour as the Squadron's Qualified Helicopter Instructor and, in particular, for converting the squadron aircrew to the Wessex helicopter.

During August the MV *Michael Murphy VC* arrived at RAF Akrotiri, having sailed over 3,400 miles from Brightlingsea in Essex. Later that month her trials began in the Air-Sea Rescue role in conjunction with 84's helicopters.

1984

THE YEAR OF THE SCORPION

On 17 January, the Squadron celebrated 12 years continuous service in support of the United Nations force in Cyprus. It was the only RAF Squadron to be able to claim such a distinction. During January the news was received that the Squadron was to be re-equipped with ex-Royal Navy Wessex HU.5s. Despite modification and refurbishment, they were still to be known as Wessex HU.5s. The first two were due to arrive in February, followed by the remainder in May. Later, February was amended to April with no definite date for the others. Further news filtered through that the replacement helicopters were to be camouflaged with a pale blue band indicating their service with the UN. Navaids were also to be upgraded by the introduction of TACAN and OMEGA.

February proved a very busy month. At one stage so many of the 1st Battalion Royal Anglians were being flown from their exercise area in Medevac flights that it was doubtful if there were any left! Three sorties were flown as part of the civil evacuation from Lebanon and 37 people of ten different nationalities were brought from RFA *Reliant* which was at anchor off the coast of Lebanon.

During the month a small party of aircrew and engineers were flown to the UK to visit Westlands to see the modifications under way. It was learnt that the work was not proceeding at the rate required and the proposed delivery date would have to be put back even farther.

Much time and effort was expended on the preparing the submission for the Wilkinson Award of the 'Sword of Peace'. The basis for this bid centred around the great variety of tasks undertaken by the Squadron. Visitors to the Squadron included a party of Chelsea pensioners who enjoyed their flight over the island.

On the UN front, a medal parade was held at the Squadron and seven aircrew were presented with the UN medal by Sqn Ldr Bob King on behalf of the Secretary-General of the United Nations. Nine aircrew paid a liaison visit to the Danish contingent of the UN at Limnitis where the hospitality lasted overnight.

On a cold and wintry afternoon in March, No.84 Squadron duty crew were called out to rescue a Canadian soldier who had been severely injured in an accident on the ski slopes of Troodos. Unfortunately, the nearest helicopter pad on Mt Olympus was at 6,400 feet and the cloudbase was at 5,500ft. The temperature of minus ten degrees prevented the Wessex from landing because of severe icing on the rotor blades. The next lower pad was at 5,800 which also proved impossible. Eventually a landing was made at the village of Trimiklini, where a slight breeze off the mountain enabled the pilot to see the landing pad. Within five minutes of landing the wounded soldier was on his way to hospital.

By the middle of March, Operation 'Pulsator' in Lebanon had been officially completed although the squadron stood by for occasional supply runs to Beirut and the possible evacuation of the remaining British Embassy staff.

On 23 March, one of the Squadron Wessexes added to the flypast flown on the occasion of the BRITCON UN medal parade. A week later, three Wessexes, complete with smoke, were provided for a farewell flypast for the station commander, Group

XT675 delivering supplies to the Danish contingent in the Buffer Zone

Captain J F Willis. The new station commander, Gp Capt A E Ryle, being an ex-Wessex man, had already expressed his interest in flying with the Squadron.

The emphasis during April was heavily on the social side. On the 8th, No.84 Squadron had an Open Day and the Squadron was able to realise a long-standing ambition in getting all of the Squadron wives airborne. Later, the Danish contingent invited many from the Squadron to a barbecue. The following weekend, the Squadron invited the Danes to a party, when many new friendships were made.

The versatility of the Wessex was again proved during May when a crewman was lowered to winch an Egyptian seaman with a suspected fractured skull from a ship 130 miles west of Akrotiri. Shortly afterwards, another crew flew to Beirut (135 miles) to collect a compassionate case from the British Embassy.

Disappointment was felt on the Squadron when it was announced that the submission for the Wilkinson Sword Award had been unsuccessful. However, congratulations were sent to the winners.

The first two replacement Wessexes (XT463 and XS518) arrived on board a Heavylift Air Cargo Belfast transport on 21 June. The two aircraft were unloaded by air movements personnel with the assistance of the Mobile Aircraft Repair Transport and Salvage Unit (MARTSU). XR522 and XT675, the two aircraft they were to replace, were then loaded on to the Belfast for transportation to RAF Sek Kong in Hong Kong.

July 1984 saw the tenth anniversary of the Turkish invasion of Cyprus and the Squadron maintained an extra stand-by commitment in case of trouble.

Throughout August, discussion took place over the preparation of two aircraft for a Royal Flight which the Squadron was expected to perform in October. The choice lay between two of the Squadron's older aircraft which would necessitate 5,500 man-hours of work or the two 'new' aircraft which would need 4,000 man-hours. Eventually the two HU.5s were chosen. In order to do this, the repair teams had a leave ban imposed and the men worked 12-14 hours a day so they would not need to work all weekends.

On 7 August, a premature baby, Leah Hillhouse, was born at the Princess Mary's RAF Hospital. Because the hospital did not have the specialist equipment to ensure her survival (she weighed only 1.2 kgs and had severe respiratory problems), she was flown in an 84 Squadron helicopter to the Beilinson Intensive Care Clinic for Premature Babies at Tel Aviv, Israel. After initial problems, the Israeli authorities proved very helpful.

During August it was learnt that the hours flown in support of the UN was under review. It was eventually decided that the

number of hours was to be fixed at 25, increasing to 30 if the need arose. Preparations for the proposed reunion in October continued with the distribution of jobs to be done. Finally, in August, a happy event was announced when the Squadron's pet scorpion gave birth to six little ones. Bad news followed when their cannibalistic tendencies occurred and they were all eaten by their elders.

On Battle of Britain Sunday, the Squadron Standard was paraded into church and the Standard bearer skillfully avoided hitting the fans - which was more than could be said for the RAF Regiment Standard bearer who managed to ricochet and clatter his Standard off the fans twice, accompanied by some very unchristian words!

October saw the culmination of all the hard work that had gone into preparing the two Wessexes for the Royal Flights. HRH The Duke of Edinburgh was flown from Air House to the UN buffer zone for a visit to the Royal Marines and then back to Akrotiri. Later in the month, the Secretary of State for Foreign Affairs, Mr Geoffrey Howe MP, was flown to President Gemayel's summer residence in the Lebanon for talks.

The highlight of the month was a reunion when a good cross-section of ground and aircrew with ages ranging from the mid-30s to the mid-70s arrived for the festivities. It all started as a casual remark made in late 1983. It had originally been hoped to hold it on 8 April 1984 but commitments made this impossible. A tremendous amount of interest had been shown by some of the old boys and eventually 24 travelled to Akrotiri to join in the celebrations. Amongst those attending were Wg Cdr Harry Guile and his wife, Sqn Ldr George Puddy and his wife (both ex-COs), Mr and Mrs Richard Green (a survivor from the 30s) and an ex-Vengeance pilot, Flt Lt Chris Holbrook and Mrs Holbrook. For six days the celebrations continued, with dinners, barbecues and cocktail parties being laid on with the local dignitaries in attendance. All in all, it was a very worthwhile 'exercise' and a great success.

At the end of the month, Leah Hillhouse, the daughter of Sgt and Mrs J Hillhouse of the Royal Signals, returned to her home at Episkopi. On the 30th, the General Service Medal for Lebanon was presented to six of the aircrew. Once again, the criteria specified meant that few qualified for the award.

November started off with six days of extreme thunderstorms which led to power cuts, floods, waterspouts and vast areas of the island becoming inaccessible. The same month brought the news that a 10% cut in fuel was to be imposed on the Squadron, cutting monthly flying from 125 to 65 hours. In December, haggling continued over the number of hours to be flown and it was eventually agreed that 86 hours per month, the absolute minimum,

Wessex HU.5 XS518 in camouflage

should be allowed. Fuel continued to be a major consideration during January. However, by the end of the month the Squadron was placed in the ridiculous situation of having vast quantities of fuel available which had to be used by the end of February. An extra 200 hours were permitted over and above the original 125. The Squadron were then told as from the 1 March it could expect a 15% reduction until further notice.

In January 1985, the news came that a second pair of replacement Wessexes were being flown out from the UK. They had reached Naples where they were grounded due to engine and gearbox problems. At the end of February they were still there, having had a new engine, main rotor gearbox, new rotor head and new blades fitted in attempts to solve vibration problems. March saw the arrival of the two Wessexes, the first after 47 days and the second ten days later. The latter, XS498, had reached Athens International Airport with severe vibration and a secondary hydraulic pack leak. Eventually a No.84 Squadron detachment was sent to repair the aircraft and it arrived on 19 March. Meanwhile, XT606 and XV721 had left for the UK. In April, the last of the Wessex 5s arrived aboard the MV *Project America*. With a great deal of co-operation, the aircraft was lifted off at once on to a RCL of No.10 Port Sqn and ferried to Akrotiri mole, hauled up the ramp and then towed to the Squadron. There only remained Mk 2 XV719 to pack up and return aboard the MV *Hans Berens*.

At the beginning of May, the Squadron were told that once again two helicopters were to be brought up to Royal Flight standard for the visit of HRH the Duke of Kent. This occurred on the 22nd and the visit went smoothly. During the month a Wessex, equipped with a load of electronic equipment, flew around to measure the radiation hazard from the mass of aerials around Akrotiri. It was on such a flight that Flt Lt Ken McGuire achieved his 4,000 hours on the Wessex.

During the month, Whirlwind XD184 was retrieved from the dump, refurbished and given a fresh coat of yellow paint. It was then mounted in a flying position near the main gate at RAF Akrotiri.

In June, the name of MALM Peter Barwell appeared in the Queen's Birthday Honours List with the award of the Meritorious Service Medal for good, faithful and meritorious service, with irreproachable character and conduct.

July brought welcome news concerning the restriction in flying hours. Initially they were increased to 110 and then towards the end of the month they were restored to the original 125 hours. Two interesting sorties were flown in co-operation with the civil authorities. First a search for a boat which was suspected of being hi-jacked by armed terrorists. The second a clandestine operation to assist the police in arresting two boats from the Lebanon which had made arrangements to pass twelve tons of hashish to another vessel.

During July, it is believed that a record was set for a Wessex task when a seaman was airlifted from his ship 142 miles west of Akrotiri. This was the first time that external overload fuel tanks had been used operationally. The rescue took place at night in a Force 7 gale and navigational assistance was provided by an US Navy Hawkeye aircraft which located the ship and guided the helicopter in. It was believed to be, not only the record non-stop distance but also the longest flight time by a Wessex.

On 23 August 1985, Sqn Ldr Paul Critchley assumed command of No.84 Squadron, Sqn Ldr Bob King returning home to join the Royal Flight at Benson. A month later, on 28

September, the Station held an Open Day when 84's contribution included a winching display and the flying-in of troops for a noisy mock battle. In October, winchman Peter Barwell was presented with his Meritorious Service Medal by Air Cdre Offord.

In early December, a plan was put forward to visit the Lebanon. Sqn Ldr Critchley with his crew of Dai Evans and Frank Haggerty took off to make an overt flight to meet Government forces north of Beirut. Reaching the coast they took some time checking their position; never was the need for long-range navigational aids more obvious. Landing on a road airstrip they were welcomed by members of the Christian forces armed with pistols and ushered into the heavily sand-bagged operations room.

On Christmas Day, the newly arrived Commander, British Forces Cyprus, AVM Ken Hayr, decided he would pay a courtesy call on the troops on the buffer zone. Paul Critchley and his navigator Chris Gibbons spent their Christmas morning performing the honours.

During January, Air Cdre Offord left the island. For his farewell, four Wessexes were flown in a box formation in his honour. Two months later, on 11 March, a dispersal exercise was flown, entailing flying the squadron's helicopters to small landing pads within the airfield perimeter. In May, Sqn Ldr Critchley completed his 4,000 hours on helicopters.

On 3 August 1986, the Station came under attack by a group of terrorists outside the Ladies Mile gate. Families who were on the beach ran for cover as they came under fire. The whole attack was over in a matter of minutes before the terrorists sped off along the beach. Later a claim was made in a Beirut newspaper by the United Nasserite Organisation claiming the attack was a success and that helicopters and transport aircraft had been destroyed. The truth was that one car was damaged and two women were injured by shrapnel. Although a helicopter was scrambled within minutes, no one was arrested. The attack changed the atmosphere of the whole camp and brought to the notice of the authorities how unprepared the Station was.

A 'May Day' message was received on 11 September from a small freighter, the *Liberty I*, stating that she was sinking but that her crew were being picked up by another vessel. A helicopter was scrambled which flew to the scene and brought ashore some of the injured crew. Later, the captain of the ship was interviewed in Limassol hospital and he was convinced that some of his crew had been overlooked. A further flight was flown but it was learnt later that all of the crew had been accounted for.

On 15 October, two helicopters flew on the last two sorties in support of the United Nations troops in Section One on the Green Line. The first, crewed by Sqn Ldr Critchley, Flt Lt Mason and MALM Barwell, carried the Commander, AVM Ken Hayr and the station commander, Gp Capt Colin Addams, whilst the second, crewed by Flt Lt Wilson, Flt Lt Broome and MALM Furness, carried all of the spare air and groundcrew who were available. Later a farewell lunch was organised to commemorate the occasion. The guests included the UN Force Commander, General Greindle and the Commander DANCON Lt Col Schunk.

On 5 November, the duty crew of XS518 was called out in the early hours to collect a pregnant woman from Dekhelia and fly her to Princess Mary's hospital at Akrotiri. Shortly after take-off the helicopter crashed in Limassol Bay. A full Search and Rescue was carried out immediately it was found to be overdue. The pilot was rescued by a fishing boat but the crew of three, Flt Lt Fiona Johnstone, MALM Peter Barwell MSM and Cpl Martin Cook PMRAFNS, were missing presumed dead. The pilot said afterwards that he had had problems closing the main door, as well as difficulties with Air Traffic Control necessitating him flying over the sea. A memorial service was held on the station on 14 November.

During January, the Chief of Air Staff, Air Marshal Sir David Craig CGB OBE ADC MA, talked with members of the Squadron when he visited Akrotiri. Later in the month a 70th Anniversary Open Day was organised. It was followed by an all-ranks guest night with wives. Paul Critchley commented in letters that considering many of the Squadron members had never attended one of these dinners and knew little of what to expect, it went off surprisingly well.

On 20 February, XT479 arrived after a somewhat chequered career at No. 707 Squadron at RNAS Yeovilton before transfer to RAF Wyton for Tacan trials. From there it was due to go to A & AEE at Boscombe Down for further trials. Instead, it was ferried to Cyprus as deck cargo to replace the one lost in November. The following month, the Squadron provided a food distribution service to personnel snowed in at Mount Olympus and villages in the area.

The first trials were carried out on 1 May of the 'Rainmaker',

A Wessex undergoing maintenance in a hangar at Akrotiri

large glass fibre bucket designed to carry water to bush fires. Initial problems were soon ironed out and the attachment soon provided an essential part of the Squadron's equipment. The same month the Squadron provided transportation to HRH The Princess Alexandra who was paying a three day visit to Akrotiri.

During September the Station played host to HRH The Princess Royal. No.84 Squadron had the honour of flying her to Nicosia on the 15th and to Dhekelia the following day. On 4 December, the Squadron held an Open Day for the wives. Flights were arranged and flying suits and 'bonedomes' provided. The same month Flt Lt Paul Todd flew some First Day Covers in aid of the RAF Museum.

In March 1988, a second dispersal exercise was held with half the Squadron being ordered to Dekhelia whilst the remainder stayed at Akrotiri. On 6 May 1988, Sqn Ldr Paul Critchley handed over command of the Squadron to Sqn Ldr Mike Leaming.

During the summer of 1988, No.84 Squadron rehearsed its role with the Lebanese Armed Forces under the command of General Aoun, refuelling from LAF bases and flying with Lebanese liaison officers aboard. Exercises under the name 'Lion Sun' was held regularly in Cyprus. These entailed the deployment of British troops from the UK and Germany for training in Cyprus.

During 1989, Flt Lt Henry Pottle took a group of air and groundcrew on a sailing expedition to southern Turkey. Not quite the voyage of the HMRAFS *Scorpion* but nevertheless a great success.

Over the following months the SAR helicopter was scrambled on numerous occasions in aid of both the local civilian population and the Army and RAF personnel on the island. The Squadron justified its presence on the island during November 1989 when a lorry transporting soldiers of the Coldstream Guards in the Troodos mountains plunged off the road and down a steep ravine. Within minutes, three Wessexes were airborne and five critically injured soldiers were airlifted to the RAF Hospital at Akrotiri after crewmen had administered first-aid. As a result of the Squadron's efforts, a letter was received from the Commanding Officer who

wrote that his battalion would forever be indebted to No.84 Squadron.

In February 1990, a number of squadron personnel were taking advantage of the snow on Mount Olympus when news came through that 84 Squadron had undertaken the rescue of injured passengers and crew from the Beirut-bound ferry, the *Baroness M*. The ferry had been shelled by an unidentified gunboat and was heading back to Larnaca, asking for assistance. At 0652 hours on 24 February, the Rescue Co-ordination Centre Cyprus had received a request from the *Baroness M*, then 30 miles west of the port of Jounieh in the Lebanon, to evacuate casualties.

As the ferry was returning with nine dead and 29 injured, RCCC alerted 84 Squadron, the Princess Mary's hospital and a 201 Squadron Nimrod for a rescue plan to be undertaken at very short notice. At 0840 the first of 84's Wessexes lifted off and was followed by two others at five-minute intervals. The first aircraft was flown by Flt Lt Dick Bardon, Flt Lt Graham Clark and winchman Mark Tait; on board were doctors Sqn Ldr Garth Manning and Flt Lt Steve Scott. The second helicopter was crewed by Flt Lt Kim Best, Flt Lt Bob Lander and MALM Ken Tucker, the third by Flt Lt Dave Holmyard, Flt Lt Pete Ritchie and Flt Lt Paul Todd. At 0925 the first aircraft was above the vessel and the two doctors and the winchman were winched on board. Later, Ken Tucker, a paramedic, and Paul Todd were lowered to assist the doctors by helping to classify the casualties and administer first aid. All casualties were suffering from blast injuries, ranging from superficial shrapnel wounds, head injuries and lower limb fractures. The front lounge of the ferry and several of the cabins had received direct hits and were scenes of devastation. In all, 15 were airlifted from the ferry, 12 by Neil Robertson stretcher, the remainder by winch or bosun's chair. Flt Lt Dick Bardon commented later: "It was a routine deck rescue with no complications".

On 28 March 1990, eight keen past members of the Squadron met in a pub near Bristol and formed 'No.84 Squadron RAF Association'. Owen Greenwood was chosen to be the Association's

142

A Wessex gives a lift to a stricken Alouette

first president; Arthur Gill as Chairman; Sam Crocker the Reunion Organiser; Jack Partington as Secretary and Treasurer, and Doug Weir as News Editor. Harry Guile and Barry Paterson also attended the meeting to give their support. Due to illness, Doug Weir later had to resign from the committee and Barry Paterson volunteered to become the Association's first News Editor. The formation of the Association was officially ratified and the committee officially elected by members at the first annual general meeting held at RAF Brize Norton on 22 September 1990. The aim of the Association, as laid down in the Constitution, is 'To keep alive and to foster the unique spirit of No.84 Squadron and to encourage ex-members of the Squadron, especially the younger members, to keep in touch with their old comrades' and to attend the reunions. Membership of the Association was to be open to all members of No.84 Squadron past and present. The Squadron Commander, Squadron Leader Mike Leaming, was notified of the formation of the Association, gave his blessings and promised his support.

Wg Cdr Leaming, in correspondence, writes, "One occurrence which does stick in my mind during my period as OC was the Army Families Day held in Happy Valley near Episkopi during June 1990. The organiser had asked for a helicopter rescue demonstration as part of the day's activities. We, on the station, were quite surprised when, 15 minutes after the 'chopper' left it came tearing back requesting that a fire bucket be made ready. The actual chain of events is still not clear but it seems that the 'survivor' who was to be rescued let off a flare which ignited a nearby bush. Within seconds the fire had spread in the tinder-dry scrub and was soon beyond the ability of those on the hillside to extinguish it. At that time the helicopter crew thought that it was time to change from demonstration to reality. Eventually two helicopters were needed to bring the fire under control, but not before it had damaged a large area of Happy Valley, which included some of the nearby quarters. I cannot recall whether we were asked back the following year!"

The same month the Squadron provided three helicopters as part of the flypast for the Queen's Birthday Parade held at Episkopi. As a prelude to the flypast, the Squadron put all five Wessexes into the air in formation. This on paper may not seem a problem but to have all the squadron aircraft airborne at the same time spoke a lot for the servicing crews. Amongst visitors to the station were Mr Tom King MP, Secretary of State for Defence, and Paul Jackson who was drafting an article for the RAF Year Book on the duties of No.84 Squadron.

The late summer of 1990 brought a rush of intense scrub fires which raged along the buffer zone. The Squadron picked up water from the Turkish side and flew over the UN buffer zone to 'bomb' the fire on the Greek side. After two days of these activities, the Squadron ended up by dropping water on Greek, Turkish and UN soldiers to keep them cool as they fought the blaze. On the 50th Anniversary of The Battle of Britain and, somewhat curtailed by

the activities of Operation 'Granby', the Squadron provided a lift for the free-fall parachute teams to open the show. Prior to the actual day, the Squadron raised money for the RAF Benevolent Fund by winching some very brave and heavily-sponsored wives out of Limassol Bay.

In October, Sqn Ldr Mike Leaming was invited by the Hellenic Air Force to attend the unveiling of a memorial at Eleusis to the airmen of the RAF and the Hellenic Air Force who had fought and died in the Greek Campaign 1940-41. The memorial, inscribed simply 'All the world is a resting place fit for heroes' is a fitting tribute to those who fought and died during that campaign.

During the month, as the finale to a week's adventure training, the Squadron Commander arranged for two teams to be picked up after a night navigation exercise and flown back by Wessex to the base camp. Unfortunately the flight commander had other ideas. He had arranged for the RAF Regiment to be waiting for them as the teams were dropped off. The teams, which included the Squadron Commander were unceremoniously trussed up, blindfolded and driven around the countryside for hours before being released to walk back to the camp. The Regiment officer in charge was quite non-plussed when the CO arrived back at camp, footsore and fuming. He had thought that it was the Squadron Commander's idea in the first place. Mike Leaming writes: "I still have to get my revenge on the flight commander!" Another effort by the squadron personnel for raising money for charity was leap-frogging the entire 6,000-foot length of the Akrotiri runway, all wearing red noses (as was the Victor tanker which overshot the runway to allow the men to complete their task).

Security of the base was still one of 84 Squadron's responsibilities. Ground patrols from No.34 Squadron RAF Regiment were flown to dropping-off points and later retrieved after their mission had ended. Similar operations involving troops and the locally-employed Cypriot policemen who set up check points in the hope of catching the occasional smuggler, are undertaken for the local authorities.

In the early months of 1991, the Squadron's diverse flying jobs included picking up a couple of Phantom crews who had bailed out over the sea and searching for, and finding half a million pounds worth of cannabis in the area. The year also brought to new OC to 84 Squadron, when Sqn Ldr Hugh Pierce assumed command from Sqn Ldr Mike Leaming. The strength of No.84 Squadron at that time numbered 50 serving men. Thirteen were officers and NCO aircrews, including the Squadron Commander. There were 12 airframe, seven engine and four dual-trade fitters, four electricians, four communications experts, two safety equipment operators and an adjutant. Added to this number were the wives and children, making a family of nearly 150.

In March 1991, it was proposed by the committee of the No. 84 Squadron Association that their members should visit the Squadron in Cyprus in May 1992 to help the Squadron celebrate its 75th Anniversary. Unfortunately, Sqn Ldr Hugh Pierce, after starting the ball rolling, relinquished his command in early December for personal and family reasons. Sqn Ldr Mike Faulkner assumed command on 5 December 1991.

During the latter months of 1991, a number of visits were made by senior officers, including the Chief of Air Staff, Air Chief Marshal Sir Peter Harding GCB ADC DSc FRAeS CBIM. It also involved the carriage of HRH The Princess Royal to Dekhelia and back which entailed a month of preparation and hard work by the engineers to bring the two helicopters up to VIP standard. The Royal flights were carried out exactly on time, despite an unserviceable aircraft on the return leg. So smooth was the flying that rumour has it the Princess Royal nodded off on both trips!.

An achievement of note was the award of an 'A' category to MALM Graham Goosey, signifying his excellence as a winchman. His award was a great credit to the Squadron as there was only one other 'A' category winchman in the whole of the RAF SAR force. One of the highlights in the period was undoubtedly the presentation of a sheep to Flt Lt Frank Haggerty. The story goes that Frank and his crew were involved in some deck winching practice with some of the commercial shipping that passes the Akrotiri peninsula. On this occasion Flt Lt Haggerty was winched down on to an Arabian vessel transporting sheep to Beirut. The captain of the vessel was most friendly to Frank with a great deal of traditional kissing on greeting. When the time came to leave, the captain insisted that Frank accepted a sheep as a gift! He was naturally unable to refuse and in due course the sheep was winched aboard. Needless to say the sheep did not appreciate this treatment and left his 'calling card' all over the floor of the helicopter. On return to Akrotiri, the Customs were rather upset over the illegal importation of the sheep, with the result that it had to be

A Wessex of No. 84 Squadron visits HMS Invincible *in October 1991*

13 May 1986. Sqn Ldr Paul Critchley reaches 4,000 hours on the Wessex.
Right to left: Whitehead, Jones, S Mason, F Haggerty, Gp Capt Colin Adams, Paul Critchley, C Gibbons, Dai Evans, unidentified, Wg Cdr Pat Herbert

slaughtered. However, the Squadron fund benefited by £20.00.

1992 started cold and wet in surprisingly untypical weather. It also meant the airlifting of supplies into Mount Olympus radar station which was snowed-in. February and March gave the Squadron a chance to have a larger than normal presence in the annual Pink Flamingo Exercise.

In April, HRH Prince Michael of Kent visited the station. The same month heralded the start of the 75th Anniversary celebrations. On 29 April, 57 members of No.84 Squadron Association and their wives led by their Chairman, Wg Cdr Arthur Gill, flew from the UK to Cyprus. On arrival at their hotel at Limassol they were welcomed by Sqn Ldr Mike Faulkner. On the Friday evening, the Squadron entertained the party at a local Greek taverna. On arrival, every member of 84 Squadron rose and applauded the guests, an unexpected and moving tribute to the 'old boys'. For the next week they were the guests of the Squadron. An Open Day was followed by the presentation to the Squadron of two oil paintings depicting its most famous son, Captain A W Beauchamp Proctor 'dog fighting' with the enemy. Session followed session, accompanied by the station 'German Oompah Band'. It was indeed an occasion to remember.

Owen Greenwood, the Squadron Association's first president, died on 1 November 1991 aged 81. He had joined the Royal Air Force in early 1938, having worked for a stock-broker in the City of London after leaving school, trained as an armourer and served with 84 at Shaibah from January 1940 until he became a Japanese prisoner-of-war in Java in 1942. Fortunately he was one of the few to survive. From 1946, for 30 years he organised the annual post-war reunions of 84 Squadron members. The Squadron and past members owe much to his unstinting hard work and dedication in trying to keep them together. He fitted in so well in any surroundings and in any company - from princes to paupers. In the early days it was not uncommon to see half a dozen Air Marshals chatting and laughing with the younger members about their fascinating adventures with '84' in the 'good old days'; such distinguished figures as MRAF Lord Douglas of Kirtleside, ACM Sir Francis Fogarty, ACM Sir Denis Barnett, ACM Sir Walter Dawson, AM Sir Richard Peck, AM Sir Hugh Saunders, AVM Stanley Vincent and Air Cdre Vernon Brown.

It had been my original intention to end the history of No.84 Squadron to date with the Squadron's 75th Anniversary celebrations. However, over the last few months two incidents of note have brought the fame of 84 to the fore in the national newspapers.

On the morning of Wednesday 4 November 1992, the Lebanese Government requested assistance in fighting fires which were rapidly enveloping the cedar-clad mountains to the north and east of the capital, Beirut. It was decided to send one Wessex complete with a Sims 'Rainmaker' which can hold 150 gallons of water, with two aircrews and engineering and logistic back-up; a total of 17 personnel. That evening HMAV *Arromanches* left Cyprus complete with fire buckets, a fuel bowser, engineering supplies, a four-ton truck, a Land Rover, camp beds and sleeping bags. By now the operation had a name and Operation 'Lacrimosa' was under way.

The helicopter departure time was carefully planned to coincide with the arrival of the support personnel aboard the *Arromanches*. The deployment site chosen was the Lebanese Armed Forces base at Jounie, 5 miles north of Beirut. Any apprehension about visiting Lebanon was quickly dispelled when the crews saw the size of the reception party. the British Ambassador and the Admiral of the Lebanese Navy along with many members of the media. After an initial recce, the crew returned to connect up the bucket and deliver the first load of water. Flying continued over the next six hours, and during that time, two large fires were extinguished in the mountains which were inaccessible to those on the ground. By the middle of the Friday afternoon the Civil Defence authorities announced that they had the situation under control. Later the crews were stood down and prepared to return to Akrotiri which they reached in time for Sunday lunch. In that short but interesting operation. 45,000 gallons of water were dropped on the Lebanon.

On 21 January 1993, Britain were requested by the International Committee of the Red Cross to evacuate mistakenly-deported Palestinians back to Israel and take those requiring urgent medical attention to hospital. Friday saw HQ British Forces Cyprus, 84 Squadron and other units at RAF Akrotiri in a hive of activity. Crews were briefed and aircraft were hurriedly painted with large red crosses on three panels of the fuselage. The arrival at Haifa after a 100-minute flight was marred only by industrial smoke which obscured the runway. The reception team was efficient and Operation 'Befriend' was under way. The destination was the camp in the Beka'a Valley, overlooked by the snow-covered Golan Heights. Landing on a nearby road, the two helicopters off-loaded the Red Cross team, medical supplies and mail and returned to Haifa. Eventually word came through that clearance for the sick was imminent but so was the prospect of having to carry out the rescue by night. The order came that the ambulance helicopters were to proceed.

At the camp they found a seething mass of cameramen and deportees being controlled by a single ICRC represent-ative. Surrounded by deportees kneeling in prayer, the crew had to physically ease the crowd back before they could take off. The first rescue aircraft departed with its passengers and headed south. The second and third helicopters met similar chaotic scenes. The last 13 deportees and ICRC members left for Haifa just as dusk was descending. The final radio message "Cyprus Flight Watch, this is Rescue 50 Combine. Task Complete" signalled the end of another episode in the Squadron's history. Later the head of the ICRC delegation to Israel described the Squadron's role as fundamental to the success of the mission and he praised the professional expertise and the seriousness of the crews throughout the operation. The three crews, led by the OC, Sqn Ldr Mike Faulkner, consisted of the following, Flt Lts Tony Dewhurst, Ian Marston, Phil Boothby, Ian McFarlane, and Frank Haggerty, MALM Keith Edwards and Sgts Mark Stevens and Mark O'Leary with Fg Off Guy Hallam as reserve pilot.

From the last chapters it will be seen that, although the base at Akrotiri is one of the more pleasant RAF stations, many of the operations are far from easy. So long as British Forces are stationed on Cyprus, with continuous flying training visits and aircraft passing through in transit, there will always be a major operational role for the Squadron.

My story ends here. Thank You 84, it has been a real pleasure getting to know you.

Presentation of the United Nations Medal 9 February 1984
Right to left: Sqn Ldr R F King, Flt Lt K McGuire, R Farley, M Hurrell, Flt Lt C Gibbons, Flt Sgt D Lloyd, MALM T Freeman, FO Neil Macdonnell

APPENDIX 1

No. 84 SQUADRON COMMANDING OFFICERS

Major H R Nicholl (later AVM Sir Hazleton Nicholl KBE CB)	15 Feb	1917
Major W Sholto Douglas (later MRAF Lord Douglas of Kirtleside GCB MC DFC)	10 Aug	1917
Major G E M Pickthorne MC	18 Nov	1918
Captain C M Crowe MC DFC	13 Jul	1919
Sqn Ldr B L Huskisson DSO DCM (later Commodore RN)	2 May	1920
Sqn Ldr W Sowrey AFC (later Air Cdre CBE DFC AFC)	1 Oct	1921
Sqn Ldr V S Brown (later Hon Air Cdre Sir Vernon Brown Kt CB OBE)	6 May	1922
Sqn Ldr E D Atkinson DFC AFC	18 Feb	1924
Sqn Ldr R H Peck OBE (later AM Sir Richard Peck KCB OBE)	10 May	1924
Sqn Ldr D E Stodart DSO DFC	2 Nov	1924
Sqn Ldr W B Farrington DSO (later Gp Capt)	8 May	1925
Sqn Ldr D E Stodart DSO DFC	13 Dec	1925
Sqn Ldr F J Vincent AFC (later Air Cdre CBE DFC)	5 May	1927
Sqn Ldr J J Breen (later Air Marshal CB OBE)	22 Oct	1928
Sqn Ldr H Stewart	30 Oct	1929
Sqn Ldr R C Hardstaff (later Wg Cdr)	12 Jan	1931
Sqn Ldr P L Plant	13 Sep	1932
Sqn Ldr S F Vincent (later AVM CB DFC AFC)	26 May	1933
Sqn Ldr F J Fogarty DFC AFC (later ACM Sir Francis Fogarty CBE KCB DFC AFC)	21 Feb	1935
Sqn Ldr C H A Stevens (later Gp Capt OBE)	12 May	1937
Sqn Ldr D H F Barnett (later ACM Sir Denis Barnett GCB CBE DFC MA)	14 Apr	1938
Sqn Ldr D L Thomson (later Air Cdre DSO DFC)	21 Nov	1938

Sqn Ldr D G Lewis (later Air Cdre DFC)	28 Jan	1940
Sqn Ldr H D Jones	1 Mar	1941
Sqn Ldr W T Russell (later Wg Cdr)	19 Apr	1941
Wg Cdr C D C Boyce (later AVM CB CBE)	31 Aug	1941
Wg Cdr J R Jeudwine (later Gp Capt DSO OBE DFC)	11 Jan	1942
Sqn Ldr A M Gill (later Wg Cdr OBE DFC AE)	30 Apr	1942
Flt Lt G R Plumb	25 Sep	1944
Wg Cdr I L B Aitkens	28 Oct	1944
Wg Cdr R E Jay	12 Nov	1944
Wg Cdr M H Constable-Maxwell DSO DFC MA	8 Jun	1945
Wg Cdr F Gomersall OBE	9 Dec	1946
Sqn Ldr M J Gloster DFC	15 Sep	1947
Sqn Ldr D R Turley-George DFC	15 Nov	1947
Sqn Ldr G T Dodgshun	10 Feb	1948
Sqn Ldr S G Nunn OBE DFC AE (later Gp Capt)	25 Oct	1948
Sqn Ldr G C Unwin DFM (later Wg Cdr DSO DFM)	16 Sep	1949
Sqn Ldr A P Norman DFC (later Wg Cdr)	4 Aug	1951
Sqn Ldr L L Johnston DSO	15 Jul	1952
Sqn Ldr H H Jenkins	20 Feb	1953
Sqn Ldr J H Dunn	31 Oct	1954
Sqn Ldr F L Spencer	26 Sep	1956
Sqn Ldr K R Bowhill OBE BA (later Wg Cdr)	28 Dec	1956
Sqn Ldr E W Talbot DFC and bar (later Wg Cdr)	28 Apr	1957
Sqn Ldr H W Guile (later Wg Cdr)	18 Jun	1958
Sqn Ldr K H Perry DSO AFC	9 Sep	1960
Sqn Ldr K J Parfit (later Gp Capt)	21 Sep	1962
Sqn Ldr R J Barnden (later Gp Capt)	14 Oct	1964
Sqn Ldr S Hitchen AFC (later Wg Cdr)	24 Oct	1966
Sqn Ldr A E Radnor (later Wg Cdr)	31 Oct	1967
Sqn Ldr D S Gates	4 Sep	1968
Sqn Ldr I G C Chalmers (later Wg Cdr)	22 Oct	1969
Sqn Ldr A B Stephens BA (later Gp Capt)	20 Nov	1970
Sqn Ldr D R Ikin	20 Dec	1970
Sqn Ldr G S Puddy AFC	17 Jan	1972
Sqn Ldr L Banham MBE	29 Apr	1974
Sqn Ldr S M St C Collins MBE	16 Dec	1976
Sqn Ldr M W P Chapple AFC (later Wg Cdr)	15 Jan	1979
Sqn Ldr N R W Hibberd	26 Aug	1980
Sqn Ldr R F King	25 Feb	1983
Sqn Ldr P G Critchley	19 Aug	1985
Sqn Ldr M W Leeming BSc	2 May	1988
Sqn Ldr H R Pierce BA	7 Jan	1991
Sqn Ldr M Faulkner BA	5 Dec	1991

Shaibah

APPENDIX II

STATIONS

	Jan	1917	Founded at Beaulieu, Hants.; nucleus from No. 16 Reserve Squadron
22	Mar	1917	To Lilbourne
23	Sep	1917	To Liettres
12	Nov	1917	To Le Hameau
29	Dec	1917	To Flez
22	Mar	1918	To Champien
23	Mar	1918	To Vert Galand
28	Mar	1918	To Conteville
4	Apr	1918	To Bertangles
8	Sep	1918	To Assevillers
8	Oct	1918	To Bouvincourt
25	Oct	1918	To Bertry West
3	Dec	1918	To Thuilles
13	May	1919	To Bickendorf
6	Jul	1919	To Eil
12	Aug	1919	To Tangmere as a cadre
8	Oct	1919	To Croydon
	Jan	1920	to Kenley
30	Jan	1920	Disbanded
13	Aug	1920	Ref at Baghdad West
20	Sep	1920	To Shaibah - dets at Baghdad West, Nasiriyah, Bushire
	Feb	1939	Dets Sharjah
24	Sep	1940	To Heliopolis- dets at Fuka, Qotafiyah, Tatoi
16	Nov	1940	To Menidi - det Paramythia
	Apr	1941	To Heraklion
	Apr	1941	To Heliopolis

26	Apr	1941	To Aqir - dets Habbaniyah, H4
24	May	1941	To Habbaniya
7	Jun	1941	To Mosul - det Shaibah
27	Sep	1941	To Habbaniya - dets Aqir, Amiriya
9	Nov	1941	To Amiriya
25	Nov	1941	To LG 116
26	Nov	1941	To LG 75
18	Dec	1941	To Gambut
2	Jan	1942	To Heliopolis
14	Jan	1942	En route FE
23	Jan	1942	P.1 Palembang
26	Jan	1942	P.2
16	Feb	1942	To Kalidjati
1	Mar	1942	Sqn dispersed
18	Mar	1942	Re-established at Drigh Rd
3	Jun	1942	To Quetta
17	Nov	1942	To Vizagapatam
13	Jan	1943	To Cholavaram
8	Apr	1943	To Ratmalana - det Yelahanka
28	Aug	1943	To Ranchi - det Drigh Rd
7	Dec	1943	To Maharajpur
10	Feb	1944	To Khumbirgram
22	Jul	1944	To Samungli
31	Oct	1944	To Yelahanka
23	Apr	1945	To Chharra - det St Thomas Mount
2	Sep	1945	To Baigachi
10	Sep	1945	To Hwambi
12	Sep	1945	To Kallang
22	Sep	1945	To Seletar - dets Kemajoram, Soerabaya

16 Jan	1946	To Kemajoram
21 May	1946	To Kuala Lumpur
11 Sep	1946	To Seletar
26 Sep	1947	To Changi
1 Feb	1948	To Tengah - det Kuala Lumpur
11 Oct	1948	En route ME
28 Nov	1948	To Habbaniya
Mar	1950	Det Mogadishu
8 Apr	1950	To Tengah
20 Feb	1953	Squadron disbanded
20 Feb	1953	Ref at Fayid; No. 204 Sqn renumbered
3 Dec	1955	To Abu Sueir

11 Mar 1956	To Nicosia
31 Dec 1956	Squadron disbanded
31 Dec 1956	Ref at Khormaksar - Aden Protectorate and Communications Squadron renumbered
3 Dec 1967	To Sharjah
30 Dec 1970	To Muharraq
1 Oct 1971	Squadron disbanded
17 Jan 1972	Ref at Akrotiri from No. 1536 Flight and a detachment from No. 230 Sqn
Jan 1972	Det Nicosia
Mar 1982	Both flights now based at Akrotiri

APPENDIX III

SHAIBAH BLUES

(Verses sung to the tune of 'A little bit of heaven'

Sure a little bit of mhutti fell
  From out the sky one day
And it nestled in the ocean
  In a spot 3,000 miles away
And when the Air Force saw it
  Sure it looked so bleak and bare
They said,"Thats what we're looking for,
  We'll build our station there.

So they sent our river gunboats
  Armoured cars and AHQ
And they sent the 'Famous Eighty Four'
  Way out there in the blue
But pichi I'll be going

To a land that's far remote
And until then you'll hear me say
  'Roll on that bloomin' boat'.

I've got those Shaibah Blues, Shaibah Blues
  I'me fed up and I'me brassed off and I'me browned
I've been living here for close upon three year
  And I wish I was in my coffin underground
I've tried to learn the lingo, but it fairly got my goat
  The only words that I know are 'Roll on that bloomin' boat
I've got those Shaibah Blues, Shaibah Blues
  I'me fed up and I'me brassed off and I'me browned..

I am assured by members in the know that this is the only version suitable for publishing.

D.H.9As preparing for a raid, Shaibah, 1 April 1928 (via A Thomas)

D.H.9A J7021 of No.84 Squadron

APPENDIX IV

Aircraft used by No.84 Squadron

S.E.5, S.E.5A

A4563, A4851, A8342, A8904, A8942, A8946, B1, B45, B120, B156, B524, B527, B539, B546, B558, B559, B560, B561, B562, B564, B566, B568, B569, B571, B579, B597, B612, B627, B631, B638, B675, B682, B699, B4853, B4865, B4866, B4872, B4874, B4876, B4886, B4894, B5463, B6410, B8010, B8233, B8272, B8337, B8399, B8403, B8408, B8420, B8491, C156, C259, C1075, C1077, C1084, C1097, C1694, C1772, C1794, C1834, C1868, C1871, C1874, C1911, C5303, C5310, C5313, C5314, C5324, C5326, C5329, C5333, C5335, C5346, C5364, C5384, C5399, C5400, C6410, C6430, C6442, C6449, C6455, C6457, C6465, C6490, C6496, C8693, C8719, C8732, C8895, C9039, C9263, C9267, C9500, C9519, C9869, D259, D260, D270, D276, D333, D6149, D6856, D6857, D6882, D6890, D6897, D6906, D6914, D6917, D6920, D6926, D6928, D6980, D6987, D8223, E4012, E4071, E5073, E5937, E5963, E6008, E6024, E6429, F855, F904, F5477, F5489, F5625, F6420, H685

Westland Wapiti

J9078, J9079, J9080 (Heart, later Diamond marking), J9081, J9085, J9086, J9087, J9088, J9089, J9090, J9091, J9092, J9097, J9098, J9099, J9100, J9408, J9413, J9488, J9514, J9592, J9594, J9619, J9635, J9835, J9838, J9839, J9840,

J9844, J9849, J9850, J9851, J9852, J9853 (Joker on tail), J9854, K1127, K1135 (Spade on tailplane), K1130 (Diamond on tailplane), K1405, K1407, K1408

Vickers Vincent

K4106, K4107, K4108, K4109, K4110, K4111, K4112, K4113, K4114, K4115, K4116, K4117, K4118, K4119, K4120, K4121, K4122, K4123, K4124, K4125, K4126, K6338, K6339, K6340, K6341, K6342, K6343, K6344, K6345, K6346, K6358

Bristol Blenheim I

L1378, L1379, L1380, L1381, L1382, L1383, L1384, L1385, L1386, L1387, L1389, L1390, L1391, L1392, L1393, L1394, L1395, L1396, L1432, L1434, L1535, L1536, L4819, L4833, L4834, L4835, L4878, L6662, L8362, L8374, L8452, L8453, L8454, L8455, L8457, L8467, L8468, L8469, L8471, L8474, L8501, L8510, L8511, L8513, L8514, L8537,

Bristol Blenheim IV

L9216, L9230, L9335, L9342, N3532, N3539, T1872, T2063, T2116, T2340, T2382, T2394, T2427, V5425, V5422, V5443, V5445, V5578, V5579, V5581, V5629,

V6094, V6229, V5892, V5893, V5840, V5850, V5897, V5505, V5860, V5861, V5791, V5897, V5891, Z5865, Z5893, Z5891, Z5892, Z5981, Z9577

Vultee Vengeance

AN917, AN900, EZ875, AN939, AN992, AN945, AN948, AN706, AN934, AN713, AN739 (F), AN669, AN944, FB954, FB944, FB981, FB962, AN975 (F), AP137 (Y), EZ801 (A *Queen of Shaibah III*), AP131 (X), AN958 (E), AN996 (D), AP106 (C), EZ833 (W), AP113

Also used Supermarine Spitfire Vc MA290 *The Looker*

De Havilland Mosquito

Mosquito FB.VI: HR526 (B), HR523, HR530, HR438, HR547, HR553, HR561 (R), HR565 (R), HR567 (A), HR583, HR628 (F), HR634, HR635, HR617, HR638, HR630, LR311 (D), RF 656 (U), RF689 (W), RF696 (F), RF943 (H), RF698 (C), RF726 (P), RF766 (A), RF955 (S), RF759 (F), RF961 (T), RF942, RF960, TA478 (K), TA487 (X), TA447 (J), TA497 (X), TA137 (C), TE604, TE618, TE607 (F), TE667 (X and C), TE601 (Q), TE616, TE617, TE749, TE699, TE618.

Mosquito PR.34: RG124, RG132.

Also used;
Airspeed Oxford; NM424, NM455, NM465, NM470, LX768.

North American Harvard; FT193, FE473.

The Squadron coding PY was not painted on every aircraft. It is believed that the number of Mosquitos used by the Squadron were far in excess of those numbered. All of the above serials are either visible on photographs or mentioned in log books.

Bristol Beaufighter

RD744, RD761, RD774, RD770 (A), RD786, RD801, RD803, RD804, RD816, RD818, RD822 (D), RD824, RD826, RD819, RD836, RD857, RD858.

Also used North American Harvard; FS845, FX483, KF636.

Photographs show that many of No. 84 Squadron's Beaufighters were not painted with either Squadron or single letter codes. They also show, on occasion, aircraft were flown belonging to No. 45 Sqdn (OB).

Bristol Brigand

RH750, RH755, RH756, RH761, RH776 (K Spade on fin), RH785 (E Club on fin), RH792, RH796, RH798 (J Heart on fin), RH801, RH804, RH809, RH810 (C), RH811 (G), RH812 (B), RH813 (C), RH814 (H), RH815 (E), RH816(A), RH817 (A), RH818 (B), RH823 (R Heart on fin), RH826, RH828 (K), RH831 (H Heart on fin), RH832, RH844, VS812, VS823, VS832, VS836 (D Club on fin), VS851, VS854 (G Diamond on fin), VS861 (B Club on fin), VS865, VS868 (A Club on fin), VS869, WB236 (K)

Also used:
Bristol Buckmaster; RP194, RP198, RP233, RP235.
North American Harvard; FS845, FS854, FX476, KF103, KF350

Vickers Valetta C.1

VW140, VW141, VW154, VW155, VW157, VW162, VW165, VW184, VW186, VW192, VW196, VW200, VW202, VW803, VW818, VW821, VW826, VW832, VW829, VW837, VW836, VW841, VW845, VW847, VW851, VW860, VX506, VX579

Also used Valetta T.3; WG257

Blackburn Beverley

XM105 (E), XM106 (R,H,X,S), XM107 (S,R), XM108 (T), XM109 (U,R), XM110 (V), XM111 (W,D), XM112 (V), XB266 (X,V), XL151 (L), XL150, XH121 (Z), XL149 (X), XM103 (U), XH120, XB284 (H), XL130 (Y), XH122

Hawker-Siddeley Andover C.1

XS595 (A), XS641 (B), XS642 (C), XS643 (D), XS645 (E), XS646 (F)

Westland Whirlwind HAR.10

XD184 (Spade), XJ437 (Heart/diamond), XK386 (N), XJ764 (Diamond), XK970 (P, 3, Club), XK986 (U, 5), XP398 (Heart), XR454 (Diamond), XP329 (V, 4), XL110 (T), XP346, XP345 (N, 2)

Westland Wessex HC.2

XT675 (Spade), XR522 (Club), XV721 (Heart), XT606 (Diamond), XV719 (The Joker)

Westland Wessex HU.5

XS417 (Diamond), XS485 (Heart), XS498 (The Joker), XS518 (Spade), XT463 (Club), XT479 (Spade)

D.H.9A E8650 crumples its undercarriage

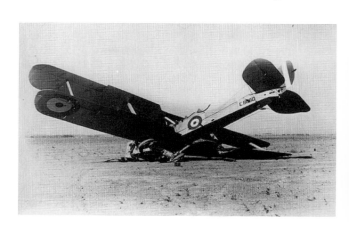

APPENDIX V

No.84 SQUADRON VICTORIES

The following list was kindly compiled by Gordon Page from records held by the Public Record Office. Contemporary abbreviations used are BU = Broke up in air; COL = Crashed on landing; DD = Driven down; FTL = Forced to land; KB = Kite Balloon; OOC = out of control. C, after Albatross, DFW and LVG = two-seater but exact mark not recognised.

21.10.17 B562 Albatros D.III OOC Gheluvelt 08.52 (Capt J M Child)

21.10.17 B4866 Albatros D.III OOC Roulers 14.10 (2/Lt P J Maloney)

21.10.17 B4874 Red & yellow 2-str OOC E of Roulers-Menin road 14.40 (Capt K Leask)

31.10.17 B4853 Albatros D.V probably OOC Menin 14.50-15.40 (Lt J S Ralston)

31.10.17 B579 Albatros D.V probably OOC Menin 14.50-15.40 (Capt K Leask)

8.11.17 B562 Albatros D.V OOC E of Poelcappelle 14.15, shared B513 (Capt J M Child)

8.11.17 B513 same (Lt F E Brown)

22.11.17 B4886 KB in flames N of Bourlon Wood 08.50 (Capt E R Pennell)

22.11.17 B562 Albatros D.V OOC E of Bourlon Wood & green DFW C.V in British lines nr Flesquières 11.45 (Capt J M Child)

26.11.17 B559 Albatros D.V OOC Fonsomme 08.00 (2/Lt W H Brown)

26.11.17 B612 Albatros D.V in vertical dive with engine full on Fonsomme 08.00 (Lt J F Larson)

30.11.17 B4886 DFW C OOC N of Honnecourt 10.00 (Capt E R Pennell)

30.11.17 B4865 DFW C OOC N of Honnecourt 10.00 (2/Lt C T Travers) [appears to be B4886's victory shared]

30.11.17 B637 Albatros D.V FTL SE of Gouzeaucourt 14.30 (Capt K Leask)

6.12.17 C5310 2-str OOC Cambrai 14.30, shared Lt R A Grosvenor, 2/Lt H A Payne & 2/Lt T G Jackson (Lt J S Ralston)

12.12.17 B637 2-str DD damaged believed crashed Hendecourt 13.45 (Capt K Leask)

23.12.17 C5310 2-str OOC St.Quentin 13.00 (Lt J S Ralston)

23.12.17 B4886 Albatros C OOC N of St.Quentin 13.00, shared B559 (Capt E R Pennell)

23.12.17 B559 same (2/Lt W H Brown)

3.1.18 A8942 2-str in flames 3m NE of St.Quentin 15.00 (Lt J F Larson)

3.1.18 B539 2-str OOC N of St.Quentin 15.00 (2/Lt A F W Beauchamp Proctor)

13.1.18 B4886 2-str OOC Bentouzelle 10.25 (Capt E R Pennell)

13.1.18 C5310 2-str crashed Crèvecoeur 11.15 (Lt J S Ralston)

13.1.18 A4563 Red 2-str crashed NW of Graincourt 11.30 (2/Lt J V Sorsoleil)

13.1.18 A4851 2-str OOC Masnières 13.1.18 (2/Lt H A Payne)

25.1.18 C5333 2-str in flames Malincourt 14.40 (2/Lt E O Krohn)

25.1.18 C9500 2-str possibly OOC Malincourt 14.40 (2/Lt H W L Saunders)

29.1.18 B627 2-str in flames SE of Bellicourt 13.25 (2/Lt E A Clear)

30.1.18 C5310 Scout OOC S of Cambrai 11.45 (2/Lt J A McCudden)

30.1.18 B637 Albatros D.V OOC Villers Outreaux 11.45 & KB DD damaged 12.10 (Capt K Leask)

30.1.18 C5310 Rumpler C OOC Le Câtelat 15.45 (2/Lt J A McCudden)

15.2.18 B539 Rumpler C probably crashed nr Bellicourt 15.45, shared C5310 (2/Lt A F W Beauchamp Proctor)

15.2.18 C5310 as above (2/Lt J A McCudden)

16.2.18 C5310 Rumpler C crashed St.Quentin 09.40 (2/Lt J A McCudden)

16.2.18 A4563 Albatros D.V in flames St.Quentin 09.40 (2/Lt J C Sorsoleil)

16.2.18 A8942 Albatros D.V OOC La Fère 10.20 (Lt J F Larson)

16.2.18 C5346 2 Albatros D.V OOC St.Quentin & 1-str crashed N of La Fère 10.30-11.10 (Capt F E Brown)

16.2.18 C5313 Albatros D.V crashed SE of St.Quentin 11.15 (Lt G O Johnson)

17.2.18 B4886 2-str OOC NE of St.Gobain 10.00 (2/Lt C T Travers)

17.2.18 B539 Albatros D.V OOC E of St.Quentin 10.45 (2/Lt A F W Beauchamp Proctor)

17.2.18 C5310 Fokker Dr.I crashed NE of St.Quentin 11.15 (2/Lt J A McCudden)

18.2.18 C5346 Albatros D.V OOC SE of Beaurevoir 11.00 (Lt G O Johnson)

18.2.18 B527 2-str OOC 5m E of St.Quentin 11.00 (Capt R A Grosvenor)

18.2.18 A8942 Albatros DD E of St.Quentin 11.00 (Lt J Larson)

18.2.18 C5313 Albatros D.V OOC Beaurevoir 11.00 (Lt P K Hobson)

18.2.18 C5303 2-str OOC Beaurevoir 11.00 (2/Lt C L Stubbs)

18.2.18 C9500 LVG C OOC Beaurevoir 11.00 (2/Lt H W L Saunders)

19.2.18 B539 Albatros D.V crashed St.Gobain 10.10 (2/Lt A F W Beauchamp Proctor)

19.2.18 A4563 2 Albatros D.V crashed St.Gobain woods & 1 Albatros D.V OOC N of St.Gobain woods 10.15 (2/Lt J V Sorsoleil)

19.2.18 A8942 Albatros DD E of La Fère 10.15 (Lt J F Larson)

19.2.18 C5310 Albatros D.V crashed N of La Fère 10.15 & another OOC St.Gobain woods 10.20 (2/Lt J A McCudden)

19.2.18 B527 2-str crashed, then Albatros D.V crashed, both St.Gobain woods 10.30 (Capt R A Grosvenor)

28.2.18 B539 Pfalz D.III OOC SE of La Fère 16.20 (2/Lt A F W Beauchamp Proctor)

6.3.18 B637 Albatros D.V OOC Renensart 09.40 (Capt K Leask)

10.3.18 C5326 2-str FTL W of Estrées & crashed 14.20 (Lt E A Clear)

10.3.18 C5384 2-str OOC with observer killed Bellicourt 14.20 (2/Lt W H Brown)

11.3.18 C5346 Albatros D.V crashed La Vergies 10.40, shared B699 (Capt F E Brown)

11.3.18 B699 as above (Lt G O Johnson)

13.3.18 B8337 Albatros D.V crashed NE of St.Quentin 12.10 (Capt F.E Brown)

13.3.18 C5308 Albatros D.V OOC NE of St.Quentin 12.10 (2/Lt C L Stubbs)

13.3.18 D260 Albatros D.V BU NE of S.Quentin 12.10 (2/Lt P K Hobson)

15.3.18 D259 DFW C shot down in our lines S of Villaret 08.20 (2/Lt A F W Beauchamp Proctor) [numbered G.150]

15.3.18 C1077 Pfalz D.III OOC NE of Ribemont 09.20 (Lt J F Larson)

15.3.18 C1075 Albatros D.V crashed Mesnil St.Laurent 09.45 (2/Lt E A Clear)

15.3.18 C5395 Albatros D.V in flames SE of Bellincourt 10.10 (2/Lt C T Travers)

16.3.18 B699 LVG C crashed between Serain & Villers Outreaux 11.25, shared D260 (Lt G O Johnson)

16.3.18 D260 as above (2/Lt P K Hobson)

17.3.18 D259 Albatros D.V OOC 11.25, Pfalz D.III OOC 11.30 & Pfalz D.III BU 11.45, all Busigny (2/Lt A F W Beauchamp Proctor)

17.3.18 B8337 Albatros D.V OOC Fresnoy Le Grande & another OOC 11.40 W of Busigny 11.45 (Capt F E Brown)

17.3.18 B8233 Pfalz D.III crashed 1m E of Moretz 11.40 (2/Lt J V Sorsoleil)

17.3.18 C5308 Albatros D.V crashed Becquigny 11.45 (2/Lt C L Stubbs)

17.3.18 C1075 Fokker Dr.I attacked which collided with an Albatros D.V, both BU Crèvecoeur 17.30 (2/Lt E A Clear)

17.3.18 C9623 Fokker Dr.I OOC Crèvecoeur 17.30 (2/Lt W H Brown)

18.3.18 C1075 Fokker Dr.I OOC W of Busigny 11.05 (2/Lt E A

Clear)

18.3.18 B8337 Albatros D.V OOC St.Souplet 11.30 (Capt F E Brown)

18.3.18 C1099 Fokker Dr.I OOC Le Cateau 11.30 (Lt J F Larson)

18.3.18 B637 Albatros D.V OOC N of Wassigny 11.30 (Capt K Leask)

18.3.18 B699 Albatros D.V OOC Sequehart 11.40 (Lt G O Johnson)

18.3.18 C9623 Fokker Dr.I crashed 11.30 & Albatros D.V OOC St.Souplet 11.40 (2/Lt W H Brown)

22.3.18 B8337 Pfalz D III crashed W of Fayet 14.15 (Capt F E Brown)

23.3.18 B637 DFW C DD smoking St.Quentin 18.25 (Capt K Leask)

25.3.18 C9623 LVG C in flames Combles, then shared with C1077 LVG C crashed in flames, both c.09.30 (2/Lt W H Brown)

25.3.18 C1077 LVG C as above (Capt R A Grosvenor)

30.3.18 C1075 Albatros D.V crashed S of Somme at Cerisy 09.30 (2/Lt E A Clear)

1.4.18 D276 2-str OOC S of Denuin 13.50 (2/Lt W E Lunnon)

3.4.18 B8408 Pfalz D.III in flames then Albatros D.V DD attempting to land overshot and crashed, German ALG at Rosières 11.50 (Capt R A Grosvenor)

3.4.18 C9623 Albatros D.V OOC E of Villers Bretonneux 11.00-12.00 (2/Lt W H Brown)

3.4.18 C1772 Albatros D.V OOC then Pfalz D.III crashed E of Rodières 11.55-13.00 (Lt J F Larson)

3.4.18 C1794 Pfalz D.III crashed S of Rosières 12.30 (2/Lt H W L Saunders)

6.4.18 C1772 LVG C crashed in No Mans Land N of Hangard 11.20, shared C1794, C9519 & C6410 11.20 (Lt J F Larson)

6.4.18 C1794 as above (2/Lt H W L Saunders)

6.4.18 C9519 as above (2/Lt C L Stubbs)

6.4.18 C6410 as above (2/Lt H O MacDonald)

10.4.18 B8408 Pfalz D.III OOC E of Albert 11.00 (Capt R A Grosvenor)

11.4.18 D270 Fokker Dr.I OOC E of Albert 17.05 (Capt E H Tatton)

11.4.18 B8403 Pfalz D.III OOC E of Albert 17.05 (Lt L Duke)

11.4.18 B8233 Fokker Dr.I OOC E of Albert 17.05 (Lt J V Sorsoleil)

12.4.18 D270 DFW C OOC Le Sars 11.15 (Capt E H Tatton)

12.4.18 B8233 Hannover C top right hand plane broke off nr Albert 11.50 (Lt E A Clear)

12.4.18 C9519 DFW C OOC E of Albert 11.50, shared D276 (Lt C L Stubbs)

12.4.18 D276 as above (Lt W E Lunon)

12.4.18 C1097 DFW C OOC E of Albert 11.50 (Lt G O Johnson)

12.4.18 C1075 Pfalz D.III DD which COL W of Plessier 18.10 (Lt E A Clear)

12.4.18 B8408 Albatros D.V crashed E of Hangard Wood, then another in flames 18.10 (Capt R A Grosvenor)

20.4.18 C6410 Albatros D.V OOC Marcelcave 09.20 (Lt F K Hobson)

21.4.18 C6410 Albatros C BU SW of Mezières 11.55-13.20 (Lt F K Hobson)

23.4.18 B8403 Fokker Dr.I OOC NE of Framerville 16.35, then pilot wounded (Lt L Duke wounded)

23.4.18 C1772 Fokker Dr.I crashed 3m E of Framerville 16.40 (Capt A F W Beauchamp Proctor)

23.4.18 C9519 Fokker Dr.I crashed E of Framerville 16.40 (Lt C L Stubbs)

23.4.18 C6410 Fokker Dr.I OOC Framerville 16.40 (Lt F K Hobson)

24.4.18 B8408 2-str in vertical dive Villers Bretonneaux aerodrome 18.10 (Capt R A Grosvenor)

25.4.18 B8408 Pfalz D.III BU, Pfalz D.III OOC & Albatros D.V OOC E of Wiencourt 17.00 (Capt R A Grosvenor)

25.4.18 B8233 Pfalz D.III in flames & Albatros D.V OOC E of Wiencourt 17.00 (Capt J V Sorsoleil)

25.4.18 D259 Albatros D.V BU N of Abancourt 17.00 (Lt R Manzer)

25.4.18 C1075 Pfalz D.III crashed S of Hangard Wood 17.00, then 2-str in flames 17.30 SE of Hangard Wood (Lt E A Clear)

25.4.18 B8403 Pfalz D.III in slow spin apparently OOC E of Wiencourt 17.00 (Lt H W L Saunders)

29.4.18 B8403 DFW C in British lines nr St.Gratien 19.00, shared B8271 & C6449 (Lt H W L Saunders)

29.4.18 B8272 as above (Lt C F Falkenberg)

29.4.18 C6440 as above (Lt Smith)

2.5.18 C5399 Albatros D.V OOC E of Abancort 14.50 (Lt W A Southey)

7.5.18 B8233 Fokker Dr.I OOC smoking Bray sur Somme 19.15 (Capt J V Sorsoleil)

9.5.18 C1772 Albatros D.V OOC W of Villers Bretonneux aerodrome 15.10 (Capt A F W Beauchamp Proctor)

9.5.18 C6442 Albatros D.V OOC Villers Bretonneux aerodrome 15.10 (Lt B Stephenson)

10.5.18 C1772 Rumpler dest S of Bray 14.10 (Capt A F W Beauchamp Proctor)

15.5.18 D259 DFW C OOC Vauvillers 11.50 (Lt R Manzer)

16.5.18 B8405 Albatros D.V OOC Chipilly 10.45 (Lt H W L Saunders)

16.5.18 C5399 Fokker Dr.I crashed NNW of Abancourt 16.20 (Lt W A Southey)

16.5.18 C1847 Albatros D.V OOC nr Rosières 18.00, then attacked by Fokker Dr.I; pilot wounded, petrol tank hit, engine stopped; crossed enemy lines at 100ft and crashed in No Man's Land (Capt H P Smith wounded. Wounded twice more trying to extricate himself from wreckage, then sheltered in a slight depression and finally rescued by Australian troops. A Corporal was badly wounded in the attempt and was not expected to live.

16.5.18 B8403 Fokker Dr.I with checkerboard wings OOC S of Herleville 18.05 (Lt H W L Saunders)

16.5.18 D259 Fokker Dr.I checkerboard wings crashed S of Herleville 18.05 (Lt R Manzer)

17.5.18 B8403 Albatros D.V crashed SE of Hangest 13.30 (Lt H W L Saunders)

17.5.18 C1772 Albatros D.V crashed Hangest 13.30 (Capt A.F.W Beauchamp Proctor)

17.5.18 C6442 Albatros D.V OOC nr Hangest 13.30 (Lt E Biccard)

17.5.18 C6465 Albatros D.V OOC Hangest 13.30 (Lt H O MacDonald)

18.5.18 B8408 Albatros D.V OOC Chaulnes 11.30 & DFW C OOC NE of Moreuil 12.00 (Capt R A Grosvenor MC)

19.5.18 B682 Fokker Dr.I OOC SE of Warfusée 09.50 (Lt A F Mathews USAS)

19.5.18 C1772 2-str OOC Vauvillers 09.45 & Albatros D.V OOC Wiencourt 10.00 (Capt R A Grosvenor MC)

19.5.18 C1772 2-str OOC Vauvillers 09.45 & Albatros D.V crashed Wiencourt 10.00 (Capt A F W Beauchamp Proctor MC)

19.5.18 C1772 Albatros D.V crashed Cachy 18.35 (Capt A F W Beauchamp Proctor MC)

19.5.18 C1772 2 Albatros D.V crashed SE of Villers Bretonneux 18.35, shared C6465, C9519 & C6442 (Capt A F W Beauchamp Proctor MC)

19.5.18 C6465 as above (Lt H O MacDonald)

19.5.18 C9519 as above (Lt B Oliver)

19.5.18 C6442 as above (Lt E E Biccard)

27.5.18 C9519 Albatros D.V yellow fuselage, green wings OOC S of Mezières 19.45 (Lt B Olier USAS)

27.5.18 C1772 Albatros D.V OOC S of Mezières 19.50 (Capt A F W Beauchamp Proctor)

28.5.18 D259 Albatros D.V OOC, then another had its top right plane carried away when struck by left wheel of D259's u/c SE of Warfusée-Abancourt 09.20 (Lt R Manzer)

28.5.18 B8403 Albatros OOC S of Wiencourt 09.20 (Lt H W L Saunders)

28.5.18 B8233 Albatros D.V OOC S of Wiencourt 09.20 (Lt C F C Wilson)

28.5.18 C1075 Albatros D.V OOC SE of Villers Bretonneux 13.25 (Lt S B Eckert USAS)

28.5.18 C1871 Albatros D.V crashed NE of Moreuil 13.30 (Lt E A Clear MC)

28.5.18 C6465 Albatros D.V smoking S of Villers Bretonneux 13.30 (Lt H O MacDonald)

28.5.18 C6457 Albatros D.V OOC Hengard 13.40 (Lt W E Lunnon)

29.5.18 D333 Albatros D.V OOC SE of Fricourt 18.50 (Capt A F W Beauchamp Proctor)

31.5.18 D333 Albatros D.V OOC Beaufort aerodrome 12.40 (Capt A F W Beauchamp Proctor)

1.6.18 D333 KB in flames SE of Albert 12.25 (Capt A F W Beauchamp Proctor)

3.6.18 B8233 Fokker Dr.I top plane shot off & another OOC E of Montdidier 20.10 (Capt J V Sorsoleil MC)

5.6.18 D333 Rumpler C BU 1m W of Moreuil 12.55, shared C5399 (Capt A F W Beauchamp Proctor)

5.6.18 C5399 as above (Lt W A Southey)

6.6.18 D333 KB in flames W of Proyart 10.10 & another in flames N of Bray 10.25 (Capt A F W Beauchamp Proctor)

11.6.18 D6882 Albatros D.V crashed Montdidier 13.45 (Lt C F Falkenberg)

11.6.18 D333 Albatros D.V OOC 5m E of Montdidier 13.50 & Pfalz D.III crashed N of Cayeaux 14.30 (Capt A F W Beauchamp Proctor)

13.6.18 D333 KB in flames E of Contoire 08.00 (Capt A F W Beauchamp Proctor)

16.6.18 D6149 Pfalz D.III OOC Beaucourt 20.00 (Lt G A Vaughn USAS)

17.6.18 C1834 Fokker Dr.I intent on stalking a D.H.4 which had fallen behind, mistook the S.E.5As for German machines and joined the formation; shot down OOC Chaulnes 09.40, shared D6890 & B682 (Capt J V Sorsoleil MC)

17.6.18 D6890 as above (Lt C F Falkenberg)

17.6.18 B682 as above (Lt A F Mathews USAS)

18.6.18 C1871 Blue Fokker Dr.I left hand planes crumpled up SE of Warfusée 10.55 (2/Lt R Manzer)

18.6.18 D333 Fokker D.VII OOC Villers Bretonneux 10.55 (Capt J S Ralston)

18.6.18 C5399 Fokker D.VII OOC Abancourt 10.55 (Lt W A Southey)

25.6.18 C1874 Pfalz D.III OOC Chipilly 13.30 (Capt J V Sorsoleil MC)

25.6.18 C6890 Pfalz D.III OOC Chipilly 13.30 (Lt C F Falkenberg)

27.6.18 D333 Enemy Aircraft OOC NE of Villers Bretonneux 09.00; then attacked himself; engine damaged and aircraft caught fire at 2,000ft; managed to forceland and caught fire near Cachy (Capt J S Ralston OK)

27.6.18 D6857 Albatros D.V OOC 2m E of Villers Bretonneux 09.45 (2/Lt W J B Nel)

27.6.18 C1834 Pfalz D.III crashed 2m E of Villers Bretonneux 10.15 (Capt J V Sorsoleil MC)

28.6.18 C6496 LVG C crashed nr Fricourt 06.50 & another DD under control which crashed on landing in shell crater, Orvillers 07.00 (Capt H W L Saunders)

29.6.18 C8732 Pfalz D.III OOC SE of Wiencourt 08.45 (2/Lt R Manzer)

16.7.18 C6496 KB in flames W of Proyart 13.45 (Capt H W Saunders)

16.7.18 C6914 KB in flames Mericourt 13.50 (Capt J S Ralston MC)

17.7.18 D6917 KB in flames Proyart 10.35 (Lt N W R Mawle)

19.7.18 C8732 KB in flames Foucaucourt 18.15 (2/Lt R Manzer)

20.7.18 D6917 Fokker D.VII crashed NE of Morcourt 09.10 & KB in flames SW of Proyart 09.15 (Lt N W R Mawle)

20.7.18 D6914 KB in flames Warvillers 09.10, shared E5937 (Capt J S Ralston)

20.7.18 E5937 as above (Lt J E Boudwin USAS)

20.7.18 C6496 Fokker D.VII crashed Morcourt 10.15 (Capt H W L Saunders)

22.7.18 C6496 KB in flames N of Fricourt 13.45 (Capt H W L Saunders)

24.7.18 D6914 Fokker D.VII BU Warfusée 11.15, shared C1868 (Capt J S Ralston)

24.7.18 C1868 as above (Lt N W R Mawle)

24.7.18 D6926 Fokker D.VII crashed SE of Warfusée 11.15 (2/Lt W J B Nel)

24.7.18 C6457 Fokker D.VII yellow tail white rudder OOC E of Bray 20.35 (Lt G A Vaughn USAS)

24.7.18 D6928 Albatros D.V OOC, pilot believed killed Péronne 20.45 (Lt C F Falkenberg)

25.7.18 D6914 shot down KB in flames S of Warvillers 06.30, then wounded by ground fire; fainted & crashed N of Amiens-St.Quentin road (Capt J S Ralston MC killed)

28.7.18 D6920 Halberstadt C crashed S of Foucaucourt 09.30 (Lt C F Falkenberg)

28.7.18 C6457 Rumpler C crashed Harbonnières 09.40, shared C8732 (Lt G A Vaughn USAS)

28.7.18 C8732 as above (2/Lt R Manzer)

29.7.18 D6917 LVG C crashed SE of Proyart 07.55, shared C8895 (Lt N W R Mawle)

29.7.18 C8895 as above (Lt A C Lobley)

29.7.18 C6496 LVG C yellow fuselage crashed just N of Bois des Tailles 08.00 (Capt H W L Saunders)

30.7.18 D6917 Fokker D.VII OOC, then Fokker D.VII half rolled into another Fokker D.VII trying to get on to Mawle's tail, both in flames S of Warvillers 10.15 (Lt N W R Mawle)

30.7.18 D6926 Fokker D.VII OOC Wancourt-Caix 10.15 (2/Lt W J B Nel)

1.8.18 D6920 Fokker D.VII in flames Suzanne aerodrome 10.00 (Lt C F Falkenberg)

1.8.18 E5963 Fokker D.VII in flames Suzanne aerodrome 10.00 (2/Lt E E Biccard)

1.8.18 B682 Pfalz D.III OOC in vicinity of Suzanne aerodrome 10.05 (Lt A F Mathews USAS)

1.8.18 C1834 Fokker D.VII in flames Suzanne aerodrome 10.05 (Capt W A Southey)

3.8.18 C8732 Fokker D.VII in flames nr Bray 06.55 (2/Lt R Manzer)

4.8.18 D6917 KB in flames SE of Proyart 05.50 (Lt N W R Mawle)

4.8.18 C8732 Albatros D.V crashed 3m E of Warfusée 08.30 (2/Lt R Manzer)

4.8.18 D6906 Albatros D.V crashed E of Warfusée 08.30 (2/Lt C R Thompson)

7.8.18 D6917 Fokker D.VII OOC & another in flames S of Caix 08.50 (Lt N W R Mawle)

7.8.18 D6926 Fokker D.VII OOC NE of Le Quesnel 09.10 (Lt W J B Nel)

7.8.18 C8732 Pfalz D.III crashed E of Le Quesnel 09.10 (2/Lt R Manzer)

7.8.18 D6906 Pfalz D.III OOC smoking E of Le Quesnel 09.10 (2/Lt C R Thompson)

7.8.18 C1834 Rumpler C crashed E of Arvillers 09.55 (Capt W A Southey)

8.8.18 D6917 KB being towed by horses at a height of 25ft in flames E of Harbonnières 10.00; pilot then wounded in stomach by ground fire attacking enemy trenches (Lt N W R Mawle)

8.8.18 D6856 KB being towed by horses in flames Rosières 14.40 (Capt A F W Beauchamp Proctor MC DFC)

8.8.18 C6496 Fokker D.VII OOC N of Foucaucourt 18.30 (2/Lt S W Highwood)

10.8.18 C1834 Fokker D.VII OOC Péronne 18.00 (Capt W A Southey)

11.8.18 D6920 KB DD deflated Estrées 06.40 (Lt C F Falkenberg)

11.8.18 D6920 Fokker D.VII crashed nr Villers Carbonnel 18.00 (2/Lt C R Thompson)

11.8.18 B8420 Fokker D.VII crashed and burnt Villers Carbonnel 18.10 (Capt D Carruthers)

11.8.18 D6856 Fokker D.VII OOC Villers Carbonnel 18.10 (Capt A F W Beauchamp Proctor MC DFC)

11.8.18 C9069 Fokker D.VII OOC Villers Carbonnel 18.10 (2/Lt S W Highwood)

11.8.18 E5937 Fokker D.VII OOC Villers Carbonnel 18.10 (Lt J E Boudwin USAS)

11.8.18 C1834 Fokker D.VII BU Villers Carbonnel 18.10 (2/Lt C F Falkenberg)

14.8.18 E5937 Fokker D.VII OOC Villers Carbonnel 10.55-11.20 (Capt D Carruthers)

14.8.18 D6856 Fokker D.VII in flames Villers Carbonnel & another OOC Estrées c.11.10 (Capt A F W Beauchamp Proctor MC DFC)

16.8.18 D6920 Fokker D.VII crashed E of Foucaucourt 09.45 (Capt C F Falkenberg)

16.8.18 D6856 DFW C in flames S of Misery 10.15 (Capt A F W Beauchamp Proctor MC DFC)

17.8.18 C1834 Fokker D.VII in flames, Estrées 09.00 (Capt A W Southey)

21.8.18 D6856 Albatros C crashed E of Estrées 15.30 (Capt A F W Beauchamp Proctor MC DFC)

22.8.18 D6856 KB in flames Assévillers 09.40 & KB in flames Hems 09.45 (Capt A F W Beauchamp Proctor MC DFC)

22.8.18 E4012 Rumpler C crashed SE of Villers Carbonnel 11.00, shared C9069 (Lt G A Vaughn USAS)

22.8.18 C9069 as above (2/Lt S W Highwood)

23.8.18 E4012 KB in flames Hem 10.15 (Lt G A Vaughn USAS)

23.8.18 E4012 Rumpler C crashed Mericourt 11.00, shared D6920 (Lt G A Vaughn USAS)

23.8.18 D6920 as above (Capt C F Falkenberg)

24.8.18 D6856 Fokker D.VII OOC Brie 18.10 & another in

flames 18.30 E of Brie (Capt A F W Beauchamp Proctor MC DFC)

25.8.18 C1834 LVG C OOC smoking Foucaucourt-Herleville 09.45, shared B8420 (Capt W A Southey)

25.8.18 B8420 as above (2/Lt C F C Wilson)

25.8.18 D6856 Fokker D.VII crashed S of Tempeux 10.00 (Capt A F W Beauchamp Proctor MC DFC)

25.8.18 E5937 Fokker D.VII crashed Tempeux 10.50, shared C8895 (2/Lt W J B Nel)

25.8.18 D6856 Rumpler C in flames crashed in British lines S of Vrely 11.20, shared D6917 & D6897 (Capt A F W Beauchamp Proctor MC DFC)

25.8.18 D6917 as above (2/Lt M H Goudie)

25.8.18 D6897 as above (2/Lt I P Corse USAS)

27.8.18 D6856 KB in flames Flaucourt 08.40, shared E5937 & D6987, then KB in flames Mt St.Quentin 09.45 not shared (Capt A F W Beauchamp Proctor MC DFC)

27.8.18 E5937 KB in flames Flaucourt 08.40, shared D6856 (Lt S E Boudwin USAS)

27.8.18 D6987 KB in flames Flaucourt 08.40, shared D6856 (2/Lt I P Corse USAS)

29.8.18 Fokker D.VII OOC W of Athies 14.45 (Capt W A Southey)

29.8.18 Fokker D.VII crashed 1m E of Somme, S of Brie 19.25, shared D6920 (Capt A F W Beauchamp Proctor MC DFC)

29.8.18 D6920 as above (Capt C F Falkenberg)

3.9.18 C1834 Rumpler C crashed Bapaume-Péronne 06.15, shared B8420, E5963, D6997 & D6982 (Capt W A Southey)

3.9.18 B8420 as above (2/Lt C F C Wilson)

3.9.18 E5963 as above (Lt E R W Millar)

3.9.18 D6997 as above (2/Lt F R Christiani)

3.9.18 D6982 as above (2/Lt A E Hill)

3.9.18 C1834 KB in flames nr Fins 06.45 (Capt W A Southey)

3.9.18 C1834 KB in flames N of Fins 15.30 (Capt W A Southey)

4.9.18 D6920 KB in flames Douvieux 13.30, shared F6420 2/Lt S W Highwood

4.9.18 F6420 as above (2/Lt C R Thompson)

5.9.18 F6420 KB in flames S of Poeuilly 09.50 (2/Lt C R Thompson)

5.9.18 C9069 KB in flames S of Poeuilly 09.50 (2/Lt S W Highwood)

7.9.18 D6920 KB in flames Bellenglise 11.30 (2/Lt S W Highwood)

7.9.18 D6987 KB in flames nr St.Quentin 11.30 (2/Lt I P Corse USAS)

7.9.18 D6856 KB in flames nr Cambrai 11.35 (Capt A F W Beauchamp Proctor MC DFC)

7.9.18 D6997 KB in flames Cambrai-St.Quentin 11.40 (2/Lt F R Christiani)

14.9.18 D6920 KB in flames Bantouzelle 10.30 (2/Lt S W Highwood)

14.9.18 E6008 KB in flames Gonnelieu 10.30 (Capt W A Southey)

14.9.18 B7902 KB set adrift Bantouzelle, last seen drifting E at 15,000ft 10.30 (2/Lt D C Rees)

15.9.18 C1911 KB in flames Bellicourt 08.50 (Capt A F W Beauchamp Proctor MC DFC)

15.9.18 F6420 KB in flames E of St.Quentin 09.35 (2/Lt C R Thompson wounded before victory)

16.9.18 C6480 Rumpler C crashed Selenoy 06.30, shared B8420 (2/Lt S W Highwood)

16.9.18 B8420 as above (2/Lt C F C Wilson)

18.9.18 E6024 Fokker D.VII OOC Montigny 14.00 (Capt C F Falkenberg DFC)

20.9.18 F6428 Fokker D.VII crashed Mont d'Origny 09.30-10.20 (2/Lt W J B Nel)

20.9.18 E6024 Fokker D.VII crashed 1m E of Mont d'Origny, another in slow spin on its back, and a third shot off Beauchamp Proctor's tail treated as DD 09.30-10.45 (Capt C F Falkenberg DFC)

21.9.18 C9293 Fokker D.VII crashed Levergies, NNE of St.Quentin 17.45 (2/Lt D C Rees)

21.9.18 D6972 Fokker D.VII OOC Levergies, NNE of St.Quentin 17.45 (2/Lt J A Jackson)

24.9.18 C1911 KB in flames Gouy 09.15 (Capt A F W Beauchamp Proctor MC DFC)

24.9.18 B7902 KB in flames NE of Gouy 09.15 (2/Lt D C Rees)

24.9.18 E4071 KB in flames Gouy 09.15 (2/Lt S W Highwood)

24.9.18 B8491 Fokker D.VII in flames, crashed Estrées 09.15 (2/Lt W J B Nel)

24.9.18 E4071 2 KB in flames Cambrai 13.50 (2/Lt S W Highwood)

24.9.18 E6024 KB in flames Cambrai 13.50 (Capt C F Falkenberg DFC)

24.9.18 D6982 2 KB in flames Cambrai 13.50 (2/Lt F R Christiani)

27.9.18 C1911 KB in flames 2m W of Crèvecoeur 08.50 (Capt A F W Beauchamp Proctor DSO MC DFC)

29.9.18 F5489 KB in flames N of Villers Outreaux 09.50 (2/Lt J G Coots)

29.9.18 E5963 KB in flames N of Montbrehain 10.10 (Lt E R W Millar)

29.9.18 E4071 KB in flames Beaurevoir, shared C9293, then KB in flames L'Espagne not shared 10.10 (2/Lt S W Highwood)

29.9.18 C9293 KB in flames Beaurevoir 10.10, shared E4071 (2/Lt D C Rees)

29.9.18 D6982 KB in flames Villers Outreaux 10.10 (2/Lt F R Christiani)

29.9.18 E6024 Red-nosed Fokker D.VII in flames Beaurevoir 10.50 (Capt C F Falkenberg DFC)

1.10.18 C1911 Fokker D.VII blue striped tail crashed SE of Fontaine, then Fokker D.VII red striped tail in flames SE of Ramicourt 16.05-16.40 (Capt A F W Beauchamp Proctor DSO MC DFC)

2.10.18 C1911 KB in flames Selvigny 08.30 (Capt A F W Beauchamp Proctor DSO MC DFC)

3.10.18 E4071 Fokker D.VII crashed & burst into flames nr Mont d'Origny 11.25 (2/Lt S W Highwood)

3.10.18 C1911 Fokker D.VII OOC c.11.25 & KB in flames c.11.45 nr Mont d'Origny (Capt A F W Beauchamp Proctor DSO MC DFC)

3.10.18 F5489 Fokker D.VII crashed E of Fresnoy 18.05, shared E4071, then Fokker D.VII crashed nr Fresnoy 18.15 not shared (2/Lt J G Coots)

3.10.18 E4071 as above (2/Lt SW Highwood)

4.10.18 E6024 Fokker D.VII OOC Cambrai 08.45 (Capt C F Falkenberg DFC)

5.10.18 C1911 KB in flames W of Bohain 11.55, shared F5477 (Capt A F W Beauchamp Proctor DSO MC DFC)

5.10.18 F5477 as above (2/Lt A E Hill)

8.10.18 C1911 Rumpler C crashed & burst into flames NE of Mametz 11.30 (Capt A F W Beauchamp Proctor DSO MC DFC)

9.10.18 D6972 Fokker D.VII crashed 2km N of Troisvilles 15.25 (Sgt H W Dowdell)

14.10.18 E4071 Fokker D.VII in flames E of Mont d'Origny 07.00-09.00 (Capt W.A Southey DFC)

22.10.18 F5625 KB in flames Prisches 09.15 (Capt W.A Southey DFC)

23.10.18 F5625 Fokker D.VII crashed just S of Fontaine 11.15 (Capt WA Southey DFC)

27.10.18 E4071 Fokker D.VII OOC Esqueheries 09.10 (Capt W.A Southey DFC)

27.10.18 E5709 Fokker D.VII crashed Mormal Forest 10.50 (Mjr W Sholto Douglas MC)

28.10.18 E5963 LVG C crashed into side of house just W of the La Queue de Boue 07.50 (Capt W A Southey DFC)

30.10.18 E6008 Fokker D.VII crashed just W of Lechelles 09.30 (Lt H O MacDonald)

30.10.18 H685 Fokker D.VII with red cross on fuselage OOC Forêt de Nouvion 09.30 (Capt W A Southey DFC)

30.10.18 E5793 Fokker D.VII crashed Lechelle Forest 09.45 (Capt S W Highwood DFC)

30.10.18 F5477 Fokker D.VII OOC N of Mormal Forest 10.30 (Lt E R W Millar)

30.10.18 B8010 Halberstadt C OOC N of Mormal Forest 10.30 (Lt H L Stubbs)

3.11.18 E6008 Grey Fokker D.VII down in flames, pilot parachuted, Mormal Forest, 15.30 (2/Lt C F C Wilson)

3.11.18 F855 Grey Fokker D.VII OOC Mormal Forest 15.30 (Lt F H Taylor MC)

4.11.18 H685 LVG C last seen diving steeply, then had to break off combat as main petrol tank hit, treated as DD indecisive 16.00 (Sgt A J Wing)

10.11.18 F904 Fokker D.VII crashed E of Matagne 10.00 (Mjr E M Pickthorn MC)

10.11.18 F855 Fokker D.VII crashed SE of Fagnolle 10.00 (Lt F H Taylor MC)

APPENDIX VI

No.84 SQUADRON NOMINAL ROLE

February - March 1942

Wg Cdr J R Jeudwine	Left Tjilatjap 7 Mar 1942
Sqn Ldr T James	Left Padang; HMS *Danae* reached Australia on *Aberkerk*.
Sqn Ldr A K Passmore	Left Tjilatjap 7 Mar 1942
Sqn Ldr J E D Tayler	Bandoeng- Changi
Flt Lt B Ashmole	Evacuated on the *Yoma*
Flt Lt H M Bongard	Bandoeng 10 Oct 42
Flt Lt A M Gill	Evacuated on the *Yoma*
Flt Lt M K Holland	Bandoeng- Singapore 12 Feb 45
Flt Lt G H Milson	Bandoeng- Singapore- Changi
Flt Lt W F Tierney	Bandoeng
Flt Lt J V C Wyllie	Bandoeng- Singapore
Fg Off J W Bott	Last seen Kalidjati 1 Mar 42
Fg Off A S Brentnall	Missing, believed drowned 27 Nov 43
Fg Off H R G Jebb	Bandoeng-
Fg Off M Keble-White	Bandoeng-
Plt Off E R Bishop	Batavia 7 Sep 1943
Plt Off B Fiheely	Batavia- overseas 15 Apr 43
Plt Off J Goldfinch	Never reached Sumatra; rejoined Sqn
Plt Off J Hawke	Never reached Sumatra; Rejoined Sqn
Plt Off D W Kewish	Last seen Kalidjati 1 Mar 42
Plt Off M Macdonald	Left Tjilatjap 7 Mar 42
Plt Off G Maurice	Evacuated on the *Yoma*
Plt Off J M McNally	Batavia- Soerabaya
Plt Off R D Millar	Batavia 25 Sep 43
Plt Off C P Streatfeild	Left Tjilatjap 7 Mar 42
Plt Off S Turner	Left Tjilatjap 7 Mar 42

NCOs and Airmen

ACl T Allaway	Batavia 7 Sep 43
LAC W Allen	Evacuated on the *Yoma*
Sgt W Amy	Evacuated on the *Yoma*
LAC J W Archer	Soerabaya 16 Apr 43
Sgt D G Argent	Bandoeng- Changi
LAC J W Armstrong	Soerabaya 16 Apr 43
LAC A Arrowsmith	Soerabaya Feb 43; Ambon; died 1990
LAC A Ashley	Changi 30 Mar 43
LAC R Atkinson	Batavia- Overseas 29 Oct 42
AC J Austin	Soerabaya 16 Apr 43
LAC D Ball	Died Ambon 4 Aug 43
Cpl Ball	Soerabaya 14 Apr 43
LAC C V Barter	Changi
LAC H Bartlett	Batavia 28 Nov 42
LAC H W Baugh	Died Hintok River 26 Jul 43
F/Sgt J R Barker	Batavia 7 Sep 43; Hakodate-Sapporo
LAC C Bean	Bandoeng Oct 43
LAC Beardshaw	Kuching 9 Oct 42
Cpl M Beatty	Missing, believed drowned 27 Nov 43
LAC W J Beckerley	Batavia- Changi
LAC G C Bell	Batavia Hosp 20 Jul 43
Sgt G Bell	Missing; killed Tjilatjap 9 Mar 42
Sgt R C H Bennett	Changi-
LAC A Berlin	Left Batavia Sep 42 - Japan?
ACl F C Biddulph	Batavia- Changi
Sgt A M Blackburn	Left Padang with Sqn Ldr T James
ACl H E Blackerby	Palembang- Batavia
Sgt Blount RAAF	
ACl Bovingdon	Killed in Sumatra 16 Feb 42
Sgt R W Bowers	Tjimahi 1 Sep 43
ACl J B Booth	Kuching 9 Oct 43
LAC Bradman	Java?
LAC J Brennan	Bandoeng Oct 43
LAC J Brett	Batavia 7 Sep 43; Sumatra Jul 44
LAC Broadhead	Java?
LAC T Bromley	Batavia 7 Sep 43
Cpl Brooks	Rangoon 1 Feb 42; rejoined Sqn India
AC H V Brown	Soerabaya 16 Apr 43
F/Sgt A Brown	Tjimahi 27 Jul 43; left Batavia Oct 43
LAC J W Brooker	Batavia 7 Sep 43; Sumatra Jul 44
Cpl Brumbey	Batavia; Pakan Baroe Rly Jul 44
LAC Bryer	Java?
AC E R Burdon	Soerabaya 16 Apr 43

Sgt O Burlock	Changi 29 Mar 45
LAC G M Byng	Batavia - Changi
Sgt F Cameron RAAF	Left Bandoeng 7 Nov 42; died 1992
ACl R Carr	Batavia 7 Sep 43
AC2 H Carrington	Batavia 7 Sep 43
Cpl H Chandler	Garoet 5 Mar 42; missing believed drowned 27 Nov 43
Cpl Cherry	Tjimahi 27 Apr 43; left Cycle Camp Batavia 10 Sep 43
LAC A A Childs	Batavia 7 Sep 43
LAC E Clement	Kuching 9 Oct 42; died 1945
Cpl R Clegg	Soerabaya 16 Apr 43; Ambon
ACl B Coates	Batavia 7 Sep 43
Cpl Cockin	Last seen Kalidjati Mar 42
AC Cole	
LAC D Collins	
LAC Mc L Collins	Batavia 7 Sep 43
LAC S Collingwood	Missing, believed drowned 27 Nov 43
LAC S Coleman	Changi 30 Mar 45
AC Connety	To Japan?
LAC Coo	Never reached Sumatra; rejoined Sqn
LAC E Cooper	
Sgt W H Cosgrove	Left Tjilatjap 7 Mar 42
AC2 J Corbett	Soerabaya 16 Apr 43
Sgt Craddock	Evacuated on the *Yoma*
Cpl C W Crocker	Java, Ambon, Singapore
LAC C Crocker	Batavia 7 Sep 43
ACl H Cressling	
Cpl Cross	Evacuated on the *Yoma*
Sgt J H Cruickshank	Changi; Kranji 29 Mar 45
ACl J Curtis	Boel Glodok, Ambon; died early 70s
LAC R W Cox	Soerabaya 16 Apr 43
AC C Cummings	Tjilatjap 4 Mar 42
Sgt D Curran RAAF	
Sgt E J Daley	Killed. Tjilatjap 10 Apr 42
LAC G J Daniels	Missing after evacuation 1 Mar 42
LAC B Dann	Batavia Apr 43
Sgt W J Davie	Killed in a/c crash 16 Feb 42
AC K C Davies	Soerabaya 16 Apr 43
Cpl J Darwin	Garoet 5 Mar 42; Batavia 20 Jul 43
LAC R Davidson	Java
ACl J Dawson	Batavia 7 Sep 43
AC A Davis	
LAC W Dempster	Batavia 7 Sep 43
LAC J Dickey	Changi 9 Feb 43
AC2 J Dobson	Soerabaya 16 Apr 43
AC J Dolan	Bandoeng
AC J H Drew	Kuching 9 Oct 42
AC2 J Drysdale	Batavia 20 Jul 43
Cpl Duffin	Batavia Hosp 20 Jul 43
LAC R W Duffield	Died Sime Road 7 Feb 44
LAC R Duncan	Left Batavia Sep 42; Japan ?
LAC J E Dunn	Garoet 5 Mar 42; Batavia 7 Sep 42
LAC J Edis	Missing, believed drowned 27 Nov 43
LAC G Edwards	Missing after evac of Kalidjati Mar 42
Sgt J Ellis	Evacuated on the *Yoma*
Sgt Engall	Evacuated on the *Yoma*
Cpl A Y Evans	Batavia 7 Sep 43; River Valley Rly
AC2 E J Evans	Changi 9 Feb 43
Cpl G Evans	Soerabaya 14 Apr 43; Batavia 7.9.43
Cpl Fairgreaves	Japan? Sep 42
Sgt Farrer	Evacuated on the *Yoma*
AC J W Fell	Changi 30 Mar 45; died Feb 91
Cpl Fiargray	Kuching 9 Oct 42
Sgt A B Firby	Bandoeng Oct 43
Cpl R Finning	Bandoeng Oct 43
LAC A Fisher	Soerabaya 16 Apr 43
LAC J Fisher	Batavia 7 Sep 43
AC J H Forsythe	Java 1 Sep 44
LAC F W Fox	Last seen Palembang Feb 42
LAC A Fretwell	Last seen Kalidjati 28 Feb 42
AC J R Frost	Bandoeng Oct 43
Cpl F Gabb	Died 13 Jul 43, Ambon

LAC Galvin	Died 13 Jul 43, Ambon
Sgt P S Gardner	No details
Sgt N Geappen RAAF	Killed in a/c crash, Sumatra 16 Feb 42
AC R Gedling	Died Boel Glodok 18 Apr 42
LAC Gillott	Soerabaya 16 Apr 43
LAC Godfrey	Garoet 5 Mar 42
F/Sgt T Gomme	Soerabaya 16 Apr 43; Ambon; died 1991
LAC T Gorringe	Japan? Batavia 7 Sep 43
LAC R Gorst	Missing, believed drowned 27 Nov 43
Sgt D Gosbell RAAF	Killed in a/c crash, Sumatra 16 Feb 42
AC Gray	
Cpl O Greenwood	Java, Pakan Baroe Rly; died 1991
Cpl J Greenbank	Japan 42; Batavia 7 Sep 43
LAC F Hadrick	Bandoeng Oct 43
AC K W Hall	Bandoeng Oct 43
Sgt J Hall	Batavia Sep 42; Japan?
AC2 R Hall	Died, Kamburi Hosp 8 Jul 43
AC1 F Halliwell	Batavia 27 Oct 42; died 11 Apr 92
LAC Hamilton	Missing, believed drowned 27 Nov 43
LAC W J Hammond	Changi
Sgt 'Ticker' Harding RAAF	Evacuated on the *Yoma*
LAC Hardy	Missing, believed drowned 27 Oct 43
Sgt H Harding	Bandoeng, Changi, Overseas Oct 43.
AC J Harbron	Batavia 28 Nov 42
AC Harris	Batavia Aug 42
Sgt L Hart	Evacuated on the *Yoma*
LAC F Hartley	Soerabaya 14 Apr 43
LAC Harding	Died 22 May 43, Ambon
LAC W T Hassall	Soerabaya 16 Apr 43
W.O W Havard	Soerabaya, Ambon, Java
Cpl H Hayes	Missing believed drowned
Sgt Headlam RAAF	Killed a/c crash, Mingaladon
LAC A Hembridge	Ambon 44
LAC J C Henderson	Bandoeng Oct 43
LAC J E Herbert	Soerabaya 16 Apr 43
Cpl A G Hewitt	Batavia Sep 42, Japan?
Sgt H Hill	Java?
Sgt G P Hirst RAAF	Bandoeng 7 Nov 42
LAC A T Howard	Soerabaya 16 Apr 43
AC J Holden	Died Ambon
Sgt D R Hooper RAAF	Left Bandoeng 7 Nov 42
Sgt M K Holmes	
LAC E Horrobin	Died 25 Apr 44 Ambon
AC R F Hosier	Left Bandoeng 26 Oct 42
Sgt H H Hough RAAF	Left Bandoeng 26 Oct 42
Sgt M Howarth	Soerabaya 16 Apr 43
LAC H Howarth	Pakan Baroe Rly 44
AC1 F Hoyle	Java Apr 43
LAC S O Hughes	Last seen Bandoeng 3 Mar 42
Cpl W J Hughes	Batavia 27 Oct 42 Japan?
AC2 V M Hutchins	Tjimahi Hosp 1 Sep 43
LAC S Hutchinson	
Sgt J Hyatt RAAF	Killed in a/c crash
Sgt K Irwin	Evacuated on the *Yoma*
Sgt D Irvine	Injured in a/c crash, Sumatra
AC J Jackson	Bandoeng
Cpl N Jeanes	Soerabaya Feb 43; Kranji Mar 45
AC J Jenner	Soerabaya 16 Apr 43
LAC C Jones	Missing, believed drowned 27 Nov 43
LAC L Jones	Left Batavia 28 Nov 42
AC H Jones	Soerabaya 16 Apr 43
Sgt D A Jones	Left Bandoeng Oct 43
W O C E Jones	Garoet 5 Mar 42; Pakan Baroe Rly
LAC J Johnson	Soerabaya 16 Apr 43; Japan
LAC J Johnstone	
AC T Keeny	Missing, Kalidjati 28 Feb 42
Sgt L E Keane	Left Bandoeng Oct 43
Sgt M Kester	Left Batavia 15 Apr 43
AC W Kidd	Changi
LAC Kitson	Evacuated on the *Yoma*
LAC Kidson	River Valley Rly; Singapore Feb 45
Sgt J W Kinerhan	Bandoeng Oct 43
Sgt J King	Bandoeng, Changi 44
Sgt J M Lamsberg	Java 1 Sep 44
A C Launder	River Valley Rly; Singapore Feb 45
Cpl T A Lawson	Changi
LAC K Leary	OVS 27 Oct 43, Hakodate, Japan
AC J G Lee	Soerabaya 16 Apr 43
LAC J Leaver	Japan, Mukaishaina
AC W Legg	

AC W Lewis	Changi
Sgt H Lewis	Batavia Hosp Staff 31 Mar 43
Sgt K Lister	Evacuated on the *Yoma*
Sgt Lloyd	Killed in a/c crash, Mingaladon
AC1 R G Lindsay	River Valley Rly Feb 45
Sgt A Longmore RAAF	Left Tjilatjap 7 Mar 42; died 1989
LAC H Lovell	Soerabaya 16 Apr 43
AC1 M G Lansdell	OVS 10 Oct 43
LAC H Luck	Died, Kamburi Hosp 20 Oct 43
AC Lynch	Soerabaya 16 Apr 43
AC A J Maber	Died Batavia 18 Sep 42
Cpl A Mackay	Only reached Rangoon
Cpl McLean	"
LAC R S Malpas	Soerabaya, River Valley Rly, Changi
LAC F J Marland	Died, Hintok River 17 Jul 43
LAC R H Masson	Bandoeng, Changi.
LAC R Massey	Japan Sep 43
LAC Mackie	Batavia 27 Oct 42
LAC Martin	Batavia Hosp 20 Jul 43; RVR Feb 45
Sgt Martin	Killed in a/c crash 16 Feb 42
AC Mason	Batavia Hosp, Sumatra Jul 44
LAC J J Mason	Changi, Sumatra.
Cpl G W Matthews	Java
Cpl R W Matthews	River Valley Rly Feb 45
LAC Matthews	Last seen Kalidjati 28 Feb 42
LAC Mayes	Last seen Kalidjati 28 Feb 42
AC H McKinley	Left Bandoeng 26 Oct 42; died 1990
AC McKay	Japan ?
AC Mcfadyen	Batavia 27 Oct 43
AC P C McGrogan	Soerabaya 16 Apr 43
AC R McElvin	Changi 21 Sep 43
Cpl R E McLoughlin	Batavia 27 Oct 43 Japan
Cpl J McCoy	Last seen Kalidjati 28 Feb 42
Sgt McKillop	Missing, believed drowned 27 Nov 43
Sgt McBride	Last seen Kalidjati 28 Feb 42
Sgt R McLeod RAAF	Believed died in captivity
LAC E Merrick	Soerabaya 14 Apr 43
Cpl L Merralls	Left Batavia 27 Oct 43.
LAC C Middleton	Kranji 30 Mar 45
Cpl J Minshull	Batavia Feb 43
Sgt W Miller	Left Bandoeng Oct 43
LAC E Milne	Changi, Sumatra Jul 44
AC Milner	Last seen Kalidjati 28 Feb 42
AC Meredith	
AC2 Mockford	Batavia 20 Jul 43; Kranji 30 Mar 44
AC2 L E Mortimer	Soerabaya 16 Apr 43
Cpl A Morton	Soerabaya Feb 43; Changi
AC Morgan	Missing, believed drowned 27 Nov 43
Sgt R D Mohr DFM	Java
Sgt M Morris	Evacuated on the *Yoma*
Sgt D O Morris	Evacuated on the *Yoma*
Cpl F T Morriss	Ambon, Java.
AC G Money	Changi 7 Feb 43
Cpl Murphy	Left at Rangoon, rejoined Sqn Imdia
Sgt G Mutton RAAF	Killed in a/c crash Sumatra
LAC Mytton	Batavia Hosp; RVR Sumatra Jul 44
Cpl S Naylor	Changi 9 Feb 43
Cpl N Naylow	Batavia Oct 42
AC T Newman	Batavia Oct 42; Pakan Baroe Rly 44
AC K Newson	Soerabaya 16 Apr 43
LAC H Nicholson	Batavia 7 Sep 43; Japan
AC Nix	Last seen Kalidjati 28 Feb 42
Cpl M Norris	Soerabaya 16 Apr 43
LAC E V Norton	Died 13 Jun 43, Ambon.
LAC Northwood	Missing, believed killed, Tjilatjap
Sgt A Nourse RAAF	Evacuated on the *Yoma*
Sgt Odgers	Killed in a/c crash, Mingaladon
AC2 L Oldcorn	Soerabaya 16 Apr 43; died Ambon
Sgt E Oliver	Changi
LAC Osbourne	Evacuated on the *Yoma* ?
Sgt S Owen	Left Padang 16 Feb 42; rejoined Sqn
Sgt G C Palmer	Bandoeng, Changi.
Cpl Parkes	
AC1 T Passey	Changi 9 Feb 43
Cpl A Pate	Kranji 30 Mar 45
LAC B Paterson	Kuching 43
AC D Peden	Left Batavia 27 Oct 43; Japan
Sgt A Pedlar RAAF	Never reached Sumatra; rejd Sqn India
Sgt J Phillips	Bandoeng, Changi
LAC D Phillips	Last seen Kalidjati 28 Feb 42
AC2 A V Phillip	River Valley Rly June 44

AC M W Piggott	Java ?
Sgt R Pile	Evacuated *Yoma*; killed in crash 1944
AC C J Pont	Last seen Palembang Feb 42
AC J K Poole	Soerabaya 16 Apr 43
AC P Pope	Java ?
LAC Porter	
Cpl J Porter	Soerabaya 16 Apr 43; died returning from Ambon
LAC V Potter	Soerabaya 16 Apr 43
Sgt J Prentice	Never reached Sumatra; rejoined Sqn
LAC J Price	Died Changi Jan 43
Sgt J Pritchard	Left Padang 16 Feb 42; rej'd Sqn
LAC H Prime	Left Batavia Apr 43
Sgt W Proctor	Bandoeng, Changi.
AC N E Pryke	Sumatra, Changi.
AC2 R W Pugh	Sumatra, Pakan Baroe Rly 44
AC Pycott	Soerabaya 16 Apr 43
Cpl J G Ramsden	Soerabaya 16 Apr 43; Horoekoe.
LAC J Ratcliffe	Missing, believed drowned 27 Nov 43
AC1 J B Reagan	Batavia 7 Sep 43; Japan
LAC T Record	Batavia Oct 42; Hokkaido
Sgt J R Reid RAAF	Killed in a/c crash, Sumatra 16 Feb 42
AC S Reuben	Batavia 7 Sep 43
AC C Rhodes	Soerabaya 16 Apr 43
F/Sgt E Rice	Boel Glodok Ambon, Java; died Oct 1992
Sgt B Riddell	Evacuated on the *Yoma*
AC H Ridge	Java, Ambon; died 1988
AC Richards	Batavia Sep 42
LAC L Richardson	Batavia 7 Sep 43
AC2 A Richardson	Batavia 7 Sep 43
AC2 W P Ring	Last seen Palembang 16 Feb 42
Sgt M Roberts	Never reached Sumatra
Cpl W Roberts	Batavia Sep 42; died Hintok River Jul 1943
LAC R Roberts	Soerabaya 16 Apr 43
LAC Roberts	Last seen Kalidjati 28 Feb 42
AC T J Roberts	Changi; River Valley Rly Jul 44
LAC F Robinson	Soerabaya 16 Apr 43
LAC R T Robinson	Batavia 7 Sep 43
AC1 A Robertson	
Cpl R R Robson	Soerabaya, Horoekoe.
LAC J Rogers	Japan
LAC G Rogers	Evacuated on the *Yoma*
Cpl R F Rooksby	Sumatra; Batavia 7 Sep 43
Cpl L Rough	Soerabaya 16 Apr 43
Cpl F Round	Java, Changi
Sgt A Ross	Left Bandoeng 7 Nov 42; Changi
Sgt D Russell	Bandoeng, Changi.
LAC Russell	Last seen Kalidjati 3 Mar 42
AC1 J Saint	Batavia 7 Sep 43; Japan
LAC Salmon	Last seen Kalidjati 28 Feb 42
Sgt C Samuels	Batavia, Ambon; died 1963
Sgt G Sayers RAAF	Left Tjilatjap 7 Mar 42; killed flying Beaufighters, 30 Sqn RAAF 1943.
AC1 W Scaife	Batavia 7 Sep 43; died
AC F L Scruby	Soerabaya 16 Apr 43
Cpl Shand	
Sgt A Sharrott	Evacuated on the *Yoma*
Cpl R F Shaw	Sole survivor of a/c crash 16 Feb 42 Batavia; River Valley Rly; died Japan
LAC F Shaw	Java, Changi, OVS 21 Sep 43
AC D Shea	Killed in train ambush 6 Mar 42
AC J A T Shine	Batavia 20 Jul 43; Changi Jun 44
LAC Shepherd	
LAC C M Shillabeer	Bandoeng, Changi
F/Sgt Sharley	Killed Tjilatjap 9 Mar 42
LAC G W Shuker	Soerabaya 16 Apr 43
LAC R Silcock	Palembang?
LAC J E Sissons	Batavia, Changi, Japan.
F/Sgt W Slee	Missing, believed killed, Kalidjati
F/Sgt L H Small	Missing, Tjilatjap 9 Mar 42
LAC S Small	Missing, believed drowned 27 Nov 43
LAC R W Smart	River Valley Rly 14 Feb 45
AC Smile	
Sgt A Smith	Garoet 5 Mar 42; reported dead
Cpl D W Smith	Soerabaya 16 Apr 43
LAC L N Smith	Left Batavia 27 Oct 42
AC2 A E Smith	Soerabaya 16 Apr 43
Cpl B Spector	River Valley Rly, Sumatra Jul 44
AC Stansfield	
LAC G Standen	Soerabaya 16 Apr 43
AC A F Stearn	Left Java Apr 43
Cpl Street	Garoet 5 Mar 42; to Japan Sep 42
Cpl Stonebridge	Tjilatjap 4 Mar 42
LAC B Stuart	Batavia 7 Sep 43.
AC1 Swainson	Batavia 27 Oct 42; Japan
AC A Tame	Died Ambon
AC2 R H Taylor	Batavia 7 Sep 43
LAC F Taylor	Batavia 7 Sep 43
AC T Taylor	Soerabaya 16 Apr 43
Sgt A Thomas	Never reached Sumatra; rejd Sqn
Sgt S Thomson RAAF	Batavia, Changi.
Cpl Thomas	Never reached Sumatra; rejd Sqn
LAC N F Thomas	Batavia 7 Sep 43
LAC F G Thomas	Batavia 7 Sep 43
AC O Thomas	Died Soerabaya Nov 42.
LAC Tobey	Tjilatjap 4 Mar 42; Batavia 1 July 43
LAC Todd	Missing believed died, Kalidjati 1 Mar
LAC Tourle	Never reached Sumatra; rejd Sqn
AC H Tovey	Java?
Sgt Treadenick	Left Bandoeng 7 Nov 42
Cpl Turnbull	Sumatra; Pakan Baroe Rly.
Sgt W Tully	Missing, believed drowned 27 Nov 43
Cpl Tweedie	Missing after evacuation I Mar 42
LAC W J Uden	Bandoeng, Pakan Baroe Rly Jul 44
LAC C Waite	Changi, Pakan Baroe Rly July 44
Sgt A W Wakefield	Bandoeng, Changi Oct 43
Cpl J W Waller	Batavia Feb 44
LAC Ward	
Cpl S Ward	Bandoeng 21 Sep 43
AC Warner	Missing, believed drowned 27 Nov 43
Cpl C W Warren	Soerabaya; died Ambon
LAC L A Warren	Soerabaya 16 Apr 43
LAC Warwick	Last seen Kalidjati 28 Feb 42
F/Sgt Watkins	Left Sumatra HMS *Danae*; to Australia on SS *Aberkerk*; rejoined Sqn at Quetta
AC1 H Watkins	Pakan Baroe Jul 44
AC1 R Watson	Batavia 7 Sep 43
LAC Waugh	Last seen Kalidjati 28 Feb 42
LAC Webb	Never reached Sumatra; rejd Sqn.
LAC R Webster	Soerabaya 16 Apr 43; died Ambon.
AC1 D Weltzer	Batavia 7 Sep 43
LAC C H Westfield	Batavia 7 Sep 43, River Valley Rly
Cpl L R West	Soerabaya 16 Apr 43
LAC F Wharfe	Batavia 1 Sep 44, Japan
Sgt K H Whibley	Bandoeng, Changi.
AC Wilkinson	Evacuated on the *Yoma*.
LAC Wilkinson	Missing believed drowned 27 Nov 43
LAC J G Williams	Missing believed drowned 27 Nov 43
AC Williams	Last seen Kalidjati 28 Feb 42
Cpl G Williams	Soerabaya 16 Apr 43; died Hintok River 21 Aug 43
LAC Wiltshire	Left in Hospital, Heliopolis.
Sgt B Winchester RAAF	Never reached Java; rejd Sqn
AC K E Winter	
Cpl W Woodhouse	Batavia 16 Apr 43
LAC H Woolford	Japan 43, Batavia 1 Sep 44
WO G C Wright	Missing, believed drowned 27 Nov 43
Sgt H Wright	Bandoeng, Changi.
Cpl R W Wright	Soerabaya 16 Apr 43
LAC Wright	Left Malang for Batavia 1 Sep 44
Cpl W L Wright	Died Hintok River 11 Jul 43
AC1 D R Vincent	
Sgt W G Young	Evacuated on the *Yoma*
AC1 J R Yabsley	Batavia 7 Sep 43; died 1990

It is a possibility that some of those mentioned did not serve with No.84 Squadron. Brief details give dates as far as known

A S.E.5A with Hispano-Suiza engine

APPENDIX VII

NOMINAL ROLE OF OFFICERS AND SGT PILOTS, NO.84 SQUADRON, 1917-1919

Maj H R Nicholl	17 Feb 1917 - 8 Aug 1917	Comm Off.
Lt R A Denne	17 Feb 1917 - 12 Jul 1917	Instructor
Capt S Dalrymple	17 Mar 1917 - Jul 1917	Instructor
Lt H B Hope	Mar 1917 - Jul 1917	Instructor
2nd Lt O W Manning	Mar 1917 - Jul 1917	Instructor
2nd Lt C F Jex	Mar 1917 - Jul 1917	Instructor
Maj W Sholto Douglas	8 Aug 1917 - 8 Nov 1918	Comm Off.
Lt A C Workman	13 Jul 1917 - 26 Feb 1918	Adjutant
Capt K St G Leask	18 Jul 1917 - 3 Apr 1918	Flt Cdr to HE
2nd Lt R Shepherd	1 Apr 1917 - 30 Mar 1918	Equip Off
Capt J M Child	26 Jul 1917 - 5 Feb 1918	Flt Cdr to HE
Capt E R Pennell	23 Jul 1917 - 6 Feb 1918	To hospital
2nd Lt C T Travers	23 May 1917 - 3 Apr 1918	To hospital
2nd Lt P J Maloney	21 Mar 1917 - 22 Nov 1917	W in A
2nd Lt F A Swoffer	Jul 1917	Gunnery Off.
2nd Lt A E Hempel	14 Aug 1917 - 21 Oct 1917	Missing POW
2nd Lt J S Ralston	14 Aug 1917 - 29 Jan 1918	To 24 Sqn
Reposted as Capt;	13 Jun 1918 - 25 Jul 1918	W in A
2nd Lt W R Kingsland	13 Aug 1917 - 8 Nov 1917	Missing POW
2nd Lt A W Proctor	18 Jun 1917 - 15 Jun 1918	To HE
Reposted;	6 Aug 1918 - 8 Oct 1918	W in A
2nd Lt E O Krohn	19 Jun 1917 - 22 Feb 1918	K in A
2nd Lt R W Mathewson	18 Jun 1917 - 19 Sep 1917	To 25th Wing
2nd Lt C L Stubbs	21 Jun 1917 - 6 Nov 1917	To Hospital
Reposted;	26 Jan 1918 - 8 May 1918	
2nd Lt W E Watts	6 May 1917 - 20 Oct 1917	Missg POW
2nd Lt F L Yeomans	21 Jun 1917 - 21 Oct 1917	Missg POW
Lt F Larsen	31 Jul 1917 - 11 Apr 1918	To Hospital
2nd Lt S M Park	31 Jul 1917 - 18 Oct 1917	Missing POW
2nd Lt W H Brown	6 Aug 1917 - 8 Apr 1918	To HE
2nd Lt J O Priestly	14 Aug 1917 - 28 Sep 1917	To No 1 AD
2nd Lt H B Parkinson	12 Sep 1917-	To No 1 AD
Lt A Dodds	13 Sep 1917-	To No 1 AD
2nd Lt R B Steele	16 Oct 1917 - 21 Oct 1917	Missing P D
2nd Lt G R Gray	19 Oct 1917 - 31 Oct 1917	Missing P D
2nd Lt E A Clear	19 Oct 1917 - 15 Jun 1918	To HE
2nd Lt E W Powell	21 Oct 1917 - 31 Oct 1917	Missing P D
2nd Lt G O Johnson	22 Oct 1917 - 18 Apr 1918	To 24 Sqn
2nd Lt H A Payne	22 Oct 1917 - 18 Mar 1918	Missing P D
2nd Lt P K Hobson	22 Oct 1917 - 11 May 1918	To H E
2nd Lt D J Rollo	29 Oct 1917 - 23 Nov 1917	W in A
Lt F E Brown	1 Nov 1917 - 28 Mar 1918	W in A
2nd Lt J Hetherington	1 Nov 1917 - 13 Nov 1917	W in acc
2nd Lt T G Jackson	8 Nov 1917- 5 Feb 1918	To 48 Sqn
2nd Lt E J Dickie	9 Nov 1917 - 30 Nov 1917	K in accident
2nd Lt H E Davies	9 Nov 1917 - 13 Jan 1918	Missing POW
2nd Lt J V Sorsoleil	16 Nov 1917 - 13 Jul 1918	To H E
2nd Lt H D Barton	23 Nov 1917 - 3 Jan 1918	To 24 Sqn
Lt R A Grosvenor	27 Nov 1917 - 25 May 1918	To hospital
2nd Lt H W Saunders	1 Dec 1917 - 6 Aug 1918	To H E
Capt J Hatton-Burke	21 Dec 1917 - 19 Mar 1918	To HQ
2nd Lt T F Northcote	23 Dec 1917 -	Admin Off.
2nd Lt J A McCudden	3 Jan 1918 - 18 Mar 1918	Missing R D
Lt R E Duke	28 Jan 1918 - 6 Mar 1918	Missg POW.
2nd Lt W J Nel	3 Feb 1918 - 27 Sep 1918	To H E
2nd Lt H O McDonald	3 Feb 1918 - 6 Jul 1918	Inj in Acc
Reposted ;	Sep 1918 - To Armistice	
2nd Lt W E Lunnon	4 Feb 1918 - 4 Jun 1918	Inj in acc
Lt L de S Duke	10 Feb 1918 - 23 Apr 1918	W in A
Reposted ;	To Armistice	
Lt S H Winkley	2 Mar 1918 - 1 Apr 1918	Missing P D
Lt C F Falkenberg	7 Mar 1918 - 10 May 1918	Acc Inj
Returned to Sqn and posted to Home Establishment Nov 1918		
Capt G Aste	13 May 1918 - 3 Aug 1918	Adjutant
Lt R Manzer	19 Mar 1918 - 8 Aug 1918	Missing POW
2nd Lt N G Bray	19 Mar 1918 - 20 Apr 1918	To H E
1st Lt A B Lapsley	19 Mar 1918 -	To USAS
2nd Lt E E Biccard	1 Apr 1918 -	To H E
Capt Lister-Kaye	3 Apr 1918 - 25 Apr 1918	W in A
Capt E H Tatton	3 Apr 1918 - 20 Apr 1918	K in A

Name	Dates	Remarks
Lt W A Southey	4 Apr 1918 -	To H E
Lt C M McCann	4 Apr 1918 - 12 Apr 1918	K in A
Lt W L Sumison	4 Apr 1918 - 24 Apr 1918	W in A POW
2nd Lt B Earlham	30 Mar 1918 - 18 Apr 1918	To HQ
Lt C F Wilson	14 Apr 1918 - 17 Jun 1918	W in A
Reposted to Sqn;		To Armistice
Capt H P Smith	15 Apr 1918 - 16 May 1918	W in A
Sgt A Jex	15 Apr 1918 -	To H E
Reposted to Sqn;	3 Sep 1918 - 17 Sep 1918	Missing POW
Lt B Stefansson	20 Apr 1918 - 28 May 1918	W in A
Lt A B Mathews	21 Apr 1918 - 24 Aug 1918	K in air raid
Lt B Oliver	24 Apr 1918 - 29 Jun 1918	To 148 USAS
Lt M Newhall	25 Apr 1918 - 2 Jun 1918	To 3 US Sqn
Lt E M Hammer	27 Apr 1918 - 19 May 1918	K in A
Lt S B Eckart	27 Apr 1918 - 2 Jun 1918	To 80 Sqn
Lt R J Fyfe	9 May 1918 - 18 Jun 1918	Missing P D
Lt S T Tipper	15 May 1918 - 20 May 1918	To Hospital
2nd Lt J E Reid	17 May 1918 - 14 Sep 1918	Missing POW
2nd Lt C R Thompson	20 May 1918 - 15 Sep 1918	W in A
2nd Lt S W Highwood	20 May 1918 - To Armistice	
Lt G A Vaughn	29 May 1918 - 28 Aug 1918	To 17 USAS
Lt D C Henderson	2 Jun 1918 - 14 Jun 1918	To Hospital
Lt D B Jones	2 Jun 1918 - 27 Jun 1918	DOW
Lt P Nielson	10 Jun 1918 - 18 Jun 1918	Missing P D
2nd Lt J Chesters	10 Jun 1918 - 10 Aug 1918	W in A
2nd Lt L W Pooley	17 Jun 1918 - 22 Jul 1918	To H E
Lt N W Mawle	18 Jun 1918 - 8 Aug 1918	W in A
Lt R Watts	19 Jun 1918 - 13 Aug 1918	To Hospital
Lt C W Rivers	22 Jun 1918 - 29 Jun 1918	To Hospital
2nd Lt C S Bateman	28 Jun 1918 - 24 Aug 1918	W in air raid
2nd Lt J Barker	30 Jun 1918 - 9 Jul 1918	To H E
Lt A C Lobley	30 Jun 1918 - 18 Aug 1918	To Hospital
2nd Lt J E Boudwin	3 Jul 1918 -	To USAS
Lt C H Pain	6 Jul 1918 - 20 Jul 1918	Inj in acc
2nd Lt A E Brown	7 Jul 1918 - 1 Aug 1918	To H E
Lt J A Gordon	10 Jul 1918 - 15 Jul 1918	To 41 Sqn
Lt W E Huxtable	15 Jul 1918 - 25 Jul 1918	To 41 Sqn
Lt I P Corse	18 Jul 1918 -	To 17 USAS
Sgt H J Guy	25 Jul 1918 - 7 Aug 1918	W in A
Lt J A Jackson	27 Jul 1918 - To Armistice	
Lt A E Ansell	29 Jul 1918 - To Armistice	Adjutant
2nd Lt M H Gaudie	1 Aug 1918 - 27 Aug 1918	W in A
2nd Lt A E Hill	8 Aug 1918 - To Armistice	
Lt I C Simpson	5 Aug 1918 -	To Hospital
Lt J L Peyton	8 Aug 1918 - 16 Aug 1918	Missing P D
Capt D Carruthers	8 Aug 1918 - 18 Oct 1918	To 24 Sqn
2nd Lt D C Rees	17 Aug 1918 - 29 Sep 1918	Missing P D
Lt J C Rorison	8 Aug 1918 - 14 Aug 1918	To 24 Sqn
Lt E R Millar	18 Aug 1918 - To Armistice	
2nd Lt J E Robbins	17 Aug 1918 -	To H E
2nd Lt W E Gemmell	20 Aug 1918 - To Armistice	
Lt F R Christiani	25 Aug 1918 - 29 Sep 1918	Missing P D
Lt E C Bateman	25 Aug 1918 - 7 Sep 1918	Missing P D
2nd Lt W B Aldred	29 Aug 1918 - 7 Sep 1918	DOW
2nd Lt R A Whyte	29 Aug 1918 - To Armistice	
2nd Lt J G Coots	1 Sep 1918 - To Armistice	
Sgt A J Wing	5 Sep 1918 - 5 Nov 1918	Missing P D
Sgt A M Stewart	4 Sep 1918 - 16 Sep 1918	Killed in Acc
Sgt H W Dowdell	5 Sep 1918 - To Armistice	
Sgt F S Thompson	5 Sep 1918 - 17 Sep 1918	Missing POW
Sgt W G Brown	7 Sep 1918 - 22 Oct 1918	To H E
Lt A E Cribbs	18 Sep 1918 - 25 Sep 1918	To 2nd Bgde
2nd Lt S H Sippe		Equip Off
2nd Lt C W Kerr	18 Sep 1918 - 1 Oct 1918	W in A
2nd Lt H W Thorn	23 Sep 1918 - 30 Oct 1918	DOW
2nd Lt G W Ireland	30 Sep 1918 -	To 85 Sqn
2nd Lt J C Collins	3 Oct 1918 - 24 Oct 1918	Missing POW
Sgt Tarver	5 Oct 1918 - 30 Oct 1918	W in A
Sgt P J Palmer	14 Oct 1918 - To Armistice	
Sgt J G Ewart	14 Oct 1918 - To Armistice	
Sgt R E Surman	25 Oct 1918 - To Armistice	
Capt T E Laing	31 Oct 1918 - To Armistice	
2nd Lt A M Rosenbleet	31 Oct 1918 - 10 Nov 1918	Missing POW
2nd Lt J M Bacon	31 Oct 1918 - To Armistice	
Maj C E Pickthorne	4 Nov 1918 - 5 Apr 1919	Comm Off
Sgt F T Dove	7 Nov 1918 - To Armistice	
Sgt A Heaps	7 Nov 1918 - To Armistice	
2nd Lt R Johnstone	11 Nov 1918 - To Armistice	
Lt C E Kelly	15 Nov 1918 -	
2nd Lt A Cruickshank	15 Nov 1918 -	
2nd Lt R D Hunnon	2 Dec 1918 -	
2nd Lt M L Hall	2 Feb 1919 -	From 56 Sqn
2nd Lt C V Forsythe	2 Feb 1919 -	From 60 Sqn
Lt R Kilpatrick	4 Feb 1919 -	From 74 Sqn
Lt J E Ferrand	4 Feb 1919 -	From 74 Sqn
Lt R H Barrett	27 Feb 1919 -	From 15 Sqn
2nd Lt C F Williams	1 Mar 1919 -	From 56 Sqn
Lt H Egan	1 Mar 1919 -	From 92 Sqn
Capt O M Faure	8 Mar 1919 -	
2nd Lt E S Banfield	1 Apr 1919 -	From 32 Sqn
Lt A N Abbott	1 Apr 1919 -	
2nd Lt L W Robins	1 Apr 1919 -	
Maj C M Crowe MC	5 Apr 1919 -	Comm Off.
2nd Lt W R Bannister	28 Apr 1919 -	From 43 Sqn
2nd Lt A S Birss	23 Apr 1919 -	
Flt Lt P W Lingwood	23 Apr 1919 - 8 Aug 1919	To 70 Sqn
Fg Off A Clarke	- Jun 1919	Killed in Acc

ACKNOWLEDGEMENTS

To all of the following I would like to offer my thanks, without their help this history could never have been written.

From 84 Squadron: P J Adams, Sqn Ldr D Addicott, J W Adkin, W Amy, The late Sqn Ldr R W J Andrusikiewicz DFC AFC, A G Arnold, P Ault, Flt Lt J W Babbington, the late ACM Sir Denis Barnett GCB CBE DFC MA, D L Baxter, Wg Cdr C H Beeton, R C Bennett, Fg Off F V Bird OBE, Flt Lt A M Blackburn DFC, W M Bond, Wg Cdr K Bowhill OBE BA, S Brookes, C Burrell, J Bush, Cpl T Butcher RAF, Flt Lt R G Cameron, A E Carter, Sqn Ldr D Cheeseborough, Flt Lt J M Clyne, J P Collins, A Copus, R Cox, Sqn Ldr P G Critchley, C W Crocker, Sqn Ldr J H Cruickshank MBE, S Davis, G Dewey, the late Wg Cdr L de S Duke RCAF, Sqn Ldr K F Dicks DFC, R G Duncan, Sqn Ldr P Elton, M A Fish MBE, R Finning, J French, J Gatley, Wg Cdr A M Gill OBE DFC AE, P B Godfrey, R Green, the late O W Greenwood, Wg Cdr H W Guile, Sqn Ldr M Hadley, D Hamshire, Sqn Ldr P Hancock, Flt Lt M Harris, P Haynes OBE JP, Sqn Ldr F W Heap, R P Hedley, B Hill, Wg Cdr S Hitchen MVO, S D Holloway, S D Hughes, S C Humphrey, J M Hutcheson, T Ingham-Brown, Flt Lt K Irwin, G Isaacs, the late Sqn Ldr H R G Jebb, Sqn Ldr H H Jenkins, the late AM G O Johnson CB MC C de G RCAF, M Kester, Sqn Ldr R F King RAF, R Kite, Flt Lt B Lambert, Wg Cdr M W Leeming BSc RAF, K J Leary, AVM K M Leask CB MC and bar, J Leaver, Wg Cdr K Lister DFC, Flt Lt R Livermore AFM, R Livesey, J Lovegrove, the late H Lowe, Flt Lt G Luckins, G Maplesden, Flt Lt H Martin, J Maskery, Flt Lt G Maurice, H McGinley, M/Eng P McWhirter, Flt Lt W A McLean, R Millar, W Miller, Flt Lt G W Milson DFC, Flt Lt D O Morris, G Money, Flt Lt A Myers, Air Cdre A A N Nicholson CBE, Gp Capt S G Nunn OBE DFC AE, E Oliver, A R Padgett, Wg Cdr C E B Papps DFC MBE RNZAF, Gp Capt K J Parfit, A W Parker, J Partington, D Pasco, B Paterson, Flt Lt A W Pedler, Sqn Ldr F Pennycott, Sqn Ldr F A Plinston DFC, Fg Off M Ponder, Fg Off R Ponting, D Poulter, R Powell, R Price, W Proctor, Gp Capt J H Ramsden OBE, T Record, E Rice, K Rimmer, G E Rogers, J N Rogers, A Ross, Comm P Rover, H Rowlands, D Russell, R E Russell, Wg Cdr W T Russell, C Scarth, Sqn Ldr S W Sills DFM, Sqn Ldr A J F Smith MBE, Wg Cdr D W Smith, Flt Lt P Snook RAF, R Startin, T Stringer, K G Styan, Wg Cdr E W Talbot DFC and bar, J Talkington, Flt Lt A W Thomas, C E Thomas, T Thompson, S Thomson, Sqn Ldr G J Thwaites MBE, the late Sqn Ldr J Tinker, Gp Capt H Tudor, Sqn Ldr C R Turner AFC, E Tutt, Wg Cdr G C Unwin DSO DFM and bar, Fg Off M J S Verschoyle, Sqn Ldr B Wade, A W Wakefield, W J Wheeler, Sqn Ldr C F Whitelock, Gp Capt R Whittam, K Wild, I P Wolstenholme, Plt Off T Woodard LVO FSG, I P Woodward, S J Wright, Flt Lt J V C Wylie DFC, No 84 Squadron RAF Akrotiri

****

Others who have helped included R C B Ashworth, K J Bickell, J Bruce, C Bowyer, M Bowyer, Mrs L Bristow, P Cooksley, B Cull, R H Dargue, J J Halley, E Hardy, Mrs R I Haynes (for translating Dutch text), B Holt, Wg Cdr J Jefford, Terence Kelly, R Larden, H Liffen, S Leslie, T Mellor-Ellis, C Minney, T O'Brien, the late W Overton, G Page, N Parker, R Phillips, B Robertson, Miss E Small (sister of Sgt L Small), R Sturtivant, R E Van Wijngaarten, The Public Record Office

****

Without wishing to single any one person out, I would like to offer a special 'Thank you' to three of the above: Wg Cdr A M Gill for his willingness in checking the entire script for grammar and spelling mistakes, for his help in preparing the two chapters covering his own service with the Squadron and, for putting up with my continual calls on the telephone. To the late Owen Greenwood for his willingness to share with me his own researches into the Squadron's history and allowing me access to letters written to him from many of the very well-known senior officers who served with the Squadron during the 1920s and 1930s. And finally Rob van Wijngaarten who spent a considerable amount of time researching the Dutch archives for details of the Squadron's service in Java and Sumatra in 1942 and 1946 and in forwarding to me the very interesting maps and photographs which add considerable interest to the chapters.

****

LITERATURE CONSULTED

Above the Trenches	Chris Shores, Norman Franks, Russell Guest
Action Stations Overseas	Sqn Ldr T Fairbairn
Air War for Yugoslavia, Greece and Crete,	Chris Shores, Brian Cull, Nicola Malizia.
Blackburn Beverley	W A Overton
Bloody Shambles Vol 2,	Chris Shores, Brian Cull, Yasuho Izawa
De Sumatra Spoorteg	H Neumann
Flight from the Middle East	ACM Sir David Lee GBE CB
Glory in Chaos	Gp Capt E R Hall
Press on Regardless	S C Humphrey
RAF Operations 1918-1938	Chaz Bowyer
The Squadrons of the Royal Air Force	James J Halley
The £500 Adventure	Julian Rogers
The War that Never Was	AVM A G Dudgeon
Vickers Aircraft	C F Andrews and E B Morgan
Westland Aircraft	Derek N James
Various copies of Flight, Flypast, Cross and Cockade.	
Various Air-Britain publications	